GLOBALIZATION
THE GREATEST HITS

GLOBALIZATION
THE GREATEST HITS
A GLOBAL STUDIES READER

EDITED BY
MANFRED B. STEGER

OXFORD
UNIVERSITY PRESS

OXFORD

UNIVERSITY PRESS

Oxford University Press, Inc., publishes works that further
Oxford University's objective of excellence in research, scholarship,
and education.

Oxford New York
Auckland Cape Town Dar es Salaam Hong Kong Karachi
Kuala Lumpur Madrid Melbourne Mexico City Nairobi
New Delhi Shanghai Taipei Toronto

With offices in
Argentina Austria Brazil Chile Czech Republic France Greece
Guatemala Hungary Italy Japan Poland Portugal Singapore
South Korea Switzerland Thailand Turkey Ukraine Vietnam

Copyright © 2010 by Paradigm Publishers

First published by Paradigm Publishers
Published by Oxford University Press,
198 Madison Avenue, New York, New York 10016
http://www.oup.com

Library of Congress Cataloging-in-Publication Data available

ISBN 978-0-19-994607-5

CONTENTS

INTRODUCTION

THE EMERGENCE OF GLOBAL STUDIES

Manfred B. Steger

Emerging as a rather amorphous buzzword in the 1980s, "globalization" rules the public discourse of the early twenty-first century as one of its core concepts. In less than three decades, it has gripped the imagination of billions around the world who find themselves witnesses to one of the most rapid yet precarious social transformations in human history. Regardless of their geographic location and socioeconomic status, most people by now have formed some opinion about "globalization" and related terms such as "globality" and "globalism." Indeed, most of us also hold strong normative views about whether the extension and intensification of social relations across world-time and world-space should be seen as a "good" or as a "bad" thing. As a reader of this book, you probably have your own opinions about this ongoing struggle over the meaning of today's dramatic globalization dynamics. But whether you are a so-called hyperglobalizer who considers the death of the modern nation-state a foregone conclusion, or a "skeptic" with regard to the significance and impact of the current compression of time and space, or a "modifier" disputing the alleged novelty of planetary interdependence, or even a "rejectionist" who dismisses the prospect of a global-ized future as nothing more than "globaloney," you nonetheless stand to benefit from a close reading of some of the seminal writings on globalization that have shaped our understanding of this phenomenon over the last quarter century.

But this is where the problem starts. Where can you find such an authoritative collection of writings produced by first-rate thinkers? Although thousands of scholarly books and journal articles on the topic have been published since the 1980s, few have taken the form of comprehensive Globalization Readers. But even these rare compilations are rather eclectic, often mixing terse journalistic pieces with dense academic articles, tedious policy reports with fiery declarations of principles, and detached social science treatises with engaged polemics. In addition, these voluminous Readers tend to cram dozens of writings on nearly all conceivable aspects of globalization into hundreds of pages of text, subdivided into multiple sections headed by separate introductions. On the opposite end, one finds some useful introductions to globalization that manage to present the "big picture" in accessible prose. But these compressed treatments are hardly designed to bring together a manageable number of primary sources of proven quality that might stimulate your global imagination.

Fortunately, you need not look any further, for you are already holding the solution to the problem in your hands! The three basic ideas behind the creation of this Globalization Reader are simple. First, it has been designed to bring together in a single mid-size volume some of the best pieces on the subject written by pioneers of globalization studies. Second, these seminal contributions have been kept to an easily digestible length, while at the same time covering the three major dimensions of globalization: economics, politics, and culture. Third, this Reader contains no editorial comments or further introductions that might interrupt the conceptual flow of the writings, so that readers can draw their own conclusions about the viewpoints and arguments presented here. These three principles are based on the efforts of record companies to produce high-quality selections of representative songs by popular solo artists and bands that have been making music for decades. Thus, we enjoy listening to *Janet Jackson: Design of a Decade, The Very Best of Cat Stevens, Madonna: Greatest Hits, The Beatles 1,* and so on.

Likewise, this Reader contains what I consider to be twenty of the "greatest hits" of globalization published in the last thirty years. I readily concede that choosing the "best" of anything always remains a subjective and incomplete endeavor—in addition to being a rather contentious task. After all, at some point in our lives haven't we all wondered why a supposed *Greatest Hits of...* album did not include our favorite song? Invariably, some readers will be disappointed in my selection for this very reason. However, I trust that, in addition to finding several personal favorites in a single collection, most will enjoy exploring unfamiliar pieces of striking significance.

In the remaining pages of this introduction, let me highlight some crucial features of the pieces compiled in this Reader by placing them in their proper academic context. This brief preview will also give you a first glimpse of how "global studies"—the new transdisciplinary field dedicated to the study of globalization—has emerged over the last thirty years.

Theodore Levitt's "The Globalization of Markets"

Most of the earliest academic coiners of "globalization" writing in the 1980s linked the term to material processes of growing interdependence driven by economics and technology. In their view, the digital revolution provided the means for what came to be known as the "globalization of markets." Indeed, this influential association of terms appeared for the first time in 1983 in the title of the opening "greatest hit" of this collection. The huge impact of the seminal essay penned by the late Harvard marketing professor Theodore Levitt for the *Harvard Business Review* is perhaps best illustrated by the fact that American "globalization guru" Thomas Friedman adopted one of its subheadings as the title for his bestseller, *The World Is Flat* (Farrar, Straus and Giroux, 2007). Levitt's essay laid the foundation for the dominant depiction of globalization as a techno-economic process destined to give birth to a "global market for standardized consumer products on a previously unimagined scale of magnitude." But the marketing professor's description of what he considers "indisputable empirical trends" is inseparable from his ideological prescriptions. For example, he insists that multinational companies have no choice but to transform themselves into global corporations capable of operating in a more cost-effective way by standardizing their products. The necessary elimination of costly adjustments to various national markets depends, according to Levitt, on the swift adoption of a "global approach," that is, the willingness of CEOs to think and act "as if the world were one large market—ignoring superficial regional and national differences.... It [the global corporation] sells the same things in the same way everywhere." The article spawned hundreds of similar pieces in business magazines and journals that sought to convince the world's leading companies to "go global." The advertising industry, in particular, set about creating "global brands" by means of global commercial campaigns. One of these early examples for this new practice of attaching the signifiers "world" and "global" to every conceivable commodity or service was the British Airways slogan, "The world's favorite airline," unleashed on "global customers" by the advertising giant Saatchi & Saatchi. Unsurprisingly, its founder had been one of Ted Levitt's most fervent disciples.

Arjun Appadurai's "Disjuncture and Difference in the Global Cultural Economy"

The second hit in our collection links the ongoing transformation of capitalism caused by globalization dynamics to the larger framework of a "global cultural economy." Authored by Arjun Appadurai, a cultural anthropologist and multilingual scholar of South Asian cultures and languages, this essay constitutes the intellectual basis of what would six years later become *Modernity at Large* (University of Minnesota Press, 1996), one of the most influential academic books exploring the cultural dimensions of globalization. Rejecting the then-dominant opposing views that globalization would result in either cultural sameness ("Americanization" or "McDonaldization") or greater differentiation (proliferation and/or fragmentation of cultures), Appadurai employs concrete South Asian examples to argue that increasing global interdependence has produced neither of these extremes. Rather, it seemed to favor an "infinitely varied mutual contest of sameness and difference" characterized by "radical disjunctures between different sorts of global flows and the uncertain landscapes created in and through these disjunctures." The pioneering intellectual contribution made by this essay lies in the author's introduction of a five-dimensional conceptual model by which to analyze these fundamental "disjunctures" among economy, culture, and politics. Appadurai's five "scapes"—ethnoscapes, mediascapes, technoscapes, finanscapes, and ideoscapes—represent particular "perspectives" or "mentalities" that allow individuals and groups to make sense of their shrinking world. Thus, the discerning anthropologist shows how an increasingly "global imagination" provides new resources for identities that are no longer exclusively anchored in the modern nation or the traditional tribe.

Anthony Giddens's "The Globalization of Modernity"

In the third contribution to this collection, the prominent British sociologist Anthony Giddens argues for the embeddedness of globalizing processes in the overarching framework of Western modernity. Taking as his point of departure his celebrated definition of globalization—"the intensification of worldwide social relations which link distant localities in such a way that local happenings are shaped by events occurring many miles away and vice-versa"—the former director of the London School of Economics goes on to examine two competing bodies of literature that discuss globalization either in the context of international relations or within an overarching "capitalist world-system." Finding both perspectives wanting, Giddens puts forward a novel classification scheme that identifies four major dimensions of globalization: the nation-state system, the world-capitalist economy, the international division of labor, and the world military order. Ending with a short discussion of the crucial role of technology and the media, this essay stimulated vigorous debates on globalization in academic journals and conferences in the early 1990s. The popularity of Giddens's ideas and definitions also contributed to the increasing influence of sociologists in shaping the contours of an embryonic transdisciplinary field dedicated to the study of globalization.

Roland Robertson's "Mapping the Global Condition"

Produced exclusively by sociologists and political scientists, the next six contributions of this collection confirm the shifting locus of these globalization debates from business schools to social science departments. Wrestling with some of the same cultural and socioeconomic themes raised by both Appadurai and Giddens, Roland Robertson's essay offers a penetrating analysis of the evolution of "world consciousness"—the awareness of "the contemporary world as a whole [and] as a single place"—both within academic literature and in concrete historical settings over the last five centuries. The British sociologist of religion introduces a powerful temporal-historical model that delineates these thickening forms of "global density" and "global complexity" in five discrete phases culminating in the dramatic heightening of global consciousness between the late 1960s and early 1990s. Originally published as a journal article in 1990, this piece was republished two years later as a book chapter in *Globalization: Social Theory and Global Culture* (Sage, 1992). Hailed as an instant classic and widely cited across the humanities and social sciences, Robertson's seminal study became a cornerstone in the growing interdisciplinary literature on globalization.

Paul Hirst and Grahame Thompson's "Globalization: A Necessary Myth?"

Conceding that "globalization" had emerged by the mid-1990s as a "fashionable concept in the social sciences," two skeptical British political economists nonetheless emphasized that the widespread image of a "global economy" was the product of an exaggerated narrative rather than an empirical reality. In other words, their detailed historical analysis of economic globalization suggests that the world economy is not a truly global phenomenon, but rather one centered on Europe, eastern Asia, and North America. Paul Hirst and Grahame Thompson emphasize that the majority of economic activity around the world still remains primarily national in origin and scope. Presenting relevant data on trade, foreign direct investment, and financial flows, the authors warn against drawing premature "global" conclusions from increased levels of economic interaction in advanced industrial countries. Their argument against the existence of a globalized economy squarely attacks what they see as the general misuse of the term. Without a truly global economic system, Hirst and Thompson insist, "globalization" represents, at best, a limited form of regionalism: "[A]s we proceeded, our skepticism deepened until we became convinced that globalization, as conceived by the more extreme globalizers, is largely a myth." In spite of its focus on empirical "data," one can detect a critical-normative message in the influential "Hirst–Thompson Thesis": it is to show that exaggerated accounts of an "iron logic of economic globalization" tend to produce disempowering political effects. Indeed, the authors suggest that certain political players have used the thesis of economic globalization to propose national economic deregulation and the reduction of welfare programs. Thus, the implementation of such policies stands to benefit pro-market forces. Although critics have identified a number of problems with the Hirst–Thompson thesis, it has had a tremendous impact on the evolution of global studies. It is thus not surprising that *Globalization in Question* (Blackwell, 1996)—the book from which this contribution has been taken—has recently been published in its expanded and revised third edition (Polity, 2009).

Michael Hardt and Antonio Negri's Preface to *Empire*

Hailed by sympathetic reviewers as "*The Communist Manifesto* for our time" and condemned by scathing critics as an "impenetrable work of absolute abstraction," *Empire* exploded on an unsuspecting international academic scene in 2000. Written by Michael Hardt, an American literary scholar, and Antonio Negri, a radical Italian philosopher with close ties to the militant "autonomist movement" within 1970s Italian communism, the book sold tens of thousands of copies. Virtually overnight, it became the subject of major debates in academia and the popular media around the world. Our collection reproduces the preface, in which the authors introduce "empire" as a potent metaphor for a radically new paradigm of authority and control. In their view, this "new global order" is composed of a series of national and supranational organisms that supersede old, nation-state–centered forms of sovereignty. And yet, Hardt and Negri insist that "empire" is not only a metaphor but also a promising theoretical concept signifying a "political subject that effectively regulates these global exchanges, the sovereign power that governs the world." This single logic of globalization, they insist, operates in all spheres of social life, and perhaps most visibly in the regulation of human interaction, the formation of global markets, the creation of new technologies, the expansion of vast circuits of material and immaterial production, and the generation of massive cultural flows. No longer opposed by an extra-systemic "outside," this new form of sovereignty constitutes a regime that effectively encompasses the "spatial totality" of the entire globe. Thus, Hardt and Negri clearly side with "hyperglobalizers" like Anthony Giddens who argue that globalization defines a new epoch of human history—a fundamental reconfiguration of the framework of human action in which nation-states are becoming increasingly less important actors. Perhaps the most important contribution of this book to the rapidly growing global studies literature of the 2000s lies in its authors' ability to construct a new "grand narrative" of globalization that synthesized insights drawn from diverse left traditions such as Marxism, anarchism, existentialism, poststructuralism, critical theory, critical race theory, subaltern studies, and feminist theory.

Saskia Sassen's "The Global City Model"

Less polemical but surpassing even Hardt and Negri's considerable interdisciplinary skills, the Dutch American sociologist Saskia Sassen has emerged in the last two decades as one of the most influential voices in global studies. The greatest hit included in this collection is a key excerpt taken from the conclusion of the revised 2001 edition of *The Global City* (Princeton University Press, 1991). This pathbreaking study chronicles why and how New York, London, and Tokyo became command centers of the global economy, in the process undergoing significant changes. Analyzing the interaction of economic and spatial dynamics in urban settings, the New York–based social scientist convincingly demonstrates that "the global" can often be studied better by focusing on the local rather than the supranational. Indeed, one of Sassen's seminal contributions to global studies is to highlight the dangers of conceptualizing globalization dynamics according to rigidly nested geographical scales that separate the global from the regional, national, and local. The methodological implications of her recognition that manifestations of the global exist on all geographical scales are truly remarkable: if the national and the local are neither the opposite nor the equivalent of the global, then global studies scholars face the complex task of describing and analyzing interdependent geographies of power that defy the conventional spatial hierarchies that tend to rely on the nation-state as *the* core category for social and political analysis. Thus, Sassen's exposition of the "global city model" offered here foreshadowed the growing prominence of political geographers and spatial analysts in the fledgling field of global studies.

Dennis Altman's "The Globalization of Sexual Identities"

Our parade of greatest hits continues with an excerpt from *Global Sex* (University of Chicago Press, 2001), a powerful study that explores the impact of globalization on identity formation through the lenses of sexuality and gender. Penned by Australian sociologist Dennis Altman, this book has been praised by scores of leading academic and public figures such as the 1991 Nobel Prize–winning writer Nadine Gordimer, who described it as an "enlightening examination of the many unrecognized consequences of contemporary life that conventional concepts of globalization don't acknowledge." Altman's landmark study represents the first major academic treatment of the globalization of sexuality, especially the ways in which desire and pleasure have been shaped and commodified by a global economy that has brought distant cultures into close contact with each other. The author sheds light on these intricate connections between globalization and the formation of sexual subjectivities by examining—like Saskia Sassen—the myriad inscriptions of global dynamics on local identities. One of the book's major insights into these processes lies in its discerning treatment of various "paradoxes of globalization" reflected in the unexpected combination of modern and premodern elements in various constructions of sex and gender that have proven to hold tremendous global appeal.

James H. Mittelman's "Globalization: An Ascendant Paradigm?"

Next, the American political scientist James Mittelman investigates the evolving relationship between the traditional academic field of "international relations" (or "international studies") and the ascending transdisciplinary constellation of "globalization studies" (or "global studies"). Distinguishing between so-called para-keepers—scholars who deny that globalization offers a fresh way of thinking about the world—and "para-makers"—academics who emphasize the creative potential of globalization—Mittelman argues that conventional international studies is less equipped to capture the novel global processes of our time than the rising field of global studies. Drawing on Thomas Kuhn's perspective on the rise and fall of scientific "paradigms," the essay offers crucial insights into the changing academic landscape of the dawning twenty-first century. Although the author concedes that the short lifespan of "globalization studies" does not yet allow it to claim more than the status of a "proto-paradigm," he nonetheless warns against the mistake of underestimating the impact of theorizing globalization on current and future academic developments. The 2002 publication of Mittelman's article marked a critical moment in the evolution of global studies as an increasingly self-conscious field of knowledge.

Joseph Stiglitz's "The Promise of Global Institutions"

The opening chapter of Joseph Stiglitz's international bestseller *Globalization and Its Discontents* (W. W. Norton, 2003) represents the midpoint of our greatest hits collection. Winner of the 2001 Nobel Prize in economics and chief economist of the World Bank from 1997 to 2000, the current professor of economics at Columbia University has done much to enlighten audiences beyond the often-detached ivory towers of academia about the economic dimensions of globalization. In some respects, Stiglitz's book amounts to an insider's "confession" to the vast shortcomings of neoliberal economic policies he himself helped elevate to global dominance during the "Roaring Nineties." Making transparent the intricate dynamics of decision making on the part of powerful elites who inhabit the privileged spaces of global institutions and influential national governments, the former chair of President Bill Clinton's Council of Economic Advisers concedes that the liberalization of trade and the global integration of markets often did not work for billions of people living in the impoverished global South. A strong advocate for a more socially conscious reform of international economic institutions—particularly the International Monetary Fund and its neoliberal "market fundamentalism"—Stiglitz anticipated the massive criticisms directed at these organizations in the wake of the devastating global economic crisis of 2008/2009. Although the chapter's focus is squarely on global economic processes and institutions, its author explicitly acknowledges the importance of *ideological* aspects of globalization in the form of politically charged narratives that put before the public certain interpretations and claims about the phenomenon itself. The existence of these discourses shows that globalization is not merely an objective process, but also a plethora of metaphors and stories that define, describe, and analyze that very process.

Mary Kaldor's "Five Meanings of Global Civil Society"

Mary Kaldor has emerged as a prominent voice in the growing chorus of scholars exploring the reinvention of civil society in the context of globalization. In the opening chapter of her critically acclaimed study *Global Civil Society* (Polity Press, 2003), the British political scientist introduces and discusses five different versions of the concept of civil society and how these distinct perspectives relate to the formation of our globalizing world. Most importantly, she shows how the novel phenomenon of a "global civil society"—often also referred to as a worldwide network of social activists advocating the Left alternative of "globalization-from-below"—is linked to efforts of minimizing violence in social relations. Seen through the eyes of "alter-globalization" activists, then, the building of a "global civil society" is not only about the struggle to rectify economic inequities created by global capitalism but also about finding a permanent solution to the perennial problem of war. A clear testimony to the strong impact of social movement scholars on the development of global studies, Kaldor's contribution also reflected the peace- and security-related context of a destabilized post-9/11 world on the eve of the U.S.-led invasion of Iraq in March 2003.

Olivier Roy's "Al Qaeda and the New Terrorists"

The next two contributions elaborate on the relationship between global terrorism and "American Empire." The first piece is a key excerpt taken from Olivier Roy's seminal study, *Globalized Islam* (Columbia University Press, 2004), which explores the modern expansion of Islam beyond its traditional regions. This process often fans the spread of "re-Islamization," that is, strong attempts to assert a Muslim identity in a non-Muslim context, which strengthen existing radical "fundamentalist" Islamist groups such as Al Qaeda. Tracing the evolution of Al Qaeda–style terrorist organizations in several successive waves from the early 1980s to the 2000s, the French sociologist of religion argues that Al Qaeda's desired Islamization of modernity has been taking place in global space emancipated from the confining territoriality of "Egypt" or the "Middle East" that once constituted the political framework of religious nationalists fighting modern secular regimes in the twentieth century. Since the Muslim *ummah* (community of believers) is no longer confined to a specific territorial entity, Osama bin Laden, Ayman al-Zawahiri, and other radical Islamists have succeeded in articulating an imagined community in rather abstract and moralistic terms. Thus, Roy argues that a proper understanding of the formation, operation, and objectives of Islamist terrorist networks must be built around a sophisticated analysis of contemporary processes of "deterritorialization."

Manfred B. Steger's "From Market Globalism to Imperial Globalism"

The second piece focusing on the post-9/11 security discourse is my own attempt to explain the ideological transformation of neoliberal "market globalism" in the 1990s into the "imperial globalism" of the 2000s—a process reflected in the unilateral and imposing policy postures of the Bush administration. One of the most frequently downloaded articles of the prominent academic journal *Global-*

izations, my 2005 essay seeks to shed light on the crucial ideological dimensions of globalization. Providing readers with a conceptual map of "globalism" and its six major ideological claims, I trace the ideological shift from a "soft power" discourse centered on the liberalization of trade and global integration of markets to the tough imperial language of American hegemony anchored in the concepts of "terror," "war," and "security." The broader academic objective of my essay was to contribute to the ongoing intellectual project of assembling a "critical theory of globalization" dedicated to a comprehensive analysis of the shifting ideological landscape of our global age. This task found its culmination in my recent study, *The Rise of the Global Imaginary* (Oxford University Press, 2008).

Jared Diamond's "The World as a Polder"

Perhaps the most serious security issue threatening humanity in the twenty-first century is not transnational terrorism but the rapid degradation of our planet's elaborate ecosystems and the related problems of global climate change, reduction of biodiversity, transboundary pollution, lavish consumption patterns in the global North paralleling deprivation in the global South, and rapid population growth. Our next greatest hit, the concluding chapter of Jared Diamond's international bestseller *Collapse* (Viking, 2005), introduces twelve major sets of environmental problems facing modern societies. The Pulitzer Prize–winning evolutionary biologist and geographer argues that at least eight of these problems were already significant threats in the past and contributed to the collapse of such complex societies as the Easter Islanders, the Anasazi in the Four Corners area of the U.S. Southwest, the Mayas, and the Norse Greenlanders. These grim historical lessons of man-made environmental collapse suggest that a similar trajectory on the global level has the potential to destroy human life as we know it. Still, Diamond assures us that such a catastrophe does not necessarily have to happen. Identifying clear links between the environmental trouble spots of our contemporary world and socially devastated areas, the excerpt ends by pointing to the centrality of politics in returning our planet to an ecologically sustainable condition. *Collapse* was one among a growing number of key books published in the mid-2000s that infused global studies with a vital ecological perspective.

Valentine Moghadam's "The Spectre That Haunts the Global Economy?"

Our hit parade continues with a key chapter taken from Valentine Moghadam's award-winning study, *Globalizing Women* (Johns Hopkins University Press, 2005).

Drawing on global studies, social movements research, and the scholarship on women's organizations, the Iranian American sociologist and women's studies scholar examines the rise of a specific segment of "global civil society": "transnational feminist networks" (TFNs). Tracing the formation and evolution of these networks in the context of a rapidly globalizing economy, she notes that female labor and women's organizations have been crucial elements of globalization in all its dimensions. One of the most surprising findings of her research is that social movements of women often project "a more radical and transformative vision of the socio-economic and political order than do many of the 'new social movements' that have been the focus of much sociological research." Confirming insights presented in this collection by both Mary Kaldor and Jackie Smith, Moghadam emphasizes that TFNs are not "anti"-globalization but rather "alter"-globalization, for they articulate the rising global imaginary as an alternative political agenda that challenges neoliberal market globalism while at the same time advancing the cause of women's rights around the world.

Paul James's "Arguing Globalizations"

Addressing some of the same issues raised in Mittelman's essay regarding the academic study of globalization, Paul James's influential article begins with an astute assessment of the conceptual difficulties involved in defining "globalization." The Australian social theorist and global studies scholar then proceeds to show how such definitional issues often hide a multitude of methodological problems that relate directly to the study of complex globalization dynamics. The core of James's article is taken up with a series of propositions about the nature of globalization that focus on the changing framework of spatiality and temporality in our global age. Proposing a layered methodological framework that combines four levels of analysis—empirical analysis, conjectural analysis, integrational analysis, and categorical analysis—the author offers an innovative approach to the development of a coherent social theory of globalization. James's essay is one of the most downloaded articles of the influential journal *Globalizations*. Indeed, the broadening appeal of such academic journals as *Globalizations, Global Networks,* and *New Global Studies* in the 2000s reflects the coming of age of global studies as a vital field of study drawing interest from scholars working in both social science and humanities disciplines.

Mike Davis's "The Urban Climacteric"

The outset of the twenty-first century constitutes a period in which urban living has, for the first time in human history, supplanted rural life. This is a momentous shift. However, cities, for all their vibrancy and dynamism, face the growing challenge of providing secure and sustainable places to live. In his best-selling book on the world's growing population relegated to shantytowns, *Planet of Slums* (Verso, 2006), Mike Davis predicts that today's radically unequal and unstable urban growth has created explosive social environments in many of the global South's sprawling megacities. Included in our collection, the opening chapter of this study brilliantly integrates a wealth of terrifying empirical data into a powerful narrative explaining how global forces facilitate rapid urban growth in the developing world, which, "in the context of structural adjustments, currency devaluations, and state retrenchment, has been an inevitable recipe for the mass production of slums." The prominent American historian and political geographer warns that large regions of our planet have entered into an "urban climacteric" that might be the harbinger of a future very different from the one envisioned by urban planners only a few decades ago. Rather than being dominated by postmodern "cities of light" constructed of glass and steel, our cityscapes are turning into disease-ridden, environmental disaster zones, cobbled "out of crude brick, recycled plastic, cement blocks, and scrap wood" and surrounded by "pollution, excrement, and decay."

Manuel Castells's "The New Public Sphere"

Picking up on the theme of "global civil society" previously raised in Mary Kaldor's contribution, Manuel Castells's recent article (2008) suggests that public debates on new forms of global governance have decisively shifted from the national domain to a global arena created by global communications networks. Author of the seminal *The Information Age* (Blackwell, 1996–1998), a pathbreaking, three-volume study on the rise of a globalized "network society," Castells argues that the rise of the new global public sphere is inextricably linked to a world-encompassing media system composed of "television, radio, and the print press, as well as a variety of multimedia and communications systems, among which the Internet and horizontal networks of communication now play a decisive role." Reaffirming key insights articulated by Saskia Sassen, the Spanish sociologist and political economist emphasizes that this media system operates simultaneously on local and global levels, making it easier for non-state actors to influence people's minds and foster social change. Ending with a brief reflection on the role of public diplomacy in the emerging global public sphere, Castells's essay represents a sophisticated example of how today's global studies scholars manage to marshal insights from a variety of disciplines to analyze the pivotal transnational flows of the twenty-first century.

Jackie Smith and Marina Karides et al.'s "Globalization and the Emergence of the World Social Forums"

The penultimate contribution to our collection comes from a project coordinated by American sociologists Jackie Smith and Marina Karides, prominent analysts of today's "global justice movements." Coauthored by a dozen scholars working on related issues, the excerpt from their study *Global Democracy and the World Social Forums* (Paradigm, 2007) offers a useful history of the evolution of the regional and global "World Social Forums" (WSFs). Constituting progressive ideological and organizational meeting places, these WSFs are composed of hundreds of leftist groups and alliances dedicated to forms of globalization anchored in egalitarian values and principles. Intentionally established as "counter-forums" to the dominant neoliberal World Economic Forum held annually in Davos, Switzerland, these alternative public spaces were designed to allow excluded and marginalized voices "to speak and act in plurality." Usually held annually in the global South, the global WSF thus serves as an open discussion space for social activists engaged in a "new form of politics that breaks with the historical sequence of events that led to the dominance of neoliberal globalization." This essay brilliantly succeeds in compressing a wealth of empirical and historical information into a discerning analysis of today's global justice movements.

William H. McNeill's "Globalization: Long Term Process or New Era in Human Affairs?"

Fittingly, our greatest hits parade ends with William H. McNeill's reflection on the historical dimensions of globalization. A pioneer of "global history"—a new branch of historical studies increasingly intertwined with the field of global studies—the American historian ponders the crucial question of whether globalization should be seen as a long-term process or as a new era in human affairs. Summarizing crucial milestones in the evolution of human societies, McNeill offers a seemingly paradoxical response to his overarching question: although the world has always been one interacting whole, the recent extension and proliferation of contemporary networks of interdependence point to a dramatic acceleration and intensification of social relations and consciousness across world-time and world-space. McNeill's conclusions are symptomatic of what might be seen as a "historical turn" in global studies—the growing attention to evolving historical patterns and shifting temporal and cultural contexts. For example, recent periodization efforts have yielded much-revised chronologies that tend to eschew conventional Eurocentric historical narratives and instead present globalization not merely as a linear, diffusionist process starting in the West in the 1970s (or the late nineteenth century, or the early sixteenth century) but as a multinodal, multidirectional dynamic full of unanticipated surprises, violent twists, sudden punctuations, and dramatic reversals.

It is with this important insight of the unpredictability of globalization processes that our hit parade ends. I hope that these short previews have whetted your appetite and you are now ready to give the full versions your full attention. So dive in and enjoy!

CHAPTER 1
THE GLOBALIZATION OF MARKETS

Theodore Levitt

A powerful force drives the world toward a converging commonality, and that force is technology. It has proletarianized communication, transport, and travel. It has made isolated places and impoverished peoples eager for modernity's allurements. Almost everyone everywhere wants all the things they have heard about, seen, or experienced via the new technologies.

The result is a new commercial reality—the emergence of global markets for standardized consumer products on a previously unimagined scale of magnitude. Corporations geared to this new reality benefit from enormous economies of scale in production, distribution, marketing, and management. By translating these benefits into reduced world prices, they can decimate competitors that still live in the disabling grip of old assumptions about how the world works.

Gone are accustomed differences in national or regional preference. Gone are the days when a company could sell last year's models—or lesser versions of advanced products—in the less-developed world. And gone are the days when prices, margins, and profits abroad were generally higher than at home.

The globalization of markets is at hand. With that, the multinational commercial world nears its end, and so does the multinational corporation.

The multinational and the global corporation are not the same thing. The multinational corporation operates in a number of countries, and adjusts its products and practices in each—at high relative costs. The global corporation operates with resolute constancy—at low relative cost—as if the entire world (or major regions of it) were a single entity; it sells the same things in the same way everywhere.

Which strategy is better is not a matter of opinion but of necessity. Worldwide communications carry everywhere the constant drumbeat of modern possibilities to lighten and enhance work, raise living standards, divert, and entertain. The same countries that ask the world to recognize and respect the individuality of their cultures insist on the wholesale transfer to them of modern goods, services, and technologies. Modernity is not just a wish but also a widespread practice among those who cling, with unyielding passion or religious fervor, to ancient attitudes and heritages.

Who can forget the televised scenes during the 1979 Iranian uprisings of young men in fashionable French-cut trousers and silky body shirts thirsting for blood with raised modern weapons in the name of Islamic fundamentalism?

In Brazil, thousands swarm daily from preindustrial Bahian darkness into exploding coastal cities, there quickly to install television sets in crowded corrugated huts and, next to battered Volkswagens, make sacrificial offerings of fruit and fresh-killed chickens to Macumban spirits by candlelight.

During Biafra's fratricidal war against the Ibos, daily televised reports showed soldiers carrying bloodstained swords and listening to transistor radios while drinking Coca-Cola.

In the isolated Siberian city of Krasnoyarsk, with no paved streets and censored news, occasional Western travelers are stealthily propositioned for cigarettes, digital watches, and even the clothes off their backs.

The organized smuggling of electronic equipment, used automobiles, western clothing, cosmetics, and pirated movies into primitive places exceeds even the thriving underground trade in modern weapons and their military mercenaries.

A thousand suggestive ways attest to the ubiquity of the desire for the most advanced things that the world makes and sells—goods of the best quality and reliability at the lowest price. The world's needs and desires have been irrevocably homogenized. This makes the multinational corporation obsolete and the global corporation absolute.

Living in the Republic of Technology

Daniel J. Boorstin, author of the monumental trilogy *The Americans,* character-ized our age as driven by "the Republic of Technology [whose] supreme law ... is convergence, the tendency for everything to become more like everything else."

In business, this trend has pushed markets toward global commonality. Corporations sell standardized products in the same way everywhere—autos, steel, chemicals, petroleum, cement, agricultural commodities and equipment, industrial and commercial construction, banking and insurance services, com-puters, semiconductors, transport, electronic instruments, pharmaceuticals, and telecommunications, to mention some of the obvious.

Nor is the sweeping gale of globalization confined to these raw material or high-tech products, where the universal language of customers and users facilitates standardization. The transforming winds whipped up by the proletarianization of communication and travel enter every crevice of life.

Commercially, nothing confirms this as much as the success of McDonald's from the Champs Elysées to the Ginza, of Coca-Cola in Bahrain and Pepsi-Cola in Moscow, and of rock music, Greek salad, Hollywood movies, Revlon cosmet-ics, Sony televisions, and Levi jeans everywhere. "High-touch" products are as ubiquitous as high-tech.

Starting from opposing sides, the high-tech and the high-touch ends of the commercial spectrum gradually consume the undistributed middle in their cos-mopolitan orbit. No one is exempt and nothing can stop the process. Everywhere everything gets more and more like everything else as the world's preference structure is relentlessly homogenized.

Consider the cases of Coca-Cola and Pepsi-Cola, which are globally stan-dardized products sold everywhere and welcomed by everyone. Both successfully cross multitudes of national, regional, and ethnic taste buds trained to a variety of deeply ingrained local preferences of taste, flavor, consistency, effervescence, and aftertaste. Everywhere both sell well. Cigarettes, too, especially American-made, make year-to-year global inroads on territories previously held in the firm grip of other, mostly local, blends.

These are not exceptional examples. (Indeed their global reach would be even greater were it not for artificial trade barriers.) They exemplify a general drift toward the homogenization of the world and how companies distribute, finance, and price products.[1] Nothing is exempt. The products and methods of the industrialized world play a single tune for all the world, and all the world eagerly dances to it.

Ancient differences in national tastes or modes of doing business disappear. The commonality of preference leads inescapably to the standardization of products, manufacturing, and the institutions of trade and commerce. Small nation-based markets transmogrify and expand. Success in world competition turns on efficiency in production, distribution, marketing, and management, and inevitably becomes focused on price.

The most effective world competitors incorporate superior quality and reliability into their cost structures. They sell in all national markets the same kind of products sold at home or in their largest export market. They compete on the basis of appropriate value—the best combinations of price, quality, reliability, and delivery for products that are globally identical with respect to design, function, and even fashion.

That, and little else, explains the surging success of Japanese companies dealing worldwide in a vast variety of products—both tangible products like steel, cars, motorcycles, hi-fi equipment, farm machinery, robots, microprocessors, carbon fibers, and now even textiles, and intangibles like banking, shipping, general contracting, and soon computer software. Nor are high-quality and low-cost operations incompatible, as a host of consulting organizations and data engineers argue with vigorous vacuity. The reported data are incomplete, wrongly analyzed, and contradictory. The truth is that low-cost operations are the hallmark of corporate cultures that require and produce quality in all that they do. High quality and low costs are not opposing postures. They are compatible, twin identities of superior practice.[2]

To say that Japan's companies are not global because they export cars with left-side drives to the United States and the European continent, while those in Japan have right-side drives, or because they sell office machines through distributors in the United States but directly at home, or speak Portuguese in Brazil is to mistake a difference for a distinction. The same is true of Safeway and Southland retail chains operating effectively in the Middle East, and to not only native but also imported populations from Korea, the Philippines, Pakistan, India, Thailand, Britain, and the United States. National rules of the road differ, and so do distribution channels and languages. Japan's distinction is its unrelenting push for economy and value enhancement. That translates into a drive for standardization at high quality levels.

Vindication of the Model T

If a company forces costs and prices down and pushes quality and reliability up—while maintaining reasonable concern for suitability—customers will prefer its world-standardized products. The theory holds at this stage in the evolution of globalization—no matter what conventional market research and even common sense may suggest about different national and regional tastes, preferences, needs, and institutions. The Japanese have repeatedly vindicated this theory, as did Henry Ford with the Model T. Most important, so have their imitators, including companies from South Korea (television sets and heavy construction), Malaysia (personal calculators and microcomputers), Brazil (auto parts and tools), Colombia (apparel), Singapore (optical equipment), and, yes, even the United States (office copiers, computers, bicycles, castings), Western Europe (automatic washing machines), Rumania (housewares), Hungary (apparel), Yugoslavia (furniture), and Israel (pagination equipment).

Of course, large companies operating in a single nation or even a single city don't standardize everything they make, sell, or do. They have product lines instead of a single product version, and multiple distribution channels. There are neighborhood, local, regional, ethnic, and institutional differences, even within metropolitan areas. But although companies customize products for particular market segments, they know that success in a world with homogenized demand requires a search for sales opportunities in similar segments across the globe in order to achieve the economies of scale necessary to compete. Such a search works because a market segment in one country is seldom unique; it has close cousins everywhere precisely because technology has homogenized the globe. Even small local segments have their global equivalents everywhere and become subject to global competition, especially on price.

The global competitor will seek constantly to standardize its offering everywhere. It will digress from this standardization only after exhausting all possibilities to retain it, and will push for reinstatement of standardization whenever digression and divergence have occurred. It will never assume that the customer is a king who knows his own wishes.

Trouble increasingly stalks companies that lack clarified global focus and remain inattentive to the economics of simplicity and standardization. The most endangered companies in the rapidly evolving world tend to be those that dominate rather small domestic markets with high value-added products for which there are smaller markets elsewhere. With transportation costs proportionately low, distant competitors will enter the now-sheltered markets of those companies with goods produced more cheaply under scale-efficient conditions. Global competition spells the end of domestic territoriality, no matter how diminutive the territory may be.

When the global producer offers its lower costs internationally, its patronage expands exponentially. It not only reaches into distant markets, but also attracts customers who previously held to local preferences and now capitulate to the attractions of lower prices. The strategy of standardization not only responds to worldwide homogenized markets but also expands those markets with aggressive low pricing. The new technological juggernaut taps an ancient motivation—to make one's money go as far as possible. This is universal—not simply a motivation but actually a need.

The Hedgehog Knows

The difference between the hedgehog and the fox, wrote Sir Isaiah Berlin in distinguishing between Dostoevski and Tolstoy, is that the fox knows a lot about a great many things, but the hedgehog knows everything about one great thing. The multinational corporation knows a lot about a great many countries and congenially adapts to supposed differences. It willingly accepts vestigial national differences, not questioning the possibility of their transformation, not recognizing how the world is ready and eager for the benefit of modernity, especially when the price is right. The multinational corporation's accommodating mode to visible national differences is medieval.

By contrast, the global corporation knows everything about one great thing. It knows about the absolute need to be competitive on a worldwide basis as well as nationally and seeks constantly to drive down prices by standardizing what it sells and how it operates. It treats the world as composed of few standardized markets rather than many customized markets. It actively seeks and vigorously works toward global convergence. Its mission is modernity and its mode is price competition, even when it sells top-of-the-line, high-end products. It knows about the one great thing all nations and people have in common: scarcity.

Nobody takes scarcity lying down; everyone wants more. This in part explains division of labor and specialization of production. They enable people and nations to optimize their conditions through trade. The median is usually money.

Experience teaches that money has three special qualities: scarcity, difficulty of acquisition, and transience. People understandably treat it with respect. Everyone in the increasingly homogenized world market wants products and features that everybody else wants. If the price is low enough, they will take highly standardized world products, even if these aren't exactly what one's parents said was suitable, what immemorial custom decreed was right, or what market-research fabulists asserted was preferred.

The implacable truth of all modern production—whether of tangible or intangible goods—is that large-scale production of standardized items is generally cheaper within a wide range of volume than small-scale production. Some argue that computer-aided design and manufacturing (CAD/CAM) will allow companies to manufacture customized products on a small scale—but cheaply. But the argument misses the point. (For a more detailed discussion, see Exhibit 1.1.) If a company treats the world as one or two distinctive product markets, it can serve the world more economically than if it treats it as three, four, or five product markets.

Exhibit 1.1 Economies of Scope

One argument that opposes globalization says that flexible factory automation will enable plants of massive size to change products and product features quickly, without stopping the manufacturing process. These factories of the future could thus produce broad lines of customized products without sacrificing the scale economies that come from long production runs of standardized items. CAD/CAM, combined with robotics, will create a new equipment and process technology (EPT) that will make small plants located close to their markets as efficient as large ones located distantly. Economies of scale will not dominate, but rather economies of scope—the ability of either large or small plants to produce great varieties of relatively customized products at remarkably low costs. If that happens, the customers will have no need to abandon special preferences.

I will not deny the power of these possibilities. But possibilities do not make probabilities. There is no conceivable way in which flexible factory automation can achieve the scale economies of a modernized plant dedicated to mass production of standardized lines. The new digitized equipment and process technologies are available to all. Manufacturers with minimal customization and narrow product-line breadth will have costs far below those with more customization and wider lines.

Why Remaining Differences?

Different cultural preferences, national tastes and standards, and business institutions are vestiges of the past. Some inheritances die gradually; others prosper and expand into mainstream global preferences. So-called ethnic markets are a good example. Chinese food, pita bread, country and western music, pizza, and jazz are everywhere. They are market segments that exist in world-wide proportions. They don't deny or contradict global homogenization but confirm it.

Many of today's differences among nations as to products and their features actually reflect the respectful accommodation of multinational corporations to what they believe are fixed local preferences. They *believe* preferences are fixed, not because they are but because of rigid habits of thinking about what actually is. Most executives in multinational corporations are thoughtlessly accommodating. They falsely presume that marketing means giving customers what they say they want rather than trying to understand exactly what they would like. So the corporations persist with high-cost, customized multinational products and practices instead of pressing hard and pressing properly for global standardization.

I do not advocate the systematic disregard of local or national differences. But a company's sensitivity to such differences does not require that it ignore the possibilities of doing things differently or better.

There are, for example, enormous differences among Middle Eastern countries. Some are socialist, some monarchies, some republics. Some take their legal heritage from the Napoleonic Code, some from the Ottoman Empire, and some from British common law; except for Israel, all are influenced by Islam. Doing business means personalizing the business relationship in an obsessively intimate fashion. During the month of Ramadan, business discussions can start only after 10 o'clock at night, when people are tired and full of food after a day of fasting. A company must almost certainly have a local partner; a local lawyer is required (as, say, in New York), and irrevocable letters of credit are essential. Yet, as Coca-Cola's senior vice president Sam Ayoub noted, "Arabs are much more capable of making distinctions between cultural and religious purposes on the one hand and economic realities on the other than is generally assumed. Islam is compatible with science and modern times."

Barriers to globalization are not confined to the Middle East. The free transfer of technology and data across the boundaries of the European Common Market countries is hampered by legal and financial impediments. And there is resistance to radio and television interference ("pollution") among neighboring European countries.

But the past is a good guide to the future. With persistence and appropriate means, barriers against superior technologies and economics have always fallen. There is no recorded exception where reasonable effort has been made to overcome them. It is very much a matter of time and effort.

A Failure in Global Imagination

Many companies have tried to standardize world practice by exporting domestic products and processes without accommodation or change—and have failed miserably. Their deficiencies have been seized on as evidence of bovine stupidity in the face of abject impossibility. Advocates of global standardization see them as examples of failures in execution.

In fact, poor execution is often an important cause. More important, however, is failure of nerve—failure of imagination.

Table 1.1   Consumer Preferences as to Automatic Washing Machine Features in the 1960s

Features	Great Britain	Italy	W. Germany	France	Sweden
Shell Dimensions*	34" and narrow	Low and narrow	34" and wide	34" and narrow	34" and wide
Drum Material	Enamel	Enamel	Stainless steel	Enamel	Stainless steel
Loading	Top	Front	Front	Front	Front
Front Porthole	Yes/no	Yes	Yes	Yes	Yes
Capacity	5 kilos	4 kilos	6 kilos	5 kilos	6 kilos
Spin Speed	700 rpm	400 rpm	850 rpm	600 rpm	800 rpm
Water-heating System	No[†]	Yes	Yes[††]	Yes	No[†]
Washing Action	Agitator	Tumble	Tumble	Agitator	Tumble
Styling Features	Inconspicuous appearance	Brightly colored	Indestructible appearance	Elegant appearance	Strong appearance

*34" height was in the process of being adopted as a standard work-surface height in Europe.
[†]Most British and Swedish homes had centrally heated hot water.
[††]West Germans preferred to launder at temperatures higher than generally provided centrally.

Consider the case for the introduction of fully automatic home laundry equipment in Western Europe at a time when few homes had even semiautomatic machines. Hoover, Ltd., whose parent company was headquartered in North Canton, Ohio, had a prominent presence in Britain as a producer of vacuum cleaners and washing machines. Due to insufficient demand in the home market and low exports to the European continent, the large washing machine plant in England operated far below capacity. The company needed to sell more of its semiautomatic or automatic machines.

Because it had a "proper" marketing orientation, Hoover conducted consumer preference studies in Britain and each major continental country. The results showed feature preferences clearly enough among several countries (see Table 1.1).

The incremental unit variable costs (in pounds sterling) of customizing to meet just a few of the national preferences were:

	£	s.	d.
Stainless steel vs. enamel drum	1	0	0
Porthole window		10	0
Spin speed of 800 rpm vs. 700 rpm		15	0
Water heater	2	15	0
6 vs. 5 kilos capacity	1	10	0
	£6	10s	0d

$18.20 at exchange rate of that time

Considerable plant investment was needed to meet other preferences.

The lowest retail prices (in pounds sterling) of leading locally produced brands in the various countries were approximately:

U.K.	£110
France	114
West Germany	113
Sweden	134
Italy	57

Product customization in each country would have put Hoover in a poor competitive position on the basis of price, mostly due to the higher manufacturing costs incurred by short production runs for separate features. Because Common Market tariff reduction programs were then incomplete, Hoover also paid tariff duties in each continental country.

How to Make a Creative Analysis

In the Hoover case, an imaginative analysis of automatic washing machine sales in each country would have revealed that

1. Italian automatics, small in capacity and size, low-powered, without built-in heaters, with porcelain enamel tubs, were priced aggressively low and were gaining large market shares in all countries, including West Germany.
2. The best-selling automatics in West Germany were heavily advertised (three times more than the next most promoted brand), were ideally suited to national tastes, and were also by far the highest-priced machines available in that country.
3. Italy, with the lowest penetration of washing machines of any kind (manual, semiautomatic, or automatic), was rapidly going directly to automatics, skipping the pattern of first buying hand-wringer, manually assisted machines and then semiautomatics.
4. Detergent manufacturers were just beginning to promote the technique of cold-water and tepid-water laundering then used in the United States.

The growing success of small, low-powered, low-speed, low-capacity, low-priced Italian machines, even against the preferred but highly priced and highly promoted brand in West Germany, was significant. It contained a powerful message that was lost on managers confidently wedded to a distorted version of the marketing concept according to which you give customers what they say they want. In fact, the customers *said* they wanted certain features, but their behavior demonstrated they'd take other features provided the price and the promotion were right.

In this case, it was obvious that, under prevailing conditions, people preferred a low-priced automatic over any kind of manual or semiautomatic machine and certainly over higher-priced automatics, even though the low-priced automatics failed to fulfill all their expressed preferences. The supposedly meticulous and demanding German consumers violated all expectations by buying the simple, low-priced Italian machines.

It was equally clear that people were profoundly influenced by promotions of automatic washers; in West Germany, the most heavily promoted ideal machine also had the largest market share despite its high price. Two things clearly influenced customers to buy: low price regardless of feature preferences, and heavy promotion regardless of price. Both factors helped customers get what they most wanted—the superior benefits bestowed by fully automatic machines.

Hoover should have aggressively sold a simple, standardized high-quality machine at a low price (afforded by the 17% variable cost reduction that the elimination of £6–10-0 worth of extra features made possible). The suggested retail prices could have been somewhat less than £100. The extra funds "saved" by avoiding unnecessary plant modifications would have supported an extended service network and aggressive media promotions.

Hoover's media message should have been: *this* is the machine that you, the homemaker, *deserve* to have to reduce the repetitive, heavy daily household burdens, so that *you* may have more constructive time to spend with your children and your husband. The promotion should also have targeted the husband to give him, preferably in the presence of his wife, a sense of obligation to provide an automatic washer for her even before he bought an automobile for himself. An aggressively low price, combined with heavy promotion of this kind, would have overcome previously expressed preferences for particular features.

The Hoover case illustrates how the perverse practice of the marketing concept and the absence of any kind of marketing imagination let multinational attitudes survive when customers actually want the benefits of global standardization. The whole project got off on the wrong foot. It asked people what features they wanted in a washing machine rather than what they wanted out of life. Selling a line of products individually tailored to each nation is thoughtless. Managers who took pride in practicing the marketing concept to the fullest did not, in fact, practice it at all. Hoover asked the wrong questions, then applied neither thought nor imagination to the answers. Such companies are like the ethnocentricists in the Middle Ages who saw with everyday clarity the sun revolving around the earth and offered it as Truth. With no additional data but a more searching mind, Copernicus, like the hedgehog, interpreted a more compelling and accurate reality. Data do not yield information except with the intervention of the mind. Information does not yield meaning except with the intervention of imagination.

Accepting the Inevitable

The global corporation accepts for better or for worse that technology drives consumers relentlessly toward the same common goals—alleviation of life's burdens and the expansion of discretionary time and spending power. Its role is profoundly different from what it has been for the ordinary corporation during its brief, turbulent, and remarkably protean history. It orchestrates the twin vectors of technology and globalization for the world's benefit. Neither fate, nor nature, nor God but rather the necessity of commerce created this role.

In the United States, two industries became global long before they were consciously aware of it. After over a generation of persistent and acrimonious labor shutdowns, the United Steelworkers of America had not called an industrywide strike since 1959; the United Auto Workers had not shut down General Motors since 1970. Both unions realize that they have become global; shutting down all or most of U.S. manufacturing would not shut out U.S. customers. Overseas suppliers are there to supply the market.

Cracking the Code of Western Markets

Since the theory of the marketing concept emerged a quarter of a century ago, the more managerially advanced corporations have been eager to offer what customers clearly wanted rather than what was merely convenient.

They have created marketing departments supported by professional market researchers of awesome and often costly proportions. And they have proliferated extraordinary numbers of operations and product lines—highly tailored products and delivery systems for many different markets, market segments, and nations.

Significantly, Japanese companies operate almost entirely without marketing departments or market research of the kind so prevalent in the West. Yet in the colorful words of General Electric's chairman John E. Welch, Jr., the Japanese, coming from a small cluster of resource-poor islands, with an entirely alien culture and an almost impenetrably complex language, have cracked the code of Western markets. They have done it not by looking with mechanistic thoroughness at the way markets are different but rather by searching for meaning with a deeper wisdom. They have discovered the one great thing all markets have in common— an overwhelming desire for dependable, world-standard modernity in all things, at aggressively low prices. In response, they deliver irresistible value everywhere, attracting people with products that market-research technocrats described with superficial certainty as being unsuitable and uncompetitive.

The wider a company's global reach, the greater the number of regional and national preferences it will encounter for certain product features, distribution

---

Exhibit 1.2 The Shortening of Japanese Horizons

One of the most powerful yet least celebrated forces driving commerce toward global standardization is the monetary system, along with the international investment process. Today money is simply electronic impulses. With the speed of light it moves effortlessly between distant centers (and even lesser places). A change of 10 basis points in the price of a bond causes an instant and massive shift of money from London to Tokyo. The system has a profound impact on the way companies operate throughout the world.

Take Japan, where high debt-to-equity balance sheets are "guaranteed" by various societal presumptions about the virtue of "a long view," or by government policy in other ways. Even here, upward shifts in interest rates in other parts of the world attract capital out of the country in powerful proportions. In recent years more and more Japanese global corporations have gone to the world's equity markets for funds. Debt is too remunerative in high-yielding countries to keep capital at home to feed the Japanese need. As interest rates rise, equity becomes a more attractive option for the issuer.

The long-term impact on Japanese enterprise will be transforming. As the equity proportion of Japanese corporate capitalization rises, companies will respond to the shorter-term investment horizons of the equity markets. Thus the much-vaunted Japanese corporate practice to taking the long view will gradually disappear.

Reality is not a fixed paradigm, dominated by immemorial customs and derived attitudes, heedless of powerful and abundant new forces. The world is becoming increasingly informed about the liberating and enhancing possibilities of modernity. The persistence of the inherited varieties of national preferences rests uneasily on increasing evidence of, and restlessness regarding, their inefficiency, costliness, and confinement. The historic past, and the national differences respecting commerce and industry it spawned and fostered everywhere, is now subject to relatively easy transformation.

Cosmopolitanism is no longer the monopoly of the intellectual and leisure classes; it is becoming the established property and defining characteristic of all sectors everywhere in the world. Gradually and irresistibly it breaks down the walls of economic insularity, nationalism, and chauvinism. What we see today as escalating commercial nationalism is simply the last violent death rattle of an obsolete institution.

Companies that adapt to and capitalize on economic convergence can still make distinctions and adjustments in different markets. Persistent differences in the world are consistent with fundamental underlying commonalities; they often complement rather than oppose each other—in business as they do in physics. There is, in physics, matter and antimatter simultaneously working in symbiotic harmony.

The earth is round, but for most purposes it's sensible to treat it as flat. Space is curved, but not much for everyday life here on earth.

Divergence from established practice happens all the time. But the multinational mind, warped into circumspection and timidity by years of stumbles and transnational troubles, now rarely challenges existing overseas practices. More often it considers any departure from inherited domestic routines as mindless, disrespectful, or impossible. It is the mind of a bygone day.

The successful global corporation does not abjure customization or differentiation for the requirements of markets that differ in product preferences, spending patterns, shopping preferences, and institutional or legal arrangements. But the global corporation accepts and adjusts to these differences only reluctantly, only after relentlessly testing their immutability, after trying in various ways to circumvent and reshape them, as we saw in the cases of Outboard Marine in Europe, SmithKline in Japan, and Komatsu in the United States.

There is only one significant respect in which a company's activities around the world are important, and this is in what it produces and how it sells. Everything else derives from, and is subsidiary to, these activities.

The purpose of business is to get and keep a customer. Or, to use Peter Drucker's more refined construction, to *create* and keep a customer. A company must be wedded to the ideal of innovation—offering better or more preferred products in such combinations of ways, means, places, and at such prices that prospects *prefer* doing business with the company rather than with others.

Preferences are constantly shaped and reshaped. Within our global commonality, enormous variety constantly asserts itself and thrives, as can be seen within the world's single largest domestic market, the United States. But in the process of world homogenization, modern markets expand to reach cost-reducing global proportions. With better and cheaper communication and transport, even small local market segments hitherto protected from distant competitors now feel the pressure of their presence. Nobody is safe from global reach and the irresistible economies of scale.

Two vectors shape the world—technology and globalization. The first helps determine human preferences; the second, economic realities. Regardless of how much preferences evolve and diverge, they also gradually converge and form markets where economies of scale lead to reduction of costs and prices.

The modern global corporation contrasts powerfully with the aging multinational corporation. Instead of adapting to superficial and even entrenched differences within and between nations, it will seek sensibly to force suitably standardized products and practices on the entire globe. They are exactly what the world will take, if they come also with low prices, high quality, and blessed reliability. The global company will operate, in this regard, precisely as Henry Kissinger wrote in *Years of Upheaval* about the continuing Japanese economic success: "voracious in its collection of information, impervious to pressure, and implacable in execution."

Given what is everywhere the purpose of commerce, the global company will shape the vectors of technology and globalization into its great strategic fecundity. It will systematically push these vectors toward their own convergence, offering everyone simultaneously high-quality, more or less standardized products at optimally low prices, thereby achieving for itself vastly expanded markets and profits. Companies that do not adapt to the new global realities will become victims of those that do.

Notes

Theodore Levitt, "The Globalization of Markets," *Harvard Business Review* (May–June 1983): 92–102. Reprinted with permission of Harvard Business School Publishing.

1. In a landmark article, Robert D. Buzzell pointed out the rapidity with which barriers to standardization were falling. In all cases they succumbed to more advanced and cheaper ways of doing things. *See* "Can You Standardize Multinational Marketing?" *Harvard Business Review* (November–December 1968).

2. There is powerful new evidence for this, even though the opposite has been urged by analysts of PIMS data for years. *See* "Product Quality: Cost Production and Business Performance—A Test of Some Key Hypotheses" by Lynn W. Phillips, Dae Chang, and Robert D. Buzzell, Harvard Business School Working Paper No. 83–13.

3. For a discussion of multinational reorganization, *see* Christopher A. Bartlett, "MNCs: Get Off the Reorganization Merry-Go-Round," *Harvard Business Review* (March–April 1983).

CHAPTER 2
DISJUNCTURE AND DIFFERENCE IN THE GLOBAL
CULTURAL ECONOMY

Arjun Appadurai

The central problem of today's global interactions is the tension between cultural homogenization and cultural heterogenization. A vast array of empirical facts could be brought to bear on the side of the 'homogenization' argument, and much of it has come from the left end of the spectrum of media studies (Hamelink, 1983; Mattelart, 1983; Schiller, 1976), and some from other, less appealing, perspectives (Gans, 1985; Iyer, 1988). Most often, the homogenization argument subspeciates into either an argument about Americanization, or an argument about 'commoditization', and very often the two arguments are closely linked. What these arguments fail to consider is that at least as rapidly as forces from various metropolises are brought into new societies they tend to become indigenized in one or other way: this is true of music and housing styles as much as it is true of science and terrorism, spectacles and constitutions. The dynamics of such indigenization have just begun to be explored in a sophisticated manner (Barber, 1987; Feld, 1988; Hannerz, 1987, 1989; Ivy, 1988; Nicoll, 1989; Yoshimoto, 1989), and much more needs to be done. But it is worth noticing that for the people of Irian Jaya, Indonesianization may be more worrisome than Americanization, as Japanization may be for Koreans, Indianization for Sri Lankans, Vietnamization for the Cambodians, Russianization for the people of Soviet Armenia and the Baltic Republics. Such a list of alternative fears to Americanization could be greatly expanded, but it is not a shapeless inventory: for polities of smaller scale, there is always a fear of cultural absorption by polities of larger scale, especially those that are near by. One man's imagined community (Anderson, 1983) is another man's political prison.

This scalar dynamic, which has widespread global manifestations, is also tied to the relationship between nations and states, to which I shall return later in this essay. For the moment let us note that the simplification of these many forces (and fears) of homogenization can also be exploited by nation-states in relation to their own minorities, by posing global commoditization (or capitalism, or some other such external enemy) as more 'real' than the threat of its own hegemonic strategies.

The new global cultural economy has to be understood as a complex, overlapping, disjunctive order, which cannot any longer be understood in terms of existing center-periphery models (even those that might account for multiple centers and peripheries). Nor is it susceptible to simple models of push and pull (in terms of migration theory) or of surpluses and deficits (as in traditional models of balance of trade), or of consumers and producers (as in most neo-Marxist theories of development). Even the most complex and flexible theories of global development which have come out of the Marxist tradition (Amin, 1980; Mandel, 1978; Wallerstein, 1974; Wolf, 1982) are inadequately quirky, and they have not come to terms with what Lash and Urry (1987) have recently called 'disorganized capitalism'. The complexity of the current global economy has to do with certain fundamental disjunctures between economy, culture and politics which we have barely begun to theorize.[1]

I propose that an elementary framework for exploring such disjunctures is to look at the relationship between five dimensions of global cultural flow which can be termed: (a) ethnoscapes; (b) mediascapes; (c) technoscapes; (d) finanscapes; and (e) ideoscapes.[2] I use terms with the common suffix scape to indicate first of all that these are not objectively given relations which look the same from every angle of vision, but rather that they are deeply perspectival constructs, inflected very much by the historical, linguistic and political situatedness of different sorts of actors: nation-states, multinationals, diasporic communities, as well as subnational groupings and movements (whether religious, political or economic), and even intimate face-to-face groups, such as villages, neighborhoods and families. Indeed, the individual actor is the last locus of this perspectival set of landscapes, for these landscapes are eventually navigated by agents who both experience and constitute larger formations, in part by their own sense of what these landscapes offer. These landscapes thus, are the building blocks of what, extending Benedict Anderson, I would like to call 'imagined worlds', that is, the multiple worlds which are constituted by the historically situated imaginations of persons and groups spread around the globe (Appadurai, 1989). An important fact of the world we live in today is that many persons on the globe live in such imagined 'worlds' and not just in imagined communities, and thus are able to contest and sometimes even subvert the 'imagined worlds' of the official mind and of the entrepreneurial mentality that surround them. The suffix scape also allows us to point to the fluid, irregular shapes of these landscapes, shapes which characterize international capital as deeply as they do international clothing styles.

By 'ethnoscape', I mean the landscape of persons who constitute the shifting world in which we live: tourists, immigrants, refugees, exiles, guestworkers and other moving groups and persons constitute an essential feature of the world, and appear to affect the politics of and between nations to a hitherto unprecedented degree. This is not to say that there are not anywhere relatively stable communities and networks, of kinship, of friendship, of work and of leisure, as well as of birth, residence and other filiative forms. But it is to say that the warp of these stabilities is everywhere shot through with the woof of human motion, as more persons and groups deal with the realities of having to move, or the fantasies of wanting to move. What is more, both these realities as well as these fantasies now function on larger scales, as men and women from villages in India think not just of moving to Poona or Madras, but of moving to Dubai and Houston, and refugees from Sri Lanka find themselves in South India as well as in Canada, just as the Hmong are driven to London as well as to Philadelphia. And as international capital shifts its needs, as production and technology generate different needs, as nation-states shift their policies on refugee populations, these moving groups can never afford to let their imaginations rest too long, even if they wished to.

By 'technoscape', I mean the global configuration, also ever fluid, of technology, and of the fact that technology, both high and low, both mechanical and informational, now moves at high speeds across various kinds of previously impervious boundaries. Many countries now are the roots of multinational enterprise: a huge steel complex in Libya may involve interests from India, China, Russia and Japan, providing different components of new technological configurations. The odd distribution of technologies, and thus the peculiarities of these technoscapes, are increasingly driven not by any obvious economies of scale, of political control, or of market rationality, but of increasingly complex relationships between money flows, political possibilities and the availability of both low and highly skilled labor. So, while India exports waiters and chauffeurs to Dubai and Sharjah, it also exports software engineers to the United States (indentured briefly to Tata-Burroughs or the World Bank), then laundered through the State Department to become wealthy 'resident aliens', who are in turn objects of seductive messages to invest their money and know-how in federal and state projects in India. The global economy can still be described in terms of traditional 'indicators' (as the World Bank continues to do) and studied in terms of traditional comparisons (as in Project Link at the University of Pennsylvania), but the complicated technoscapes (and the shifting ethnoscapes), which underlie these 'indicators' and 'comparisons' are further out of the reach of the 'queen of the social sciences' than ever before. How is one to make a meaningful comparision of wages in Japan and the United States, or of real estate costs in New York and Tokyo, without taking sophisticated account of the very complex fiscal and investment flows that link the two economies through a global grid of currency speculation and capital transfer?

Thus it is useful to speak as well of 'financescapes', since the disposition of global capital is now a more mysterious, rapid and difficult landscape to follow than ever before, as currency markets, national stock exchanges, and commodity speculations move mega-monies through national turnstiles at blinding speed, with vast absolute implications for small differences in percentage points and time units. But the critical point is that the global relationship between ethnoscapes, technoscapes and financescapes is deeply disjunctive and profoundly unpredictable, since each of these landscapes is subject to its own constraints and incentives (some political, some informational and some techno-environmental), at the same time as each acts as a constraint and a parameter for movements in the other. Thus, even an elementary model of global political economy must take into account the shifting relationship between perspectives on human movement, technological flow, and financial transfers, which can accommodate their deeply disjunctive relationships with one another.

Built upon these disjunctures (which hardly form a simple, mechanical global 'infrastructure' in any case) are what I have called 'mediascapes' and 'ideoscapes', though the latter two are closely related landscapes of images. 'Mediascapes' refer both to the distribution of the electronic capabilities to produce and disseminate information (newspapers, magazines, television stations, film production studios, etc.), which are now available to a growing number of private and public interests throughout the world; and to the images of the world created by these media. These images of the world involve many complicated inflections, depending on their mode (documentary or entertainment), their hardware (electronic or pre-electronic), their audiences (local, national or transnational) and the interests of those who own and control them. What is most important about these mediascapes is that they provide (especially in their television, film and cassette forms) large and complex repertoires of images, narratives and 'ethnoscapes' to viewers throughout the world, in which the world of commodities and the world of 'news' and politics are profoundly mixed. What this means is that many audiences throughout the world experience the media themselves as a complicated and interconnected repertoire of print, celluloid, electronic screens and billboards. The lines between the 'realistic' and the fictional landscapes they see are blurred, so that the further away these audiences are from the direct experiences of metropolitan life, the more likely they are to construct 'imagined worlds' which are chimerical, aesthetic, even fantastic objects, particularly if assessed by the criteria of some other perspective, some other 'imagined world'.

'Mediascapes', whether produced by private or state interests, tend to be image-centered, narrative-based accounts of strips of reality, and what they offer to those who experience and transform them is a series of elements (such as characters, plots and textual forms) out of which scripts can be formed of imagined lives, their own as well as those of others living in other places. These scripts can and do get disaggregated into complex sets of metaphors by which people live (Lakoff and Johnson, 1980) as they help to constitute narratives of the 'other' and proto-narratives of possible lives, fantasies which could become prolegomena to the desire for acquisition and movement.

'Ideoscsapes' are also concatenations of images, but they are often directly political and frequently have to do with the ideologies of states and the counter-ideologies of movements explicitly oriented to capturing state power or a piece of it. These ideoscapes are composed of elements of the Enlightenment worldview, which consists of a concatenation of ideas, terms and images, including 'freedom', 'welfare', 'rights', 'sovereignty', 'representation' and the master-term 'democracy'. The master-narrative of the Enlightenment (and its many variants in England, France and the United States) was constructed with a certain internal logic and presupposed a certain relationship between reading, representation and the public sphere (for the dynamics of this process in the early history of the United States, see Warner, 1990). But their diaspora across the world, especially since the nineteenth century, has loosened the internal coherence which held these terms and images together in a Euro-American master-narrative, and provided instead a loosely structured synopticon of politics, in which different nation-states, as part of their evolution, have organized their political cultures around different 'keywords' (Williams, 1976).

As a result of the differential diaspora of these keywords, the political narratives that govern communication between elites and followings in different parts of the world involve problems of both a semantic and a pragmatic nature: semantic to the extent that words (and their lexical equivalents) require careful translation from context to context in their global movements; and pragmatic to the extent that the use of these words by political actors and their audiences may be subject to very different sets of contextual conventions that mediate their translation into public politics. Such conventions are not only matters of the nature of political rhetoric (viz. what does the aging Chinese leadership mean when it refers to the dangers of hooliganism? What does the South Korean leadership mean when it speaks of 'discipline' as the key to democratic industrial growth?).

These conventions also involve the far more subtle question of what sets of communicative genres are valued in what way (newspapers versus cinema for example) and what sorts of pragmatic genre conventions govern the collective 'readings' of different kinds of text. So, while an Indian audience may be attentive to the resonances of a political speech in terms of some key words and phrases reminiscent of Hindi cinema, a Korean audience may respond to the subtle codings of Buddhist or neo-Confucian rhetorical strategy encoded in a political document. The very relationship of reading to hearing and seeing may vary in important ways that determine the morphology of these different 'ideoscapes' as they shape themselves in different national and transnational contexts. This globally variable synaesthesia has hardly even been noted, but it demands urgent analysis. Thus 'democracy' has clearly become a master-term, with powerful echoes from Haiti and Poland to the Soviet Union and China, but it sits at the center of a variety of ideoscapes (composed of distinctive pragmatic configurations of rough 'translations' of other central terms from the vocabulary of the Enlightenment). This creates ever new terminological kaleidoscopes, as states (and the groups that seek to capture them) seek to pacify populations whose own ethnoscapes are in motion, and whose mediascapes may create severe problems for the ideoscapes with which they are presented. The fluidity of ideoscapes is complicated in particular by the growing diasporas (both voluntary and involuntary) of intellectuals who continuously inject new meaning-streams into the discourse of democracy in different parts of the world.

This extended terminological discussion of the five terms I have coined sets the basis for a tentative formulation about the conditions under which current global flows occur: *they occur in and through the growing disjunctures between ethnoscapes, technoscapes, finanscapes, mediascapes and ideoscapes.* This formulation, the core of my model of global cultural flow, needs some explanation. First, people, machinery, money, images, and ideas now follow increasingly non-isomorphic paths: of course, at all periods in human history, there have been some disjunctures between the flows of these things, but the sheer speed, scale and volume of each of these flows is now so great that the disjunctures have become central to the politics of global culture. The Japanese are notoriously hospitable to ideas and are stereotyped as inclined to export (all) and import (some) goods, but they are also notoriously closed to immigration, like the Swiss, the Swedes and the Saudis. Yet the Swiss and Saudis accept populations of guestworkers, thus creating labor diasporas of Turks, Italians and other circum-Mediterranean groups. Some such guestworker groups maintain continuous contact with their home-nations, like the Turks, but others, like high-level South Asian migrants, tend to desire lives in their new homes, raising anew the problem of reproduction in a deterritorialized context.

Deterritorialization, in general, is one of the central forces of the modern world, since it brings laboring populations into the lower class sectors and spaces of relatively wealthy societies, while sometimes creating exaggerated and intensified senses of criticism or attachment to politics in the home-state. Deterritorialization, whether of Hindus, Sikhs, Palestinians or Ukrainians, is now at the core of a variety of global fundamentalisms, including Islamic and Hindu fundamentalism. In the Hindu case for example (Appadurai and Breckenridge, forthcoming) it is clear that the overseas movement of Indians has been exploited by a variety of interests both within and outside India to create a complicated network of finances and religious identifications, in which the problems of cultural reproduction for Hindus abroad has become tied to the politics of Hindu fundamentalism at home.

At the same time, deterritorialization creates new markets for film companies, art impresarios and travel agencies, who thrive on the need of the deterritorialized population for contact with its homeland. Naturally, these invented homelands, which constitute the mediascapes of deterritorialized groups, can often become sufficiently fantastic and one-sided that they provide the material for new ideoscapes in which ethnic conflicts can begin to erupt. The creation of 'Khalistan', an invented homeland of the deterritorialized Sikh population of England, Canada and the United States, is one example of the bloody potential in such mediascapes, as they interact with the 'internal colonialisms' (Hechter, 1974) of the nation-state. The West Bank, Namibia and Eritrea are other theaters for the enactment of the bloody negotiation between existing nation-states and various deterritorialized groupings.

The idea of deterritorialization may also be applied to money and finance, as money managers seek the best markets for their investments, independent of national boundaries. In turn, these movements of monies are the basis of new kinds of conflict, as Los Angelenos worry about the Japanese buying up their city, and people in Bombay worry about the rich Arabs from the Gulf States who have not only transformed the prices of mangoes in Bombay, but have also substantially altered the profile of hotels, restaurants and other services in the eyes of the local population, just as they continue to do in London. Yet, most residents of Bombay are ambivalent about the Arab presence there, for the flip side of their presence is the absence of friends and kinsmen earning big money in the Middle East and bringing back both money and luxury commodities to Bombay and other cities in India. Such commodities transform consumer taste in these cities, and also often end up smuggled through air and sea ports and peddled in the gray markets of Bombay's streets. In these gray markets, some members of Bombay's middle classes and of its lumpenproletariat can buy some of these goods, ranging from cartons of Marlboro cigarettes, to Old Spice shaving cream and tapes of Madonna. Similarly gray routes, often subsidized by the moonlighting activities of sailors, diplomats, and airline stewardesses who get to move in and out of the country regularly, keep the gray markets of Bombay, Madras and Calcutta filled with goods not only from the West, but also from the Middle East, Hong Kong and Singapore.

It is this fertile ground of deterritorialization, in which money, commodities and persons are involved in ceaselessly chasing each other around the world, that the mediascapes and ideoscapes of the modern world find their fractured and fragmented counterpart. For the ideas and images produced by mass media often are only partial guides to the goods and experiences that deterritorialized populations transfer to one another. In Mira Nair's brilliant film, *India Cabaret*, we see the multiple loops of this fractured deterritorialization as young women, barely competent in Bombay's metropolitan glitz, come to seek their fortunes as cabaret dancers and prostitutes in Bombay, entertaining men in clubs with dance formats derived wholly from the prurient dance sequences of Hindi films. These scenes cater in turn to ideas about Western and foreign women and their 'looseness', while they provide tawdry career alibis for these women. Some of these women come from Kerala, where cabaret clubs and the pornographic film industry have blossomed, partly in response to the purses and tastes of Keralites returned from the Middle East, where their diasporic lives away from women distort their very sense of what the relations between men and women might be. These tragedies of displacement could certainly be replayed in a more detailed analysis of the relations between the Japanese and German sex tours to Thailand and the tragedies of the sex trade in Bangkok, and in other similar loops which tie together fantasies about the other, the conveniences and seductions of travel, the economics of global trade and the brutal mobility fantasies that dominate gender politics in many parts of Asia and the world at large.

While far more could be said about the cultural politics of deterritorialization and the larger sociology of displacement that it expresses, it is appropriate at this juncture to bring in the role of the nation-state in the disjunctive global economy of culture today. The relationship between states and nations is everywhere an embattled one. It is possible to say that in many societies, the nation and the state have become one another's projects. That is, while nations (or more properly groups with ideas about nationhood) seek to capture or co-opt states and state power, states simultaneously seek to capture and monopolize ideas about nationhood (Baruah, 1986; Chatterjee, 1986; Nandy, 1989). In general, separatist, transnational movements, including those which have included terror in their methods, exemplify nations in search of states: Sikhs, Tamil Sri Lankans, Basques, Moros, Quebecois, each of these represent imagined communities which seek to create states of their own or carve pieces out of existing states. States, on the other hand, are everywhere seeking to monopolize the moral resources of community, either by flatly claiming perfect coevality between nation and state, or by systematically museumizing and representing all the groups within them in a variety of heritage politics that seems remarkably uniform throughout the world (Handler, 1988; Herzfeld, 1982; McQueen, 1988). Here, national and international mediascapes are exploited by nation-states to pacify separatists or even the potential fissiparousness of all ideas of difference. Typically, contemporary nation-states do this by exercising taxonomical control over difference; by creating various kinds of international spectacle to domesticate difference; and by seducing small groups with the fantasy of self-display on some sort of global or cosmopolitan stage. One important new feature of global cultural politics, tied to the disjunctive relationships between the various landscapes discussed earlier, is that state and nation are at each other's throats, and the hyphen that links them is now less an icon of conjuncture than an index of disjuncture. This disjunctive relationship between nation and state has two levels: at the level of any given nation-state, it means that there is a battle of the imagination, with state and nation seeking to cannibalize one another. Here is the seedbed of brutal separatisms, majoritarianisms that seem to have appeared from nowhere, and micro-identities that have become political projects within the nation-state. At another level, this disjunctive relationship is deeply entangled with the global disjunctures discussed throughout this essay: ideas of nationhood appear to be steadily increasing in scale and regularly crossing existing state boundaries: sometimes, as with the Kurds, because previous identities stretched across vast national spaces, or, as with the Tamils in Sri Lanka, the dormant threads of a transnational diaspora have been activated to ignite the micro-politics of a nation-state.

In discussing the cultural politics that have subverted the hyphen that links the nation to the state, it is especially important not to forget its mooring in the irregularities that now characterize 'disorganized capital' (Lash and Urry, 1987; Kothari, 1989). It is because labor, finance and technology are now so widely separated that the volatilities that underlie movements for nationhood (as large as transnational Islam on the one hand, or as small as the movement of the Gurkhas for a separate state in the North-East of India) grind against the vulnerabilities which characterize the relationships between states. States find themselves pressed to stay 'open' by the forces of media, technology, and travel which had fueled consumerism throughout the world and have increased the craving, even in the non-Western world, for new commodities and spectacles. On the other hand, these very cravings can become caught up in new ethnoscapes, mediascapes, and eventually, ideoscapes, such as 'democracy' in China, that the state cannot tolerate as threats to its own control over ideas of nationhood and 'people-hood'. States throughout the world are under siege, especially where contests over the ideoscapes of democracy are fierce and fundamental, and where there are radical disjunctures between ideoscapes and technoscapes (as in the case of very small countries that lack contemporary technologies of production and information); or between ideoscapes and finanscapes (as in countries, such as Mexico or Brazil where international lending influences national politics to a very large degree); or between ideoscapes and ethnoscapes (as in Beirut, where diasporic, local and translocal filiations are suicidally at battle); or between ideoscapes and mediascapes (as in many countries in the Middle East and Asia) where the lifestyles represented on both national and international TV and cinema completely overwhelm and undermine the rhetoric of national politics: in the Indian case, the myth of the law-breaking hero has emerged to mediate this naked struggle between the pieties and the realities of Indian politics, which has grown increasingly brutalized and corrupt (Vachani, 1989).

The transnational movement of the martial arts, particularly through Asia, as mediated by the Hollywood and Hongkong film industries (Zarilli, forthcoming) is a rich illustration of the ways in which long-standing martial arts traditions, reformulated to meet the fantasies of contemporary (sometimes lumpen) youth populations, create new cultures of masculinity and violence, which are in turn the fuel for increased violence in national and international politics. Such violence is in turn the spur to an increasingly rapid and amoral arms trade which penetrates the entire world. The worldwide spread of the AK-47 and the Uzi, in films, in corporate and state security, in terror, and in police and military activity, is a reminder that apparently simple technical uniformities often conceal an increasingly complex set of loops, linking images of violence to aspirations for community in some 'imagined world'.

Returning then to the 'ethnoscapes' with which I began, the central paradox of ethnic politics in today's world is that primordia (whether of language or skin color or neighborhood or of kinship) have become globalized. That is, sentiments whose greatest force is in their ability to ignite intimacy into a political senti- ment and turn locality into a staging ground for identity have become spread over vast and irregular spaces, as groups move, yet stay linked to one another through sophisticated media capabilities. This is not to deny that such primordia are often the product of invented traditions (Hobsbawm and Ranger, 1983) or retrospective affiliations, but to emphasize that because of the disjunctive and unstable interplay of commerce, media, national policies and consumer fantasies, ethnicity, once a genie contained in the bottle of some sort of locality (however large), has now become a global force, forever slipping in and through the cracks between states and borders.

But the relationship between the cultural and economic levels of this new set of global disjunctures is not a simple one-way street in which the terms of global cultural politics are set wholly by, or confined wholly within, the vicissitudes of international flows of technology, labor and finance, demanding only a modest modification of existing neo-Marxist models of uneven development and state- formation. There is a deeper change, itself driven by the disjunctures between all the landscapes I have discussed, and constituted by their continuously fluid and uncertain interplay, which concerns the relationship between production and consumption in today's global economy. Here I begin with Marx's famous (and often mined) view of the fetishism of the commodity, and suggest that this fetishism has been replaced in the world at large (now seeing the world as one, large, interactive system, composed of many complex sub-systems) by two mutually supportive descendants, the first of which I call production fetishism, and the second of which I call the fetishism of the consumer.

By production fetishism I mean an illusion created by contemporary trans- national production loci, which masks translocal capital, transnational earning- flows, global management and often faraway workers (engaged in various kinds of high-tech putting out operations) in the idiom and spectacle of local (some- times even worker) control, national productivity and territorial sovereignty. To the extent that various kinds of Free Trade Zone have become the models for production at large, especially of high-tech commodities, production has itself become a fetish, masking not social relations as such, but the relations of production, which are increasingly transnational. The locality (both in the sense of the local factory or site of production and in the extended sense of the nation-state) becomes a fetish which disguises the globally dispersed forces that actually drive the production process. This generates alienation (in Marx's sense) twice intensified, for its social sense is now compounded by a complicated spatial dynamic which is increasingly global.

As for the fetishism of the consumer, I mean to indicate here that the consumer has been transformed, through commodity flows (and the mediascapes, especially of advertising, that accompany them) into a sign, both in Baudrillard's sense of a simulacrum which only asymptotically approaches the form of a real social agent; and in the sense of a mask for the real seat of agency, which is not the consumer but the producer and the many forces that constitute production. Global advertising is the key technology for the worldwide dissemination of a plethora of creative, and culturally well-chosen, ideas of consumer agency. These images of agency are increasingly distortions of a world of merchandising so subtle that the consumer is consistently helped to believe that he or she is an actor, where in fact he or she is at best a chooser.

The globalization of culture is not the same as its homogenization, but globalization involves the use of a variety of instruments of homogenization (armaments, advertising techniques, language hegemonies, clothing styles and the like), which are absorbed into local political and cultural economies, only to be repatriated as heterogeneous dialogues of national sovereignty, free enterprise, fundamentalism, etc. in which the state plays an increasingly delicate role: too much openness to global flows and the nation-state is threatened by revolt—the China syndrome; too little, and the state exits the international stage, as Burma, Albania and North Korea in various ways have done. In general, the state has become the arbiter of this *repatriation of difference* (in the form of goods, signs, slogans, styles, etc.). But this repatriation or export of the designs and commodities of difference continuously exacerbates the 'internal' politics of majoritarianism and homogenization, which is most frequently played out in debates over heritage.

Thus the central feature of global culture today is the politics of the mutual effort of sameness and difference to cannibalize one another and thus to proclaim their successful hijacking of the twin Enlightenment ideas of the triumphantly universal and the resiliently particular. This mutual cannibalization shows its ugly face in riots, in refugee-flows, in state-sponsored torture and in ethnocide (with or without state support). Its brighter side is in the expansion of many individual horizons of hope and fantasy, in the global spread of oral rehydration therapy and other low-tech instruments of well-being, in the susceptibility even of South Africa to the force of global opinion, in the inability of the Polish state to repress its own working classes, and in the growth of a wide range of progressive, transnational alliances. Examples of both sorts could be multiplied. The critical point is that both sides of the coin of global cultural process today are products of the infinitely varied mutual contest of sameness and difference on a stage characterized by radical disjunctures be-

tween different sorts of global flows and the uncertain landscapes created in
and through these disjunctures.

Notes

Reproduced by permission of Sage Publications, London, Los Angeles, New Delhi, and
Singapore, from Arjun Appadurai, "Disjuncture and Difference in the Global Cultural
Economy." In *Modernity at Large: Cultural Dimensions of Globalization* (Minneapolis:
University of Minnesota Press, 1996): 27–43.

A longer version of this essay appears in *Public Culture* 2 (2), Spring 1990. This
longer version sets the present formulation in the context of global cultural traffic in
earlier historical periods, and draws out some of its implications for the study of cultural
forms more generally.

1. One major exception is Fredric Jameson, whose (1984) essay on the relationship between postmodernism and late capitalism has in many ways inspired this essay.
However, the debate between Jameson (1986) and Ahmad (1987) in *Social Text* shows
that the creation of a globalizing Marxist narrative, in cultural matters, is difficult territory indeed. My own effort, in this context, is to begin a restructuring of the Marxist
narrative (by stressing lags and disjunctures) that many Marxists might find abhorrent.
Such a restructuring has to avoid the dangers of obliterating difference within the 'third
world', of eliding the social referent (as some French postmodernists seem inclined to
do) and of retaining the narrative authority of the Marxist tradition, in favor of greater
attention to global fragmentation, uncertainty and difference.

2. These ideas are argued more fully in a book I am currently working on, tentatively
entitled *Imploding Worlds: Imagination and Disjuncture in the Global Cultural Economy*.

References

Ahmad, A. (1987) 'Jameson's Rhetoric of Otherness and the "National Allegory"', *Social
        Text* 17: 3–25.
Amin, S. (1980) *Class and Nation: Historically and in the Current Crisis*. New York and
        London: Monthly Review.
Anderson, B. (1983) *Imagined Communities: Reflections on the Origin and Spread of
        Nationalism*. London: Verso.
Appadurai, A. (1989) 'Global Ethnoscapes: Notes and Queries for a Transnational An-
        thropology', in R.G. Fox (ed.), *Interventions: Anthropology of the Present*.
Appadurai, A. and Breckenridge, C.A. (forthcoming) *A Transnational Culture in the
        Making: The Asian Indian Diaspora in the United States*. London: Berg.
Barber, K. (1987) 'Popular Arts in Africa', *African Studies Review* 30(3).

Baruah, S. (1986) 'Immigration, Ethnic Conflict and Political Turmoil, Assam 1979–1985', *Asian Survey* 26(11).

Chatterjee, P. (1986) *Nationalist Thought and the Colonial World: A Derivative Discourse.* London: Zed Books.

Feld, S. (1988) 'Notes on World Beat', *Public Culture* 1(1): 31–7.

Gans, E. (1985) *The End of Culture: Toward a Generative Anthropology.* Berkeley: University of California.

Hamelink, C. (1983) *Cultural Autonomy in Global Communications.* New York: Longman.

Handler, R. (1988) *Nationalism and the Politics of Culture in Quebec.* Madison: University of Wisconsin.

Hannerz, U. (1987) 'The World in Creolization,' *Africa* 57(4): 546–59.

Hannerz, U. (1989) 'Notes on the Global Ecumene', *Public Culture* 1(2): 66–75.

Hechter, M. (1974) *Internal Colonialism: The Celtic Fringe in British National Development, 1536–1966.* Berkeley and Los Angeles: University of California.

Herzfeld, M. (1982) *Ours Once More: Folklore, Ideology and the Making of Modern Greece.* Austin: University of Texas.

Hobsbawm, E. and Ranger, T. (eds.) (1983) *The Invention of Tradition.* New York: Columbia University Press.

Ivy, M. (1988) 'Tradition and Difference in the Japanese Mass Media', *Public Culture* 1(1): 21–9.

Iyer, P. (1988) *Video Night in Kathmandu.* New York: Knopf.

Jameson, F. (1984) 'Postmodernism, or the Cultural Logic of Late Capitalism', *New Left Review* 146(July–August): 53–92.

Jameson, F. (1986) 'Third World Literature in the Era of Multi-National Capitalism', *Social Text* 15(Fall): 65–88.

Kothari, R. (1989) *State Against Democracy: In Search of Humane Governance.* New York: New Horizons.

Lakoff, G. and Johnson, M. (1980) *Metaphors We Live By.* Chicago and London: University of Chicago.

Lash, S. and Urry, J. (1987) *The End of Organized Capitalism.* Madison: University of Wisconsin.

Mandel, E. (1978) *Late Capitalism.* London: Verso.

Mattelart, A. (1983) *Transnationals and Third World: The Struggle for Culture.* South Hadley, MA: Bergin and Garvey.

McQueen, H. (1988) 'The Australian Stamp: Image, Design and Ideology', *Arena* 84(Spring): 78–96.

Nandy, A. (1989) 'The Political Culture of the Indian State', *Daedalus* 118(4): 1–26.

Nicoll, F. (1989) 'My Trip to Alice', *Criticism, Heresy and Interpretation (CHAT)* 3: 21–32.

Schiller, H. (1976) *Communication and Cultural Domination.* White Plains, NY: International Arts and Sciences.

Vachani, L. (1989) 'Narrative, Pleasure and Ideology in the Hindi Film: An Analysis of the Outsider Formula', MA thesis, The Annenberg School of Communication, University of Pennsylvania.

Wallerstein, I. (1974) *The Modern World-System* (2 volumes). New York and London: Academic Press.

Warner, M. (1990) *The Letters of the Republic: Publication and the Public Sphere*. Cambridge, MA: Harvard.

Williams, R. (1976) *Keywords*. New York: Oxford.

Wolf, E. (1982) *Europe and the People Without History*. Berkeley: University of California.

Yoshimoto, M. (1989) 'The Postmodern and Mass Images in Japan', *Public Culture* 1(2): 8–25.

Zarilli, P. (Forthcoming) 'Repositioning the Body: An Indian Martial Art and Its Pan-Asian Publics' in C.A. Breckenridge (ed.), *Producing the Postcolonial: Trajectories to Public Culture in India*.

Chapter 3
The Globalization of Modernity

Anthony Giddens

Modernity is inherently globalising—this is evident in some of the most basic characteristics of modern institutions, including particularly their disembeddedness and reflexivity. But what exactly is globalisation, and how might we best conceptualise the phenomenon? I shall consider these questions at some length here, since the central importance of globalising processes today has scarcely been matched by extended discussions of the concept in the sociological literature. We can begin by recalling some points made earlier. The undue reliance which sociologists have placed upon the idea of "society," where this means a bounded system, should be replaced by a starting point that concentrates upon analysing how social life is ordered across time and space—the problematic of time-space distanciation. The conceptual framework of time-space distanciation directs our attention to the complex relations between *local involvements* (circumstances of co-presence) and *interaction across distance* (the connections of presence and absence). In the modern era, the level of time-space distanciation is much higher than in any previous period, and the relations between local and distant social forms and events become correspondingly "stretched." Globalisation refers essentially to that stretching process, in so far as the modes of connection between different social contexts or regions become networked across the earth's surface as a whole.

Globalisation can thus be defined as the intensification of worldwide social relations which link distant localities in such a way that local happenings are shaped by events occurring many miles away and vice versa. This is a dialectical process because such local happenings may move in an obverse direction from the very distanciated relations that shape them. *Local transformation* is as much a part of globalisation as the lateral extension of social connections across time and space. Thus whoever studies cities today, in any part of the world, is aware that what happens in a local neighbourhood is likely to be influenced by factors—such as world money and commodity markets—operating at an indefinite distance away from that neighbourhood itself. The outcome is not necessarily, or even usually, a generalised set of changes acting in a uniform direction, but consists in mutually opposed tendencies. The increasing prosperity of an urban area in Singapore might be causally related, via a complicated network of global economic ties, to the impoverishment of a neighbourhood in Pittsburgh whose local products are uncompetitive in world markets.

Another example from the very many that could be offered is the rise of local nationalisms in Europe and elsewhere. The development of globalised social relations probably serves to diminish some aspects of nationalist feeling linked to nation-states (or some states) but may be causally involved with the intensifying of more localised nationalist sentiments. In circumstances of accelerating globalisation, the nation-state has become "too small for the big problems of life, and too big for the small problems of life."[1] At the same time as social relations become laterally stretched and as part of the same process, we see the strengthening of pressures for local autonomy and regional cultural identity.

Two Theoretical Perspectives

Apart from the work of Marshall McLuhan and a few other individual authors, discussions of globalisation tend to appear in two bodies of literature, which are largely distinct from one another. One is the literature of international relations, the other that of "world-system theory," particularly as associated with Immanuel Wallerstein, which stands fairly close to a Marxist position.

Theorists of international relations characteristically focus upon the development of the nation-state system, analysing its origins in Europe and its subsequent worldwide spread. Nation-states are treated as actors, engaging with one another in the international arena—and with other organisations of a transnational kind (intergovernmental organisations or non-state actors). Although various theoretical positions are represented in this literature, most authors paint a rather similar picture in analysing the growth of globalisation.[2] Sovereign states, it is presumed, first emerge largely as separate entities, having more or less complete administrative control within their borders. As the European state system matures and later becomes a global nation-state system, patterns of interdependence become increasingly developed. These are not only expressed in the ties states form with one another in the international arena, but in the burgeoning of intergovernmental organisations. These processes mark an overall movement towards "one world," although they are continually fractured by war. Nation-states, it is held, are becoming progressively less sovereign than they used to be in terms of control over their own affairs—although few today anticipate in the near future the emergence of the "world-state" which many in the early part of this century foresaw as a real prospect.

While this view is not altogether wrong, some major reservations have to be expressed. For one thing, it again covers only one overall dimension of globalisation as I wish to utilise the concept here—the international coordination of states. Regarding states as actors has its uses and makes sense in some contexts. However, most theorists of international relations do not explain *why* this usage makes sense; for it does so only in the case of nation-states, not in that of pre-modern states. The reason has to do with a theme discussed earlier—there is a far greater concentration of administrative power in nation-states than in their precursors, in which it would be relatively meaningless to speak of "governments" who negotiate with other "governments" in the name of their respective nations. Moreover, treating states as actors having connections with each other and with other organisations in the international arena makes it difficult to deal with social relations that are not between or outside states, but simply crosscut state divisions.

A further shortcoming of this type of approach concerns its portrayal of the increasing unification of the nation-state system. The sovereign power of modern states was not formed prior to their involvement in the nation-state system, even in the European state system, but developed in conjunction with it. Indeed, the sovereignty of the modern state was from the first *dependent upon the relations between states,* in terms of which each state (in principle if by no means always in practice) recognised the autonomy of others within their own borders. No state, however powerful, held as much sovereign control in practice as was enshrined in legal principle. The history of the past two centuries is thus not one of the progressive loss of sovereignty on the part of the nation-state. Here again we must recognise the dialectical character of globalisation and also the influence of processes of uneven development. Loss of autonomy on the part of some states or groups of states has often gone along with an *increase* in that of others, as a result of alliances, wars, or political and economic changes of various sorts. For instance, although the sovereign control of some of the "classical" Western nations may have diminished as a result of the acceleration of the global division of labour over the past thirty years, that of some Far Eastern countries—in some respects at least—has grown.

Since the stance of world-system theory differs so much from international relations, it is not surprising to find that the two literatures are at arm's distance from one another. Wallerstein's account of the world system makes many contributions, in both theory and empirical analysis.[3] Not least important is the fact that he skirts the sociologists' usual preoccupation with "societies" in favour of a much more embracing conception of globalised relationships. He also makes a clear differentiation between the modern era and preceding ages in terms of the phenomena with which he is concerned. What he refers to as "world economies"—networks of economic connections of a geographically extensive sort—have existed prior to modern times, but these were notably different from the world system that has developed over the past three or four centuries. Earlier world economies *were* usually centred upon large imperial states and never covered more than certain regions in which the power of these states was concentrated. The emergence of capitalism, as Wallerstein analyses it, ushers in a quite different type of order, for the first time genuinely global in its span and based more on economic than political power—the "world capitalist economy." The world capitalist economy, which has its origins in the sixteenth and seventeenth centuries, is integrated through commercial and manufacturing connections, not by a political centre. Indeed, there exists a multiplicity of political centres, the nation-states. The modern world system is divided into three components, the core, the semi-periphery, and the periphery, although where these are located regionally shifts over time.

According to Wallerstein, the worldwide reach of capitalism was established quite early on in the modern period: "Capitalism was from the beginning an affair of the world economy and not of nation-states.... Capital has never allowed its aspirations to be determined by national boundaries."[4] Capitalism has been such a fundamental globalising influence precisely because it is an economic rather than a political order; it has been able to penetrate far-flung areas of the world which the states of its origin could not have brought wholly under their political sway. The colonial administration of distant lands may in some situations have helped to consolidate economic expansion, but it was never the main basis of the spread of capitalistic enterprise globally. In the late twentieth century, where colonialism in its original form has all but disappeared, the world capitalist economy continues to involve massive imbalances between core, semi-periphery, and periphery.

Wallerstein successfully breaks away from some of the limitations of much orthodox sociological thought, most notably the strongly defined tendency to focus upon "endogenous models" of social change. But his work has its own shortcomings. He continues to see only one dominant institutional nexus (capitalism) as responsible for modern transformations. World-system theory thus concentrates heavily upon economic influences and finds it difficult satisfactorily to account for just those phenomena made central by the theorists of international relations: the rise of the nation-state and the nation-state system. Moreover, the distinctions between core, semi-periphery, and periphery (themselves perhaps of questionable value), based upon economic criteria, do not allow us to illuminate political or military concentrations of power, which do not align in an exact way to economic differentiations.

Dimensions of Globalisation

I shall, in contrast, regard the world capitalist economy as one of four dimensions of globalisation, following the four-fold classification of the institutions of modernity mentioned above (see Figure 3.1).[5] The nation-state system is a second dimension; as the discussion above indicated, although these are connected in various ways, neither can be explained exhaustively in terms of the other.

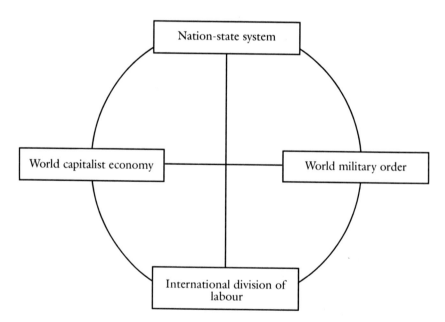

Figure 3.1   The Dimensions of Globalisation.

If we consider the present day, in what sense can world economic organisation be said to be dominated by capitalistic economic mechanisms? A number of considerations are relevant to answering this question. The main centres of power in the world economy are capitalist states—states in which capitalist economic enterprise (with the class relations that this implies) is the chief form of production. The domestic and international economic policies of these states involve many forms of regulation of economic activity, but, as noted, their institutional organisation maintains an "insulation" of the economic from the political. This allows wide scope for the global activities of business corporations, which always have a home base within a particular state but may develop many other regional involvements elsewhere.

Business firms, especially the transnational corporations, may wield immense economic power, and have the capacity to influence political policies in their home bases and elsewhere. The biggest transnational companies today have budgets larger than those of all but a few nations. But there are some key respects in which their power cannot rival that of states—especially important here are the factors of territoriality and control of the means of violence. There is no area on the earth's surface, with the partial exception of the polar regions, which is not claimed as the legitimate sphere of control of one state or another. All modern states have a more or less successful monopoly of control of the means of violence within their own territories. No matter how great their economic power, industrial corporations are not military organisations (as some of them were during the colonial period), and they cannot establish themselves as political/legal entities which rule a given territorial area.

If nation-states are the principal "actors" within the global political order, corporations are the dominant agents within the world economy. In their trading relations with one another, and with states and consumers, companies (manufacturing corporations, financial firms, and banks) depend upon production for profit. Hence the spread of their influence brings in its train a global extension of commodity markets, including money markets. However, even in its beginnings, the capitalist world economy was never just a market for the trading of goods and services. It involved, and involves today, the commodifying of labour power in class relations which separate workers from control of their means of production. This process, of course, is fraught with implications for global inequalities.

All nation-states, capitalist and state socialist, within the "developed" sectors of the world are primarily reliant upon industrial production for the generation of the wealth upon which their tax revenues are based. The socialist countries form something of an enclave within the capitalist world economy as a whole, industry being more directly subject to political imperatives. These states are scarcely post-capitalist, but the influence of capitalistic markets upon the distribution of goods and labour power is substantially muted. The pursuit of growth by both Western and East European societies inevitably pushes economic interests to the forefront of the policies which states pursue in the international arena. But it is surely plain to all, save those under the sway of historical materialism, that the material involvements of nation-states are not governed purely by economic considerations, real or perceived. The influence of any particular state within the global political order is strongly conditioned by the level of its wealth (and the connection between this and military strength). However, states derive their power from their sovereign capabilities, as Hans J. Morgenthau emphasises.[6] They do not operate as economic machines, but as "actors" jealous of their territorial rights, concerned with the fostering of national cultures, and having strategic geopolitical involvements with other states or alliances of states.

The nation-state system has long participated in that reflexivity characteristic of modernity as a whole. The very existence of sovereignty should be understood as something that is reflexively monitored, for reasons already indicated. Sovereignty is linked to the replacement of "frontiers" by "borders" in the early development of the nation-state system: autonomy inside the territory claimed by the state is sanctioned by the recognition of borders by other states. As noted, this is one of the major factors distinguishing the nation-state system from systems of states in the pre-modern era, where few reflexively ordered relations of this kind existed and where the notion of "international relations" made no sense.

One aspect of the dialectical nature of globalisation is the "push and pull" between tendencies towards centralisation inherent in the reflexivity of the system of states on the one hand and the sovereignty of particular states on the other. Thus, concerted action between countries in some respects diminishes the individual sovereignty of the nations involved, yet by combining their power in other ways, it increases their influence within the state system. The same is true of the early congresses which, in conjunction with war, defined and redefined states' borders—and of truly global agencies such as the United Nations. The global influence of the U.N. (still decisively limited by the fact that it is not territorial and does not have significant access to the means of violence) is not purchased solely by means of a diminution of the sovereignty of nation-states—things are more complicated than this. An obvious example is that of the "new nations"— autonomous nation-states set up in erstwhile colonised areas. Armed struggle against the colonising countries was very generally a major factor in persuading the colonisers to retreat. But discussion in the U.N. played a key role in setting up ex-colonial areas as states with internationally recognised borders. However weak some of the new nations may be economically and militarily, their emergence *as* nation-states (or, in many cases, "state-nations") marks a net gain in terms of sovereignty, as compared to their previous circumstances.

The third dimension of globalisation is the world military order. In specifying its nature, we have to analyse the connections between the industrialisation of war, the flow of weaponry and techniques of military organisation from some parts of the world to others, and the alliances which states build with one another. Military alliances do not necessarily compromise the monopoly over the means of violence held by a state within its territories, although in some circumstances they certainly can do so.

In tracing the overlaps between military power and the sovereignty of states, we find the same push-and-pull between opposing tendencies noted previously. In the current period, the two most militarily developed states, the United States and the Soviet Union, have built a bipolar system of military alliances of truly global scope. The countries involved in these alliances necessarily accept limitations over their opportunities to forge independent military strategies externally. They may also forfeit complete monopoly of military control within their own territories, in so far as American or Soviet forces stationed there take their orders from abroad. Yet, as a result of the massive destructive power of modern weaponry, almost all states possess military strength far in excess of that of even the largest of pre-modern civilisations. Many economically weak Third World countries are militarily powerful. In an important sense there is no "Third World" in respect of weaponry, only a "First World," since most countries maintain stocks of technologically advanced armaments and have modernised the military in a thoroughgoing way. Even the possession of nuclear weaponry is not confined to the economically advanced states.

The globalising of military power obviously is not confined to weaponry and alliances between the armed forces of different states—it also concerns war itself. Two world wars attest to the way in which local conflicts became matters of global involvement. In both wars, the participants were drawn from virtually all regions (although the Second World War was a more truly worldwide phenomenon). In an era of nuclear weaponry, the industrialisation of war has proceeded to a point at which, as was mentioned earlier, the obsolescence of Clausewitz's main doctrine has become apparent to everyone.[7] The only point of holding nuclear weapons—apart from their possible symbolic value in world politics—is to deter others from using them.

While this situation may lead to a suspension of war between the nuclear powers (or so we all must hope), it scarcely prevents them from engaging in military adventures outside their own territorial domains. The two superpowers in particular engage in what might be called "orchestrated wars" in peripheral areas of military strength. By these I mean military encounters, with the governments of other states or with guerilla movements or both, in which the troops of the superpower are not necessarily even engaged at all, but where that power is a prime organising influence.

The fourth dimension of globalisation concerns industrial development. The most obvious aspect of this is the expansion of the global division of labour, which includes the differentiations between more and less industrialised areas in the world. Modern industry is intrinsically based on divisions of labour, not only on the level of job tasks but on that of regional specialisation in terms of type of industry, skills, and the production of raw materials. There has undoubtedly taken place a major expansion of global interdependence in the division of labour since the Second World War. This has helped to bring about shifts in the worldwide distribution of production, including the deindustrialisation of some regions in the developed countries and the emergence of the "Newly Industrialising Countries" in the Third World. It has also undoubtedly served to reduce the internal economic hegemony of many states, particularly those with a high level of industrialisation. It is more difficult for the capitalist countries to manage their economies than formerly was the case, given accelerating global economic interdependence. This is almost certainly one of the major reasons for the declining impact of Keynesian economic policies, as applied at the level of the national economy, in current times.

One of the main features of the globalising implications of industrialism is the worldwide diffusion of machine technologies. The impact of industrialism is plainly not limited to the sphere of production, but affects many aspects of day-to-day life, as well as influencing the generic character of human interaction with the material environment.

Even in states which remain primarily agricultural, modern technology is often applied in such a way as to alter substantially preexisting relations between human social organisation and the environment. This is true, for example, of the use of fertilisers or other artificial farming methods, the introduction of modern farming machinery, and so forth. The diffusion of industrialism has created "one world" in a more negative and threatening sense than that just mentioned—a world in which there are actual or potential ecological changes of a harmful sort that affect everyone on the planet. Yet industrialism has also decisively conditioned our very sense of living in "one world." For one of the most important effects of industrialism has been the transformation of technologies of communication.

This comment leads on to a further and quite fundamental aspect of globalisation, which lies behind each of the various institutional dimensions that have been mentioned and which might be referred to as cultural globalisation. Mechanised technologies of communication have dramatically influenced all aspects of globalisation since the first introduction of mechanical printing into Europe. They form an essential element of the reflexivity of modernity and of the discontinuities which have torn the modern away from the traditional.

The globalising impact of media was noted by numerous authors during the period of the early growth of mass circulation newspapers. Thus one commentator in 1892 wrote that, as a result of modern newspapers, the inhabitant of a local village has a broader understanding of contemporary events than the prime minister of a hundred years before. The villager who reads a paper "interests himself simultaneously in the issue of a revolution in Chile, a bush-war in East Africa, a massacre in North China, a famine in Russia."[8]

The point here is not that people are contingently aware of many events, from all over the world, of which previously they would have remained ignorant. It is that the global extension of the institutions of modernity would be impossible were it not for the pooling of knowledge which is represented by the "news." This is perhaps less obvious on the level of general cultural awareness than in more specific contexts. For example, the global money markets of today involve direct and simultaneous access to pooled information on the part of individuals spatially widely separated from one another.

Notes

1. Daniel Bell, "The World and the United States in 2013," *Daedalus* 116 (1987).

2. See for example James N. Rosenthau, *The Study of Global Interdependence* (London: Pinter, 1980).

3. Immanuel Wallerstein, *The Modern World System* (New York: Academic, 1974).

4. Immanuel Wallerstein, "The Rise and Future Demise of the World Capitalist System: Concepts for Comparative Analysis," in his *The Capitalist World Economy* (Cambridge, U.K.: Cambridge University Press, 1979), p. 19.

5. This figure (and the discussion which accompanies it) supersedes that which appears on p. 277 of *Nation-State and Violence*.

6. H. J. Morgenthau, *Politics Among Nations* (New York: Knopf, 1960).

7. Clausewitz was a subtle thinker, however, and there are interpretations of his ideas which continue to insist upon their relevance to the present day.

8. Max Nordau, *Degeneration* (New York: Fertig, 1968), p. 39; orig. ed. 1892.

CHAPTER 4
MAPPING THE GLOBAL CONDITION

Roland Robertson

Nothing will be done anymore, without the whole world meddling in it. (Paul Valéry), in Lesourne, 1986: 103)

We are on the road from the evening-glow of European philosophy to the dawn of world philosophy. (Karl Jaspers, 1957: 83–4)

Insofar as [present realities] have brought us a global present without a common past [they] threaten to render all traditions and all particular past histories irrelevant. (Hannah Arendt, 1957: 541)

The transformation of the medieval into the modern can be depicted in at least two different ways. In one sense it represents the trend towards the consolidation and strengthening of the territorial state ... In another sense it represents a reordering in the priority of international and domestic realms. In the medieval period the world, or transnational, environment was primary, the domestic secondary. (Richard Rosencrance, 1986: 77)

My primary concern here is to continue the discussion of the analytical and empirical aspects of globalization. I also want to raise some general questions about social theory. As far as the main issue is concerned, I set out the grounds for systematic analysis and interpretation of globalization since the mid-fifteenth century, indicating the major phases of globalization in recent world history and exploring some of the more salient aspects of the contemporary global circumstance from an analytical point of view. On the general-theoretical front I argue again that much of social theory is both a product of and an implicit reaction to, as opposed to a direct engagement with, the globalization process.

While there is rapidly growing interest in the issue of globalization, much of it is expressed very diffusely. It has become a widely used term in a number of theoretical, empirical and applied areas of intellectual inquiry, including the various 'policy sciences,' such as business studies and strategic studies. There is also a danger that 'globalization' will become an intellectual 'play zone,' a site for the expression of residual social-theoretical interests, interpretive indulgence, or the display of world-ideological preferences. I think we must take very seriously Immanuel Wallerstein's (1987: 309) contention that 'world-systems' analysis is not a theory about the world. 'It is a protest against the ways in which social scientific inquiry was structured for all of us at its inception in the middle of the nineteenth century.' Even though I do not, as I have said, subscribe to world-systems theory in the conventional sense of the term, primarily because of its economism, and am not pessimistic about the possibility of our being able to accomplish significant theoretical work *vis-à-vis* the world as a whole, I consider it to be of the utmost importance for us to realize fully that much of the conventional sociology which has developed since the first quarter of the twentieth century has been held in thrall by the virtually global institutionalization of the idea of the culturally cohesive and sequestered national society during the main phase of 'classical' sociology. Ironically, the global aspect of that phenomenon has received relatively little attention (Meyer, 1980).

Globalization and the Structuration of the World

The present discussion, in this and the following chapters, is a continuation of previous efforts to theorize the topic of globalization, a task made all the more difficult by the recent and continuing events in the territories of the old USSR, Eastern and Central Europe, China and elsewhere, which have disrupted virtually all of the conventional views concerning 'world order.' At the same time those events and the circumstances they have created make the analytical effort even more urgent. We have entered a phase of what appears to us in the 1990s to be great global uncertainty—so much so that the very idea of uncertainty promises to become globally institutionalized. Or, to put it in a very different way, there is an eerie relationship between postmodernist theories and the idea of postmodernity, on the one hand, and the geopolitical 'earthquakes' that we (the virtually *global we)* have recently experienced, on the other.

We need to enlarge our conception of 'world politics' in such a way as to facilitate systematic discussion, but not conflation, of the relationship between politics in the relatively narrow sense and the broad questions of 'meaning' which can only be grasped by wide-ranging, empirically sensitive interpretations of the global-human condition as a whole. Specifically, I argue that what is often called world politics has in the twentieth century hinged considerably upon the issue of the interpretation of and the response to modernity, aspects of which were politically and internationally thematized as the standard of 'civilization' (Gong, 1984) during the late nineteenth and early twentieth centuries with particular reference to the inclusion of non-European (mainly Asian) societies in Eurocentric 'international society' (Bull and Watson, 1984a).

Communism and 'democratic capitalism' have constituted alternative forms of acceptance of modernity (Parsons, 1964), although some would now argue that the recent and dramatic ebbing of communism can in part be attributed to its 'attempt to preserve the integrity of the premodern system' (Parsons, 1967: 484–5) by invoking 'socialism' as the central of a series of largely 'covert gestures of reconciliation … toward both the past and the future' (Parsons, 1967: 484).[1] On the other hand fascism and neofascism have, in spite of their original claims to the establishment of *new* societal and international 'orders' (as was explicitly the case with the primary Axis powers of World War II: Germany and Japan), been directly interested in *transcending or resolving* the problems of modernity. That issue has certainly not disappeared. The world politics of the global debate about modernity has rarely been considered of relevance to the latter and yet it is clear that, for example, conceptions of the past by the major belligerents in World War I illustrated a sharp contrast between 'the temporalities of the nations of each alliance system and underlying causes of resentment and misunderstanding' (Kern, 1983: 277), with the nations whose leaders considered themselves to be relatively deprived—notably Germany and Japan—being particularly concerned to confront the problem of modernity in political and military terms.[2] Sociologists and philosophers are familiar with many intellectual developments of the 1920s and 1930s, but these have not been linked to the broad domain of *Realpolitik.* It may well be that the Cold War that developed after the defeat of great-power Fascism constituted an interruption and partial freezing of the world-cultural politics of modernity and that with the ending of the Cold War as conventionally understood those politics will now be resumed in a situation of much greater global complexity, in the interrelated contexts of more intense globalization, the growing political presence of Islam, the discourse of postmodernity and 'the ethnic revival' (A.D. Smith, 1981), which itself may be considered as *an aspect of* the contemporary phase of globalization (Lechner, 1984).

Any attempt to theorize the general field of globalization must lay the grounds for relatively patterned discussion of the politics of the global-human condition, by attempting to indicate the structure of any viable discourse about the shape and 'meaning' of the world as a whole. I regard this as an urgent matter partly because much of the explicit intellectual interpretation of the global scene is being conducted by academics operating under the umbrella of 'cultural studies' with exceedingly little attention to the issue of global complexity and structural contingency, except for frequently invoked labels such as 'late capitalism,' 'disorganized capitalism,' or the salience of 'the transnational corporation.' This is not at all to say that the economic factor is unimportant, or that the 'textual,' 'power-knowledge,' or 'hegemonic' aspects of the 'world system' are of minor significance. Rather, I am insisting that both the economics and the culture of the global scene should be analytically connected to the general structural and actional features of the global field.

I maintain that what has come to be called globalization is, in spite of differing conceptions of that theme, best understood as indicating the problem of *the form* in terms of which the world becomes 'united,' but by no means integrated in naive functionalist mode (Robertson and Chirico, 1985). Globalization as a topic is, in other words, a conceptual entry to the problem of 'world order' in the most general sense—but, nevertheless, an entry which has no cognitive purchase without considerable discussion of historical and comparative matters. It is, moreover, a phenomenon which clearly requires what is conventionally called interdisciplinary treatment. Traditionally the general field of the study of the world as a whole has been approached via the discipline of international relations (or, more diffusely, international studies). That discipline (sometimes regarded as a subdiscipline of political science) was consolidated during particular phases of the overall globalization process and is now being reconstituted in reference to developments in other disciplinary areas, including the humanities (Der Derian and Shapiro, 1989). Indeed, the first concentrated thrust into the study of the world as a whole on the part of sociologists, during the 1960s (discussed in Nettl and Robertson, 1968), was undertaken, as has been seen, mainly in terms of the idea of the sociology of international relations. There can be little doubt that to this day the majority of social scientists still think of 'extra-societal' matters in terms of 'international relations' (including variants thereof, such as transnational relations, nongovernmental relations, supranational relations, world politics and so on). Nonetheless that tendency is breaking down, in conjunction with considerable questioning of what Michael Mann (1986) has called the unitary conception of society. While there have been attempts to carve out a new discipline for the study of the world as a whole, including the long-historical making of the contemporary 'world system' (e.g., Bergesen, 1980a), my position is that it is not so much that we need a new discipline in order to study the world as a whole but that social theory in the broadest sense—as a perspective which stretches across the social sciences and humanities (Giddens and Turner, 1987: 1) and even the natural sciences—should be refocused and expanded so as to make concern with 'the world' a central hermeneutic, and in such a way as to constrain empirical and comparative-historical research in the same direction.

Undoubtedly, as we have already seen, there *have* been various attempts in the history of social theory to move along such lines but the very structure of the globalization process has inhibited such efforts from taking off into a fully fledged research program, mostly notably during the crucial take-off period of globalization itself, 1870–1925. So we are led to the argument that exerting ourselves to develop *global* social theory is not merely an exercise 'demanded by the transparency of the processes rendering the contemporary world as a whole as a single place but also that our labors in that regard are crucial to the empirical understanding of the bases upon which the matrix of contemporary disciplinarity and interdisciplinarity rests. There has been an enormous amount of talk in recent years about self-reflexiveness, the critical-theoretic posture, and the like; but ironically much of that talk has been about as far removed from discussion of the real world—in the twofold sense of quotidian contemporary realities and differences *and* the concrete global circumstance—as it could be. Much of fashionable social theory has favored the abstract and, from a simplistic global perspective, 'the local' to the great neglect of the global and civilizational contours and bases of Western social theory itself. The distinction between the global and the local is becoming very complex and problematic, to the extent that we should now perhaps speak in such terms as the global institutionalization of the life-world and the localization of globality.

In the second half of the 1980s 'globalization' (and its problematic variant, 'internationalization') became a commonly used term in intellectual, business, media and other circles, in the process acquiring a number of meanings, with varying degrees of precision. This has been a source of frustration, but not necessarily a cause for surprise or alarm, to those of us who had sought earlier in the decade to establish a relatively strict definition of globalization as part of an attempt to come to terms systematically with major aspects of contemporary 'meaning and change' (Robertson, 1978). Nevertheless a stream of analysis and research *has* been developed around the general idea, if not always the actual concept, of globalization. It is my intention here to indicate some of the most pressing issues in this area—not so much by surveying and evaluating different approaches to the making of the contemporary world system, world society, the global ecumene, or whatever one chooses to call the late twentieth-century world as a whole; but rather by considering some relatively neglected analytical and historical themes.

I deal here with relatively recent aspects of globalization, although I want to emphasize as strongly as possible that in doing so I am not suggesting for a moment that moves and thrusts in the direction of global unicity are unique to relatively recent history. I also argue that globalization is intimately related to modernity and modernization, as well as to postmodernity and 'postmodernization' (in so far as the latter pair of motifs have definite analytical purchase). In attempting to justify that proposal I am by no means suggesting that work within the frame of 'the globalization paradigm' should be limited to the relatively recent past. All I am maintaining is that the concept of globalization *per se* is most clearly applicable to a particular series of relatively recent developments concerning *the concrete structuration of the world as a whole.* The term 'structuration' has been deliberately chosen. Although I will shortly consider some aspects of Anthony Giddens's work on 'the global scene,' I cannot address here the general problems which arise from the concept of structuration (Cohen, 1989; Bryant and Jary, 1991). I will say only that if the notion of structuration is to be of assistance to us analytically in the decades ahead it has to be moved out of its quasi-philosophical context, its confinement within the canonical discourses about subjectivity and objectivity, individual and society, and so on (Archer, 1988). It has to be made directly relevant to *the world* in which we live. It has to contribute to the understanding of how the global 'system' has been and continues to be *made.* It has to be focused on the production and reproduction of 'the world' as the most salient plausibility structure of our time (Wuthnow, 1978: 65). The same applies to the cultural-agency problematic which Margaret Archer (1988) has recently theorized.

Human history has been replete with ideas concerning the physical structure, the geography, the cosmic location and the spiritual and/or secular significance of the world (Wagar, 1971); movements and organizations concerned with the patterning and/or the unification of the world as a whole have intermittently appeared for at least the last two thousand years; and ideas about the relationship between the universal and the particular have been central to all of the major civilizations. Even something like what has recently been called 'the global-local nexus' (or the local-global nexus') was thematized as long ago as the second century BC when Polybius, in his *Universal History,* wrote with reference to the rise of the Roman empire: 'Formerly the things which happened in the world had no connection among themselves ... But since then all events are united in a common bundle' (Kohn, 1971: 121).[3] However, the crucial considerations are that it has not been until relatively recent times that it has been realistically thought that 'humanity is rapidly becoming, physically speaking, a single society' (Hobhouse, 1906: 331), and that it has not been until quite recently that considerable numbers of people living on various parts of the planet have spoken and acted in direct reference to the problem of the 'organization' of the entire, heliocentric world. It is in relation to this heavily contested problem of the concrete patterning and consciousness of the world, including resistance to globality, that I seek to center the concept and the discourse of globalization.

The world as a whole could, in theory, have become the reality which it now is in ways and along trajectories other than those that have actually obtained (Lechner, 1989). The world could, in principle, have been rendered as a 'singular system' (Moore, 1966) via the imperial hegemony of a single nation or a 'grand alliance' between two or more dynasties or nations; the victory of 'the universal proletariat'; the global triumph of a particular form of organized religion; the crystallization of 'the world spirit'; the yielding of nationalism to the ideal of 'free trade'; the success of the world-federalist movement; the worldwide triumph of a trading company; or in yet other ways. Some of these have in fact held sway at certain moments in world history. Indeed, in coming to terms analytically with the contemporary circumstance we have to acknowledge that some such possibilities are as old as world history in any meaningful sense of that phrase and have greatly contributed to the existence of the globalized world of the late twentieth century. Moreover, much of world history can be fruitfully considered as sequences of 'miniglobalization,' in the sense that, for example, historic empire formation involved the unification of previously sequestered territories and social entities. There have also been shifts in the opposite direction, as with the deunification of medieval Europe, of which Rosencrance (1986) has spoken—although the rise of the territorial state also promoted imperialism and thus conceptions of the world as a whole.

Nonetheless, when all is said and done no single possibility has, or so I claim, been more continuously prevalent than another. There may have been periods in world history when one such possibility was more of a 'globalizing force' than others—and that must certainly be a crucial aspect of the discussion of globalization in the long-historical mode—but we have not as a world-people moved into the present global-human circumstance along one or even a small cluster of these particular trajectories. Yet in the present climate of 'globality' there is a strong temptation for some to insist that the single world of our day can be accounted for in terms of one particular process or factor, such as 'Westernization,' 'imperialism' or, in the dynamic and diffuse sense, 'civilization.' As I argue more specifically in later chapters, the problem of globality is very likely to become a basis of major ideological and analytical cleavages of the twenty-first century, as the idea of 'the new world order' in its political, military and economic senses, not least because the connotations of that term as used in pre-Axis and Axis contexts are so negative. While I do not subscribe to the view that social theorists should at all costs attempt to be neutral about these and other matters, I am committed to the argument that one's moral stance should be realistic and that one should have no intrinsically vested interest in the attempt to map this or any other area of the human condition. More precisely, I argue that systematic comprehension of the structuration of world order is essential to the viability of any form of contemporary theory and that such comprehension must involve analytical separation of the factors that have facilitated the shift towards a single world—for example the spread of capitalism, Western imperialism and the development of a global media system—from the *general and global* agency-structure (and/or culture) theme. While the empirical relationship between the two sets of issues is of great importance (and, of course, complex), conflation of them leads us into all sorts of difficulties and inhibits our ability to come to terms with the basic but shifting terms of the contemporary world order, including the 'structure' of 'disorderliness.'

Thus we must return to the question of the actual form of recent and contemporary moves in the direction of global interdependence and global consciousness. In posing the basic question in this way we immediately confront the critical issue of the period during which the move towards the world as a singular system became more or less inexorable. If we think of the history of the world as consisting for a very long time in *the objectiveness* of a variety of different civilizations existing in varying degrees of separation from each other, our main task now is to consider the ways in which the world 'moved' from being merely 'in itself' to the problem or the possibility of its being 'for itself.' Before coming directly to that vital issue I must attend briefly to some basic analytical matters. This I do via the statement of Giddens (1987: 255–93) on 'Nation-States in the Global State System.'

Giddens makes much of the point that 'the development of the sovereignty of the modern state from its beginnings depends upon a reflexively monitored set of relations between states' (Giddens, 1987: 263). He argues that the period of treaty making following World War I 'was effectively the first point at which a reflexively monitored system of nation-states came to exist globally' (1987: 256). I fully concur with both the emphasis on the importance of the post–World War I period and Giddens's claim that 'if a new and formidably threatening pattern of war was established at this time, so was a new pattern of peace' (1987: 256). More generally, Giddens's argument that the development of the modern state has been guided by increasingly global norms concerning its sovereignty is, if not original, of great importance. However, he tends to conflate the issue of the homogenization of the state (in Hegel's sense)—what Giddens calls 'the universal scope of the nation-state' (1987: 264)—and the issue of relationships between states.

It is important to make a distinction between the diffusion of expectations concerning the external legitimacy and mode of operation of the state and the development of regulative norms concerning the relationships between states, while readily acknowledging that the issue of the powers and limits of the state has been *empirically* linked to the structuring of the relationships between states and, moreover, that it constitutes a crucial axis of globalization. James Der Derian (1989) has recently drawn attention to an important aspect of that theme by indicating the proximity of the formal 'Declaration of the Rights of Man' that sovereignty resides in the nation to Jeremy Bentham's declaration in the same year of 1789 that there was a need for a new word—'international'—which would 'express, in a more significant way, the branch of law which goes commonly under the name of the *law of nations'* (Bentham, 1948: 326).

So while the two issues upon which I have been dwelling via Giddens's analysis undoubtedly have been and remain closely interdependent, it is crucial to keep them analytically apart in order that we may fully appreciate variations in the nature of the empirical connections between them. In sum, the problem of contingency arising from state sovereignty and the development of relational rules between sovereign units is not the same as the issue of the crystallization and diffusion of conceptions of national statehood (A.D. Smith, 1979). Nor is it the same as the development and spread of conceptions of the shape and meaning of 'international society' (Gong, 1984). The second set of matters is on a different 'level' than that addressed by Giddens.

My primary reason for emphasizing this matter is that it provides an immediate entry to what I consider the most pressing general problem in the contemporary discussion of globalization. Giddens's analysis is a good example of an attempt to move toward the global circumstance via the conventional concerns of sociological theory. While readily conceding that it was his specific, initial concern to talk about the modern nation state and the internal and external violence with which its development has been bound up, the fact remains that in spite of all of his talk about global matters at the end of his analysis, Giddens is restricted precisely by his having to center 'the current world system' within a discussion of 'the global *state* system' (Giddens, 1987: 276–7; emphasis added). Even though he eventually separates, in analytical terms, the nation-state system (with the ambiguity I have indicated) as the political aspect of the world system from the 'global information system' (as relating to 'symbolic orders/modes of discourse'); the 'world-capitalist economy' (as the economic dimension of the world system); and the 'world military order' (as concerning 'law/modes of sanction')—along lines reminiscent of approaches of the 1960s (Nettl and Robertson, 1968) and, ironically, of a general Parsonian, functional-imperative approach—Giddens ends up with a 'map' of what he reluctantly calls the world system, which is centered upon his conflated characterization of the rise of the modern state system. Giddens (1990) has of course expanded upon and modified his thinking about what he now calls globalization, in relation to modernity and the idea of postmodernity. That will be the specific focus of Chapter 9.

'Mapping' the world social-scientifically is, of course, a common procedure; it crystallized during the 1960s both with the diffusion of perceptions concerning the existence of the Third World and with polarized First (liberal-capitalist) and Second (industrializing-communist) Worlds. Ever since that period—the beginning of the current phase of contemporary, late twentieth-century globalization—there has proliferated a large number of different and, indeed, conflicting ideological and/or 'scientific' maps of the world-system of national societies, so much so that it is reasonable to say that the discourse of mapping is a vital ingredient of global-political culture, one which fuses geography (as in the use of North–South and East–West terminology) with political, economic, cultural and other forms of placement of nations on the global-international map. Much of this overall effort has resulted in significant work—for example Johan Galtung's *The True Worlds* (1980) and Peter Worsley's (1984) lengthy discussion of the cultures of 'the three worlds.' Indeed, the kind of work which has strongly reminded us of the major cleavages and discontinuities in the world as a whole is a significant antidote to those who now speak blithely in 'global village' terms of a single world. Nonetheless there can be no denying that the world is much more singular than it was as recently as, say, the 1950s. The crucial question remains of the basic form or structure in terms of which that shift has occurred. That that form has been *imposed* upon certain areas of the world is, of course, a crucial issue, but until the matter of form (more elaborately, structuration) is adequately thematized our ability to comprehend the dynamics of the making of the world as a whole will be severely limited.

A Minimal Phase Model of Globalization

I offer here what I call and advocate as a necessarily minimal model of globalization. This model does not make grand assertions about primary factors, major mechanisms, and so on. Rather, it indicates the major constraining tendencies which have been operating in relatively recent history as far as world order and the compression of the world in our time are concerned.

One of the most pressing tasks in this regard is to confront the issue of the undoubted salience of the unitary nation state—more diffusely, the national society—since about the mid-eighteenth century and at the same time to acknowledge its historical uniqueness, in a sense its abnormality (McNeill, 1986). The homogeneous nation state—homogeneous here in the sense of a culturally homogenized, administered citizenry (B. Anderson, 1983)—is a construction of a particular form of life. That we ourselves have been increasingly subject to its constraints does not mean that for analytical purposes it has to be accepted as *the* departure point for analyzing and understanding the world. This is why I have argued not merely that national societies should be regarded as constituting but one general reference point for the analysis of the global-human circumstance, but that we have to recognize even more than we do now that the prevalence of the national society in the twentieth century is an aspect of globalization (Robertson, 1989a)—that the diffusion of *the idea of* the national society as a form of institutionalized societalism (Lechner, 1989) was central to the accelerated globalization which began to occur just over a hundred years ago. I have also argued more specifically that the two other major components of globalization have been, in addition to national systems and the system of international relations, conceptions of individuals and of humankind. It is in terms of the shifting relationships between and the 'upgrading' of these reference points that globalization has occurred in recent centuries. This pattern has certainly been greatly affected by and subject to all sorts of economic, political and other processes and actions; but my task here is to legitimize the need for an overall comprehension of the global circumstance.

I now propose, in skeletal terms, that the temporal-historical path to the present circumstance of a very high degree of global density and complexity can be delineated as follows:

Phase 1: The Germinal Phase   Lasting in Europe from the early fifteenth until the mid-eighteenth century. Incipient growth of national communities and downplaying of the medieval 'transnational' system. Expanding scope of the Catholic church. Accentuation of concepts of the individual and of ideas about humanity. Heliocentric theory of the world and beginning of modern geography; spread of Gregorian calendar.

Phase II: The Incipient Phase   Lasting—mainly in Europe—from the mid-eighteenth century until the 1870s. Sharp shift towards the idea of the homogeneous, unitary state; crystallization of conceptions of formalized international relations, of standardized citizenly individuals and a more concrete conception of humankind. Sharp increases in legal conventions and agencies concerned with international and transnational regulation and communication. International exhibitions. Beginning of problem of 'admission' of non-European societies to 'international society.' Thematization of nationalism-internationalism issue.

Phase III: The Take-off Phase   Lasting from the 1870s until the mid-1920s. 'Take-off' here refers to a period during which the increasingly manifest globalizing tendencies of previous periods and places gave way to a single, inexorable form centered upon the four reference points, and thus constraints, of national societies, generic individuals (but with a masculine bias), a single 'international society,' and an increasingly singular, but not unified conception of humankind. Early thematization of 'the problem of modernity.' Increasingly global conceptions of the 'correct outline' of an 'acceptable' national society; thematization of ideas concerning national and personal identities; inclusion of a number of non-European societies in 'international society'; international formalization and attempted implementation of ideas about humanity. Globalization of immigration restrictions. Very sharp increase in number and speed of global forms of communication. The first 'international novels.' Rise of ecumenical movement. Development of global competitions—for example the Olympics and Nobel prizes. Implementation of world time and near-global adoption of Gregorian calendar. First *world* war.

Phase IV: The Struggle-for-Hegemony Phase   Lasting from the mid-1920s until the late-1960s. Disputes and wars about the fragile terms of the dominant globalization process established by the end of the take-off period. Establishment of the League of Nations and then the United Nations. Principle of national independence established. Conflicting conceptions of modernity (Allies v. the Axis), followed by high point of the Cold War (conflict within 'the modern project'). Nature of and prospects for humanity sharply focused by the Holocaust and use of the atomic bomb. The crystallization of the Third World.

Phase V: The Uncertainty Phase   Beginning in the late 1960s and displaying crisis tendencies in the early 1990s. Heightening of global consciousness in late 1960s. Moon landing. Accentuation of 'post-materialist' values. End of the Cold War and manifest rise of the problem of 'rights' and widespread access to nuclear and thermonuclear weaponry. Number of global institutions and movements greatly increases. Sharp acceleration in means of global communication. Societies increasingly facing problems of multiculturality and polyethnicity. Conceptions of individuals rendered more complex by gender, sexual, ethnic and racial considerations. Civil rights become a global issue. International system more fluid—end of bipolarity. Concern with humankind as a species-community greatly enhanced, particularly via environmental movements. Arising of interest in world civil society and world citizenship, in spite of 'the ethnic revolution.' Consolidation of global media system, including rivalries about such. Islam as a deglobalizing/reglobalizing movement. Earth Summit in Rio de Janeiro.

This is merely an outline, with much detail and more rigorous analysis and interpretation of the shifting relationships between and the relative autonomization of each of the four major components to be worked out. Some of this is attempted in the following chapters. Clearly one of the most important empirical questions has to do with the extent to which the form of globalization which was set firmly in motion during the period 1870–1925 will 'hold' in the coming decades. In a more theoretical vein, much more needs to be done to demonstrate the ways in which the selective responses of relevant collective actors, particularly societies, to globalization play a crucial part in the making of the world as a whole. Different forms of societal participation in the globalization process make a crucial difference to its precise form. My main point is that there is a general autonomy and 'logic' to the globalization process, which operates in *relative* independence of strictly societal and other more conventionally studied sociocultural processes. The global system is not simply an outcome of processes of basically intra-societal origin *(contra* Luhmann, 1982b) or even a development of the inter-state system. Its making has been and continues to be much more complex than that.

Notes

Reproduced by permission of Sage Publications, London, Los Angeles, New Delhi, and Singapore, from Roland Robertson, "Mapping the Global Condition." In *Globalization: Social Theory and Global Culture* (London; Newbury Park, California: Sage, 1992): 49–60. Published in association with *Theory, Culture & Society* 1990. References omitted.

Allusions to chapters within this piece refer to the original book from which this chapter was taken.

1. It is of more than passing interest to note that in speaking of communism as a radical branch of one of 'the great "reform" movements of postmedieval Western history'—socialism—Talcott Parsons said in 1964 that 'it seems a safe prediction that Communism will, from its own internal dynamics, evolve in the direction of the restoration—or where it has yet not existed, the institution—of political democracy' (1964: 396–97). On the other hand, Parsons insisted, problematically, that the *internationalism* of communism had made a crucial contribution to world order.

2. Ronald Inglehart (1990: 33) observes in the course of his empirical analysis of culture in advanced industrial societies 'that the publics of the three major Axis powers, Germany, Japan, and Italy, all tend to be underachievers in life satisfaction. The traumatic discrediting of their social and political systems that accompanied their defeat in World War II may have left a legacy of cynicism that their subsequent social change and economic success has still not entirely erased.'

3. I owe the precise phrases 'local-global nexus' and 'global-local nexus' to Chadwick Alger (1988).

Chapter 5
Globalization
A Necessary Myth?

Paul Hirst and Grahame Thompson

Globalization has become a fashionable concept in the social sciences. a core dictum in the prescriptions of management gurus, and a catch-phrase for journalists and politicians of every stripe. It is widely asserted that we live in an era in which the greater part of social life is determined by global processes, in which national cultures, national economies and national borders are dissolving. Central to this perception is the notion of a rapid and recent process of economic globalization. A truly global economy is claimed to have emerged or to be in the process of emerging, in which distinct national economies and, therefore, domestic strategies of national economic management are increasingly irrelevant. The world economy has internationalized in its basic dynamics, it is dominated by uncontrollable market forces, and it has as its principal economic actors and major agents of change truly transnational corporations that owe allegiance to no nation-state and locate wherever on the globe market advantage dictates.

   This image is so powerful that it has mesmerized analysts and captured political imaginations. But is it the case? This book is written with a mixture of scepticism about global economic processes and optimism about the possibilities of control of the international economy and about the viability of national political strategies. One key effect of the concept of globalization has been to paralyse radical reforming national strategies, to see them as unfeasible in the face of the judgement and sanction of international markets. If, however, we face economic changes that are more complex and more equivocal than the extreme globalists argue, then the possibility remains of political strategy and action for national and international control of market economies in order to promote social goals.

We began this investigation with an attitude of moderate scepticism. It was clear that much had changed since the 1960s, but we were cautious about the more extreme claims of the most enthusiastic globalization theorists. In particular it was obvious that radical expansionary and redistributive strategies of national economic management were no longer possible in the face of a variety of domestic and international constraints. However, the closer we looked the shallower and more unfounded became the claims of the more radical advocates of economic globalization. In particular we began to be disturbed by three facts. First, the absence of a commonly accepted model of the new global economy and how it differs from previous states of the international economy. Second, in the absence of a clear model against which to measure trends, the tendency to casually cite examples of the internationalization of sectors and processes as if they were evidence of the growth of an economy dominated by autonomous global market forces. Third, the lack of historical depth, the tendency to portray current changes as unique and without precedent and firmly set to persist long into the future.

To anticipate, as we proceeded our scepticism deepened until we became convinced that globalization, as conceived by the more extreme globalizers, is largely a myth. Thus we argue that:

1. The present highly internationalized economy is not unprecedented: it is one of a number of distinct conjunctures or states of the international economy that have existed since an economy based on modern industrial technology began to be generalized from the 1860s. In some respects, the current international economy is *less* open and integrated than the regime that prevailed from 1870 to 1914.

2. Genuinely transnational companies appear to be relatively rare. Most companies are based nationally and trade multinationally on the strength of a major national location of assets, production and sales, and there seems to be no major tendency towards the growth of truly international companies.

3. Capital mobility is not producing a massive shift of investment and employment from the advanced to the developing countries. Rather foreign direct investment (FDI) is highly concentrated among the advanced industrial economies and the Third World remains marginal in both investment and trade, a small minority of newly industrializing countries apart.

4. As some of the extreme advocates of globalization recognize, the world economy is far from being genuinely 'global'. Rather trade, investment and financial flows are concentrated in the Triad of Europe, Japan and North America and this dominance seems set to continue.

5. These major economic powers, the G3, thus have the capacity, especially if they coordinate policy, to exert powerful governance pressures over financial markets and other economic tendencies. Global markets are thus by no means beyond regulation and control, even though the current scope and objectives of economic governance are limited by the divergent interests of the great powers and the economic doctrines prevalent among their elites.

These and other more detailed points challenging the globalization thesis will be developed in later chapters. We should emphasize that this book challenges the strong version of the thesis of *economic* globalization, because we believe that without the notion of a truly globalized economy many of the other consequences adduced in the domains of culture and politics would either cease to be sustainable or become less threatening. Hence most of the discussion here is centred on the international economy and the evidence for and against the process of globalization. However, the book is written to emphasize the possibilities of national and international governance, and as it proceeds issues of the future of the nation-state and the role of international agencies, regimes and structures of governance are given increasing prominence.

It is one thing to be sceptical about various uses of the concept of globalization, it is another to explain the widespread development and reception of the concept since the 1970s. It will not do to wheel out the concept of 'ideology' here, for this view is so widespread that it covers the most diverse outlooks and social interests. It covers the political spectrum from left to right, it is endorsed in different disciplines—economics, sociology, cultural studies and international politics—and it is advanced both by theoretical innovators and traditionalists. The literature on globalization is vast and varied. We deliberately chose not to write this book by summarizing and criticizing this literature, in part because that would be a never-ending enterprise given the scale and rate of publication on the topic, but mainly because we concluded that the great bulk of the literature that considered the international economy was based on untenable assumptions, for example, that globalization was an accomplished fact. Hence we decided to examine the evidence against concepts that could specify what a distinctive global economy would look like but which did not presuppose its existence.

We are well aware that there is a wide variety of views that use the term 'globalization'. Even among those analysts who confine themselves to strictly economic processes some make far more radical claims about changes in the international economy than others. It might therefore be argued that we are focusing too narrowly in concentrating on delineating and challenging the most extreme version of the thesis of economic globalization. Indeed, in criticizing such positions we might be held to be demolishing a straw man. On the contrary, we see these extreme views as strong, relatively coherent and capable of being developed into a clear ideal-typical conception of a globalized economic system. Such views are also important in that they have become politically highly conse-quential. The most eloquent proponents of the extreme view are very influential and have tended to set the tone for discussion in business and political circles. Views that shape the perception of key decision-makers are important, and thus are a primary target rather than a marginal one. The advocates of 'globalization' have proposed the further liberalization of the international economy and the deregulation of domestic economies. This advocacy has had serious effects in Asia and in emerging financial markets, leading to economic crisis, unemployment and impoverishment. The view we attack may have been dented by the Asian crisis but it is not dead. It remains strong in the developed countries, where it has sustained the rhetoric of 'competitiveness' and the belief that the extensive welfare states of Northern and Western Europe are a constraint on economic performance that they can no longer afford in an internationalized economy. These myths still need puncturing before they do impossible damage to both social stability and economic performance.

Some less extreme and more nuanced analyses that employ the term global-ization are well established in the academic community and concentrate on the relative internationalization of major financial markets, of technology and of certain important sectors of manufacturing and services, particularly since the 1970s. Emphasis is given in many of these analyses to the increasing constraints on national-level governance that prevent ambitious macroeconomic policies that diverge significantly from the norms acceptable to international financial markets. Indeed, we ourselves have over some time drawn attention to such phenomena in our own work.

Obviously, it is no part of our aim here to deny that such trends to increased internationalization have occurred or to ignore the constraints on certain types of national economic strategy. Our point in assessing the significance of the internationalization that has occurred is to argue that it is well short of dissolving distinct national economies in the major advanced industrial countries, or of preventing the development of new forms of economic governance at the national and international levels. There are, however, very real dangers in not distinguishing clearly between certain trends towards internationalization and the strong version of the globalization thesis. It is particularly unfortunate if the two become confused by using the same word, 'globalization', to describe both. Often we feel that evidence from more cautious arguments is then used carelessly to bolster more extreme ones, to build a community of usage when there needs to be strict differentiation of meanings. It also confuses public discussion and policy-making, reinforcing the view that political actors can accomplish less than is actually possible in a global system.

The strong version of the globalization thesis requires a new view of the international economy, as we shall shortly see, one that subsumes and subordinates national-level processes. Whereas tendencies towards internationalization can be accommodated within a modified view of the world economic system, that still gives a major role to national-level policies and economic actors. Undoubtably this implies some greater or lesser degree of change; firms, governments and international agencies are being forced to behave differently, but in the main they can use existing institutions and practices to do so. In this way we feel it makes more sense to consider the international economic system in a longer historical perspective, to recognize that current changes, while significant and distinctive, are not unprecedented and do not necessarily involve a move towards a new type of economic system. The strong economic versions of the globalization thesis have the advantage that they clearly and sharply pose the possibility of such a change. If they are wrong they are still of some value in enabling us to think out what *is* happening and why. In this sense, challenging the strong version of the thesis is not merely negative but helps us to develop our own ideas.

However, the question remains to be considered of how the myth of the globalization of economic activity became established as and when it did. In answering, one must begin with the ending of the post-1945 era in the turbulence of 1972–3. A period of prolonged economic growth and full employment in the advanced countries, sustained by strategies of active national state intervention and a managed multilateral regime for trade and monetary policy under US hegemony, was brought to an end by a number of significant changes. Thus we can point to:

1. The effects of the collapse of the Bretton Woods system and the 1973 and 1979 OPEC oil crises (which massively increased oil prices) in producing turbulence and volatility in all the major economies through the 1970s into the early 1980s. Significant in generating such turbulence

and undermining previous policy regimes was the rapid rise in inflation in the advanced countries brought about by domestic policy failures, the international impact of US involvement in the Vietnam War, and the oil price hikes of 1973 and 1979.

2. The efforts of financial institutions and manufacturers, in this period of turbulence and inflationary pressure, to compensate for domestic uncertainty by seeking wider outlets for investments and additional markets; hence the widespread bank lending to the Third World during the inflationary 1970s, the growth of the Eurodollar market, and the increasing ratios of foreign trade to GDP in the advanced countries.

3. The public policy acceleration of the internationalization of financial markets by the widespread abandonment of exchange controls and other market deregulation in the late 1970s and early 1980s, even as the more extreme forms of volatility in currency markets were being brought under control by, for example, the development of the European Monetary System (EMS) in 1979 and the Louvre and Plaza accords in the 1980s.

4. The tendency towards 'deindustrialization' in Britain and the United States and the growth of long-term unemployment in Europe, promoting fears of foreign competition, especially from Japan.

5. The relatively rapid development of a number of newly industrializing countries (NICs) in the Third World and their penetration of First World markets.

6. The shift from standardized mass production to more flexible production methods, and the change from the perception of the large, nationally rooted, oligopolistic corporation as the unchallengeably dominant economic agent towards a more complex world of multinational enterprises, less rigidly structured firms and the increased salience of smaller firms— summed up in the widespread and popular concept of 'post-Fordism'.

These changes are undoubted and they were highly disturbing to those conditioned by the unprecedented success and security of the post-1945 period in the advanced industrial states. The perceived loss of national control, the increased uncertainty and unpredictability of economic relations, and rapid institutional change were a shock to minds conditioned to believe that poverty, unemployment and economic cycles could all be controlled or eliminated in a market economy based on the profit motive. If the widespread consensus of the 1950s and 1960s was that the future belonged to a capitalism without losers, securely managed by national governments acting in concert, then the later 1980s and 1990s have been dominated by a consensus based on contrary assumptions, that global markets are uncontrollable and that the only way to avoid becoming a loser—whether as nation, firm or individual—is to be as competitive as possible. The notion of an ungovernable world economy is a response to the collapse of expectations schooled by Keynesianism and sobered by the failure of monetarism to provide an alternative route to broad-based prosperity and stable growth. 'Globalization' is a myth suitable for a world without illusions, but it is also one that robs us of hope. Global markets are dominant, and they face no threat from any viable contrary political project, for it is held that Western social democracy and socialism of the Soviet bloc are both finished.

One can only call the political impact of 'globalization' the pathology of over-diminished expectations. Many overenthusiastic analysts and politicians have gone beyond the evidence in overstating the extent of the dominance of world markets and their ungovernability. If this is so, then we should seek to break the spell of this uncomforting myth. The old rationalist explanation for primitive myths was that they were a way of masking and compensating for humanity's helplessness in the face of the power of nature. In this case we have a myth that exaggerates the degree of our helplessness in the face of contemporary economic forces. If economic relations are more governable (at both the national and international levels) than many contemporary analysts suppose, then we should explore the possible scale and scope of that governance. It is not currently the case that radical goals are attainable: full employment in the advanced countries, a fair deal for the poorer developing countries and widespread democratic control over economic affairs for the world's people. But this should not lead us to dismiss or ignore the forms of control and social improvement that could be achieved relatively rapidly with a modest change in attitudes on the part of key elites. It is thus essential to persuade reformers of the left and conservatives who care for the fabric of their societies that we are not helpless before uncontrollable global processes. If this happens, then changing attitudes and expectations might make these more radical goals acceptable.

Models of the International Economy

We can only begin to assess the issue of globalization if we have some relatively clear and rigorous model of what a global economy would be like and how it represents both a new phase in the international economy and an entirely changed environment for national economic actors. Globalization in its radical sense should be taken to mean the development of a new economic structure, and not just conjunctural change towards greater international trade and investment within an existing set of economic relations. An extreme and one-sided ideal type of this kind enables us to differentiate *degrees* of internationalization, to eliminate some possibilities and to avoid confusion between claims. Given such a model it becomes possible to assess it against evidence of international trends and thus enables us more or less plausibly to determine whether or not this phenomenon of the development of a new supranational economic system is occurring. In order to do this we have developed two basic contrasting ideal types of international economy, one that is fully globalized, and an open international economy that is still fundamentally characterized by exchange between relatively distinct national economies and in which many outcomes, such as the competitive performance of firms and sectors, are substantially determined by processes occurring at the national level. These ideal types are valuable in so far as they are useful in enabling us to clarify the issues conceptually, that is, in specifying the difference between a new global economy and merely extensive and intensifying international economic relations. Too often evidence compatible with the latter is used as though it substantiated the former. With a few honourable exceptions, the more enthusiastic advocates of globalization have failed to specify that difference, or to specify what evidence would be decisive in pointing to a structural change towards a global economy. Increasing salience of foreign trade and considerable and growing international flows of capital are not *per se* evidence of a new and distinct phenomenon called 'globalization'.

Type I: An Inter-national Economy

We shall first develop a simple and extreme version of this type. An *international economy* is one in which the principal entities are national economies. Trade and investment produce growing interconnection between these still national economies. Such a process involves the increasing integration of more and more nations and economic actors into world market relationships. Trade relations, as a result, tend to take on the form of national specializations and the international division of labour. The importance of trade is, however, progressively replaced by the centrality of investment relations between nations, which increasingly act as the organizing principle of the system. The form of interdependence between nations remains, however, of the 'strategic' kind. That is, it implies the continued relative separation of the domestic and the international frameworks for policy-making and the management of economic affairs, and also a relative separation in terms of economic effects. Interactions are of the 'billiard ball' type; international events do not directly or necessarily penetrate or permeate the domestic economy but are refracted through national policies and processes. The international and the domestic policy fields either remain relatively separate as distinct levels of governance, or they work 'automatically'. In the latter case adjustments are not thought to be the subject of policy by public bodies or authorities, but are a consequence of 'unorganized' or 'spontaneous' market forces.

Perhaps the classic case of such an 'automatic' adjustment mechanism remains the Gold Standard, which operated at the height of the Pax Britannica system from mid-nineteenth century to 1914. Automatic is put in inverted commas here to signal the fact that this is a popular caricature. The actual system of adjustment took place very much in terms of overt domestic policy interventions (see chapter 2). The flexibility in wages and prices that the Gold Standard system demanded (the international value of currencies could not be adjusted since these were fixed in terms of gold) had to be engendered by governments through domestic expenditure-reducing policies to influence the current account and through interest rate policy to influence the capital account.

Great Britain acted as the political and economic hegemon and the guarantor of this system. But it is important to recognize that the Gold Standard and the Pax Britannica system was merely one of several structures of the international economy in this century. Such structures were highly conditional on major sociopolitical conjunctures. Thus the First World War wrecked British hegemony, accelerating a process that would have occurred far more slowly merely as a consequence of British industrial decline. It resulted in a period of protectionism and national autarchic competition in the 1930s, followed by the establishment of American hegemony after the Second World War and by the reopened international economy of the Bretton Woods system. This indicates the danger of assuming that current major changes in the international economy are unprecedented and that they are inevitable or irreversible. The lifetime of a prevailing system of international economic relations in this century has been no more than thirty to forty years. Indeed, given that most European currencies did not become fully convertible until the late 1950s, the full Bretton Woods system after the Second World War only lasted upwards of thirteen to fourteen years. Such systems have been transformed by major changes in the politico-economic balance of power and the conjunctures that have effected these shifts have been large-scale conflicts between the major powers. In that sense, the international economy has been determined as to its structure and the distribution of power within it by the major nation-states.

The period of this worldwide inter-national economic system is also typified by the rise and maturity of the multinational corporation, as a transformation of the large merchant trading companies of a past era. From our point of view, however, the important aspect of these multinational companies is that they retain a clear national home base; they are subject to the national regulation of the home country, and by and large they are effectively policed by that country.

The point of this ideal type drawing on the institutions of the *belle époque* is not, however, a historical analogy: for a simple and automatically governed international economic system *like* that before 1914 is unlikely to reproduce itself now. The current international economy is relatively open, but it has real differences from that prevailing before the First World War: it has more generalized and institutionalized free trade through the WTO, foreign investment is different in its modalities and destinations—although a high degree of capital mobility is once again a possibility—the scale of short-term financial flows is greater, the international monetary system is quite different and freedom of labour migration is drastically curtailed. The pre-1914 system was, nevertheless, genuinely international, tied by efficient long-distance communications and industrialized means of transport.

The communications and information technology revolution of the late twentieth century has further developed a trading system that could make day-to-day world prices: it did not create it. In the second half of the nineteenth century the submarine intercontinental telegraph cables enabled the integration of world markets (Standage 1998). Modern systems dramatically increase the possible volume and complexity of transactions, but we have had information media capable of sustaining a genuine international trading system for over a century. The difference between a trading system in which goods and information moved by sailing ship and one in which they moved by steam ships and electricity is qualitative. If the theorists of globalization mean that we have an economy in which each part of the world is linked by markets sharing close to real-time information, then that began not in the 1970s but in the 1870s.

Type 2: A Globalized Economy

A *globalized economy* is a distinct ideal type from that of the inter-national economy and can be developed by contrast with it. In such a global system distinct national economies are subsumed and rearticulated into the system by international processes and transactions. The inter-national economy, on the contrary, is one in which processes that are determined at the level of national economies still dominate and international phenomena are outcomes that emerge from the distinct and differential performance of the national economies. The inter-national economy is an aggregate of nationally located functions. Thus while there is in such an economy a wide and increasing range of international economic interactions (financial markets and trade in manufactured goods, for example), these tend to function as opportunities or constraints for nationally located economic actors and their public regulators.

The global economy raises these nationally based interactions to a new power. The international economic system becomes autonomized and socially disembedded, as markets and production become truly global. Domestic policies, whether of private corporations or public regulators, now have routinely to take account of the predominantly international determinants of their sphere of operations. As systemic interdependence grows, the national level is permeated by and transformed by the international. In such a globalized economy the problem this poses for public authorities of different countries is how to construct policies that coordinate and integrate their regulatory efforts in order to cope with the systematic interdependence between their economic actors.

The first major consequence of a globalized economy would thus be that its governance is fundamentally problematic. Socially decontextualized global markets would be difficult to regulate, even supposing effective cooperation by the regulators and a coincidence of their interests. The principal difficulty is to construct both effective and integrated patterns of national and international public policy to cope with global market forces. The systematic economic interdependence of countries and markets would by no means necessarily result in a harmonious integration enabling world consumers to benefit from truly independent, allocatively efficient market mechanisms. On the contrary, it is more than plausible that the populations of even successful and advanced states and regions would be at the mercy of autonomized and uncontrollable (because global) market forces. Interdependence would then readily promote *disintegration*—that is, competition and conflict—between regulatory agencies at different levels. Such conflict would further weaken effective public governance at the global level. Enthusiasts for the efficiency of free markets and the superiority of corporate control compared with that of public agencies would see this as a rational world order freed from the shackles of obsolete and ineffective national public interventions. Others, less sanguine but convinced globalization *is* occurring, like Cerny (1998), see it as a world system in which there can be no generalized or sustained public reinsurance against the costs imposed on localities by unfavourable competitive outcomes or market failures.

Even if one does not accept that the full process of globalization is taking place, this ideal type can help to highlight some aspects of the importance of greater economic integration within the major regional trade blocs. Both the European Union (EU) and the North American Free Trade Area (NAFTA) will soon be highly integrated markets of continental scale. Already in the case of the EU it is clear that there are fundamental problems of the integration and coordination of regulatory policies between the different public authorities at Union, national and regional level.

It is also clear that this ideal type highlights the problem of weak public governance for the major corporations. Even if such companies were truly global, they would not be able to operate in all markets equally effectively and, like governments, would lack the capacity to reinsure against unexpected shocks relying on their own resources alone. Governments would no longer be available to assist as they have been for 'national champions'. Firms would therefore seek to share risks and opportunities through inter-corporate investments, partnerships, joint ventures, etc. Even in the current internationalized economy we can recognize such processes emerging.

A second major consequence of the notion of a globalizing international economy would be the transformation of multinational companies (MNCs) into transnational companies (TNCs) as the major players in the world economy.[1] The TNC would be genuine footloose capital, without specific national identification and with an internationalized management, and at least potentially willing to locate and relocate anywhere in the globe to obtain either the most secure or the highest returns. In the financial sector this could be achieved at the touch of a button and in a truly globalized economy would be wholly dictated by market forces, without deference to national monetary policies. In the case of primarily manufacturing companies, they would source, produce and market at the global level as strategy and opportunities dictated. The company would no longer be based on one predominant national location (as with the MNC) but would service global markets through global operations. Thus the TNC, unlike the MNC, could no longer be controlled or even constrained by the policies of particular national states. Rather it could escape all but the commonly agreed and enforced international regulatory standards. National governments could not adopt particular and effective regulatory policies that diverged from these standards to the detriment of TNCs operating within their borders. The TNC would be the main manifestation of a truly globalized economy.

Julius (1990) and Ohmae (1990, 1993), for example, both consider this trend towards true TNCs to be well established. Ohmae argues that such 'stateless' corporations are now the prime movers in an interlinked economy (ILE) centred on North America, Europe and Japan. He contends that macroeconomic and in-dustrial policy intervention by national governments can only distort and impede the rational process of resource allocation by corporate decisions and consumer choices on a global scale. Like Akio Morita of Sony, Ohmae argues that such corporations will pursue strategies of 'global localization' in responding on a worldwide scale to specific regionalized markets and locating effectively to meet the varying demands of distinct localized groups of consumers. The assumption here is that TNCs will rely primarily on foreign direct investment and the full domestication of production to meet such specific market demands. This is in contrast to the strategy of flexibly specialized core production in the company's main location and the building of branch assembly plants where needed or where dictated by national public policies. The latter strategy is compatible with nationally based companies. The evidence from Japanese corporations which are the most effective operators in world markets favours the view that the latter strategy is predominant (Williams et al. 1992). Japanese companies appear to have been reluctant to locate core functions like R&D or high value-added parts of the production process abroad. Thus national companies with an international scope of operations currently and for the foreseeable future seem more likely to be the pattern than the true TNCs. Of course, such multinational companies, although they are nationally based, are internationally orientated. Foreign markets influence their domestic strategies and foreign competitors their production processes. Although MNCs continue to trade substantially *within* their national economies, significant percentages of foreign sales influence their actions. The point, however, is that this is not new; companies in the long boom period after 1945 were influenced in this way too, and were successful only if they met the standards of international competition.

A third consequence of globalization would be the further decline in the political influence and economic bargaining power of organized labour. Globalized markets and TNCs would tend to be mirrored by an open world market in labour. Thus while companies requiring highly skilled and productive labour might well continue to locate in the advanced countries, with all their advantages, rather than merely seek areas where wages are low, the trend towards the global mobility of capital and the relative national fixity of labour would favour those advanced countries with the most tractable labour forces and the lowest social overheads relative to the benefits of labour competence and motivation. 'Social democratic' strategies of enhancement of working conditions would thus be viable only if they assured the competitive advantage of the labour force, without constraining management prerogatives, and at no more overall cost in taxation than the average for the advanced world. Such strategies would clearly be a tall order and the tendency of globalization would be to favour management at the expense of even strongly organized labour, and, therefore, public policies sympathetic to the former rather than the latter. This would be the 'disorganized capitalism' of Lash and Urry (1987) with a vengeance, or it could be seen as placing a premium on moderate and defensive strategies where organized labour remains locally strong (Scharpf 1991, 1997).

A final and inevitable consequence of globalization is the growth in fundamental multipolarity in the international political system. In the end, the hitherto hegemonic national power would no longer be able to impose its own distinct regulatory objectives in either its own territories or elsewhere, and lesser agencies (whether public or private) would thus enjoy enhanced powers of denial and evasion vis-à-vis any aspirant 'hegemon'. A variety of bodies from international voluntary agencies to TNCs would thus gain in relative power at the expense of national governments and, using global markets and media, could appeal to and obtain legitimacy from consumers/citizens across national boundaries. Thus the distinct disciplinary powers of national states would decline, even though the bulk of their citizens, especially in the advanced countries, remained nationally bound. In such a world, national military power would become less effective. It would no longer be used to pursue economic objectives because 'national' state control in respect of the economy would have largely disappeared. The use of military force would be increasingly tied to non-economic issues, such as nationality and religion. A variety of more specific powers of sanction and veto in the economic sphere by different kinds of bodies (both public and private) would thus begin to compete with national states and begin to change the nature of international politics. As economics and nationhood pulled apart, the international economy would become even more 'industrial' and less 'militant' than it is today. War would be increasingly localized; wherever it threatened powerful global economic interests the warring parties would be subject to devastating economic sanction.

Notes

Paul Hirst and Grahame Thompson, "Globalization: A Necessary Myth?" In *Globalization in Question: The International Economy and the Possibilities of Governance* (Cambridge, UK: Polity Press, 1996): 1–13. Used by permission of Polity Press Ltd.

References omitted. Allusions to chapters within this piece refer to the original book from which this chapter was taken.

1. This distinction between MNCs and TNCs is not usual. There is a tendency to use the terms interchangeably, with TNC increasingly adopted as a generally accepted term for both types. Where we use the term TNC it should be clear that we are referring to *true* TNCs in the context of discussing the strong globalizer's view.

CHAPTER 6
PREFACE TO *EMPIRE*

Michael Hardt and Antonio Negri

Empire is materializing before our very eyes. Over the past several decades, as colonial regimes were overthrown and then precipitously after the Soviet barriers to the capitalist world market finally collapsed, we have witnessed an irresistible and irreversible globalization of economic and cultural exchanges. Along with the global market and global circuits of production has emerged a global order, a new logic and structure of rule—in short, a new form of sovereignty. Empire is the political subject that effectively regulates these global exchanges, the sovereign power that governs the world.

Many argue that the globalization of capitalist production and exchange means that economic relations have become more autonomous from political controls, and consequently that political sovereignty has declined. Some celebrate this new era as the liberation of the capitalist economy from the restrictions and distortions that political forces have imposed on it; others lament it as the closing of the institutional channels through which workers and citizens can influence or contest the cold logic of capitalist profit. It is certainly true that, in step with the processes of globalization, the sovereignty of nation-states, while still effective, has progressively declined. The primary factors of production and exchange—money, technology, people, and goods—move with increasing ease across national boundaries; hence the nation-state has less and less power to regulate these flows and impose its authority over the economy. Even the most dominant nation-states should no longer be thought of as supreme and sovereign authorities, either outside or even within their own borders. *The decline in sovereignty of nation-states, however, does not mean that sovereignty as such has declined.*[1] Throughout the contemporary transformations, political controls, state functions, and regulatory mechanisms have continued to rule the realm of economic and social production and exchange. Our basic hypothesis is that sovereignty has taken a new form, composed of a series of national and supranational organisms united under a single logic of rule. This new global form of sovereignty is what we call Empire.

The declining sovereignty of nation-states and their increasing inability to regulate economic and cultural exchanges is in fact one of the primary symptoms of the coming of Empire. The sovereignty of the nation-state was the cornerstone of the imperialisms that European powers constructed throughout the modern era. By "Empire," however, we understand something altogether different from "imperialism." The boundaries defined by the modern system of nation-states were fundamental to European colonialism and economic expansion: the territorial boundaries of the nation delimited the center of power from which rule was exerted over external foreign territories through a system of channels and barriers that alternately facilitated and obstructed the flows of production and circulation. Imperialism was really an extension of the sovereignty of the European nation-states beyond their own boundaries. Eventually nearly all the world's territories could be parceled out and the entire world map could be coded in European colors: red for British territory, blue for French, green for Portuguese, and so forth. Wherever modern sovereignty took root, it constructed a Leviathan that overarched its social domain and imposed hierarchical territorial boundaries, both to police the purity of its own identity and to exclude all that was other.

The passage to Empire emerges from the twilight of modern sovereignty. In contrast to imperialism, Empire establishes no territorial center of power and does not rely on fixed boundaries or barriers. It is a *decentered* and *deterritorializing* apparatus of rule that progressively incorporates the entire global realm within its open, expanding frontiers. Empire manages hybrid identities, flexible hierarchies, and plural exchanges through modulating networks of command. The distinct national colors of the imperialist map of the world have merged and blended in the imperial global rainbow.

The transformation of the modern imperialist geography of the globe and the realization of the world market signal a passage within the capitalist mode of production. Most significant, the spatial divisions of the three Worlds (First, Second, and Third) have been scrambled so that we continually find the First World in the Third, the Third in the First, and the Second almost nowhere at all. Capital seems to be faced with a smooth world—or really, a world defined by new and complex regimes of differentiation and homogenization, deterritorialization and reterritorialization. The construction of the paths and limits of these new global flows has been accompanied by a transformation of the dominant productive processes themselves, with the result that the role of industrial factory labor has been reduced and priority given instead to communicative, cooperative, and affective labor. In the postmodernization of the global economy, the creation of wealth tends ever more toward what we will call biopolitical production, the production of social life itself, in which the economic, the political, and the cultural increasingly overlap and invest one another.

Many locate the ultimate authority that rules over the processes of globalization and the new world order in the United States. Proponents praise the United States as the world leader and sole superpower, and detractors denounce it as an imperialist oppressor. Both these views rest on the assumption that the United States has simply donned the mantle of global power that the European nations have now let fall. If the nineteenth century was a British century, then the twentieth century has been an American century; or really, if modernity was European, then postmodernity is American. The most damning charge critics can level, then, is that the United States is repeating the practices of old European imperialists, while proponents celebrate the United States as a more efficient and more benevolent world leader, getting right what the Europeans got wrong. Our basic hypothesis, however, that a new imperial form of sovereignty has emerged, contradicts both these views. *The United States does not, and indeed no nation-state can today, form the center of an imperialist project.* Imperialism is over. No nation will be world leader in the way modern European nations were.

The United States does indeed occupy a privileged position in Empire, but this privilege derives not from its similarities to the old European imperialist powers, but from its differences. These differences can be recognized most clearly by focusing on the properly imperial (not imperialist) foundations of the United States constitution, where by "constitution" we mean both the *formal constitution,* the written document along with its various amendments and legal apparatuses, and the *material constitution,* that is, the continuous formation and re-formation of the composition of social forces. Thomas Jefferson, the authors of the *Federalist,* and the other ideological founders of the United States were all inspired by the ancient imperial model; they believed they were creating on the other side of the Atlantic a new Empire with open, expanding frontiers, where power would be effectively distributed in networks. This imperial idea has survived and matured throughout the history of the United States constitution and has emerged now on a global scale in its fully realized form.

We should emphasize that we use "Empire" here not as a metaphor, which would require demonstration of the resemblances between today's world order and the Empires of Rome, China, the Americas, and so forth, but rather as a *concept,* which calls primarily for a theoretical approach.[2] The concept of Empire is characterized fundamentally by a lack of boundaries: Empire's rule has no limits. First and foremost, then, the concept of Empire posits a regime that effectively encompasses the spatial totality, or really that rules over the entire "civilized" world. No territorial boundaries limit its reign. Second, the concept of Empire presents itself not as a historical regime originating in conquest, but rather as an order that effectively suspends history and thereby fixes the existing state of affairs for eternity. From the perspective of Empire, this is the way things will always be and the way they were always meant to be. In other words, Empire presents its rule not as a transitory moment in the movement of history, but as a regime with no temporal boundaries and in this sense outside of history or at the end of history. Third, the rule of Empire operates on all registers of the social order extending down to the depths of the social world. Empire not only manages a territory and a population but also creates the very world it inhabits. It not only regulates human interactions but also seeks directly to rule over human nature. The object of its rule is social life in its entirety, and thus Empire presents the paradigmatic form of biopower. Finally, although the practice of Empire is continually bathed in blood, the concept of Empire is always dedicated to peace—a perpetual and universal peace outside of history.

The Empire we are faced with wields enormous powers of oppression and destruction, but that fact should not make us nostalgic in any way for the old forms of domination. The passage to Empire and its processes of globalization offer new possibilities to the forces of liberation. Globalization, of course, is not one thing, and the multiple processes that we recognize as globalization are not unified or univocal. Our political task, we will argue, is not simply to resist these processes but to reorganize them and redirect them toward new ends. The creative forces of the multitude that sustain Empire are also capable of autonomously constructing a counter-Empire, an alternative political organization of global flows and exchanges. The struggles to contest and subvert Empire, as well as those to construct a real alternative, will thus take place on the imperial terrain itself—indeed, such new struggles have already begun to emerge. Through these struggles and many more like them, the multitude will have to invent new democratic forms and a new constituent power that will one day take us through and beyond Empire.

The genealogy we follow in our analysis of the passage from imperialism to Empire will be first European and then Euro-American, not because we believe that these regions are the exclusive or privileged source of new ideas and historical innovation, but simply because this was the dominant geographical path along which the concepts and practices that animate today's Empire developed—in step, as we will argue, with the development of the capitalist mode of production.[3] Whereas the genealogy of Empire is in this sense Eurocentric, however, its present powers are not limited to any region. Logics of rule that in some sense originated in Europe and the United States now invest practices of domination throughout the globe. More important, the forces that contest Empire and effectively prefigure an alternative global society are themselves not limited to any geographical region. The geography of these alternative powers, the new cartography, is still waiting to be written—or really, it is being written today through the resistances, struggles, and desires of the multitude.

Notes

Reprinted by permission of the publisher from *Empire,* by Michael Hardt and Antonio Negri (Cambridge, Massachusetts: Harvard University Press, 2000): xi–xvi. Copyright © 2000 by the President and Fellows of Harvard College.

    1. On the declining sovereignty of nation-states and the transformation of sovereignty in the contemporary global system, see Saskia Sassen, *Losing Control? Sovereignty in an Age of Globalization* (New York: Columbia University Press, 1996).

    2. On the concept of Empire, see Maurice Duverger, "Le concept d'empire," in Maurice Duverger, ed., *Le concept d'empire* (Paris: PUF, 1980), pp. 5–23. Duverger divides the historical examples into two primary models, with the Roman Empire on one side and the Chinese, Arab, Mesoamerican, and other Empires on the other. Our analyses pertain primarily to the Roman side because this is the model that has animated the Euro-American tradition that has led to the contemporary world order.

    3. "Modernity is not a phenomenon of Europe as an *independent* system, but of Europe as center." Enrique Dussel, "Beyond Eurocentrism: The World System and the Limits of Modernity," in Fredric Jameson and Masao Miyoshi, eds., *The Cultures of Globalization* (Durham: Duke University Press, 1998), pp. 3–31; quotation p. 4. Two interdisciplinary texts served as models for us throughout the writing of this book: Marx's *Capital* and Deleuze and Guattari's *A Thousand Plateaus*. Ours is certainly not the only work that prepares the terrain for the analysis and critique of Empire. Although they do not use the term "Empire," we see the work of numerous authors oriented in this direction; they include Fredric Jameson, David Harvey, Arjun Appadurai, Gayatri Spivak, Edward Said, Giovanni Arrighi, and Arif Dirlik, to name only some of the best known.

CHAPTER 7

THE GLOBAL CITY MODEL

Saskia Sassen

The debate around the validity and nature of the construct [of the global city] itself raised a number of conceptual, methodological and empirical questions. Some of these questions directly or indirectly intersect with the more specific issues I present in subsequent sections. Several types of criticism are based on a conception of the global city model that is faulty and even flat wrong, while others are, in my reading, correct and yet others are constructive in the sense that they have added questions or actual empirical and theoretical elements to the research literature on the subject.

Globalization and homogenization.

A first group of critiques of the concept centered on questions linked to globalization and the associated homogenization it is supposed to bring about. One version of this critique is the assertion that in the global city model globalization is conceived of as a force coming from outside and homogenizing cities. This type of critique is fundamentally flawed in that the global city model is precisely an analytic strategy to correct the common assumption in economic approaches to globalization that the global is that which crosses borders, as in international trade and investment.

The global city represents a strategic space where global processes materialize in national territories and global dynamics run through national institutional arrangements. In this sense the model overrides the zero-sum notion about the global economy and the national economy as mutually exclusive. A key purpose of the model is to conceive of economic globalization not just as capital flows, but as the work of coordinating, managing and servicing these flows and the work of servicing the multiple activities of firms and markets operating in more than one country. This means also that globalization is not simply something that is exogenous. It comes partly from the inside of national corporate structures and elites, a dynamic I conceive of as a process of incipient de-nationalization. There are sites where global processes are indeed experienced as an invasion, as coming from the outside, but the global city is precisely the site where global processes can get activated inside a country with the participation of some of its national actors. The global city represents the endogenizing of key dynamics and conditionalities of the global economy.

Methodologically this means that globalization can also be studied through detailed sociological and anthropological examinations of these processes as they take place in cities. For me this has meant going all the way from the top levels to the bottom levels in an effort to capture the variety of work processes, work cultures, infrastructures, and so on, that are part of the global control capacity concentrated in cities, a capacity that is one of the features of the global economic system.

Furthermore, I unpack the "global economy" into a variety of highly specialized cross-border circuits corresponding to specific industries, more precisely, those components of industries which are operating across borders. Among these are a variety of financial sub-sectors, accounting, legal, advertising, construction, engineering, architecture, telecommunication services, and others. Each of these may have its own specific geography of networks, even though there will tend to be strong overlap in the case of some of these, notably finance and its sister industries.

This also means that these networks may run through distinct sets of global cities. The global circuits for gold will be different from those for oil, and those for the futures markets may be different from the major currency trading networks. Some cities which are part of these circuits may have highly specialized global city functions and be located on specialized networks that connect them with the leading global cities even though they themselves are not necessarily global cities. Kuala Lumpur is significant as a futures market and Singapore is significant for currency trading, which gives each of these cities specific global city functions; it also puts each of these cities on a different global specialized circuit. The leading global cities in the world tend to have a very large range of these specialized circuits running through them, but even these cities do not involve all specialized components of the global economy. Even the leading global cities will tend to be highly specialised for the servicing of a particular set of global markets and global firms.

The above conditions signal that there is no such entity as a single global city. This is one important difference with the capitals of earlier empires or particular world cities in earlier periods. The global city is a function of a cross border network of strategic sites. In my reading there is no fixed number of global cities, because it depends on countries deregulating their economies, privatizing public sectors (to have something to offer to international investors), and the extent to which national and foreign firms and markets make a particular city (usually an established business center of sorts) a basing point for their operations. What we have seen since the early 1990s is a growing number of countries opting or being pressured into the new rules of the game and hence a rapid expansion of the network of cities that either are global cities or have global city functions—a somewhat fuzzy distinction that I find useful in my research. The global city network is the operational scaffolding of that other fuzzy notion, the global economy.

A common critique asserts that the global city model posits convergence and homogenization among these cities. The development of global city functions in different cities across the world does indeed signal convergence of something. But this is a highly specialized, institutionally differentiated process. It is a very different process from the kind of homogenization/convergence we see in consumer markets and the global entertainment industry.

As I argued already in the first edition of this book, there is a division of functions among the major global cities rather than simply competition as was and is commonly asserted. This was certainly the case in their financial sectors. But this is not a division of labor à la Ricardo, with the ideal of mutually exclusive specializations. That was a model of comparative national advantage. This is a model of cross-border systems, each by necessity installed in multiple different national locations.

Methodologically this underlines the difference between studying a set of cities from a classical comparative approach and from a global approach. The issue of comparability in the latter is not standardizing in order to compare. It is, rather, tracking a given system or dynamic (e.g., a particular type of financial market) and its distinct incarnations (operations, institutional setting, accommodation with national laws and regulations, etc.) in different countries. Though there is some overlap, this entails different analytic categories, research techniques and interpretation standards from those of classical comparative methods. There is work to be done on the methods front, an effort that I am currently engaged in.

Further, many of the critiques along the homogenization notion are centered on an incorrect understanding of the type of convergence the model specifies. The content given to this notion is often that, according to the global city model, the various global cities around the world will become alike, and particularly, that they will resemble New York City. Put that way, I would agree with the critique: why should Paris and Tokyo become like New York. The weight of their institutional, political, cultural histories, the inertia of the built environment, the different roles played by the state in each city will diverge and have its own rich specific history. But that is not the point of convergence in the global city model: it is the development and partial importation of a set of specialized functions and the direct and indirect effects this may have on the larger city.

A second major set of issues comes out of the existence of several similar concepts. Most notably the "world city" concept, both its older meaning and the more current one formulated by John Friedmann and Goetz (1982). As mentioned briefly in the introduction to this new edition, the difference between the classic concept of the world city and the global city model is one of level of generality and historical specificity. The world city concept has a certain kind of timelessness attached to it where the global city model marks a specific socio-spatial historical phase. A key differentiating element between Friedmann and Goetz's formulation and mine is my emphasis on the "production" of the global economic system. It is not simply a matter of global coordination but one of the production of global control capacities.

A focus on the *work* behind command functions, on the actual *production process* in the finance and services complex, and on global market*places* has the effect of incorporating the material facilities underlying globalization and the whole infrastructure of jobs typically not marked as belonging to the corporate sector of the economy. What emerges from such an analysis is an economic configuration that differs sharply from that suggested by the concept information economy. We recover the material conditions, production sites, and place-boundedness that are also part of globalization and the information economy.

Another differentiation is with Castells's (1996) argument about the space of flows and the notion that the global city is not a place but a network. While I already argued in the first edition that the global city is a function of a network, I insisted that it is also a place. I briefly touch on my conception of the global city as a network in the above discussion on the unpacking of the global economy in terms of multiple specialized circuits. In chapter 5 there is a more developed presentation which focuses, among other aspects, on the network of transactions among global cities conceived of as a space of centrality that is partly deterritorialized and takes place largely in digital networks but is also partly deeply territorialized in the set of cities that constitute the network.

The place-ness of the global city is a crucial theoretical and methodological issue in my work. Theoretically it captures Harvey's notion of capital fixity as necessary for hypermobility. A key issue for me has been to introduce into our notions of globalization the fact that capital even if dematerialized is not simply hypermobile or that trade and investment and information flows are not only about flows. Further, place-ness also signals an embeddedness in what has been constructed as the "national," as in national economy and national territory. This brings with it a consideration of political issues and theorizations about the role of the state in the global economy which are excluded in more conventional accounts about the global economy. Part of the place-ness of the global city is that it is a function of a network—a condition particularly evident in certain sectors. One could say that I do not agree with the opposition space of flows vs. place. Global cities are places but they are so in terms of their functions in specific, often highly specialized networks. Finally, of the four different types of spatial correlates for spaces of centrality that I discussed in chapter 5, it is the transterritorial networks of global cities which best capture the way in which global cities are functions of networks.

A third concept is that of global city-region. As categories for analysis, these two concepts share key propositions about economic globalization but overlap only partly in the features they each capture. The focus on a region introduces a set of different variables. I find this an enormously useful concept precisely because of these different variables and hence will return below to a more detailed discussion of this specific concept.

A different kind of distinction is that between the global city construct and the city in general. Quite a few of the negative but also positive critiques fail to understand that I make a distinction between what is encompassed by the global city model and the larger urban entity called New York, Paris or Tokyo. This confusion may partly be a function of the fact that in Part Three of the book I examine the larger city. What may not have been stated with adequate clarity in the first edition is that the effort in Part Three was to understand the impact of the global city function on the larger city, to see whether this impact is beneficial for a large sector of the population or not. My assumption was not that all of the empirical conditions described are necessarily part of the global city function. Every city has its own larger materiality, polity, sociality, each often part of old lineages. The development of global city functions, the endogenising of the dynamics and conditionalities of economic globalization in the space of the city is a strategic but not all-encompassing event. An important methodological implication is that one can actually study the global city function without having to study the whole city. One methodological issue raised by this way of conceiving matters is the boundary question, to which I also return below.

Another distinction is my use of the notion of global city functions to identify a particular case, that of a city which fulfilled a fairly limited and highly specialized set of functions in the management and servicing of the global economy, rather than the multiplicity of functions evident in major global cities. I used the case of Miami as an example as it has emerged with a growing role for European, North American and Asian firms which have operations in Latin America and the Caribbean. This is not necessarily a static condition: it may disappear in a way that would be much less likely for London or New York, or it may evolve into the more complex and multifaceted condition of a global city. A certain level of complexity in global city functions has its own impact on these functions; it can ratchet them upwards into top-level capabilities. For instance, the sophistication of domestic investors in the U.S. pushed the U.S. financial services firms into becoming a state of the art sector which in turn gave it its advantage in global markets.

Finally, there is the distinction between international cities, such as Florence or Venice, and global cities. I agree completely with this differentiation and find it useful. It helps to strengthen the case for a tighter analytic conception of the global city.

The concept of the global city-region adds a whole new dimension to questions of territory and globalization. Here I want to confine myself to examining the differences between the two concepts. A first difference concerns the question of scale. The territorial scale of the region is far more likely to include a cross-section of a country's economic activities than the scale of the city. It is likely, for instance, to include as key variables manufacturing and basic infrastructure. This, in turn, brings with it a more benign focus on globalization. The concept of the global city introduces a far stronger emphasis on strategic components of the global economy, and hence on questions of power. Secondly, the concept of the global city will tend to have a stronger emphasis on the networked economy because of the nature of the industries that tend to be located there: finance and specialized services. And, thirdly, it will tend to have more of an emphasis on economic and spatial polarization because of the disproportionate concentration of very high and very low income jobs in the city compared with what would be the case for the region.

Overall, I would say, the concept of the global city is more attuned to questions of power and inequality. The concept of the global city-region is more attuned to questions about the nature and specifics of broad urbanization patterns, a more encompassing economic base, more middle sectors of both households and firms, and hence to the possibility of having a more even distribution of economic benefits under globalization. In this regard, it could be said that the concept of the global city-region allows us to see the possibilities for a more distributed kind of growth, a wider spread of the benefits associated with the growth dynamics of globalization.

Both concepts have a problem with boundaries of at least two sorts, the boundary of the territorial scale as such and the boundary of the spread of globalization in the organizational structure of industries, institutional orders, places, and so on. In the case of the global city I have opted for an analytic strategy that emphasizes core dynamics rather than the unit of the city as a container—the latter being one that requires territorial boundary specification. Emphasizing core dynamics and their spatialization (in both actual and digital space) does not completely solve the boundary problem, but it does allow for a fairly clear trade-off between emphasizing the core or center of these dynamics and their spread institutionally and spatially. In my work I have sought to deal with both sides of this trade-off: by emphasizing, on the one side of the trade-off the most advanced and globalized industries, such as finance, and, on the other side, how the informal economy in major global cities is articulated with some of the leading industries. In the case of the global city-region, it is not clear to me how Scott et al. (2001) specify the boundary question both in its territorial sense and in terms of its organization and spread.

A second difference is the emphasis on competition and competitiveness, much stronger in the global city-region construct. In my reading, the nature itself of the leading industries in global cities strengthens the importance of cross-border networks and specialized division of functions among cities in different countries and/or regions rather than international competition per se. In the case of global finance and the leading specialized services catering to global firms and markets—law, accounting, credit rating, telecommunications—it is clear that we are dealing with a cross-border system, one that is embedded in a series of cities, each possibly part of a different country. It is a de-facto global system.

The industries that are likely to dominate global city-regions, on the other hand, are less likely to be networked in this way. For instance, in the case of large manufacturing complexes, the identification with the national is stronger and the often stronger orientation to consumer markets brings to the fore the question of quality, prices and the possibility of substitution. Hence competition and competitiveness are likely to be far more prominent. Further, even when there is significant off-shoring of production and in this regard an international division of production, as in the auto industry, for instance, this type of internationalization tends to be in the form of the chain of production of a given firm. Insofar as most firms still have their central headquarters associated with a specific region and country, the competition question is likely to be prominent and, very importantly, sited—i.e., it is the U.S. versus the Japanese auto manufacturers.

Finally, the question of the competitiveness of a region is deeply centered in its infrastructure. To some extent this is also a crucial variable in the case of global cities, but it is, probably, a far more specialized type of infrastructure. The regional scale brings to the fore questions of public transport, highway construction, and kindred aspects in a way that the focus on global cities does not. Again, it reveals to what extent a focus on the region allows for a more benevolent appreciation of competitiveness in a global economy. In contrast, a focus on the global city will tend to bring to the fore the growing inequalities between highly provisioned and profoundly disadvantaged sectors and spaces of the city, and hence questions of power and inequality. A focus on the regional infrastructure is far more likely to include strong consideration of middle class needs in this regard.

A third difference, connected to the preceding one, is that a focus on networked cross-border dynamics among global cities also allows us to capture more readily the growing intensity of such transactions in other domains—political, cultural, social, criminal. We now have evidence of greater cross-border transactions among immigrant communities and communities of origin and a greater intensity in the use of these networks once they become established, including for economic activities that had been unlikely until now. We also have evidence of greater cross-border networks for cultural purposes, as in the growth of international markets for art and a transnational class of curators; and for non-formal political purposes, as in the growth of transnational networks of activists around environmental causes, human rights, and so on. These are largely city-to-city cross-border networks, or, at least, it appears at this time to be simpler to capture the existence and modalities of these networks at the city level. The same can be said for the new cross-border criminal networks. Dealing with the regional scale does not necessarily facilitate recognizing the existence of such networks from one region to the other. It is far more likely to be from one specific community in a region to another specific community in another region, thereby neutralizing the meaning of the region as such.

Perhaps deserving separate treatment, although it is yet another instance of differentiation, is the assertion that using the notion of global city to describe cities such as London is unwarranted since they were far more international in an earlier era than they are today. At its most extreme this type of critique rejects the specificity of the concept, either arguing that there is no such entity as a global city or that nothing is new, that London and New York have been international centers for a long time and, if anything, are less international today than they were in the past.

The clearest case of this is London which can indeed be represented as having much less global influence in the 1990s than it had in the era of British empire.

My response to this critique is to emphasize the intervening period, when the national state gained ascendance and cross-border economic flows took place within the framework of the inter-state system. It is against this phase of variable length for different types of countries that the emergence of global cities needs to be understood. I do not argue that this is the first time or the most acute instance of this development of intense cross-border networks among cities. My point is rather that the formation of a global economic system after a phase of national and interstate governance of economies needs to be specified theoretically and empirically and cannot be seen simply as a renewal of older forms. The global city network is one of the marking features of the organizational architecture of the current phase.

Identification and measurement.

When it comes to identification and measurement of the variables we can use to specify or understand what makes a city a global city, we enter a somewhat fuzzy domain. This is partly due to the fact that existing categories, data sets, and research techniques tend to be based on certain notions of closure and scale. The city is a difficult scale at which to have precise empirical measures. The best data sets are at the national scale.[1] Further, closure is a key feature of many data sets, including those at the urban scale. Thus attempting to measure a unit that is characterized by lack of closure brings additional problems, and when this is at the urban scale the problems escalate. One result has been a series of rather problematic indicators of global city status.

Global city functions are a specific set of processes taking place in a city. But they are not the whole urban economy, even though they have large shadow effects. Nor can these functions simply be reduced to the whole producer services sector of a city. This is a recurrent confusion when it comes to measures. I discuss these issues in greater detail in the section on producer services below.

Finally, a confusion in some of the literature is the failure to distinguish between the particular role that a global city or a city with global city functions may have in the global economy and the impact of that role on the city itself. The former may be very significant without the latter being so. The reverse case is rare. The key point regarding the research literature is that an urban economy might be largely domestic—most urban economies probably are—yet play a strategic role in multiple specialized circuits of the global economy. There tends to be a threshold effect whereby global city functions tend to reach a certain level before a city is particularly significant in the global economy. But this is to some extent an empirical question. We need more studies to specify this.

The outcomes that we capture in the concept of the global city are a result of multiple processes. Different time periods, different contents, different scales, each shape the various processes involved. All of these variables in turn feed the distinction between the significance of global city functions to a particular city's economy and to the organization of the global economy itself.

Notes

Saskia Sassen, "The Global City Model." In *The Global City: New York, London, Tokyo* (Princeton, NJ: Princeton University Press, 1991): 346–355. Reprinted by permission of Princeton University Press.

Allusions to chapters within this piece refer to the original book from which this chapter was taken.

1. In recognition of this fact and given the increasing importance of cities for a broad range of socio-scientific issues, the U.S. National Academy of Sciences has launched a major initiative to study ways of raising the quality of urban-level data.

CHAPTER 8
THE GLOBALIZATION OF SEXUAL IDENTITIES

Dennis Altman

Most of the literature about globalization and identity is concerned with the rebirth of nationalist, ethnic, and religious fundamentalism, or the decline of the labor movement.[1] (I am using "identity" to suggest a socially constructed myth about shared characteristics, culture, and history which comes to have real meaning for those who espouse it.)[2] Here I concentrate on the identity politics born of sexuality and gender, and the new social movements which arise from these, already foreshadowed in the previous chapter. These new identities are closely related to the larger changes of globalization: consider the globalization of "youth," and the role of international capitalism in creating a teenage identity in almost every country, with specific music, language, fashion, and mores.[3] In recent years this is expressed in terms of "boy" and "girl" cultures, as in references to "boy bands" or "a booming girl culture worldwide,"[4] which suggests the invention of an intermediate generational identity between "children" and "youth."

Over the past decade I've been researching and thinking about the diffusion of certain sorts of "gay/lesbian" identities, trying to trace the connections between globalization and the preconditions for certain sexual subjectivities.[5] My examples are drawn predominantly from Southeast Asia because this is the part of the "developing" world I know best, but they could even more easily be drawn from Latin America, which has a particularly rich literature exploring these questions.[6] The question is not whether homosexuality exists—it does in almost every society of which we know—but how people incorporate homosexual behavior into their sense of self. Globalization has helped create an international gay/lesbian identity, which is by no means confined to the western world: there are many signs of what we think of as "modern" homosexuality in countries such as Brazil, Costa Rica, Poland, and Taiwan. Indeed the gay world—less obviously the lesbian, largely due to marked differences in women's social and economic status—is a key example of emerging global "subcultures," where members of particular groups have more in common across national and continental boundaries than they do with others in their own geographically defined societies.

It is worth noting that even within the "first world" there is a range of attitudes toward the assertion of gay/lesbian identities. While they have flourished in the English-speaking countries and in parts of northern Europe, there is more resistance to the idea in Italy and France, where ideas of communal rights—expressed through the language of multiculturalism in Australia and Canada, and through a somewhat different tradition of religious pluralism in the Netherlands and Switzerland—seem to run counter to a universalist rhetoric of rights, which are not equated with the recognition of separate group identities.[7] The United States shares both traditions, so that its gay and lesbian movement argues for recognition of "civil rights" on the basis of being just like everyone else, and in some cases deserving of special protection along the lines developed around racial and gender discrimination.

At the same time the United States has gone farthest in the development of geographically based gay and lesbian communities, with defined areas of its large cities—the Castro in San Francisco, West Hollywood, Halsted in Chicago, the West Village in New York—becoming urban "ghettos," often providing a base to develop the political clout of the community. (In almost all large American cities politicians now recognize the importance of the gay vote.) This model has been replicated in a number of western countries, whether it is the Marais in Paris or Darlinghurst in Sydney. There is some irony in the fact that, while homosexual rights have progressed much further in the countries of northern Europe, the United States remains the dominant cultural model for the rest of the world.

This dominance was symbolized in accounts in Europe of "gay pride" events in the summer of 1999, which often ignored national histories and attributed the origins of gay political activism to the Stonewall riots of 1969, ignoring the existence of earlier groups in countries such as Germany, the Netherlands,

Switzerland, and France, and the radical gay groups which grew out of the 1968 student movements in both France and Italy. (Stonewall was a gay bar in New York City which was raided by the police, leading to riots by angry homosexuals and the birth of the New York Gay Liberation Front.) In cities as diverse as Paris, Hamburg, and Warsaw the anniversary of Stonewall was celebrated with Christopher Street Day, and the dominance of American culture is summed up by the press release from the Lisbon Gay, Lesbian, Bisexual, and Transgender Pride committee boasting of the performances of a "renowned DJ from New York City" and "Celeda—the Diva Queen from Chicago."

Thinking and writing about these questions, it became clear to me that observers, indigenous and foreign alike, bring strong personal investments to how they understand what is going on, in particular whether (in words suggested to me by Michael Tan) we are speaking of "ruptures" or "continuities." For some there is a strong desire to trace a continuity between precolonial forms of homosexual desire and its contemporary emergence, even where the latter might draw on the language of (West) Hollywood rather than indigenous culture. Such views are argued strenuously by those who cling to an identity based on traditional assumptions about the links between gender performance and sexuality, and deny the relevance of an imported "gay" or "lesbian" identity for themselves. Thus the effeminate *bakkla* in the Philippines or the *kathoey* in Thailand might see those who call themselves "gay" as hypocrites, in part because they insist on their right to behave as men, and to desire others like them.[8] For others there is a perception that contemporary middle-class self-proclaimed gay men and lesbians in, say, New Delhi, Lima, or Jakarta have less in common with "traditional" homosexuality than they do with their counterparts in western countries. As Sri Lankan author Shaym Selvadurai said of his novel *Funny Boy,* which is in part about "coming out" as gay: "The people in the novel are in a place that has been colonized by Western powers for 400 years. A lot of Western ideas—bourgeois respectability, Victorian morality—have become incorporated into the society, and are very much part of the Sri Lankan society."[9]

"Modern" ways of being homosexual threaten not only the custodians of "traditional" morality, they also threaten the position of "traditional" forms of homosexuality, those which are centered around gender nonconformity and transvestism. The title of the Indonesian gay/lesbian journal *Gaya Nusantara,* which literally means "Indonesian style," captures this ambivalence nicely with its echoes of both "traditional" and "modern" concepts of nation and sexuality, but at the same time it is clearly aimed at "modern" homosexuals rather than the "traditional" transvestite *waria.*[10]

It is often assumed that homosexuals are defined in most "traditional" societies as a third sex, but that too is too schematic to be universally useful. As

Peter Jackson points out, the same terms in Thailand can be gender *and* sexual categories.[11] Here, again, we are confronted by considerable confusion, where similar phenomena can be viewed as either culturally specific or as universal. Insofar as there is a confusion between sexuality and gender in the "traditional" view that the "real" homosexual is the man who behaves like a woman (or, more rarely, vice versa) this is consistent with the dominant understanding of homosexuality in western countries during the hundred years or so before the birth of the contemporary gay movement. The idea of a "third sex" was adopted by people like Ulrichs and Krafft-Ebing as part of an apologia for homosexuality (giving rise to Carpenter's "intermediate sex").[12] In the 1918 novel *Despised and Rejected* the hero laments: "What had nature been about, in giving him the soul of a woman in the body of a man?"[13] Similar views can be found in Radclyffe Hall's novel *The Well of Loneliness* (1928), whose female hero calls herself Stephen. Today many people who experience homosexual desires in societies which do not allow space for them will see themselves as "men trapped in women's bodies" or vice versa.

In popular perceptions something of this confusion remains today—and persists in much popular humor, such as the remarkably successful play/film *La cage aux folles* (*The Birdcage*) or the film *Priscilla, Queen of the Desert*. George Chauncey argues that the very idea of a homosexual/heterosexual divide became dominant in the United States only in the mid-twentieth century: "The most striking difference between the dominant sexual culture of the early twentieth century and that of our own era is the degree to which the earlier culture permitted men to engage in sexual relations with other men, often on a regular basis, without requiring them to regard themselves—or be regarded by others—as gay ... Many men ... neither understood nor organised their sexual practices along a hetero-homosexual axis."[14] John Rechy's landmark novel *City of Night* (1963) captures the transition to "modern" concepts: his world is full of "hustlers," "queens," "masculine" or "butch" homosexuals, whom he sometimes calls "gay."[15]

If one reads or views contemporary accounts of homosexual life in, say, Central America, Thailand, and Côte d'Ivoire,[16] one is immediately struck by the parallels. It is of course possible that the observers, all of whom are trained in particular ethnographic and sociological methods, even where, as in the case of Schifter, they are indigenous to the country of study, are bringing similar—and one assumes unconscious—preconceptions with them. Even so, it is unlikely that this itself would explain the degree of similarity they identify. In the same way, the Dutch anthropologist Saskia Wieringa has pointed to the similarities of butch-femme role-playing in Jakarta and Lima, and how they echo that of preliberation western lesbian worlds.[17] In many "traditional" societies there were complex variations across gender and sex lines, with "transgender" people (Indonesian *waria*, Thai *kathoey*, Moroccan *hassas*, Turkish *kocek*, Filipino *bayot*, Luban *kitesha* in parts of Congo) characterized by both transvestite and homosexual behavior. These terms are usually—not always—applied to men, but there are other terms sometimes used of women, such as *mati* in Suriname, which also disrupt simplistic assumptions about sex and gender.[18] As Gilbert Herdt says: "Sexual orientation and identity are not the keys to conceptualizing a third sex and gender across time and space."[19] In many societies there is confusion around the terms—for example the *hijras* of India, who were literally castrated, are sometimes considered equivalent to homosexuals even though the reality is more complex.[20]

Different people use terms such as *bayot* or *waria* in different ways, depending on whether the emphasis is on gender—these are men who wish in some way to be women—or on sexuality—these are men attracted to other men. Anthropology teaches us the need to be cautious about any sort of binary system of sex/gender; Niko Besnier uses the term "gender liminality" to avoid this trap[21] and it should also alert us against the sort of romanticized assumptions that some Americans have brought to understanding the Native American *berdarche*.[22] Besnier also stresses that such "liminality" is not the same as homosexuality: "Sexual relations with men are seen as an optional consequence of gender liminality, rather than its determiner, prerequisite or primary attribute."[23] The other side of this distinction is that there are strong pressures to define *fa'afafine* (the Samoan term) or other such groups in Pacific countries as asexual, thus leading to a particular denial in which both Samoans and outsiders are complicit.[24]

Certainly most of the literature about Latin America stresses that a homosexual *identity* (as distinct from homosexual practices) is related to rejection of dominant gender expectations, so that "a real man" can have sex with other men and not risk his heterosexual identity. As Roger Lancaster put it: "Whatever else a *cochon* might or might not do, he is tacitly understood as one who assumes the receptive role in anal intercourse. His partner, defined as 'active' in the terms of their engagement, is not stigmatized, nor does he acquire a special identity of any sort."[25] Thus the *nature* rather than the *object* of the sexual act becomes the key factor. However, there is also evidence that this is changing, and a more western concept of homosexual identity is establishing itself, especially among the middle classes.

Sexuality becomes an important arena for the production of modernity, with "gay" and "lesbian" identities acting as markers for modernity.[26] There is an ironic echo of this in the Singapore government's bulldozing of Bugis Street, once the center of transvestite prostitution in the city—and its replacement by a Disneyland-like simulacrum where a few years ago I was taken to see a rather sanitized drag show presented to a distinctly yuppie audience.[27] There is an equal irony in seeing the decline of a homosexuality defined by gender nonconformity as a "modern" trend just when transsexuals and some theorists in western countries are increasingly attracted by concepts of the malleability of gender.[28] From one perspective the fashionable replica of the stylized "lipstick lesbian" or "macho" gay man is less "postmodern" than the *waria* or the Tongan *fakaleiti*.[29]

Perhaps the reality is that androgyny is postmodern when it is understood as performance, not when it represents the only available way of acting out certain deep-seated beliefs about one's sexual and gender identity. Even so, I remain unsure just why "drag," and its female equivalents, remain a strong part of the contemporary homosexual world, even where there is increasing space for open homosexuality and a range of acceptable ways of "being" male or female. Indeed there is evidence that in some places there is a simultaneous increase in both gay/lesbian identities *and* in transgender performance, as in recent developments in Taiwan where drag shows have become very fashionable, and some of the performers, known as "third sex public relations officers," insist that they are not homosexual even when their behavior would seem to contradict this.[30] Similar comments could probably be made about *onnabe,* Japanese women who dress as men and act as the equivalent of geishas for apparently heterosexual women, and Jennifer Robertson describes the incorporation of androgyny into the "'libidinal' economy of the capitalist market" as "gender-bending" performers are turned into marketable commodities.[31] In the west it has become increasingly fashionable to depict transvestism in unmistakably heterosexual terms; what was daring (and possibly ambiguous) in the 1959 film *Some Like It Hot* becomes farce in the 1993 film *Mrs. Doubtfire*.[32] But at the same time there is, particularly in the United States, the emergence of a somewhat new form of transgender politics, in which the concern of an older generation to be accepted as the woman or man they "really" are is replaced by an assertion of a transgender identity and the malleability of gender.[33] (Western writers tend to be reasonably careful to distinguish between *transsexual* and *transvestite*. However, this distinction is often not made in parts of Asia and, I assume, other parts of the world.)

Speaking openly of homosexuality and transvestism, which is often the consequence of western influence, can unsettle what is accepted but not acknowledged. Indeed there is some evidence in a number of societies that those who proclaim themselves "gay" or "lesbian," that is, seek a public identity based on their sexuality, encounter a hostility which may not have been previously apparent. But there is a great deal of mythology around the acceptance of gender/sexual nonconformity outside the west, a mythology to which for different reasons both westerners and nonwesterners contribute. Romanticized views about homoeroticism in many nonwestern cultures, often based on travel experiences, disguise the reality of persecution, discrimination, and violence, sometimes in unfamiliar forms. Firsthand accounts make it clear that homosexuality is far from being universally accepted—or even tolerated—in such apparent "paradises" as Morocco, the Philippines, Thailand, or Brazil: "Lurking behind the Brazilians' pride of their flamboyant drag queens, their recent adulation of a transvestite chosen as a model of Brazilian beauty, their acceptance of gays and lesbians as leaders of the country's most widely practised religion and the constitutional protection of homosexuality, lies a different truth. Gay men, lesbians and transvestites face widespread discrimination, oppression and extreme violence."[34]

Just as the most interesting postmodern architecture is found in cities like Shanghai or Bangkok, so too the emphasis of postmodern theory on pastiche, parody, hybridity, and so forth is played out in a real way by women and men who move, often with considerable comfort, from apparent obedience to official norms to their own sense of gay community. The dutiful Confucian or Islamic Malaysian son one weekend might appear in drag at Blueboy, Kuala Lumpur's gay bar, the next—and who is to say which is "the real" person? Just as many Malaysians can move easily from one language to another, so most urban homosexuals can move from one style to another, from camping it up with full awareness of the latest fashion trends from Castro Street to playing the dutiful son at a family celebration.

To western gay liberationists these strategies might seem hypocritical, even cowardly (and some westerners expressed surprise at the apparent silence from Malaysian gay men after the arrest of Anwar on sodomy charges). But even the most politically aware Malaysians may insist that there is no need to "come out" to their family, while explaining that in any case their lover is accepted as one of the family—though not so identified. (The Malaysian situation is further complicated by the fact that Muslims are subject to both civil and *sharia* laws, and the latter have been used quite severely, against transvestites in particular.) Some people have suggested that everything is possible *as long as it is not stated,* but it is probably more complex than that. For many men I have met in Southeast Asia being gay does mean a sense of communal identity, and even a sense of "gay pride," but this is not necessarily experienced in the vocabulary of the west.

Middle-class English-speaking homosexuals in places like Mexico City, Istanbul, and Mumbai will speak of themselves as part of a gay (sometimes "gay and lesbian") community, but the institutions of such a community will vary considerably depending on both economic resources and political space. Thus in Kuala Lumpur, one of the richer cities of the "developing" world, there are no gay or lesbian bookstores, restaurants, newspapers, or businesses—at least not in the open way we would expect them in comparable American or European cities. There is, however, a strong sense of gay identity around the AIDS organization

Pink Triangle—its name is emblematic—and sufficient networks for a gay sauna to open and attract customers. Yet when a couple of years ago I gave some copies of the Australian gay magazine *Outrage* to the manager of the Kuala Lumpur sauna, I was told firmly there could be no display of something as overtly homosexual as these magazines—which are routinely sold by most Australian newsagents. In the same way there is also a strong lesbian network in the city, and many women use office faxes and email to arrange meetings and parties.

At that same sauna I met one man who told me he had heard of the place through a friend now living in Sydney. In conversations I have had with middle-class gay men in Southeast Asia there are frequent references to bars in Paris and San Francisco, to Sydney's Gay and Lesbian Mardi Gras, to American gay writers. Those who take on gay identities often aspire to be part of global culture in all its forms, as suggested by this quote from a Filipino anthology of gay writing: "I met someone in a bar last Saturday . . . He's a bank executive. He's mestizo (your type) and . . . loves Barbra Streisand, Gabriel García Márquez, Dame Margot Fonteyn, Pat Conroy, Isabel Allende, John Williams, Meryl Streep, Armistead Maupin, k. d. lang, Jim Chappell, Margaret Atwood and Luciano Pavarotti."[35]

Similarly magazines like *G & L* in Taiwan—a "lifestyle" magazine launched in 1996—mixes local news and features with stories on international, largely American, gay and lesbian icons. As mobility increases, more and more people are traveling abroad and meeting foreigners at home. It is as impossible to prevent new identities and categories traveling as it is to prevent pornography traveling across the Internet.

As part of the economic growth of south and east Asia the possibilities of computer-based communications have been grasped with enormous enthusiasm, and have created a new set of possibilities for the diffusion of information and the creation of (virtual) communities. Whereas the gay movements of the 1970s in the west depended heavily on the creation of a gay/lesbian press, in countries such as Malaysia, Thailand, and Japan the Internet offers the same possibilities, with the added attraction of anonymity and instant contact with overseas, thus fostering the links with the diaspora already discussed. Work by Chris Berry and Fran Martin suggests that the Internet has become a crucial way for young homosexuals to meet each other in Taiwan and Korea—and in the process to develop a certain, if privatized, form of community.[36] In Japan the Internet has become a central aid to homosexual cruising.

It is precisely this constant dissemination of images and ways of being, moving disproportionately from north to south, which leads some to savagely criticize the spread of sexual identities as a new step in neocolonialism: "The very constitution of a subject entitled to rights involves the violent capture of the disenfranchised by an institutional discourse which inseparably weaves them into the textile of global capitalism."[37] This position is argued with splendid hyperbole by Pedro Bustos-Aguilar, who attacks both "the gay ethnographer ... [who] kills a native with the charm of his camera" and "the union of the New World Order and Transnational Feminism" which asserts neocolonialism and western hegemony in the name of supposed universalisms.[38]

Bustos-Aguilar's argument is supported by the universalist rhetoric which surrounded the celebration of the twenty-fifth anniversary of Stonewall, but he could have had great fun with a 1993 brochure from San Francisco which offered "your chance to make history ... [at] the first ever gay & lesbian film festival in India & parallel queer tour"—and even more with the reporter from the *Washington Blade* who wrote of Anwar's "ostensibly being gay."[39] It finds a troubling echo in the story of an American, Tim Wright, who founded a gay movement in Bolivia, and after four years was found badly beaten and amnesiac: "And things have gone back to being what they were."[40]

A more measured critique comes from Ann Ferguson, who has warned that the very concept of an international lesbian *culture* is politically problematic, because it would almost certainly be based upon western assumptions, even though she is somewhat more optimistic about the creation of an international *movement,* which would allow for self-determination of local lesbian communities.[41] While western influences were clearly present, it is as true to see the emergence of groups in much of Latin America, in Southeast Asia, and among South African blacks as driven primarily by local forces.

It is certainly true that the assertion of gay/lesbian identity can have neo-colonial implications, but given that many anti/postcolonial movements and governments deny existing homosexual traditions it becomes difficult to know exactly whose values are being imposed on whom. Both the western outsider and the local custodians of national culture are likely to ignore existing realities in the interest of ideological certainty. Those outside the west tend to be more aware of the difference between traditional homosexualities and contemporary gay identity politics, a distinction sometimes lost by the international gay/lesbian movement in its eagerness to claim universality.[42] New sexual identities mean a loss of certain traditional cultural comforts while offering new possibilities to those who adopt them, and activists in nonwestern countries will consciously draw on both traditions. In this they may be inconsistent, but no more than western gay activists who simultaneously deploy the language of universal rights and special group status.

In practice most people hold contradictory opinions at the same time, reminding us of Freud's dictum that "it is only in logic that contradictions cannot exist." There are large numbers of men and fewer women in nonwestern countries who will describe themselves as "gay" or "lesbian" in certain circumstances, while sometimes claiming these labels are inappropriate to their situation. It is hardly surprising that people want both to identify with and to distinguish themselves from a particular western form of homosexuality, or that they will call upon their own historical traditions to do so. This ambivalence is caught in this account by a Chinese-Australian: "[Chinese] gays were determined to advance their cause but in an evolutionary rather than revolutionary way. They seized on issues such as gayness, gay culture, gay lifestyle, equal rights for gays and so on. In romantic poems the gay dreams of our ancestors were represented by two boys sharing a peach and the emperor who cut his sleeves of his gown rather than disturb his lover sleeping in his arms. To revive this dream, and enable millions of Chinese-born gays to choose their lifestyle, is a huge task. But it has happened in Taiwan, as it did in Hong Kong, and so it will in China."[43]

There are of course examples of Asian gay groups engaging in political activity of the sort associated with their counterparts in the west. Indonesia has a number of gay and lesbian groups, which have now held three national meetings. The best-known openly gay figure in Indonesia, Dede Oetomo, was a candidate of the fledgling Democratic People's Party in the 1999 elections, which followed the overthrow of Suharto. There have been several small radical gay political groups established in the Philippines in recent years, and gay demonstrations have taken place in Manila. ProGay (the Progressive Organization of Gays in the Philippines), as its name suggests, is concerned to draw links between specifically gay issues and larger questions of social justice.[44] The first lesbian conference was held in Japan in 1985,[45] and there have been lesbian organizations in Taiwan since 1990 and the Philippines since 1992.[46] The international lesbigay press carried reports of a national conference of lesbians in Beijing in late 1998 and in Sri Lanka the following year. There have been several *tongzhi* gatherings in Hong Kong (a term adopted to cover "lesbians, bisexuals, gays and transgendered people"), and a manifesto adopted by the 1996 meeting argued that "[c]ertain characteristics of confrontational politics, such as through coming out and mass protests and parades may not be the best way of achieving *tongzhi* liberation in the family-centred, community-oriented Chinese societies which stress the importance of social harmony."[47] (An odd myth, given the revolutionary upheavals in twentieth-century China.) None of these groups have the history or the reach of gay/lesbian movements in Latin America, where Brazil, Argentina, Chile, and Mexico all have significant histories of a politicized homosexuality.

In many cases homosexual identities are asserted without an apparent gay/lesbian movement. In 1998 there was a move by bar owners in Kuala Lumpur to organize a gay-pride party which was canceled after a protest by the Malaysian Youth Council. The best example of a nonpolitical gay world can probably be found in Thailand, where there is a growing middle-class gay world, based neither on prostitution nor on traditional forms of gender nonconformity (as in the person of the *kathoey*), but only a small lesbian group, Anjaree, and no gay male groups at all since the collapse of a couple of attempts to organize around HIV in the late 1980s.[48] In late 1996 controversy erupted in Thailand after the governing body of the country's teacher-training colleges decreed that "sexual deviants" would be barred from entering the colleges. While there was considerable opposition to the ban (subsequently dropped), other than Anjaree most of this came from nongay sources. In the ensuing public debate one could see contradictory outside influences at work—both an imported fear of homosexuals and a more modern emphasis on how such a ban infringed human rights. As Peter Jackson concluded: "A dynamic gay scene has emerged ... in the complete absence of a gay rights movement."[49]

Indeed it may be that a political movement is the least likely part of western concepts of homosexual identity to be adopted in many parts of the world, even as some activists enthusiastically embrace the mores and imagery of western queerdom. The particular form of identity politics which allowed for the mobilization of a gay/lesbian electoral pressure in countries like the United States, the Netherlands, and even France may not be appropriate elsewhere, even if western-style liberal democracy triumphs. The need of western lesbian/gays to engage in identity politics as a means of enhancing self-esteem may not be felt in other societies. Even so, one should read Jackson's comment about Thailand with some caution. Already when he wrote it there was an embryonic group in Bangkok around an American-owned and -run gay bookstore. At the end of 1999 one of the country's gay papers organized a gay festival and twilight parade in the heart of Bangkok, announcing it as "the first and biggest gay parade in Asia where Asian gay men have a basic human right to be who they want to be and love who they want to love."[50] Similarly, accounts of homosexual life in Japan alternate between assuming a high degree of acceptance—and therefore no reason for a political movement—and severe restrictions on the space to assert homosexual identity, though the gay group OCCUR has recently gained a certain degree of visibility.

The western gay/lesbian movement emerged in conditions of affluence and liberal democracy, where despite other large social issues it was possible to develop a politics around sexuality, which is more difficult in countries where the basic structures of political life are constantly contested.[51] Writing of contemporary South Africa Mark Gevisser notes: "Race-identification overpowers everything else—class, gender and sexuality."[52] In the same way basic questions of political economy and democratization will impact the future development of gay/lesbian movements in much of Asia and Africa. Yet in Latin America and eastern Europe gay/lesbian movements have grown considerably in the past decade, and there are signs of their emergence in some parts of Africa, for example in Botswana and in Zimbabwe, where President Mugabe has consistently attacked homosexuality as the product of colonialism.[53] Similar rhetoric has come from the leaders of Kenya,[54] Namibia, and Uganda, whose President Museveni has denounced homosexuality as "western"—using the rhetoric of the Christian right to do so.[55] Anglican bishops from Africa—though not South Africa—were crucial in defeating moves to change the Church of England's attitudes toward homosexuality at the 1998 decennial Lambeth Conference. South Africa is a crucial exception, perhaps because apartheid's denunciation of homosexuality made it easier for the African National Congress to develop a policy of acceptance as part of their general support for "a rainbow nation." Even so, some elements of the ANC are strongly homophobic, revealed in the rhetoric of many of Winnie Mandela's supporters.[56]

While many African officials and clergy maintain that homosexuality is not part of precolonial African culture, the evidence for its existence—and the slow acknowledgment of its role in African life—is emerging across the continent. One might speculate that the strong hostility from some African political and religious leaders toward homosexuality as a "western import" is an example of psychoanalytic displacement, whereby anxieties about sexuality are redirected to continuing resentment against colonialism and the subordinate position of Africa within the global economy. Western-derived identities can easily become markers of those aspects of globalization which are feared and opposed. Similarly, a 1994 conference for gay/MSMs (men who have sex with men) in Bombay was opposed by the National Federation of Indian Women, an affiliate of the Communist party of India, as "an invasion of India by decadent western cultures and a direct fallout of our signing the GATT agreement."[57] Whether the federation was aware of how close its rhetoric was to right-wing Americans such as Patrick Buchanan is unknown.

Part of the appearance of modernity is the use of western languages. Rodney Jones has noted the importance of English as part of the cultural capital of Hong Kong homosexuals,[58] and when I attended an AIDS conference in Morocco in 1996 participants complained that despite an attempt to ensure equal use of Arabic it was "easier" to talk about sexuality in French. A similar emphasis on English is noted by James Farrar in presumably heterosexual discos in Shanghai, where ironically the Village People song "YMCA" has now become "a globalized dance ritual in which the dancers are encouraged to use their hands to make shapes of the English letters, identifying themselves momentarily with a boundless global ecumene of sexy happy youth 'at the YMCA.'"[59] One assumes the Shanghai dancers are unaware of the clearly gay overtones to both the song and the group. I admit to particular pleasure in reading this piece; an early proposal for my book *The Homosexualization of America* was rejected by an editor who complained (this was in 1982) that in a year no one would remember the Village People, the image with which I began that book.

A common language is essential for networking, and the past twenty years have seen a rapid expansion of networks among lesbian and gay groups across the world. In 1978 the International Lesbian and Gay Association (ILGA) was formed at a conference in Coventry, England.[60] While ILGA has largely been driven by northern Europeans, it now has member groups in more than seventy countries and has organized international meetings in several southern cities. Other networks, often linked to feminist and AIDS organizing, have been created in the past two decades, and emerging lesbian and gay movements are increasingly likely to be in constant contact with groups across the world. The inspiration from meeting with other lesbians at international women's conferences has been a powerful factor in the creation of lesbian groups in a number of countries. Thus the Asian Lesbian Network, which now includes women from twelve or thirteen countries, began at an International Lesbian Information Service conference in Geneva in 1986.[61]

In recent years there has been some attempt to promote international networking among transgendered people—or, as Americans now call them, transfolk—with both the British-based International Gender Transient Affinity and the U.S.-based Gender Freedom International lobbying to protect transgendered people across the world from what seems to be routine harassment and persecution. The paradox of globalization is played out in constructions of sex/gender which combine the premodern with the modern, so that people identifying with "traditional" forms of transgender identity will employ modern techniques of surgery and hormone therapy to alter their bodies.

Notes

Dennis Altman, "The Globalization of Sexual Identities." In *Global Sex* (Chicago: University of Chicago Press, 2001): 86–99. Reprinted by permission of the University of Chicago Press © 2001 by the University of Chicago Press.

Allusions to chapters within this piece refer to the original book from which this chapter was taken.

1. E.g., Frances Fox Piven, "Globalizing Capitalism and the Rise of Identity Politics," in L. Panitch, ed., *Socialist Register* (London: Merlin, 1995), 102–16; Leslie Sklair, "Social Movements and Global Capitalism," in F. Jameson and M. Miyoshi, eds., *The Cultures of Globalization* (Durham: Duke University Press, 1998), 291–311; Kaldor, *New and Old Wars*, 76–86.

2. For a clear exposition of this view of social constructionism see Jeffrey Weeks, *Sexuality and Its Discontents* (London: Routledge & Kegan Paul, 1985).

3. E.g., Beverley Hooper, "Chinese Youth: The Nineties Generation," *Current History* 90:557 (1991): 269–69.

4. See Sherrie Inness, ed., *Millennium Girls* (Lanham, MD: Rowman & Little-field, 1999); Marion Leonard, "Paper Planes: Travelling the New Grrrl Geographies," in T. Skelton and G. Valentine, eds., *Cool Places: Geographies of Youth Cultures* (London: Routledge, 1998), 101–18.

5. Much of this section draws on work originally published in the mid-1990s. See especially Dennis Altman, "Rupture or Continuity? The Internationalization of Gay Identities," *Social Text* 14:3 (1996): 77–94; Altman, "On Global Queering," *Australian Humanities Review,* no. 2, July 1996 (electronic journal, www.lib.latrobe.edu.au); Altman, "Global Gaze/Global Gays," *GLQ* 3(1997): 417–36.

6. See the bibliography in Balderston and Guy, *Sex and Sexuality in Latin America,* 259–77; the chapters on Brazil and Argentina in B. Adam, J. W Duyvendak, and A. Krouwel, eds., *The Global Emergence of Gay and Lesbian Politics* (Philadelphia: Temple University Press, 1999); and the special issue of *Culture, Health, and Society* (1:3 [1999]) on "alternative sexualities and changing identities among Latin American men," edited by Richard Parker and Carlos Carceres.

7. For a discussion of the French position see David Caron, "Liberté, Egalité, Sero-positivité: AIDS, the French Republic, and the Question of Community," in Boule and Pratt, "AIDS in France," 281–93. On the Netherlands see Judith Schuyf and Andre Krouwel, "The Dutch Lesbian and Gay Movement: The Politics of Accommodation," in Adam, Duyvendak, and Krouwel, *Global Emergence of Gay and Lesbian Politics,* 158–83. On Australia see Dennis Altman, "Multiculturalism and the Emergence of Lesbian/Gay Worlds," in R. Nile, ed., *Australian Civilisation* (Melbourne: Oxford University Press, 1994), 110–24.

8. I owe thanks to a long list of people who over the years have discussed these issues with me, including Ben Anderson, Eufracio Abaya, Hisham Hussein, Lawrence Leong, Shivananda Khan, Peter Jackson, Julian Jayaseelan, Ted Nierras, Dede Oetomo, and Michael Tan.

9. Jim Marks, "The Personal Is Political: An Interview with Shaym Selvadurai," *Lambda Book Report* (Washington) 5:2 (1996): 7.

10. The original Indonesian term was *banci.* The term *waria* was coined in the late 1970s by combining the words for "woman" and "man." See Dede Oetomo, "Masculinity in Indonesia," in R. Parker, R. Barbosa, and P. Aggleton, eds., *Framing the Sexual Subject* (Berkeley: University of California Press, 2000), 58–59 n. 2.

11. See Peter Jackson, "Kathoey><Gay><Man: The Historical Emergence of Gay Male Identity in Thailand," in Manderson and Jolly, *Sites of Desire, 166–90.*

12. See Jeffrey Weeks, *Coming Out* (London: Quartet, 1977); John Lauritsen and David Thorstad, *The Early Homosexual Rights Movement* (New York: Times Change Press, 1974).

13. A. T. Fitzroy, *Despised and Rejected* (London: Gay Men's Press, 1988; originally published 1918), 223.

14. George Chauncey, *Gay New York* (New York: Basic Books, 1994), 65.

15. John Rechy, *City of Night* (New York: Grove, 1963).

16. E.g., Annick Prieur, *Mema's House, Mexico City* (Chicago: University of Chicago Press, 1998); Jacobo Schifter, *From Toads to Queens* (New York: Haworth, 1999); Peter Jackson and Gerard Sullivan, eds., *Lady Boys, Tom Boys, Rent Boys* (New York: Haworth, 1999); *Woubi Cheri* (1998), directed by Philip Brooks and Laurent Bocahut.

17. Saskia Wieringa, "Desiring Bodies or Defiant Cultures: Butch-Femme Lesbians in Jakarta and Lima," in E. Blackwood and S. Wieringa, eds., *Female Desires: Same-Sex Relations and Transgender Practices across Cultures* (New York: Columbia University Press, 1999), 206–29.

18. Gloria Wekker, "What's Identity Got to Do with It? Rethinking Identity in Light of the Mati Work in Suriname," in Blackwood and Wieringa, *Female Desires*, 119–38. Compare the very complex typologies of "same-sex" groups in Murray and Roscoe, *Boy-Wives and Female Husbands*, 279–82, and the chapter by Rudolph Gaudio on "male lesbians and other queer notions in Hausa," 115–28.

19. Herdt, *Third Sex, Third Gender*, 47.

20. See Serena Nanda, "The Hijras of India: Cultural and Individual Dimensions of an Institutionalized Third Gender Role," in E. Blackwood, ed., *The Many Faces of Homosexuality* (New York: Harrington Park Press, 1986), 35–54. And read her comments in light of Shivananda Khan, "Under the Blanket: Bisexualities and AIDS in India," in Aggleton, *Bisexualities and AIDS*, 161–77.

21. See Niko Besnier, "Polynesian Gender Liminality through Time and Space," in Herdt, *Third Sex, Third Gender*, 285–328. Note that the subtitle of Herdt's book is "Beyond Sexual Dimorphism in Culture and History."

22. See Ramon Gutierrez, "Must We Deracinate Indians to Find Gay Roots?" *Outlook* (San Francisco), winter 1989, 61–67.

23. Besnier, "Polynesian Gender Liminality," 300.

24. See Lee Wallace, *"Fa'afafine: Queens of Samoa* and the Elision of Homosexuality," *GLQ* 5:1 (1999): 25–39.

25. Roger Lancaster, "'That We Should All Turn Queer?' Homosexual Stigma in the Making of Manhood and the Breaking of Revolution in Nicaragua," in Parker and Gagnon, *Conceiving Sexuality*, 150.

26. See Henning Bech, *When Men Meet: Homosexuality and Modernity* (Chicago: University of Chicago Press, 1997); Kenneth Plummer, *The Making of the Modern Homosexual* (London: Hutchinson, 1981); Seidman, *Difference Troubles*.

27. See Laurence Wai-teng Leong, "Singapore," in West and Green, *Sociolegal Control of Homosexuality*, 134; and the remarkable Singapore film *Bugis Street* (1995), directed by Yon Fan—remarkable for having been made at all.

28. E.g., Sandy Stone, "The Empire Strikes Back: A Posttranssexual Manifesto," in P. Treichler, L. Cartwright, and C. Penley, eds., *The Visible Woman* (New York: New York University Press, 1998), 285–309.

29. See Niko Besnier, "Sluts and Superwomen: The Politics of Gender Liminality in Urban Tonga," *Ethnos* 62:1–2 (1997): 5–31.

30. Thanks to Arthur Chen of the AIDS Prevention and Research Center, Taipei, for this information.

31. Jennifer Robertson, *Takarazuka: Sexual Politics and Popular Culture in Modern Japan* (Berkeley: University of California Press, 1998), 207.

32. For some of the complications in reading cinematic versions of cross-dressing see Marjorie Garber, *Vested Interests* (New York: Routledge, 1992).

33. See Leslie Feinberg, *Transgender Warriors* (Boston: Beacon, 1996); Kate Bornstein, *Gender Outlaw* (New York: Routledge, 1993).

34. Sereine Steakley, "Brazil Can Be Tough and Deadly for Gays," *Bay Windows* (Boston), June 16, 1994.

35. Jerry Z. Torres, "Coming Out," in N. Garcia and D. Remoto, eds., *Ladled: An Anthology of Philippine Gay Wiling* (Manila: Anvil, 1994), 128.

36. Chris Berry and Fran Martin, "Queer'n'Asian on the Net: Syncretic Sexualities in Taiwan and Korean Cyberspaces," *Inqueeries* (Melbourne), June 1998, 67–93.

37. Pheng Cheah, "Posit(ion)ing Human Rights in the Current Global Conjuncture," *Public Culture* 9 (1997): 261.

38. Pedro Bustos-Aguilar, "Mister Don't Touch the Banana," *Critique of Anthropology* 15:2 (1995): 149–70.

39. Kai Wright, "Industrializing Nations Confront Budding Movement," *Washington Blade,* October 23, 1998.

40. Pedro Albornoz, "Landlocked State," *Harvard Gay and Lesbian Review* 6:1 (1999): 17.

41. Ann Ferguson, "Is There a Lesbian Culture?" in J. Allen, ed., *Lesbian Philosophies and Cultures* (Albany: State University of New York Press, 1990), 63–88.

42. See, e.g., the interview by William Hoffman with Mumbai activist Ashok Row Kavi, *Poz,* July 1998, which proclaims him "the Larry Kramer of India."

43. Bing Yu, "Tide of Freedom," *Capital Gay* (Sydney), May 1, 1998.

44. In July 1999 the paper *ManilaOUT* listed over twenty gay, lesbian, and "gay and lesbian-friendly" organizations in Manila.

45. Naeko, "Lesbian = Woman," in B. Summerhawk et al., eds., *Queer Japan* (Norwich, VT: New Victoria Publishers, 1998), 184–87.

46. Malu Merin, "Going beyond the Personal," *Women in Action* (ISIS International Manila) 1 (1996): 58–62.

47. Manifesto of Chinese Tongzhi Conference, Hong Kong, December 1996. Thanks to Graham Smith for providing this source.

48. See Andrew Matzner, "Paradise Not," *Harvard Gay and Lesbian Review* 6:1 (winter 1999): 42–44.

49. Peter Jackson, "Beyond Bars and Boys: Life in Gay Bangkok," *Outrage* (Melbourne), July 1997, 61–63.

50. Statement from *Male* magazine, quoted *in Brother/Sister* (Melbourne), September 16, 1999, 51.

51. There is a similar argument in Barry Adam, Jan Willem Duyvendak, and Andre

Krouwel, "Gay and Lesbian Movements beyond Borders?" in Adam, Duyvendak, and Krouwel, *Global Emergence of Gay and Lesbian Politics*, 344–71.

52. Mark Gevisser, "Gay Life in South Africa," in Drucker, *Different Rainbows:* 116.

53. Dean Murphy, "Zimbabwe's Gays Go 'Out' at Great Risk," *Los Angeles Times*, July 27, 1998.

54. For one view of the situation in Kenya see Wanjira Kiama, "Men Who Have Sex with Men in Kenya," in Foreman, *AIDS and Men*, 115–26.

55. Chris McGreal, "Gays Are Main Evil, Say African Leaders," *Guardian Weekly*, October 7–13, 1999, 4.

56. See Carl Stychin, *A Nation by Rights* (Philadelphia: Temple University Press, 1998), chap. 3.

57. *Times of India*, November 9, 1994, quoted by Sherry Joseph and Pawan Dhall, "No Silence Please, We're Indians!" in Drucker, *Different Rainbows*, 164.

58. Rodney Jones, "'Potato Seeking Rice': Language, Culture, and Identity in Gay Personal Ads in Hong Kong," *International Journal of the Sociology of Language* 143 (2000): 31–59.

59. James Farrar, "Disco 'Super-Culture': Consuming Foreign Sex in the Chinese Disco," *Sexualities* 2:2 (1999): 156.

60. John Clark, "The Global Lesbian and Gay Movement," in A. Hendriks, R. Tielman, and E. van der Veen, eds., *The Third Pink Book* (Buffalo: Prometheus Books, 1993), 51–61.

61. "The Asian Lesbian Network," *Breakout* (newsletter of Can't Live in the Closet, Manila) 4:3–4 (1998): 13.

CHAPTER 9

GLOBALIZATION

AN ASCENDANT PARADIGM?

James H. Mittelman

This essay explores the question, Does globalization constitute an ascendant paradigm in International Studies?[1] Put in perspective, this question goes beyond our field's three "great debates" over ontology, methodology, and epistemology. Now, another debate, which focuses on globalization as a paradigmatic challenge, is heating up, kindling theoretical controversies, and fusing the issues vetted in earlier rounds. The first debate was waged between "realists" and "idealists"; the second, "traditionalists" and "scientists"; the third, "positivists" vs. "post-positivists," or "mainstreamers" vs. "dissidents" (in the terms of Lapid, 1989; Wendt, 1999:39; and Puchala, 2000:136).

Now, it is time to move on. International Studies is on the cusp of a debate between those whom I call *para-keepers,* observers who are steadfast about maintaining the prevailing paradigms and deny that globalization offers a fresh way of thinking about the world, and *para-makers,* who bring into question what they regard as outmoded categories and claim to have shifted to an innovatory paradigm. This distinction is a heuristic for examining multiple theses. The ensuing heuristic argument does not posit a relation between two positions such that one is the absence of the other. Rather, between the keepers and the makers there are many gradations and dynamic interactions. These are tendencies, not absolutes.

In our field, ascendancy to a new *paradigm* would mark something other, or more, than the fourth, a successor, in a sequential progression of debates. True, building new knowledge may be a cumulative process; but it is not necessarily a linear one, and only occasionally involves paradigmatic rupture. To be sure, paradigms do not shift frequently, quickly, or easily. International Studies specialists are supposed to be the knowers, but, frankly speaking, often follow the doers in the sense that we trail events, even massive ones, as with our failure to anticipate the end of the Cold War, and still resist changing the paradigms in which many of us are invested.

If a paradigm in Kuhn's sense (1970) is understood to mean a common framework, a shared worldview that helps to define problems, a set of tools and methods, and modes of resolving the research questions deemed askable, then globalization studies makes for strange bedfellows. Perhaps constituting an up-and-coming subfield within International Studies, globalization research brings together different types of theorists, with varied commitments and stakes.

No one would deny that globalization is the subject of a rapidly proliferating theoretical literature. Notwithstanding its antecedents, primarily studies in classical social theory and world history, and on the rise of capitalism, a scholarly literature on globalization per se did not really exist before the 1990s. To a certain extent, globalization is a synthetic concept—a reconstruction of precursor concepts through which analysts seek to comprehend reality. Clearly, this reconstruction is of recent vintage, and the literature and contestation over its importance go to the heart of our field: What is the fundamental problematic in International Studies? Primarily peace and war? Mainly what states do to each other? Rather, states and markets, a binary in much teaching and research on International Political Economy (even though Strange [1996, 1998] and others exploded it to include a wide variety of non-state actors)? Or, if globalization really strikes a new chord, how does it change the problematic, and what are the implications for the ways in which disciplinary, cross-national, development, and area studies relate to our field?

For the purpose of addressing these issues, globalization may be best understood as a syndrome of political and material processes, including historical transformations in time and space and the social relations attendant to them. It is also about ways of thinking about the world. Globalization thus constitutes a set of ideas centered on heightened market integration, which, in its dominant form, neoliberalism, is embodied in a policy framework of deregulation, liberalization, and privatization.[2]

In this essay, then, the objective is to pull together the divergent positions, which heretofore are fragmented and may be found in many scattered sources, on the question of the ascendancy of these ideas and the formation of a new paradigm. I want to frame and sharpen the debate, and seek to strike a balance, though not necessarily midway, along a continuum, marked on either end by the resolute arguments put forward by the para-keepers and the more grandiose claims of the para-makers. In so doing, I will stake out postulates in globalization studies, disclose its inadequacies, and note the explanatory potential.

An Emerging Debate

In the evolving debate, it is worth repeating, there are fluid blends and a spectrum, not a sharp dichotomy, between para-keepers and para-makers. Indeed, in time, the para-makers may become wedded to keeping their paradigm and experience attacks by other para-makers. To discern their positions in respect to globalization, one can illustrate—not provide comprehensive coverage—by invoking explicit statements expressing the commitments of scholars and by examining logical extensions of their arguments, taking care, of course, not to do injustice to them.

The keepers are naysayers who doubt or deny that globalization constitutes an ascendant paradigm. They include realists, interdependence theorists, social democrats, and some world-system theorists. Regarding globalization as "the fad of the 1990s" and as a model lacking evidence, Waltz declares that contrary to the claims of theorists whom he calls "globalizers"—what I take to be a shorthand for globalization researchers—"politics, as usual, prevails over economics" (1999: 694, 696, 700). Clinging to the neorealist position that "national interests" continue to drive the "interstate system"—advanced two decades before (Waltz, 1979)—he does not examine the foundational theoretical literature by "globalizers" who worry about the same problems that concern him. Surprisingly, Waltz fails to identify major pioneering theoreticians (such as Giddens, 1990; Harvey, 1990; and Robertson, 1992), opposing points of view, and different schools of globalization studies. Waltz would probably find much to respect and much to correct in this work. Recalling Keohane and Nye's 1977 book, *Power and Interdependence,* Waltz's point (1999) is that the globalizers' contention about interdependence reaching a new level is not unlike the earlier claim that simple interdependence had become complex interdependence—i.e., countries are increasingly connected by varied social and political relationships and to a lesser degree by matters of security and force.

In fact, more recently, Keohane and Nye maintained that contemporary globalization is not entirely new: "Our characterization of interdependence more than 20 years ago now applies to globalization at the turn of the millennium" (2000:104). Thus, like complex interdependence, the concept of globalization can be fruitfully extended to take into account networks that operate at "multi-continental distances," the greater density of these networks, and the increased number of actors participating in them (Keohane and Nye, 2000). In comparison to Waltz, Keohane and Nye reach beyond classic themes in politics to allow for more changes, and build transnational issues into their framework. However, like Waltz, Keohane and Nye (1998) posit that the system of state sovereignty is resilient and remains the dominant structure in the world. Implicit in their formulation is that the state-centered paradigm is the best-suited approach to globalization; by inference, it can be adjusted so long as it is utilized in an additive manner—i.e., incorporates more dimensions into the analysis.

Not only do interdependence theorists (and neoliberal institutionalists, in Keohane's sense of the term [1984]) seek to assimilate globalization to tried and tested approaches in International Studies, but also social democrats have similarly argued that there is nothing really new about globalization. By extension, from this standpoint, a new theoretical departure is unwarranted. In an influential study, Hirst and Thompson (1999, echoing Gordon, 1988) claim that the world economy is not really global, but centered on the triad of Europe, Japan, and North America, as empirically demonstrated by flows of trade, foreign direct investment, and finance. They argue that the current level of internationalized activities is not unprecedented; the world economy is not as open and integrated as it was in the period from 1870 to 1914; and today, the major powers continue to harmonize policy, as they did before. Leaving aside methodological questions about the adequacy of their empirical measures and the matter of alternative indicators (Mittelman, 2000:19–24), clearly Hirst and Thompson adhere to a Weberian mode of analysis consisting of a dichotomy between two ideal types, an inter-national economy based on exchange between separate national economies versus a full-fledged global economy. Taking issue with advocates of free markets who, the authors believe, exaggerate globalizing tendencies and want to diminish regulation, Hirst and Thompson, on the contrary, favor more extensive political control of markets—greater regulation.

World-system theorists also contend that there is nothing new about global-ization, a phenomenon that can be traced back many centuries to the origins of capitalism (Wallerstein, 2000) or even longer. From this perspective, it is argued that the basic conflict is between a capitalist world-system and a socialist world-system. However, as will be discussed, the point of much globalization research is to expand binaries such as the inter-national versus the global and capitalism versus socialism so as to allow for multiple *globalizing* processes, including at the macroregional, subregional, and microregional levels as well as in localities. If anything, globalization blurs many dualities—state and non-state, legal and illegal, public and private, and so on—that are customary in our field.

Coming down differently on the debate over globalization qua paradigm are diverse theorists who resist pigeonholing into any particular tradition or traditions, yet all of them support the proposition that globalization constitutes a distinctive theoretical innovation. However difficult to categorize collectively, this transatlantic group of authors signals the stirrings of a paradigmatic challenge to International Studies. Emblematic of this position are the writings of four scholars with different commitments but whose position on new knowledge converges.

Representative of the innovatory stance is Cerny's assertion that theorists are seeking an alternative to realism and that "the chief contender for that honour has been the concept of globalization" (1996:618). Similarly, Clark's *Globalization and International Relations Theory* makes the unequivocal argument that "globalization offers a framework within which political change can be understood" and that "if globalization does anything, it makes possible a theory of change" (1999:174). Joining Cerny and Clark, Scholte holds that "[c]ontemporary globalisation gives ample cause for a paradigm shift" (1999:9), or, in another formulation, "the case that globalism warrants a paradigm shift would seem to be incontrovertible" (1999:22). Although Scholte does fill in some of the blanks, the question still is, What are the characteristics of this new paradigm?

While globalization theorists have tentatively, but not systematically, responded to this question (an issue to which we will return), there is also a more guarded intervention in the debate over globalization's status as a paradigm. Noting "parametric transformations" in world order, Rosenau clearly sides with those who affirm that globalization forms a new point of paradigmatic departure; however, he holds that his concept of globalization is "narrower in scope and more specific in content" than are many other concepts associated with changing global structures. According to Rosenau, globalization refers to "processes, to sequences that unfold either *in the mind* or in behavior" as people and organizations attempt to achieve their goals (1997:80; emphasis added). In other words, globalization is not only an objective trend, but also constitutes, or is constituted by, subjective processes. It is a mental, or intersubjective, framework that is implicated both in the exercise of power and in scholarship that informs, or is critical of, public policy. Certainly because of the need for greater theoretical, as well as empirical, precision, a qualified response to the question of the rise of a new paradigm is worthy of consideration. The route to this response will be a Kuhnian notion of what sparks paradigmatic transformations.

The Question of New Knowledge[3]

In his study of the history of the natural sciences, Kuhn (1970) famously argued that new paradigms appear through ruptures rather than through a linear accumulation of facts or hypotheses. Normal science, he claimed, is a means of confirming the type of knowledge already established and legitimized by the paradigm in which it arises. According to Kuhn, normal science often suppresses innovations because they are subversive of a discipline's fundamental commitments.

> No part of the aim of normal science is to call forth new sorts of phenomena; indeed those that will not fit the box are often not seen at all. Nor do scientists normally aim to invent new theories, and they are often intolerant of those invented by others. Instead, normal-scientific research is directed to the articulation of those phenomena and theories that the paradigm already supplies. (Kuhn, 1970:24)

Or, to extrapolate, one might say that members of a shared knowledge community not only normalize certain types of questions, but also suppress the ability to raise them. Most important, Kuhn's insight is that only rarely do intellectuals refuse to accept the evasion of anomalies: observations at odds with expectations derived from prior theoretical understandings. A new paradigm emerges when the burden of anomalous phenomena grows too great and when there is incommensurability between competing paradigms to the extent that proponents of alternative frameworks cannot accept a common ground of assumptions.

Some observers dispute whether Kuhn's thesis, derived from the natural sciences, can be imported into the social sciences—and, I might add, into a field like International Studies, which is far more heterogeneous than disciplines such as physics. My concern here, however, is not the epistemological debate over the disparate means of discovery in respective branches of knowledge (see Lakatos, 1970; Ball, 1976; Barnes, 1982). Rather, my contention—globalization is not only about "real" phenomena, but also a way of interpreting the world—is more pragmatic.

To be sure, a Kuhnian perspective of the generation of knowledge is vulnerable insofar as it is limited to social and psychological conditions within the scientific community, and does not give sufficient credence to socially constructed knowledge outside this community. The factors internal to the social sciences cannot be fully explained without reference to the external elements. There is nothing, however, to prevent joining Kuhn's insight about theoretical innovation with a broader analysis of social conditions. Moreover, unless one believes that

International Studies is rapidly approaching a Kuhnian crisis, i.e., the overthrow of a reigning paradigm or paradigms—and I do not—then it is important to grasp the dynamic interface between established knowledge sets, including the structures (curricula, professional journals, funding agencies, etc.) that maintain and undermine them, and a potentially new paradigm. It would appear that even without a paradigm crisis, an ascendant paradigm could emerge.

For Kuhn, the transition to a new paradigm is all or nothing: "Like the gestalt switch, it must occur all at once (though not necessarily in an instant) or not at all" (Kuhn, 1970:150; also pertinent are the nuances in his subsequent work, 1977a, 1977b). In explaining transformations in this manner, Kuhn falls short insofar as he underestimates the tenacity of forerunner paradigms and their ability to modify themselves. By all indications in the social sciences, they fight back, usually with gusto. Nevertheless, by identifying the propellant of a new paradigm as the refusal to accept the evasion of anomalies in conjunction with the quest for an alternative, Kuhn has contributed powerfully to understanding theoretical innovation.

In this vein, it is well to recall Weber's "'Objectivity' in Social Science and Social Policy" (1949). Like Kuhn, Weber indicated that the prevailing intellectual apparatus is in constant tension with new knowledge. According to Weber, this conflict is a propellant for creativity and discovery—concepts are and should be subject to change. However, there should also be a certain staying power in the intellectual apparatus that enables one to ferret out what is worth knowing. In other words, there is nothing worse than the fads and fashions that come in and out of vogue. In the end, Weber called for a mid-course between unyielding old concepts and unceasing shifts in paradigms.

Following Kuhn and Weber in the chase for paradigmatic advance, what are the anomalies in our field, and is globalization a viable contender for fixing these imperfections?

Discomfort with International Studies

A discipline without complaints would be a non sequitur. After all, scholars are trained in the art of debate; the skills of nuance are our stock-in-trade. That said, it is important to consider the specific anomalies within International Studies. Although some of these anomalies are perennial, it is no wonder that others have appeared, given monumental changes after the Cold War, and with the distinctive mix of global integration and disintegration at the dawn of a new millennium. While others could be cited, five anomalies seem most important, but can be considered only succinctly here.[4]

First, the term *International* Studies suggests a focus on relations between nations. But this is not so. The discipline has primarily concerned relations between states, the nation being only one of many principles of social organization (Shaw, 1994:25; also Shaw, 1999). Closely related, careful observers (e.g., Rosenau, 1997; Baker, 2000:366) have long argued that the conventional distinction between separate national and international spheres of activity is a misnomer. Nowadays, it is increasingly difficult to maintain the lines of demarcation between the domestic and the foreign realms, or between Comparative Politics and International Politics. Globalization means that the distinction between them is hard to enforce. Increasingly evident are myriad forms of interpenetration between the global and the national—global economic actors even exist within the state, as with global crime groups in Russia or the International Monetary Fund/World Bank's structural adjustment programs in developing countries.

Thus, a third discontent is opposition to the persistence of state centrism. From this angle, the case for an ontological shift springs from the anomaly between the objects of study seen through a realist or neorealist lens and globalists' vision of a polycentric, or multilevel, world order. New ontological priorities—an issue to which I will return—would consist of a series of linked processes. Toward this end, globalization researchers are attempting to design a framework for interrelating economics, politics, culture, and society in a seamless web. Hence, in large measure as a response to globalization, some scholars have shifted attention to global governance: an effort to incorporate a broader ontology of structures and agents. The state is treated as one among several actors. It is not that state sovereignty is losing meaning, but the multilevel environment in which it operates, and hence the meaning of the concept, is changing.

Methodologically, the field of *International* Studies is based on the premise of territoriality, reflected in central concepts such as state-centered nationalism, state borders, and state sovereignty. Yet, with the development of new technologies, especially in communications and transportation, the advent of a "network society" (Castells, 1996), and the emergence of a "nonterritorial region" (Ruggie, 1993), there is a marked shift toward a more deterritorialized world. Hence, Scholte has challenged "methodological territorialism"—the ingrained practice of formulating questions, gathering data, and arriving at conclusions all through the prism of a territorial framework (1999:17; and 2000). Without swinging to the opposite extreme of adopting a "globalist methodology" by totally rejecting the importance of the principle of territoriality, Scholte calls for a "full-scale methodological reorientation," and concludes: "[T]hat globalisation warrants a paradigm shift would seem to be incontrovertible" (1999:21–22).

Finally, there is the postmodernist complaint, which, arguably, has not really registered in our field.[5] As Said (1979) contends in regard to Orientalism, it is hard to erase certain representations of reality, for in Foucaultian terms, they take on the aura of authoritative expressions and are implicated in the exercise of power. Knowledge sets may thus operate as closed systems—what Caton (1999) terms "endless cycles of self-referring statements"—thwarting counterrepresentations that might have the power to challenge normal knowledge. As scholars in International Studies, perhaps we should reflect on this allegation about collectively self-referential work, for we spend an enormous amount of time engaging in intramural debates over concepts, often without sufficient attention to the phenomena themselves. Still, it would be wrong to gloss over Said's insight that representations manifest as knowledge are tied to the establishment, maintenance, and exercise of power. In International Studies, probing Said's point about reflexivity involves shifting explanatory levels above and below the state—a characteristic of globalization research.

Characteristics of Globalization Studies

Globalization theorists, of course, are not univocal. Inasmuch as their writings abound, there are different interpretations and considerable contestation. As Puchala aptly put it, "[C]onventional theories all have a table of outcomes that inventory what needs to be explained." For example, the realist table of outcomes is chiefly wars, alliances, balances of power, and arms races. For liberals, the outcomes are regimes, integration, cooperation, and hegemons (Puchala, 2001). By contrast, the problematic that globalization theorists seek to explain, while dynamic and open-ended, not invariant, may be gleaned from an emerging series of core, linked propositions. I will highlight six of them.

1. Many contemporary problems cannot be explained as interactions among nation states, i.e., as International Studies, but must be construed as global problems. Although this claim is not unique to globalization studies, at issue is a series of problems—e.g., the rise of organized crime, global warming, and the spread of infectious diseases—partly within and partly across borders, partially addressed by states and partially beyond their regulatory framework.

2. Globalization constitutes a structural transformation in world order. As such, not only is it about the here and now, it also warrants a long perspective of time and revives the study of space. A preoccupation with what Braudel called "the world of events"—the immediate moment—focuses attention on a frame that differs from the *longue durée,* an observation point that some researchers find advantageous for viewing the spatial reorganization of the global economy.

3. As a transformation, globalization involves a series of continuities and discontinuities with the past. In other words, the globalization tendency is by no means a total break—as noted, there is considerable disagreement about how much is new—but the contemporary period is punctuated by large-scale acceleration in globalizing processes such as the integration of financial markets, technological development, and intercultural contact.

4. New ontological priorities are warranted because of the emergence of a dialectic of suprastate and substate forces, pressures from above and below. The advent of an ontology of globalization is fluid, by no means fixed. It includes the global economy as an actor in its own right (as embodied, for example, in transnational corporations), states and interstate organizations, regionalist processes (at the macro, sub, and micro levels), world cities, and civil society, sometimes manifest as social movements.

5. Given shifting parameters, the state, in turn, seeks to adjust to evolving global structures. States, however, are in varied positions vis-à-vis globalizing structures, and reinvent themselves differently, the gamut of policies running from a full embrace, as with New Zealand's extreme neoliberal policies from 1984 to 1999, to resistance, illustrated by Malaysia's capital controls in 1998.

6. Underpinning such differences is a set of new, or deeper, tensions in world order, especially the disjuncture between the principle of territoriality, fundamental to the concept of state sovereignty, and the patent trend toward deterritorialization, especially, but not only, apparent in regard to transborder economic flows. The horizontal connections forged in the world economy and the vertical dimensions of state politics are two dissimilar vectors of social organization, with the latter seeking to accommodate the changing global matrix.

However schematically presented, the aforementioned, interrelated propositions put into question some of International Studies' ingrained ways of conceptualizing the world. At present, although the attempts at reconceptualization are in a preliminary stage of formulation, it is worth identifying the traps and confusions.

Discomfort with Paradigmatic Pretension

Barring caricatures of the concept *and* phenomena of globalization—e.g., it is totalizing, inevitable, and homogenizing, rather than, as many scholars maintain, partial, open-ended, and hybrid—surely there are grounds for discontent. For one thing, globalization may be seen as a promiscuous concept, variously referring to a historical scenario, interconnections, movements of capital, new technologies and information, an ideology of competitiveness, and a political response to the spread and deepening of the market. Hence, the complaint lodged earlier in this article: Observers (e.g., Kearney, 2001) are crying out and striving for more analytical precision.

Moreover, globalization is sometimes deemed overdetermined—too abstract, too structural, and insufficiently attentive to agency. From this perspective, it is thought that the logic is mechanically specified or misspecified in that it is too reductive. For some, especially scholars carrying out contextualized, fine-grained research on particular issues and distinct areas, globalization is regarded as too blunt a tool. After all, what does it leave out? What is not globalization? In response, it may be argued that globalization is mediated by other processes and actors, including the state. Furthermore, globalization has a direct or indirect impact on various levels of social organization, and becomes inserted into the local, thus complicating the distinction between the global and the local.

Another problem, then, is that the globalization literature has spawned its own binary oppositions. On the one hand, as indicated, the phenomena of globalization blur dichotomous distinctions to which International Studies has grown accustomed. For example, civil society now penetrates the state (as with members of environmental movements assuming important portfolios in government in the Philippines; and in several African countries, state substitution is abundantly evident—some so-called nongovernmental organizations are sustained by state funding or, arguably, their agendas are driven by the state or interstate organizations). On the other hand, globalization research itself presents new binary choices—"globalization from above" and "globalization from below," top-down and bottom-up globalization, and so on—that certainly have heuristic value but must be exploded in order to capture the range of empirical phenomena.

How Far Have We Come?

It would be remiss not to join a discussion of the drawbacks to globalization as an avenue of inquiry with its real gains, even if the nature of a new paradigm is tentative and being contested.

In the main, globalization studies emphasizes the historicity of all social phenomena. There is no escaping historiography: What are the driving forces behind globalization, and when did it originate? With the beginnings of intercultural contact, the dawn of capitalism in western Europe in the long sixteenth century, or in a distinct conjuncture after World War II? Research has thus opened new questions for investigation and debate. And even if one returns to old issues, such as theories of the state, there are opposing views and vexing questions, especially in the face of public representations, such as Margaret Thatcher's attack on the "nanny state." Should the state be construed as in retreat (Strange, 1996), as an agent of globalization (Cox, 1987), or, in an even more activist role, as the author of globalization (Panitch, 1996; from another perspective, Weiss, 1998)? Taken together, the writings on these issues combat the fragmentation of knowledge. Not surprisingly, given the themes that globalization embraces— technology, ecology, films, health, fast-food and other consumer goods, and so on—it is transdisciplinary, involving not exclusively the social sciences, but also the natural sciences, the humanistic sciences, and professional fields such as architecture, law, and medicine.

Arguably, within the social sciences, economic and political geographers (including Taylor, 1993; Taylor, Johnson, and Watts, 1995; Thrift, 1996; Dicken, 1998; Knox and Agnew, 1998; Harvey, 1999; Olds, 2001) have carried out some of the most sophisticated research on globalization. Even though the importance of spatial concerns is increasingly apparent, many International Studies specialists have not noticed the work of economic and political geographers.

For the purposes of teaching globalization, one way to draw students into a subject that, after all, involves thinking about big, abstract structures, is to focus on spatial issues as they relate to the changes in one's own locale. Reading a collection of essays consisting of anthropological fieldwork at McDonald's restaurants in different Asian countries (Watson, 1997), and then comparing the findings in the literature to their own fieldwork, including interviewing employees and customers at a nearby McDonald's, my students are asked to analyze the cultural political economy of globalization: a production system, the composition of the labor force (largely immigrants and members of minority groups in our locale), social technologies, and the representations conveyed by symbols. The students pursue the question of meanings—the intersubjective dimensions of globalization—in the writings of architects, e.g., on shopping malls and theme parks (Sorkin, 1992), and by visits to local sites.

Time permitting, consideration is also given to the legal and medical spheres. Cybergangs and some novel types of crime do not neatly fit into the jurisdiction of national or international law (see, e.g., Sassen, 1998). The field of public health has called attention to the nexus of social *and* medical problems, especially with the spread of AIDS. The tangible consequences of a changing global division of labor and power include new flows and directions of migration, the separation of families, a generation of orphans, and the introduction of the HIV virus into rural areas by returning emigrants. As these topics suggest, globalization studies identifies silences and establishes new intellectual space—certainly one criterion by which to gauge an ascendant paradigm.

Pushing the Agenda

Notwithstanding important innovations, as a paradigm, globalization is more of a potential than a refined framework, worldview, kit of tools and methods, and mode of resolving questions. Where then to go from here? Although these are not the only issues, the following challenges stand out as central to developing globalization studies:

1. Just as with capitalism, which has identifiable variants, there is no single, unified form of globalization. Researchers have not yet really mapped the different forms of globalization, which in the literature is sometimes preceded by adjectival designations, such as "neoliberal," "disembedded," "centralizing," "Islamic," "inner and outer," or "democratic." The adjectival labels are but hints at the need for systematic study of the varieties. Or should the object of study be globalizations?

2. Closely related is the problem of how to depict the genres of globalization research. What are the leading schools of thought? How to classify them so as to organize this massive literature and advance investigation? To catalog globalization studies according to national traditions of scholarship, by disciplinary perspective, or on single issues risks mistaking the parts for the whole. Avoiding this trap, Guillén (2001) decongests the burgeoning globalization research by organizing it into key debates: Is globalization really happening, does it produce convergence, does it undermine the authority of nation-states, is globality different from modernity, and is a global culture in the making? In another stocktaking, Held, McGrew, Goldblatt, and Perraton (1999) sort the field into hyperglobalizers who believe that the growth of world markets diminishes the role of states, skeptics who maintain that international interactions are not novel and that states have the power to regulate international economic flows, and transformationalists who claim that new patterns and an unprecedented configuration of global power relations have emerged. But there are other debates, major differences among policy research (Rodrik, 1997), structural approaches (Falk, 1999), and critical/poststructural accounts (Hardt and Negri, 2000).

3. What are the implications of globalization for disciplinary and cross-national studies? How should these domains of knowledge respond to

the globalization challenge? It would seem that in light of the distinctive combinations of evolving global structures and local conditions in various regions, globalization enhances, not reduces, the importance of the comparative method. However, there is the matter of exploring disciplinary and comparative themes within changing parameters and examining the interactions between these parameters and the localities.

4. Similarly, what does globalization mean for development and area studies? McMichael (2000:149) holds that "[t]he globalization project succeeds the development project." Surely development theory emerged in response to a particular historical moment: the inception of the Cold War, which, if anything, was an ordering principle in world affairs. After the sudden demise of this structure, development studies reached a conceptual cul de sac. Put more delicately, it may be worth revisiting development studies' basic tenets, especially apropos the dynamics of economic growth and the mechanisms of political power in the poorest countries, which have experienced a fundamental erosion of the extent of control that they had maintained—however little to begin with. This loss has been accompanied by changing priorities and reorganizations within funding agencies, a crucial consideration in terms of support for training the next generation of scholars, particularly apparent with regard to fieldwork for dissertations. Although some para-keeper area specialists have dug in their heels and have fought to protect normal knowledge in their domain, the task is to reinvent and thereby strengthen area studies.

5. Insufficient scholarly attention has centered on the ethics of globalization. The telling question is, What and whose values are inscribed in globalization? In light of the unevenness of globalization, with large zones of marginalization (not only in a spatial sense, but also in terms of race, ethnicity, gender, and who is or is not networked), there is another searching question, Is globalization ethically sustainable? What is the relationship between spirituality and globalization, an issue posed by different religious movements? Which contemporary Weberian will step forward to write The Neoliberal Ethic and the Spirit of Globalization?

6. Emanating mostly from the West, globalization studies is not really global. In terms of participating researchers and the focus of inquiry, there is a need for decentering. The literature on globalization unavailable in the English language (e.g., Ferrer, 1997; Gómez, 2000; Kaneko, 1999; Norani and Mandal, 2000; Podestà, Gómez Galán, Jácome, and Grandi, 2000) is rarely taken into account in the English-speaking world. Still, only limited work has thus far emerged in the developing world, including studies undertaken by the Council for the Development of

Economic and Social Research in Africa (1998), the National University of Singapore (Olds, Dicken, Kelly, Kong, and Yeung, 1999), the Latin American Social Sciences Council (Seoane and Taddei, 2001), and the Institute of Malaysian and International Studies at the National University of Malaysia (Mittelman and Norani, 2001).

7. Apart from the development of individual courses, there is a lack of systematic thought about the programmatic implications of globalization for the academy. Does global restructuring warrant academic restructuring in the ways in which knowledge is organized for students? If a new paradigm is emerging, then what does this mean in terms of pedagogy and curriculum? Will universities—and their International Studies specialists—be in the forefront of, or trail behind, changes in world order? Will they really open to the innovation of globalization studies?

To sum up, it is worth recalling that on more than one occasion Susan Strange held that International Studies is like an open range, home to many different types of research. Today, there is diversity, but surely one should not overlook the fences that hold back the strays. Mavericks who work in non-Western discourses, economic and political geographers, postmodernists and poststructuralists, not to mention humanists (whose contributions are emphasized by Alker, 1996; Puchala, 2000; and others), have faced real barriers.

It is in this context that globalization studies has emerged as a means to explain the intricacy and variability of the ways in which the world is restructuring and, by extension, to assess reflexively the categories used by social scientists to analyze these phenomena. The para-keepers, to varying degrees, are reluctant to embrace globalization as a knowledge set because some of its core propositions challenge predominant ontological, methodological, and epistemological commitments— what Kuhn referred to as "normal science." Again, not to dichotomize positions, but to look to the other end of the spectrum, para-makers advance a strong thesis about the extent to which a new paradigm is gaining ascendancy. The debate is fruitful in that it engages in theoretical stocktaking, locates important problem areas, and points to possible avenues of inquiry. It also helps to delimit space for investigation and to identify venues of intellectual activity. But, in the near term, there is no looming Kuhnian crisis in the sense of an impending overthrow that would quickly sweep away reigning paradigms. Given that systematic research on globalization is only slightly more than a decade in the making, it is more likely that International Studies has entered an interregnum between the old and the new.

Although globalization studies entails a putting together of bold efforts to theorize structural change, it would be wrong to either underestimate or exaggerate the achievements. Judging the arguments in the debate, on balance, a modest thesis is in order. The efforts to theorize globalization have produced a patchwork, an intellectual move rather than a movement, and more of a potential than worked-out alternatives to accepted ways of thinking in International Studies. In sum, this fledgling may be regarded as a proto-paradigm.

Notes

James H. Mittelman, "Globalization: An Ascendent Paradigm?" *International Studies Perspectives* (February 2002): 1–14. Reprinted by permission of *International Studies Perspectives*.

1. I owe a debt of gratitude to Donald J. Puchala, Linda J. Yarr, three anonymous reviewers, and the ISP editors for critical comments on drafts of this article. Thanks, too, to Patrick Jackson, who generously shared materials and insights—too numerous to pick up on entirely here.

2. The literature (e.g., Beck, 2000; Giddens, 2000) suggests a number of other ways to come to grips with what constitutes globablization.

3. This section draws from, and builds on, Mittelman (1997).

4. The question of the meaning of power and counterpower under globalization is a topic too broad to examine here. I am exploring this theme elsewhere.

5. I have the strong impression, but cannot "prove," that International Studies scholars, with notable exceptions (e.g., Der Derian, 1994; Peterson, 1992; Sylvester, 1994; Walker, 1993), have been more insular in the face of incursions from postmodernism and poststructuralism than have those in the other social sciences.

References

Alker, H. R. (1996) *Rediscoveries and Reformulations: Humanistic Methods for International Studies.* Cambridge and New York: Cambridge University Press.

Baker, A. (2000) "Globalization and the British 'Residual State.'" In *Political Economy and the Changing Global Order*, 2nd ed., edited by R. Stubbs and G. R. D. Underhill, pp. 362–372. Don Mills, Ontario: Oxford University Press.

Ball, T. (1976) From Paradigms to Research Programs: Toward a Post-Kuhnian Political Science. *American Journal of Political Science* 20(February):151–177.

Barnes, B. (1982) *T. S. Kuhn and Social Science.* New York: Columbia University Press.

Beck, U. (2000) *What Is Globalization?* Translated by Patrick Camiller. Cambridge: Polity Press.

Castells, M. (1996) *The Rise of the Network Society.* Oxford: Blackwell.

Caton, S. C. (1999) *Lawrence of Arabia: A Film's Anthropology.* Berkeley: University of California Press.

Cerny, P. G. (1996) Globalization and Other Stories: The Search for a New Paradigm for International Relations. *International Journal* 51 (Autumn):617–637.

Clark, I. (1999) *Globalization and International Relations Theory.* Oxford and New York: Oxford University Press.

Council for the Development of Economic and Social Research in Africa (1998) Social Sciences and Globalisation in Africa. *CODESRIA Bulletin* 2(December):3–6.

Cox, R. W. (1987) *Production, Power and World Order: Social Forces in the Making of History.* New York: Columbia University Press.

Der Derian, J., ed. (1994) *International Theory: Critical Investigations.* New York: New York University Press.

Dicken, P. (1998) *Global Shift: Transforming the World Economy,* 3rd ed. New York and London: Guilford Press.

Falk, R. (1999) *Predatory Globalization: A Critique.* Cambridge: Polity Press.

Ferrer, A. (1997) *Hechos y ficciones de la globalización [Facts and Fictions of Globalization].* Buenos Aires: Fondo de Cultura Economica [Collection of Economic Writings].

Giddens, A. (1990) *The Consequences of Modernity.* Cambridge: Polity Press.

Giddens, A. (2000) *Runaway World: How Globalization Is Reshaping Our Lives.* New York: Routledge.

Gómez, J. M. (2000) *Política e democracia em tempos de globalização.* Petrópolis, RJ, Brazil: Editora Vozes.

Gordon, D. (1988) The Global Economy: New Edifice or Crumbling Foundations? *New Left Review* 168(March–April):24–64.

Guillén, M. F. (2001) Is Globalization Civilizing, Destructive or Feeble? A Critique of Five Key Debates in the Social-Science Literature. *Annual Review of Sociology* 27:235–260.

Hardt, M., and A. Negri (2000) *Empire.* Cambridge, MA: Harvard University Press.

Harvey, D. (1990) *The Condition of Postmodernity.* Oxford: Blackwell.

Harvey, D. (1999) *Limits to Capital.* London: Verso.

Held, D., A. G. McGrew, D. Goldblatt, and J. Perraton (1999) *Global Transformations: Politics, Economics and Culture.* Cambridge: Polity Press.

Hirst, P., and G. Thompson (1999) *Globalization in Question: The International Economy and the Possibilities of Governance,* 2nd ed. Cambridge: Polity Press.

Kaneko, M. (1999) *Han Gurouburizumu: Shijou Kaiku no Senryakuteki Shikou [Anti-globalism: Strategic Thinking on Market Reforms].* Tokyo: Iwanami Shoten.

Kearney, A. T. (2001) Measuring Globalization. *Foreign Policy* 122(January–February):56–65.

Keohane, R. O. (1984) *After Hegemony: Cooperation and Discord in the World Political Economy.* Princeton, NJ: Princeton University Press.

Keohane, R. O., and J. S. Nye, Jr. (1977) *Power and Interdependence: World Politics in Transition.* Boston and Toronto: Little, Brown.

Keohane, R. O., and J. S. Nye, Jr. (1998) Power and Interdependence in the Information Age. New York: Council on Foreign Relations Web site, web.lexis-nexis.com/universe/printdoc/

Keohane, R. O., and J. S. Nye, Jr. (2000) Globalization: What's New? What's Not? (And So What?) *Foreign Policy* 118(Spring):104–120.

Knox, P., and J. Agnew (1998) *The Geography of the World Economy,* 3rd ed. London: Edward Arnold.

Kuhn, T. S. (1970) *The Structure of Scientific Revolutions,* 2nd ed. Chicago: University of Chicago Press.

Kuhn, T. S. (1977a) *The Essential Tension: Selected Studies in Scientific Tradition and Change.* Chicago: University of Chicago Press.

Kuhn, T. S. (1977b) "Second Thoughts on Paradigms." In *The Structure of Scientific Theories,* 2nd ed., edited by F. Suppe, pp. 459–482. Urbana: University of Illinois Press.

Lakatos, I. (1970) "Falsification and the Methodology of Scientific Research Programmes." In *Criticism and the Growth of Knowledge,* edited by I. Lakatos and A. Musgrave, pp. 91–196. Cambridge: Cambridge University Press.

Lapid, Y. (1989) The Third Debate: On the Prospects of International Theory in a Post-positivist Era. *International Studies Quarterly* 33:235–254.

McMichael, P. (2000) *Development and Social Change: A Global Perspective,* 2nd ed. Thousand Oaks, CA: Pine Forge Press.

Mittelman, J. H. (1997) "Rethinking Innovation in International Studies: Global Transformation at the Turn of the Millennium." In *Innovation and Transformation in International Studies,* edited by S. Gill and J. H. Mittelman, pp. 248–263. Cambridge: Cambridge University Press.

Mittelman, J. H. (2000) *The Globalization Syndrome: Transformation and Resistance.* Princeton, NJ: Princeton University Press.

Mittelman, J. H., and Norani Othman, eds. (2001) *Capturing Globalization.* London and New York: Routledge.

Othman, Norani, and S. Mandal, eds. (2000) *Malaysia Menangani Globalisasi: Peserata atau Mangasi? [Malaysia Responding to Globalization: Participants or Victims?]* Bangi, Malaysia: Penerbit Universiti Kebangsaan Malaysia [National University of Malaysia Press].

Olds, K (2001) *Globalization and Urban Change: Capital, Culture, and Pacific Rim Mega-Projects.* Oxford and New York: Oxford University Press.

Olds, K., P. Dicken, P. Kelly, L. Kong, and H. W. Yeung, eds. (1999) *Globalisation and the Asia-Pacific: Contested Territories.* London: Routledge.

Panitch, L. (1996) "Rethinking the Role of the State." In *Globalization: Critical Reflections,* edited by J. H. Mittelman, pp. 83–113. Boulder, CO: Lynne Rienner.

Peterson, S., ed. (1992) *Gendered States: Feminist (Re)Visions of International Relations.* Boulder, CO: Lynne Rienner.

Podestà, B., M. Gómez Galán, F. Jácome, and J. Grandi, eds. (2000) *Ciudadanía y mundialización regional: La sociedad civil ante la integración regional.* Madrid: CIDEAL.

Puchala, D. J. (2000) Marking a Weberian Moment: Our Discipline Looks Ahead. *International Studies Perspectives* 1(August):133–144.

Puchala, D. J. (2001) Personal correspondence with the author. 30 January.

Robertson, R. (1992) *Globalization: Social Theory and Global Culture.* Newbury Park, CA: Sage.

Rodrik, D. (1997) *Has Globalization Gone Too Far?* Washington, DC: Institute for International Economics.

Rosenau, J. N. (1997) *Along the Domestic-Foreign Frontier: Exploring Governance in a Turbulent World.* Cambridge: Cambridge University Press.

Ruggie, J. G. (1993) Territoriality and Beyond: Problematizing Modernity in International Relations. *International Organization* 46(Summer):561–598.

Said, E. W. (1979) *Orientalism*. New York: Vintage.

Sassen, S. (1998) *Globalization and Its Discontents*. New York: New Press.

Scholte, J. A. (1999) "Globalisation: Prospects for a Paradigm Shift." In *Politics and Globalisation: Knowledge, Ethics and Agency*, edited by M. Shaw, pp. 9–22. London and New York: Routledge.

Scholte, J. A. (2000) *Globalization: A Critical Introduction*. London: Macmillan.

Seoane, J., and E. Taddei, eds. (2001) *Resistencias mundiales [De Seattle a Porto Alegre]*. Buenos Aires: Consejo Latinamericano de Ciencias Sociales.

Shaw, M. (1994) "Introduction: The Theoretical Challenge of Global Society." In *Global Society and International Relations*, edited by M. Shaw. Oxford: Oxford University Press.

Shaw, M., ed. (1999) *Politics and Globalisation: Knowledge, Ethics and Agency*. London: Routledge.

Sorkin, M., ed. (1992) *Variations on a Theme Park: The New American City and the End of Public Space*. New York: Hill and Wang.

Strange, S. (1996) *The Retreat of the State: The Diffusion of Power in the World Economy*. Cambridge: Cambridge University Press.

Strange, S. (1998) *Mad Money: When Markets Outgrow Governments*. Ann Arbor: University of Michigan Press.

Sylvester, C. (1994) *Feminist Theory and International Relations Theory in a Postmodern Era*. Cambridge: Cambridge University Press.

Taylor, P. J. (1993) *Political Geography: World-Economy, Nation-State, and Locality*. New York: Wiley.

Taylor, P. J., R. J. Johnson, and M. J. Watts (1995) *Geographies of Global Change: Remapping the World in the Late Twentieth Century*. Oxford: Blackwell.

Thrift, N. (1996) *Spatial Formations*. London: Sage.

Walker, R. B. J. (1993) *Inside/Outside: International Relations as Political Theory*. Cambridge: Cambridge University Press.

Wallerstein, I. (2000) Globalization or the Age of Transition? A Long-Term View of the Trajectory of the World System. *International Sociology* 15(June):249–265.

Waltz, K. N. (1979) *Theory of International Politics*. Reading, MA: Addison-Wesley.

Waltz, K. N. (1999) Globalization and Governance. *PS: Political Science & Politics* 23 (December):693–700.

Watson, J. L., ed. (1997) *Golden Arches East: McDonald's in East Asia*. Stanford, CA: Stanford University Press.

Weber, M. (1949) "'Objectivity' in Social Science and Social Policy." In *The Methodology of the Social Sciences*, edited and translated by E. Shils and H. A. Finch, pp. 49–112. New York: Free Press.

Weiss, L. (1998) *State Capacity: Governing the Economy in a Global Era*. Cambridge: Polity Press.

Wendt, A. (1999) *Social Theory of International Politics*. Cambridge: Cambridge University Press.

CHAPTER 10
THE PROMISE OF GLOBAL INSTITUTIONS

Joseph Stiglitz

International bureaucrats—the faceless symbols of the world economic order—are under attack everywhere. Formerly uneventful meetings of obscure technocrats discussing mundane subjects such as concessional loans and trade quotas have now become the scene of raging street battles and huge demonstrations. The protests at the Seattle meeting of the World Trade Organization in 1999 were a shock. Since then, the movement has grown stronger and the fury has spread. Virtually every major meeting of the International Monetary Fund, the World Bank, and the World Trade Organization is now the scene of conflict and turmoil. The death of a protestor in Genoa in 2001 was just the beginning of what may be many more casualties in the war against globalization.

Riots and protests against the policies of and actions by institutions of globalization are hardly new. For decades, people in the developing world have rioted when the austerity programs imposed on their countries proved to be too harsh, but their protests were largely unheard in the West. What is new is the wave of protests in the developed countries.

It used to be that subjects such as structural adjustment loans (the programs that were designed to help countries adjust to and weather crises) and banana quotas (the limits that some European countries impose on the importing of bananas from countries other than their former colonies) were of interest to only a few. Now sixteen-year-old kids from the suburbs have strong opinions on such esoteric treaties as GATT (the General Agreement on Tariffs and Trade) and NAFTA (the North American Free Trade Area, the agreement signed in 1992 between Mexico, United States, and Canada that allows for the freer movement of goods, services, and investment—but not people—among those countries). These protests have provoked an enormous amount of soul-searching from those in power. Even conservative politicians such as France's president, Jacques Chirac, have expressed concern that globalization is not making life better for those most in need of its promised benefits.[1] It is clear to almost everyone that something has gone horribly wrong. Almost overnight, globalization has become the most pressing issue of our time, something debated from boardrooms to op-ed pages and in schools all over the world.

Why has globalization—a force that has brought so much good—become so controversial? Opening up to international trade has helped many countries grow far more quickly than they would otherwise have done. International trade helps economic development when a country's exports drive its economic growth. Export-led growth was the centerpiece of the industrial policy that enriched much of Asia and left millions of people there far better off. Because of globalization many people in the world now live longer than before and their standard of living is far better. People in the West may regard low-paying jobs at Nike as exploitation, but for many people in the developing world, working in a factory is a far better option than staying down on the farm and growing rice.

Globalization has reduced the sense of isolation felt in much of the developing world and has given many people in the developing countries access to knowledge well beyond the reach of even the wealthiest in any country a century ago. The antiglobalization protests themselves are a result of this connectedness. Links between activists in different parts of the world, particularly those links forged through Internet communication, brought about the pressure that resulted in the international landmines treaty—despite the opposition of many powerful governments. Signed by 121 countries as of 1997, it reduces the likelihood that children and other innocent victims will be maimed by mines. Similar, well-orchestrated public pressure forced the international community to forgive the debts of some of the poorest countries. Even when there are negative sides to globalization, there are often benefits. Opening up the Jamaican milk market to U.S. imports in 1992 may have hurt local dairy farmers but it also meant poor children could get milk more cheaply. New foreign firms may hurt protected state-owned enterprises but they can also lead to the introduction of new technologies, access to new markets, and the creation of new industries.

Foreign aid, another aspect of the globalized world, for all its faults still has brought benefits to millions, often in ways that have almost gone unnoticed: guerrillas in the Philippines were provided jobs by a World Bank–financed project as they laid down their arms; irrigation projects have more than doubled the incomes of farmers lucky enough to get water; education projects have brought literacy to the rural areas; in a few countries AIDS projects have helped contain the spread of this deadly disease.

Those who vilify globalization too often overlook its benefits. But the proponents of globalization have been, if anything, even more unbalanced. To them, globalization (which typically is associated with accepting triumphant capitalism, American style) *is* progress; developing countries must accept it, if they are to grow and to fight poverty effectively. But to many in the developing world, globalization has not brought the promised economic benefits.

A growing divide between the haves and the have-nots has left increasing numbers in the Third World in dire poverty, living on less than a dollar a day. Despite repeated promises of poverty reduction made over the last decade of the twentieth century, the actual number of people living in poverty has actually increased by almost 100 million.[2] This occurred at the same time that total world income increased by an average of 2.5 percent annually.

In Africa, the high aspirations following colonial independence have been largely unfulfilled. Instead, the continent plunges deeper into misery, as incomes fall and standards of living decline. The hard-won improvements in life expectancy gained in the past few decades have begun to reverse. While the scourge of AIDS is at the center of this decline, poverty is also a killer. Even countries that have abandoned African socialism, managed to install reasonably honest governments, balanced their budgets, and kept inflation down find that they simply cannot attract private investors. Without this investment, they cannot have sustainable growth.

If globalization has not succeeded in reducing poverty, neither has it succeeded in ensuring stability. Crises in Asia and in Latin America have threatened the economies and the stability of all developing countries. There are fears of financial contagion spreading around the world, that the collapse of one emerging market currency will mean that others fall as well. For a while, in 1997 and 1998, the Asian crisis appeared to pose a threat to the entire world economy.

Globalization and the introduction of a market economy have not produced the promised results in Russia and most of the other economies making the transition from communism to the market. These countries were told by the

West that the new economic system would bring them unprecedented prosperity. Instead, it brought unprecedented poverty: in many respects, for most of the people, the market economy proved even worse than their Communist leaders had predicted. The contrast between Russia's transition, as engineered by the international economic institutions, and that of China, designed by itself, could not be greater: While in 1990 China's gross domestic product (GDP) was 60 percent that of Russia, by the end of the decade the numbers had been reversed. While Russia saw an unprecedented increase in poverty, China saw an unprecedented decrease.

The critics of globalization accuse Western countries of hypocrisy, and the critics are right. The Western countries have pushed poor countries to eliminate trade barriers, but kept up their own barriers, preventing developing countries from exporting their agricultural products and so depriving them of desperately needed export income. The United States was, of course, one of the prime culprits, and this was an issue about which I felt intensely. When I was chairman of the Council of Economic Advisers, I fought hard against this hypocrisy, as had my predecessors at the Council from both parties. It not only hurt the developing countries; it also cost Americans billions of dollars, both as consumers, in the higher prices they paid, and as taxpayers, to finance the huge agricultural subsidies. The struggles were, all too often, unsuccessful. Special commercial and financial interests prevailed—and when I moved over to the World Bank, I saw the consequences to the developing countries all too clearly.

But even when not guilty of hypocrisy, the West has driven the globalization agenda, ensuring that it garners a disproportionate share of the benefits, at the expense of the developing world. It was not just that the more advanced industrial countries declined to open up their markets to the goods of the developing countries—for instance, keeping their quotas on a multitude of goods from textiles to sugar—while insisting that those countries open up their markets to the goods of the wealthier countries; it was not just that the more advanced industrial countries continued to subsidize agriculture, making it difficult for the developing countries to compete, while insisting that the developing countries eliminate their subsidies on industrial goods. Looking at the "terms of trade"— the prices which developed and less developed countries get for the products they produce—after the last trade agreement in 1995 (the eighth), the *net* effect was to lower the prices some of the poorest countries in the world received relative to what they paid for their imports.[3] The result was that some of the poorest countries in the world were actually made worse off.

Western banks benefited from the loosening of capital market controls in Latin America and Asia, but those regions suffered when inflows of speculative hot money (money that comes into and out of a country, often overnight, often little more than betting on whether a currency is going to appreciate or depreciate) that had poured into countries suddenly reversed. The abrupt outflow of money left behind collapsed currencies and weakened banking systems. The Uruguay Round also strengthened intellectual property rights. American and other Western drug companies could now stop drug companies in India and Brazil from "stealing" their intellectual property. But these drug companies in the developing world were making these life-saving drugs available to their citizens at a fraction of the price at which the drugs were sold by the Western drug companies. There were thus two sides to the decisions made in the Uruguay Round. Profits of the Western drug companies would go up. Advocates said this would provide them more incentive to innovate; but the increased profits from sales in the developing world were small, since few could afford the drugs, and hence the incentive effect, at best, might be limited. The other side was that thousands were effectively condemned to death, because governments and individuals in developing countries could no longer pay the high prices demanded. In the case of AIDS, the international outrage was so great that drug companies had to back down, eventually agreeing to lower their prices, to sell the drugs at cost in late 2001. But the underlying problems—the fact that the intellectual property regime established under the Uruguay Round was not balanced, that it overwhelmingly reflected the interests and perspectives of the producers, as opposed to the users, whether in developed or developing countries—remain.

Not only in trade liberalization but in every other aspect of globalization even seemingly well-intentioned efforts have often backfired. When projects, whether agriculture or infrastructure, recommended by the West, designed with the advice of Western advisers, and financed by the World Bank or others have failed, unless there is some form of debt forgiveness, the poor people in the developing world still must repay the loans.

If, in too many instances, the benefits of globalization have been less than its advocates claim, the price paid has been greater, as the environment has been destroyed, as political processes have been corrupted, and as the rapid pace of change has not allowed countries time for cultural adaptation. The crises that have brought in their wake massive unemployment have, in turn, been followed by longer-term problems of social dissolution—from urban violence in Latin America to ethnic conflicts in other parts of the world, such as Indonesia.

These problems are hardly new—but the increasingly vehement worldwide reaction against the policies that drive globalization is a significant change. For decades, the cries of the poor in Africa and in developing countries in other parts of the world have been largely unheard in the West. Those who labored in the developing countries knew something was wrong when they saw financial crises becoming more commonplace and the numbers of poor increasing. But they had no way to change the rules or to influence the international financial institutions that wrote them. Those who valued democratic processes saw how "conditionality"—the conditions that international lenders imposed in return for their assistance—undermined national sovereignty. But until the protestors came along there was little hope for change and no outlets for complaint. *Some* of the protestors went to excesses; *some* of the protestors were arguing for higher protectionist barriers against the developing countries, which would have made their plight even worse. But despite these problems, it is the trade unionists, students, environmentalists—ordinary citizens—marching in the streets of Prague, Seattle, Washington, and Genoa who have put the need for reform on the agenda of the developed world.

Protestors see globalization in a very different light than the treasury secretary of the United States, or the finance and trade ministers of most of the advanced industrial countries. The differences in views are so great that one wonders, are the protestors and the policy makers talking about the same phenomena? Are they looking at the same data? Are the visions of those in power so clouded by special and particular interests?

What is this phenomenon of globalization that has been subject, at the same time, to such vilification and such praise? Fundamentally, it is the closer integration of the countries and peoples of the world which has been brought about by the enormous reduction of costs of transportation and communication, and the breaking down of artificial barriers to the flows of goods, services, capital, knowledge, and (to a lesser extent) people across borders. Globalization has been accompanied by the creation of new institutions that have joined with existing ones to work across borders. In the arena of international civil society, new groups, like the Jubilee movement pushing for debt reduction for the poorest countries, have joined long-established organizations like the International Red Cross. Globalization is powerfully driven by international corporations, which move not only capital and goods across borders but also technology. Globalization has also led to renewed attention to long-established international *intergovernmental* institutions: the United Nations, which attempts to maintain peace; the International Labor Organization (ILO), originally created in 1919, which promotes its agenda around the world under its slogan "decent work"; and the World Health Organization (WHO), which has been especially concerned with improving health conditions in the developing world.

Many, perhaps most, of these aspects of globalization have been welcomed everywhere. No one wants to see their child die, when knowledge and medicines are available somewhere else in the world. It is the more narrowly defined *economic* aspects of globalization that have been the subject of controversy, and the international institutions that have written the rules, which mandate or push things like liberalization of capital markets (the elimination of the rules and regulations in many developing countries that are designed to stabilize the flows of volatile money into and out of the country).

To understand what went wrong, it's important to look at the three main institutions that govern globalization: the IMF, the World Bank, and the WTO. There are, in addition, a host of other institutions that play a role in the international economic system—a number of regional banks, smaller and younger sisters to the World Bank, and a large number of UN organizations, such as the UN Development Program or the UN Conference on Trade and Development (UNCTAD). These organizations often have views that are markedly different from the IMF and the World Bank. The ILO, for example, worries that the IMF pays too little attention to workers' rights, while the Asian Development Bank argues for "competitive pluralism," whereby developing countries will be provided with alternative views of development strategies, including the "Asian model"—in which governments, while relying on markets, have taken an active role in creating, shaping, and guiding markets, including promoting new technologies, and in which firms take considerable responsibility for the social welfare of their employees—which the Asian Development Bank sees as distinctly different from the American model pushed by the Washington-based institutions.

In this book, I focus mostly on the IMF and the World Bank, largely because they have been at the center of the major economic issues of the last two decades, including the financial crises and the transition of the former Communist countries to market economies. The IMF and the World Bank both originated in World War II as a result of the UN Monetary and Financial Conference at Bretton Woods, New Hampshire, in July 1944, part of a concerted effort to finance the rebuilding of Europe after the devastation of World War II and to save the world from future economic depressions. The proper name of the World Bank—the International Bank for Reconstruction and Development—reflects its original mission; the last part, "Development," was added almost as an afterthought. At the time, most of the countries in the developing world were still colonies, and what meager economic development efforts could or would be undertaken were considered the responsibility of their European masters.

The more difficult task of ensuring global economic stability was assigned to the IMF. Those who convened at Bretton Woods had the global depression of the 1930s very much on their minds. Almost three quarters of a century ago, capitalism faced its most severe crisis to date. The Great Depression enveloped the whole world and led to unprecedented increases in unemployment. At the worst point, a quarter of America's workforce was unemployed. The British economist John Maynard Keynes, who would later be a key participant at Bretton Woods, put forward a simple explanation, and a correspondingly simple set of prescriptions: lack of sufficient aggregate demand explained economic downturns; government policies could help stimulate aggregate demand. In cases where monetary policy is ineffective, governments could rely on fiscal policies, either by increasing expenditures or cutting taxes. While the models underlying Keynes's analysis have subsequently been criticized and refined, bringing a deeper understanding of why market forces do not work quickly to adjust the economy to full employment, the basic lessons remain valid.

The International Monetary Fund was charged with preventing another global depression. It would do this by putting international pressure on countries that were not doing their fair share to maintain global aggregate demand, by allowing their own economies to go into a slump. When necessary it would also provide liquidity in the form of loans to those countries facing an economic downturn and unable to stimulate aggregate demand with their own resources.

In its original conception, then, the IMF was based on a recognition that markets often did not work well—that they could result in massive unemployment and might fail to make needed funds available to countries to help them restore their economies. The IMF was founded on the belief that there was a need for *collective action at the global level* for economic stability, just as the United Nations had been founded on the belief that there was a need for collective action at the global level for political stability. The IMF is a *public* institution, established with money provided by taxpayers around the world. This is important to remember because it does not report directly to either the citizens who finance it or those whose lives it affects. Rather, it reports to the ministries of finance and the central banks of the governments of the world. They assert their control through a complicated voting arrangement based largely on the economic power of the countries at the end of World War II. There have been some minor adjustments since, but the major developed countries run the show, with only one country, the United States, having effective veto. (In this sense, it is similar to the UN, where a historical anachronism determines who holds the veto—the victorious powers of World War II—but at least there the veto power is shared among five countries.)

Over the years since its inception, the IMF has changed markedly. Founded on the belief that markets often worked badly, it now champions market supremacy with ideological fervor. Founded on the belief that there is a need for international pressure on countries to have more expansionary economic policies—such as increasing expenditures, reducing taxes, or lowering interest rates to stimulate the economy—today the IMF typically provides funds only if countries engage in policies like cutting deficits, raising taxes, or raising interest rates that lead to a contraction of the economy. Keynes would be rolling over in his grave were he to see what has happened to his child.

The most dramatic change in these institutions occurred in the 1980s, the era when Ronald Reagan and Margaret Thatcher preached free market ideology in the United States and the United Kingdom. The IMF and the World Bank became the new missionary institutions, through which these ideas were pushed on the reluctant poor countries that often badly needed their loans and grants. The ministries of finance in poor countries were willing to become converts, if necessary, to obtain the funds, though the vast majority of government officials, and, more to the point, people in these countries often remained skeptical. In the early 1980s, a purge occurred inside the World Bank, in its research department, which guided the Bank's thinking and direction. Hollis Chenery, one of America's most distinguished development economists, a professor at Harvard who had made fundamental contributions to research in the economics of development and other areas as well, had been Robert McNamara's confidant and adviser. McNamara had been appointed president of the World Bank in 1968. Touched by the poverty that he saw throughout the Third World, McNamara had redirected the Bank's effort at its elimination, and Chenery assembled a first-class group of economists from around the world to work with him. But with the changing of the guard came a new president in 1981, William Clausen, and a new chief economist, Ann Krueger, an international trade specialist, best known for her work on "rent seeking"—how special interests use tariffs and other protectionist measures to increase their incomes at the expense of others. While Chenery and his team had focused on how markets failed in developing countries and what governments could do to improve markets and reduce poverty, Krueger saw government as the problem. Free markets were the solution to the problems of developing countries. In the new ideological fervor, many of the first-rate economists that Chenery had assembled left.

Although the missions of the two institutions remained distinct, it was at this time that their activities became increasingly intertwined. In the 1980s, the Bank went beyond just lending for projects (like roads and dams) to providing broad-based support, in the form of *structural adjustment loans;* but it did this only when the IMF gave its approval—and with that approval came IMF-imposed conditions on the country. The IMF was supposed to focus on crises; but developing countries were always in need of help, so the IMF became a permanent part of life in most of the developing world.

The fall of the Berlin Wall provided a new arena for the IMF: managing the transition to a market economy in the former Soviet Union and the Communist bloc countries in Europe. More recently, as the crises have gotten bigger, and even the deep coffers of the IMF seemed insufficient, the World Bank was called in to provide tens of billions of dollars of emergency support, but strictly as a junior partner, with the guidelines of the programs dictated by the IMF.

In principle, there was a division of labor. The IMF was supposed to limit itself to matters of *macroeconomics* in dealing with a country, to the government's budget deficit, its monetary policy, its inflation, its trade deficit, its borrowing from abroad; and the World Bank was supposed to be in charge of *structural issues*—what the country's government spent money on, the country's financial institutions, its labor markets, its trade policies. But the IMF took a rather imperialistic view of the matter: since almost any structural issue could affect the overall performance of the economy, and hence the government's budget or the trade deficit, it viewed almost everything as falling within its domain. It often got impatient with the World Bank, where even in the years when free market ideology reigned supreme there were frequent controversies about what policies would best suit the conditions of the country. The IMF had the answers (basically, the same ones for every country), didn't see the need for all this discussion, and, while the World Bank debated what should be done, saw itself as stepping into the vacuum to provide the answers.

The two institutions could have provided countries with alternative perspectives on some of the challenges of development and transition, and in doing so they might have strengthened democratic processes. But they were both driven by the collective will of the G-7 (the governments of the seven most important advanced industrial countries),[4] and especially their finance ministers and treasury secretaries, and too often, the last thing they wanted was a lively democratic debate about alternative strategies.

A half century after its founding, it is clear that the IMF has failed in its mission. It has not done what it was supposed to do—provide funds for countries facing an economic downturn, to enable the country to restore itself to close to full employment. In spite of the fact that our understanding of economic processes has increased enormously during the last fifty years, crises around the world have been more frequent and (with the exception of the Great Depression) deeper. By some reckonings, close to a hundred countries have faced crises.[5] Every major emerging market that liberalized its capital market has had at least one crisis. But this is not just an unfortunate streak of bad luck. Many of the policies that the IMF pushed, in particular, premature capital market liberalization, have contributed to global instability. And once a country was in crisis, IMF funds and programs not only failed to stabilize the situation but in many cases actually made matters worse, especially for the poor. The IMF failed in its original mission of promoting global stability; it has also been no more successful in the new missions that it has undertaken, such as guiding the transition of countries from communism to a market economy.

The Bretton Woods agreement had called for a third international economic organization—a World Trade Organization to govern international trade relations, a job similar to the IMF's governing of international financial relations. Beggar-thy-neighbor trade policies, in which countries raised tariffs to maintain their own economies but at the expense of their neighbors, were largely blamed for the spread of the depression and its depth. An international organization was required not just to prevent a recurrence but to encourage the free flow of goods and services. Although the General Agreement on Tariffs and Trade (GATT) did succeed in lowering tariffs enormously, it was difficult to reach the final accord; it was not until 1995, a half century after the end of the war and two thirds of a century after the Great Depression, that the World Trade Organization came into being. But the WTO is markedly different from the other two organizations. It does not set rules itself; rather, it provides a forum in which trade negotiations go on and it ensures that its agreements are lived up to.

The ideas and intentions behind the creation of the international economic institutions were good ones, yet they gradually evolved over the years to become something very different. The Keynesian orientation of the IMF, which emphasized market failures and the role for government in job creation, was replaced by the free market mantra of the 1980s, part of a new "Washington Consensus"—a consensus between the IMF, the World Bank, and the U.S. Treasury about the "right" policies for developing countries—that signaled a radically different approach to economic development and stabilization.

Many of the ideas incorporated in the consensus were developed in response to the problems in Latin America, where governments had let budgets get out of control while loose monetary policies had led to rampant inflation. A burst of growth in some of that region's countries in the decades immediately after World War II had not been sustained, allegedly because of excessive state intervention in the economy. Unfortunately, the ideas that were developed to cope with problems arguably specific to Latin American countries were applied to other countries, countries with quite different economic structures, strengths, and weaknesses. Policies like capital market liberalization were pushed throughout Latin America, before there was a strong body of either theory or evidence that they promoted growth. Even as evidence mounted that such policies contributed to instability, these policies were pushed elsewhere, sometimes in situations where they were even more poorly suited.

In many cases, the Washington Consensus policies, even if they had been appropriate in Latin America, were ill-suited for countries in the early stages of development or transition. Most of the advanced industrial countries—including the United States and Japan—had built up their economies by wisely and selectively protecting some of their industries until they were strong enough to compete with foreign companies. While blanket protectionism has often not worked for countries that have tried it, neither has rapid trade liberalization. Forcing a developing country to open itself up to imported products that would compete with those produced by certain of its industries, industries that were dangerously vulnerable to competition from much stronger counterpart industries in other countries, can have disastrous consequences—socially and economically. Jobs have systematically been destroyed—poor farmers in developing countries simply couldn't compete with the highly subsidized goods from Europe and America—before the countries' industrial and agricultural sectors were able to grow strong and create new jobs. Even worse, the IMF's insistence on developing countries maintaining tight monetary policies has led to interest rates that would make job creation impossible even in the best of circumstances. And because trade liberalization occurred before safety nets were put into place, those who lost their jobs were forced into poverty. Liberalization has thus, too often, not been followed by the promised growth, but by increased misery. And even those who have not lost their jobs have been hit by a heightened sense of insecurity.

Capital controls are another example: European countries banned the free flow of capital until the seventies. Some might say it's not fair to insist that developing countries with a barely functioning bank system risk opening their markets. But putting aside such notions of fairness, it's bad economics; the influx of hot money into and out of the country that so frequently follows after capital market liberalization leaves havoc in its wake. Small developing countries are like small boats. Rapid capital market liberalization, in the manner pushed by the IMF, amounted to setting them off on a voyage on a rough sea, before the holes in their hulls have been repaired, before the captain has received training, before life vests have been put on board. Even in the best of circumstances, there was a high likelihood that they would be overturned when they were hit broadside by a big wave.

Even if the IMF had subscribed to "mistaken" economic theories, it might not have mattered if its domain of activity had been limited to Europe, the United States, and other advanced industrialized countries that can fend for themselves. But the end of colonialism and communism has given the international financial institutions the opportunity to expand greatly their original mandates. Today these institutions have become dominant players in the world economy. Not only countries seeking their help but also those seeking their "seal of approval" so that they can better access international capital markets must follow their economic prescriptions, prescriptions which reflect their free market ideologies and theories.

The result for many people has been poverty and for many countries social and political chaos. The IMF has made mistakes in all the areas it has been involved in: development, crisis management, and in countries making the transition from communism to capitalism. Structural adjustment programs did not bring sustained growth even to those, like Bolivia, that adhered to its strictures; in many countries, excessive austerity stifled growth; successful economic programs require extreme care in *sequencing*—the order in which reforms occur—and pacing. If, for instance, markets are opened up for competition too rapidly, before strong financial institutions are established, then jobs will be destroyed faster than new jobs are created. In many countries, mistakes in sequencing and pacing led to rising unemployment and increased poverty.[6] In the 1997 Asian crisis, IMF policies exacerbated the crises in Indonesia and Thailand. Free market reforms in Latin America have had one or two successes—Chile is repeatedly cited—but much of the rest of the continent has still to make up for the lost decade of growth following the so-called successful IMF bailouts of the early 1980s, and many today have persistently high rates of unemployment—in Argentina, for instance, at double-digit levels since 1995—even as inflation has been brought down. The collapse in Argentina in 2001 is one of the most recent of a series of failures over the past few years. Given the high unemployment rate for almost seven years, the wonder is not that the citizens eventually rioted, but that they suffered quietly so much for so long. Even those countries that have experienced some limited growth have seen the benefits accrue to the well-off, and especially the *very* well-off—the top 10 percent—while poverty has remained high, and in some cases the income of those at the bottom has even fallen.

Underlying the problems of the IMF and the other international economic institutions is the problem of governance: who decides what they do. The institutions are dominated not just by the wealthiest industrial countries but by commercial and financial interests in those countries, and the policies of the institutions naturally reflect this. The choice of heads for these institutions symbolizes the institutions' problem, and too often has contributed to their dysfunction. While almost all of the activities of the IMF and the World Bank today are in the developing world (certainly, all of their lending), they are led by representatives from the industrialized nations. (By custom or tacit agreement the head of the IMF is always a European, that of the World Bank an American.) They are chosen behind closed doors, and it has never even been viewed as a prerequisite that the head should have any experience in the developing world. The institutions are not representative of the nations they serve.

The problems also arise from who *speaks* for the country. At the IMF, it is the finance ministers and the central bank governors. At the WTO, it is the trade ministers. Each of these ministers is closely aligned with particular constituencies *within* their countries. The trade ministries reflect the concerns of the business community—both exporters who want to see new markets opened up for their products and producers of goods which fear competition from new imports. These constituencies, of course, want to maintain as many barriers to trade as they can and keep whatever subsidies they can persuade Congress (or their parliament) to give them. The fact that the trade barriers raise the prices consumers pay or that the subsidies impose burdens on taxpayers is of less concern than the profits of the producers—and environmental and labor issues are of even less concern, other than as obstacles that have to be overcome. The finance ministers and central bank governors typically are closely tied to the financial community; they come from financial firms, and after their period of government service, that is where they return. Robert Rubin, the treasury secretary during much of the period described in this book, came from the largest investment bank, Goldman Sachs, and returned to the firm, Citigroup, that controlled the largest commercial bank, Citibank. The number-two person at the IMF during this period, Stan Fischer, went straight from the IMF to Citigroup. These individuals naturally see the world through the eyes of the financial community. The decisions of any institution naturally reflect the perspectives and interests of those who make the decisions; not surprisingly, as we shall see repeatedly in the following chapters, the policies of the international economic institutions are all too often closely aligned with the commercial and financial interests of those in the advanced industrial countries.

For the peasants in developing countries who toil to pay off their countries' IMF debts or the businessmen who suffer from higher value-added taxes upon the insistence of the IMF, the current system run by the IMF is one of taxation without representation. Disillusion with the international system of globalization under the aegis of the IMF grows as the poor in Indonesia, Morocco, or Papua New Guinea have fuel and food subsidies cut, as those in Thailand see AIDS increase as a result of IMF-forced cutbacks in health expenditures, and as families in many developing countries, having to pay for their children's education under so-called cost recovery programs, make the painful choice not to send their daughters to school.

Left with no alternatives, no way to express their concern, to press for change, people riot. The streets, of course, are not the place where issues are discussed, policies formulated, or compromises forged. But the protests have made government officials and economists around the world think about alternatives to these Washington Consensus policies as the one and true way for growth and development. It has become increasingly clear not to just ordinary citizens but to policy makers as well, and not just those in the developing countries but those in the developed countries as well, that globalization as it has been practiced has not lived up to what its advocates promised it would accomplish—or to what it can and should do. In some cases it has not even resulted in growth, but when it has, it has not brought benefits to all; the net effect of the policies set by the Washington Consensus has all too often been to benefit the few at the expense of the many, the well-off at the expense of the poor. In many cases commercial interests and values have superseded concern for the environment, democracy, human rights, and social justice.

Globalization itself is neither good nor bad. It has the *power* to do enormous good, and for the countries of East Asia, who have embraced globalization *under their own terms,* at their own pace, it has been an enormous benefit, in spite of the setback of the 1997 crisis. But in much of the world it has not brought comparable benefits.

The experience of the United States during the nineteenth century makes a good parallel for today's globalization—and the contrast helps illustrate the successes of the past and today's failures. At that time, when transportation and communication costs fell and previously local markets expanded, new national economies formed, and with these new national economies came national companies, doing business throughout the country. But the markets were not left to develop willy-nilly on their own; government played a vital role in shaping the evolution of the economy. The U.S. government obtained wide economic latitude when the courts broadly interpreted the constitutional provision that allows the federal government to regulate interstate commerce. The federal government began to regulate the financial system, set minimum wages and working conditions, and eventually provided unemployment and welfare systems to deal with the problems posed by a market system. The federal government also promoted some industries (the first telegraph line, for example, was laid by the federal government between Baltimore and Washington in 1842) and encouraged others, like agriculture, not just helping set up universities to do research but providing extension services to train farmers in the new technologies. The federal government played a central role not only in promoting American growth. Even if it did not engage in the kinds of active redistribution policies, at least it had programs whose benefits were widely shared—not just those that extended education and improved agricultural productivity, but also land grants that provided a minimum opportunity for all Americans.

Today, with the continuing decline in transportation and communication costs, and the reduction of man-made barriers to the flow of goods, services, and capital (though there remain serious barriers to the free flow of labor), we have a process of "globalization" analogous to the earlier processes in which national economies were formed. Unfortunately, we have no world government, accountable to the people of every country, to oversee the globalization process in a fashion comparable to the way national governments guided the nationalization process. Instead, we have a system that might be called *global governance without global government,* one in which a few institutions—the World Bank, the IMF, the WTO—and a few players—the finance, commerce, and trade ministries, closely linked to certain financial and commercial interests—dominate the scene, but in which many of those affected by their decisions are left almost voiceless. It's time to change some of the rules governing the international economic order, to think once again about how decisions get made at the international level—and in whose interests—and to place less emphasis on ideology and to look more at what works. It is crucial that the successful development we have seen in East Asia be achieved elsewhere. There is an enormous cost to continuing global instability. Globalization can be reshaped, and when it is, when it is properly, fairly run, with all countries having a voice in policies affecting them, there is a possibility that it will help create a new global economy in which growth is not only more sustainable and less volatile but the fruits of this growth are more equitably shared.

Notes

Joseph Stiglitz, "The Promise of Global Institutions." In *Globalization and Its Discontents* (New York: W. W. Norton, 2003): 3–22. Used by permission of W. W. Norton & Company, Inc.

Allusions to chapters within this piece refer to the original book from which this chapter was taken.

1. J. Chirac, "The Economy Must Be Made to Serve People," address at the International Labour Conference, June 1996.

2. In 1990, 2.718 billion people were living on less than $2 a day. In 1998, the number of poor people living on less than $2 a day is estimated as 2.801 billion—World Bank, *Global Economic Prospects and the Developing Countries 2000* (Washington, DC: World Bank, 2000), p. 29. For additional data, see *World Development Report* and *World Economic Indicators,* annual publications of the World Bank. Health data can be found in UNAIDS/WHO, *Report on the HIV/AIDS Epidemic 1998.* While there has been some controversy concerning these numbers, there is little disputing three facts: there has been little progress eliminating poverty; most of the progress has been made in Asia, and especially China; and in much of the rest of the world the plight of the poor has worsened. In Sub-Saharan Africa, 46 percent of the population lives in absolute poverty (on less than a dollar a day), and in Latin America and the former Soviet Union the percentage of the population in poverty (on this very stringent definition) is 16 percent and 15 percent, respectively.

3. This eighth agreement was the result of negotiations called the *Uruguay Round* because the negotiations began in 1986 in Punta del Este, Uruguay. The round was concluded in Marrakech on December 15, 1993, when 117 countries joined in this trade liberalization agreement. The agreement was finally signed for the United States by President Clinton on December 8, 1994. The World Trade Organization came into formal effect on January 1, 1995, and over 100 nations had signed on by July. One provision of the agreement entailed converting the GATT into the WTO.

4. These are the United States, Japan, Germany, Canada, Italy, France, and the UK. Today, the G-7 typically meets together with Russia (the G-8). The seven countries are no longer the seven largest economies in the world. Membership in the G-7, like permanent membership in the UN Security Council, is partly a matter of historical accident.

5. See Gerard Caprio, Jr., et al., eds., *Preventing Bank Crises: Lessons from Recent Global Bank Failures. Proceedings of a Conference Co-sponsored by the Federal Reserve Bank of Chicago and the Economic Development Institute of the World Bank.* EDI Development Studies (Washington, DC: World Bank, 1998).

6. While there have been a host of critiques of the structural adjustment program, even the IMF's review of the program noted its many faults. This review includes three parts: internal review by the IMF staff (IMF Staff, *The ESAF at Ten Years: Economic Adjustment and Reform in Low-Income Countries.* Occasional Papers #156, February 12, 1998); external review by an independent reviewer (K. Bothway, et al., *Report by a Group of Independent Experts Review: External Evaluation of the ESAF* [Washington DC: IMF, 1998]); and a report from IMF staff to the Board of Directors of the IMF, distilling the lessons from the two reviews (IMF Staff, *Distilling the Lessons from the ESAF Reviews* [Washington, DC: IMF, July 1998]).

CHAPTER 11
FIVE MEANINGS OF GLOBAL CIVIL SOCIETY

Mary Kaldor

The terms 'global' and 'civil society' became the new buzzwords of the 1990s. In this book, I want to suggest that the two terms are interconnected and reflect a new reality, however imperfectly understood. The reinvention of 'civil society' in the 1970s and 1980s, simultaneously in Latin America and Eastern Europe, had something to do with the global context—the social, political and economic transformations that were taking place in different parts of the world and that came to the surface after 1989. Indeed, although the term 'civil society' has a long history and its contemporary meanings draw on that history, the various ways in which it is used, I shall argue, are quite different from in the past.

What is new about the concept of civil society since 1989 is globalization. Civil society is no longer confined to the borders of the territorial state. There was always a common core of meaning in the civil society literature, which still has relevance. Civil society was associated with a rule-governed society based largely on the consent of individual citizens rather than coercion. Different definitions of civil society have reflected the different ways in which consent was generated, manufactured, nurtured or purchased, the different rights and obligations that formed the basis of consent, and the different interpretations of this process. However, the fact that civil society was territorially bound meant that it was always contrasted with coercive rule-governed societies and with societies that lacked rules. In particular, as I shall argue, civil society within the territorial boundaries of the state was circumscribed by war.

This is what has changed. The end of the Cold War and growing global interconnectedness have undermined the territorial distinction between 'civil' and 'uncivil' societies, between the 'democratic' West and the 'non-democratic' East and South, and have called into question the traditional centralized war-making state. And these developments, in turn, have opened up new possibilities for political emancipation as well as new risks and greater insecurity. Whether we are talking about isolated dissidents in repressive regimes, landless labourers in Central America or Asia, global campaigns against land mines or third world debt, or even religious fundamentalists and fanatic nationalists, what has changed are the opportunities for linking up with other like-minded groups in different parts of the world, and for addressing demands not just to the state but to global institutions and other states. On the one hand, global civil society is in the process of helping to constitute and being constituted by a global system of rules, underpinned by overlapping inter-governmental, governmental and global authorities. In other words, a new form of politics, which we call civil society, is both an outcome and an agent of global interconnectedness. And on the other hand, new forms of violence, which restrict, suppress and assault civil society, also spill over borders so that it is no longer possible to contain war or lawlessness territoriality.

In the aftermath of the revolutions of 1989, the term 'civil society' was taken up in widely different circles and circumstances. Yet there is no agreed definition of the term. Indeed its ambiguity is one of its attractions. The fact that neoliberals, Islamicists, or post-Marxists use the same language provides a common platform through which ideas, projects and policy proposals can be worked out. The debate about its meaning is part of what it is about. As John Keane suggests, the global spread of the term and the discussion about what it betokens is, in itself, a signal of an emerging global civil society.[1]

This global discussion has involved the resurrection of a body of civil society literature. The search for classic texts has provided what might be called a legitimizing narrative, which has had the advantage of conferring respectability on the term but has also often weakened our understanding of the novel aspects of the discovery of the term. By clothing the concept in historical garb, it is possible that the past has imposed a kind of straitjacket which obscures or even confines the more radical contemporary implications. Comaroff and Comaroff talk about the 'archaeology' of civil society 'usually told, layer upon layer, as a chronological epic of ideas and authors' starting with an 'origin story' in the late 1700s. They argue that the term has become a 'neo-modern myth: consider the extent to which a diverse body of works—some of them analytic, some pragmatic and prescriptive, some purely philosophical—have begun to tell about the genesis and genealogy of the concept, even as they argue over its interpretation, its telos, its theoretical and socio-moral virtues'.[2]

The 'neo-modern myth' does obscure the implications of the break with territorially bound civil society. On the other hand, agreement about the history of the concept is part of what provides a common basis for a global conversation. The civil society literature is so diverse that it allows for selectivity; the choice of texts to be studied can be used to justify one interpretation rather than another. While the debate about earlier literature can reify particular meanings that are no longer applicable, it can also serve as a way of investigating the idea, exploring the answers to questions which were faced in earlier periods as well as today, finding out what questions were different and how they were distinguished from the present situation.

This is a book then about a political idea. It is an idea that expresses a real phenomenon, even if the boundaries of the phenomenon vary according to different definitions, and even if the shape and direction of the phenomenon are constantly changing. The investigation of these different definitions, the study of past debates as well as the actions and arguments of the present, are a way of directly influencing the phenomenon, of contributing to a changing reality, if possible for the better.

This book is subtitled an 'answer to war'. This is because the concept of civil society has always been linked to the notion of minimizing violence in social relations, to the public use of reason as a way of managing human affairs in place of submission based on fear and insecurity, or ideology and superstition. The word 'answer' does not imply that global civil society is some sort of magic formula—a solution or alternative to war. Rather it is a way of addressing the problem of war, of debating, arguing about, discussing and pressing for possible solutions or alternatives.

I will start by briefly recapitulating the context in which the term was 're-invented'. I will then set out five different meanings of global civil society, two historical and three contemporary. And in the last section, I will outline my plan for the book, how I will investigate these different meanings and their implications for our understanding of the changing political world.

Context

Developments variously known as globalization, post-industrialism and information society came to the surface in the aftermath of the end of the Cold War. Two aspects of these developments are of particular significance in providing a context for the evolution of the concept of global civil society.

First of all, concern about personal autonomy, self-organization, private space became salient not only in Eastern Europe as a way of getting around the totalitarian militaristic state but also in other parts of the world where the paternalism and rigidity of the state in the post-war period were called into question. In the United States and Western Europe, these concerns had already surfaced in the 1960s and 1970s, with the emergence of movements concerned about civil rights, feminism or the environment. Giddens and Beck emphasize the growing importance of these concerns in societies which are increasingly complex, vulnerable to manufactured risk, and where expert systems no longer hold unquestioned sway.[3] The rediscovery of the term 'civil society' in Eastern Europe in the 1980s, therefore, had a resonance in other parts of the world. The term 'civil society' and related terms such as 'anti-politics' or 'power of the powerless' seemed to offer a discourse within which to frame parallel concerns about the ability to control the circumstances in which individuals live, about substantive empowerment of citizens. Indeed, East European thinkers like Václav Havel believed their ideas were not only applicable to Eastern Europe; they were a response to what Havel called the 'global technological civilization'.[4] While Western elites seized upon the language as evidence for the victory of actually existing democracies, the inheritors of the so-called new social movements began to use the term to express a demand for a radical extension of democracy for political as well as economic emancipation.[5]

Even though these ideas had echoes of the eighteenth-century preoccupation with restraints on state power, it seems to me that they were responses to an entirely novel situation. It was a situation characterized by the actual experience of an overbearing state, which reached into everyday life far more widely than ever before. In the case of Eastern Europe, it was experience of arbitrary power and the extension of state activity into every sphere of social life, even, at least during the Stalinist period, private life. Elsewhere, it was both the extension of state power and the rigidity and lack of responsiveness to social, economic and cultural change. As I shall argue, the character of the state has to be understood in terms of the heritage of war and Cold War. It was also a time of social, economic, technological and cultural transformations in life styles, ranging from work (greater insecurity, greater flexibility and greater inequality) to gender and family relations, which called into question institutional loyalties and assumptions about collective or traditional behaviour.

Secondly, growing interconnectedness and the end of the last great global inter-state conflict have eroded the boundaries of civil society. It was growing interconnectedness that allowed the emergence of 'islands of civic engagement' in Eastern Europe and in those Latin American countries suffering from military dictatorships. The activists of that period were able to seek international allies both at governmental and non-governmental levels and pierce through the closed societies in which they lived, even before the great advances in information and communications technology. On the one hand, the extension of transnational legal arrangements from above, for example the Helsinki Agreement of 1975, provided an instrument for opening up autonomous spaces in Eastern Europe and elsewhere. On the other hand, the inheritors of the 'new' social movements, the European peace movements and the North American human rights movements were able to link up with groups and individuals in Eastern Europe and Latin America to provide some kind of support and protection. Keck and Sikkink use the term the 'boomerang effect' to describe the way civil society groups by-passed the state and appealed to transnational networks and institutions as well as foreign governments, so that their demands bounced back, as it were, on their own situation.[6] In effect, these movements and their successors made use of and contributed to global political and legal arrangements; they were an essential part of the process of constructing a framework for global governance.

The end of the Cold War has contributed to the breakdown of the sharp distinction between internal and external, what is often called in the International Relations literature the Great Divide.[7] Some argue that something like a global civil society (however this is defined) exists in the North Atlantic region but not elsewhere.[8] Hence the boundaries of civil society have merely moved outwards. This could perhaps have been said to be true during the Cold War where the boundaries of the West were pushed outwards to protect a North Atlantic group of nations. But, in the aftermath of the Cold War, I would suggest that something different is happening. It is no longer possible to insulate territory from anarchy and disorder. In place of vertical territorial-based forms of civil society, we are witnessing the emergence of horizontal transnational global networks, both civil and uncivil. What one might call zones of civility and zones of incivility exist side by side in the same territorial space; North Atlantic space may have more extensive zones of civility than other parts of the world but such sharp geographic distinctions can no longer be drawn. The events of September 11 were a traumatic expression of the fact that territorial borders no longer define the zones of civility. In other words, the territorial restructuring of social, economic and political relations has profound implications for how we think about civil society.[9]

To sum up, I want to suggest that the discussion about global civil society has to be understood in terms of what one might call deepening and widening, a move away from state-centred approaches, combining more concern with individual empowerment and person autonomy, as well as a territorial restructuring of social and political relations in different realms.

Definitions of Global Civil Society

I propose to set out five different versions of the concept of civil society in common usage and to say something about what they imply in a global context. This is a non-exhaustive and abbreviated (but not altogether arbitrary) list. As I try to show in chapter 2, the civil society literature is much richer and more complex than this summary would suggest; the aim is to set up some parameters for the rest of the book.

The first two versions are drawn from past versions of the concept; the last three are contemporary versions, with echoes of historical usage. It is not straightforward to transpose the concept of civil society into the concept of global civil society, since, as I have argued, the key to understanding what is new about contemporary meanings is precisely their global character. Yet the exercise may be illuminating since I do believe that there is a common core of meaning and we can investigate the nature of the contemporary phenomenon by trying to understand the relevance of past meanings.

Societas Civilis

Here I am referring to what could be described as the original version of the term—civil society as a rule of law and a political community, a peaceful order based on implicit or explicit consent of individuals, a zone of 'civility'. Civility is defined not just as 'good manners' or 'polite society' but as a state of affairs where violence has been minimized as a way of organizing social relations. It is public security that creates the basis for more 'civil' procedures for settling conflicts—legal arrangements, for example, or public deliberation. Most later definitions of civil society are predicated on the assumption of a rule of law and the relative absence of coercion in human affairs at least within the boundaries of the state. Thus, it is assumed that such a *societas civilis* requires a state, with a public monopoly of legitimate violence. According to this definition, the meaning of civil society cannot be separated from the existence of a state. Civil society is distinguished not from the state but from non-civil societies—the state of nature or absolutist empires—and from war.

One of the main objections to the notion of global civil society is the absence of a world state.[10] However, it can be argued that the coming together of humanitarian and human rights law, the establishment of an international criminal court, the expansion of international peacekeeping, betoken an emerging framework of global governance, what Immanuel Kant described as a universal civil society, in the sense of a cosmopolitan rule of law, guaranteed by a combination of international treaties and institutions.

Bourgeois Society (Bürgerliche Gesellschaft)

For Hegel and Marx, civil society was that arena of ethical life in between the state and the family. It was a historically produced phenomenon linked to the emergence of capitalism. They drew on the insights of the Scottish enlightenment, especially Adam Smith and Adam Ferguson, who argued that the advent of commercial society created the individuals who were the necessary condition for civil society. Markets, social classes, civil law and welfare organizations were all part of civil society. Civil society was, for the first time, contrasted with the state. For Hegel, civil society was the 'achievement of the modern age'. And for Marx, civil society was the 'theatre of history'.

Transposed to a global level, civil society could be more or less equated with 'globalization from below'—all those aspects of global developments below and beyond the state and international political institutions, including transnational corporations, foreign investment, migration, global culture, etc. [11]

The Activist Version

The activist perspective is probably closest to the version of civil society that emerged from the opposition in Central Europe in the 1970s and 1980s. It is sometimes described as the post-Marxist or utopian version of the concept. It is a definition that presupposes a state or rule of law, but insists not only on restraints on state power but on a redistribution of power. It is a radicalization of democracy and an extension of participation and autonomy. On this definition, civil society refers to active citizenship, to growing self-organization outside formal political circles, and expanded space in which individual citizens can influence the conditions in which they live both directly through self-organization and through political pressure.

What is important, according to this definition, at a transnational level is the existence of a global public sphere—a global space where non-instrumental communication can take place, inhabited by transnational advocacy networks like Greenpeace or Amnesty International, global social movements like the protestors in Seattle, Prague and Genoa, international media through which their campaigns can be brought to global attention, new global 'civic religions' like human rights or environmentalism.

The Neoliberal Version

In the aftermath of 1989, neoliberals claimed their victory and began to popularize the term 'civil society' as what the West has, or even what the United States has. This version might be described as 'laissez-faire politics', a kind of market in politics. According to this definition, civil society consists of associational life—a non-profit, voluntary 'third sector'—that not only restrains state power but also actually provides a substitute for many of the functions performed by the state. Thus charities and voluntary associations carry out functions in the field of welfare which the state can no longer afford to perform. This definition is perhaps the easiest to transpose to the global arena; it is viewed as the political or social counterpart of the process of globalization understood as economic globalization, liberalization, privatization, deregulation and the growing mobility of capital and goods. In the absence of a global state, an army of NGOs (non-governmental organizations) perform the functions necessary to smooth the path of economic globalization. Humanitarian NGOs provide the safety net to deal with the casualties of liberalization and privatization strategies in the economic field. Funding for democracy-building and human rights NGOs is somehow supposed to help establish a rule of law and respect for human rights. Thus critics have charged that the term is reactionary, a way of evading the responsibilities of states for welfare or security.[12]

The Postmodern Version

The postmodern definition of civil society departs from the universalism of the activist and neoliberal versions, although even this version requires one universal principle—that of tolerance.[13] Civil society is an arena of pluralism and contestation, a source of incivility as well as civility. Some postmodernists criticize the concept of civil society as Eurocentric, a product of a specific Western culture that is imposed on the rest of the world. Others suggest a reformulation so as to encompass other more communalist understandings of political culture. In particular, it is argued that classic Islamic society represented a form of civil society in the balance between religion, the bazaar and the ruler.

For the activist version, the inhabitants of civil society can be roughly equated with civic-minded or public-spirited groups. Those active in civil society would be those concerned about public affairs and public debate. For the postmodernists, civic-minded groups are only one component of civil society. In particular, postmodernists emphasize the importance of national and religious identities as well as multiple identities as a precondition for civil society, whereas for the activists, a shared cosmopolitanism is more important. Whether or not groups advocating violence should be included is open to question.

From this perspective, it is possible to talk about global civil society in the sense of the global spread of fields of contestation. Indeed, one might talk about a plurality of global civil societies through different globally organized networks. These might include Islam, nationalist Diaspora networks, as well as human rights networks, etc.

These five versions are summarized in table 11.1. My own understanding of global civil society, which I shall explore in this book, incorporates much of these different meanings. I do believe that both the first two versions, a rule of law and a market society, or at least the aspiration for a rule of law and for economic autonomy, are constituted and constituted by what we now tend to mean by civil society; for civil society to exist there has to be a relationship with markets, which secure economic autonomy, and the rule of law, which provides security. I also think that the various actors that inhabit contemporary versions of civil society are all part of global civil society—the social movements and the civic networks of the activist version; the charities, voluntary associations and what I shall call the 'tamed' NGOs of the neoliberal version; and the nationalist and fundamentalist groups that are included in the postmodern version.

In terms of normative considerations, however, I am closest to the activist version. All versions of civil society are both normative and descriptive. They describe a political project i.e., a goal, and at the same time an actually existing

Table 11.1 The Five Versions of Civil Society

Type of Society	Territorially Bounded	Global
Societas civilis	Rule of law/Civility	Cosmopolitan order
Bürgerliche Gesellschaft	All organized social life between the state and the family	Economic, social and cultural globalization
Activist	Social movements, civic activists	A global public sphere
Neoliberal	Charities, voluntary associations, third sector	Privatization of democracy building, humanitarianism
Postmodern	Nationalists, fundamentalists as well as above	Plurality of global networks of contestation

reality, which may not measure up to the goal. *Societas civilis* expressed the goal of public security, of a civilized, i.e., non-violent, society. *Bürgerliche Gesellschaft* was about the rise of market society as a condition for individual freedom, and the balance between the state and the market. For Hegel, this was the *telos* (end goal) of history; for Marx, civil society was merely a stage towards the *telos* of communism.

The contemporary versions of civil society all have normative goals, which can only be fully explained in the context of globalization. The neoliberal version is about the benefits of Western, especially American, society; thus the goal is the spread of this type of society to the rest of the world. Globalization, the spread of global capitalism, is viewed as a positive development, the vehicle, supplemented by global civil society, for achieving global Westernization or 'the end of history'.

The postmodern version has to be related to the break with modernity of which a key component was the nation-state. Even though the postmodernists are anti-teleological, they would see the contestation that is currently taking place on a global scale as a way of breaking with grand narratives, teleological political projects that were associated with states. The rise of the Internet allows for a riot of virtuality and for a denial of the existence of something called the real.

The activist version is about political emancipation. It is about the empowerment of individuals and the extension of democracy. I will argue that war and the threat of war always represented a limitation on democracy. Globalization offers the possibility of overcoming that limitation and, at the same time, the global extension of democracy has become, as a consequence of globalization, the necessary condition for political emancipation. For activists, globalization is not an unqualified benefit. It offers possibilities for emancipation on a global scale. But in practice, it involves growing inequality and insecurity and new forms of violence. Global civil society, for the activists, therefore, is about 'civilizing' or democratizing globalization, about the process through which groups, movements and individuals can demand a global rule of law, global justice and global empowerment. Global civil society does, of course, in my own version, include those who are opposed to globalization and those who do not see the need for regulation. Thus my version of global civil society is based on the belief that a genuinely free conversation, a rational critical dialogue, will favour the 'civilizing' option.

Notes

Mary Kaldor, "Five Meanings of Global Civil Society" (2003). In *Global Civil Society: An Answer to War* (Cambridge, UK: Polity Press, 2003): 1–12. Used by permission of Polity Press Ltd.

Allusions to chapters within this piece refer to the original book from which this chapter was taken.

1. John Keane, *Civil Society: Old Images, New Visions* (Polity, Cambridge, 1998).

2. John L. Comaroff and Jean Comaroff (eds.), *Civil Society and the Political Imagination in Africa: Critical Perspectives* (University of Chicago Press, Chicago, 1999), p. 4.

3. Anthony Giddens, *Runaway World: How Globalisation Is Reshaping Our Lives* (Profile, London, 1999); and Ulrich Beck, *World Risk Society* (Polity, Cambridge, 1999).

4. Václav Havel, "The Power of the Powerless" in John Keane (ed.), *The Power of the Powerless: Citizens against the State in Central-Eastern Europe* (Hutchinson, London, 1985).

5. Jean Cohen and Andrew Arato, *Civil Society and Political Theory* (Verso, London, 1992).

6. Margaret Keck and Kathryn Sikkink, *Activists Beyond Borders: Advocacy Networks in International Politics* (Cornell University Press, Ithaca, NY, 1998).

7. See Ian Clark, *Globalisation and International Relations Theory* (Oxford University Press, Oxford, 1999).

8. Chris Brown, "Cosmopolitanism, World Citizenship and Global Civil Society," *Critical Review of International Social and Political Philosophy*, 3 (2000).

9. Saskia Sassen, *Globalisation and Its Discontents* (New Press, New York, 1998).

10. Brown, "Cosmopolitanism"; David Rieff, "The False Dawn of Civil Society," *Nation*, 22 Feb. 1999.

11. This version of global civil society is exemplified in John Keane's essay "Global Civil Society?" in Helmut Anheier, Marlies Glasius and Mary Kaldor (eds.), *Global Civil Society 2001* (Oxford University Press, Oxford, 2001). The term 'globalization from below' is sometimes used in a narrow sense to refer to global social movements, NGOs and networks. See Mario Piantia, *Globalizzazione dal Bass: Economia Mondiale e Movimenti Sociali* (Manifestolibri, Rome, 2001).

12. Rieff, "The False Dawn."

13. Keane, "Global Civil Society?"

CHAPTER 12
AL QAEDA AND THE NEW TERRORISTS[1]

Olivier Roy

Al Qaeda is an organisation and a trademark. It can operate directly, in a joint venture, or by franchising. It embodies, but does not have the monopoly of, a new kind of violence. Many groups (such as the Kelkal network in France) are acting along the same lines without necessarily having a direct connection with Al Qaeda. In the pages below we shall concentrate on Al Qaeda but also mention other groups and actors, focusing more on new patterns of Islam-related violence than on Al Qaeda itself.

The strength of Al Qaeda is that it is made up of veterans of the Afghan wars, who know each other and have developed an *esprit de corps* in the Afghan 'trenches' (*sangar*) or training camps. This comrade-based solidarity between people from different countries has been translated into a flexible and mobile international organisation where the chain of command duplicates personal ties. The weaknesses of Al Qaeda are, first, that it needs a sanctuary to create such a spirit of brotherhood and, second, that the uprootedness of these militants makes it difficult for them to establish a social and political basis among Muslim populations in areas where they do not benefit from the support of some sort of indigenous subcontractors.

The First Wave: From Abdullah Azzam to Al Qaeda

The forerunner of Al Qaeda was the Office of Services (Maktab al-Khidamat, also called Bayt al-Ansar, or House of Auxiliaries) established in the early 1980s in Peshawar by Abdullah Azzam, a Palestinian Muslim Brother with a Jordanian passport (a refugee of 1967), who broke with the PLO in protest against its nationalist and secular stand. Azzam (correctly) understood that nationalism was superseding the religious dimension in the Palestinian *jihad* as in all Islamist movements in the Middle East. He concluded that the only legitimate *jihad* was for the sake of the entire *ummah* and picked the Afghan resistance against the Soviet invasion as the exemplary model. Azzam was not an ideologue or a theologian. He was an activist whose thinking revolved entirely around the concepts of *jihad* and *ummah*. Nor was he a Salafi or a Wahhabi. He used to quote all the classical schools of law and to debate using the traditional concepts of the classical *fiqh*. When extolling *jihad*, Azzam held an intermediary position between the classical view that *jihad* is only a collective duty and is not a pillar of Islam, and the view of the modern jihadists, for whom it is both a pillar of the faith and a personal duty.[2] In this sense he was not a neofundamentalist and requested (vainly) that the volunteers going into Afghanistan not meddle with Afghan religious customs.

Did Azzam have a coherent long-term strategic view when sending young Muslim volunteers into Afghanistan? Not necessarily. Of course the ultimate goal of *jihad* is to provide the *ummah* with a secure territory. But Afghanistan was seen by Azzam less as a frontier that had to be defended than as a training ground to breed the vanguard that would spark an overall resistance against the encroachments of the infidels on the *ummah*. The first virtue of *jihad* is to magnify the faith and commitment of believers, whatever its real success on the ground. *Jihad* is a religious duty first: 'Jihad is the most excellent form of worship, and by means of it the Muslim can reach the highest of ranks.'[3] *Jihad* in Afghanistan was aimed at setting up the vanguard of the *ummah*, not at creating an Islamic state there. Nor did Azzam favour supporting a given Afghan faction; he seldom interfered in *mujahedin* politics and earned great respect among the Afghan fighters. He eschewed terrorist attacks (including targeting civilians) and restrained his activities to the Afghan battlefield, avoiding strikes on Soviet interests outside Afghanistan.

The shift to the Al Qaeda of the 1990s was done under Bin Laden's supervision after Abdullah Azzam died in a mysterious car bombing in Peshawar in

November 1989. His death, which is still shrouded in mystery, was beneficial to Bin Laden, who took charge of what remained of the organisation, sidelining the would-be heir of Azzam, his son-in law, Abdullah Anas.[4] The transfer of power was undertaken with the obvious blessing of the Pakistani and Saudi sponsors, who maintained their support for Bin Laden till 1998 in the case of the Saudis, and 9/11 in that of the Pakistanis. The United States ceased even to monitor closely the chain of events after February 1989, and woke up belatedly in August 1998—ten years of neglect that would prove very costly.

To enhance their legitimacy and belittle the role of Abdullah Azzam, Bin Laden's disciples developed a kind of 'foundation myth': the battle of Masada, or 'the Lion's Den' (a camp near Jaji that was besieged by Soviet troops in June 1987, during the sacred month of Ramadan). According to the legend, Bin Laden and a handful of fighters succeeded in breaking the siege. Many of the founding fathers of Al Qaeda participated in the battle (such as Enaam Arnaut, a Syrian-born US citizen; Ayman al-Zawahiri; Abu Zubair al-Madani, who was killed in Bosnia in 1992; and the Saudi Abu Abdurrahman, or Hassan as-Sarehi).

Tens of thousands of militants went to Afghanistan through the Islamic networks for training and *jihad*. They were called 'Arabs' by the Afghans and 'Afghans' by their compatriots after they had returned to their country of origin. The three prominent nationalities among the 'Afghans' (if we exclude the Pakistanis who were not under Bin Laden's control) were the Saudis, the Egyptians and the Algerians. If we consider the ratio of militants to population, the Saudis are clearly overrepresented in Al Qaeda's ranks.[5]

Interestingly there were almost no Syrians, no 'actual' Palestinians (that is, those living in West Bank or Gaza; the Palestinians in Al Qaeda all came from refugee families), no Iraqi Arabs (Iraqi 'Afghans' were all Kurds) and very few Turks. It is also important to note that there were no 'real' Afghans among the 'Afghans', and no Iranians at all. Al Qaeda did not circumvent the Sunni/Shia divide. Many of the volunteers were killed in action. Some stayed in Afghanistan or Pakistan after the Soviet withdrawal in 1989, while others returned to their own country and helped to establish more radical splinter groups from the mainstream Islamist movements.

In Algeria many 'Afghans' were among the founders of the FIS—Said Mekhloufi, Kamar Eddine Kherbane and Abdullah Anas, for example. The 'Afghans' were even more numerous in the radical GIA, of which all the first wave of leaders had returned from Afghanistan: Tayyeb el Afghani (killed in 1992), Jaffar el Afghani (killed in 1994) and Sherif Gusmi (killed in 1994). The founders of the FIS had been with Commander Massoud and the GIA's founders with Gulbuddin Hekmatyar. In Yemen, Sheikh Tariq al-Fadli founded an Islamic Jihad organisation, while Zayn al-Abidin Abu Bakr al-Mihdar created the Aden-Abyan

Islamic Army. In Jordan, Khalil al-Deek established the Army of Muhammad, while in Libya, Abu Shartila, alias Abu Tariq Darnaw, heads the Mohammed al Hami battalion. In the Philippines, Abubakar Janjalani (killed in 1997) launched the Abu Sayyaf Group (named after an Afghanistan veteran killed in action). Abu Hamza al-Masri (the Egyptian Mustafa Kamel) lost one eye and a hand in Afghanistan and ended up as a radical *imam* in London, where he founded the Supporters of Sharia. Ibn ul-Khattab, one of the youngest volunteers for Afghanistan, joined the Chechen resistance, where he played an important role in triggering the second war in August 1999. He was reportedly assassinated by a Russian secret service poisoned letter in 2003.

Less often the Afghanistan veterans came from existing organisations and gave them a more radical twist when they returned to their home countries, as did Riduan Isamuddin (also known as Hambali), who joined Jemaah Islamiah in Indonesia. From Egypt, Muhammad al-Islambuli, brother of the murderer of Sadat, went to Afghanistan, as did Sheikh Omar Abdurrahman (sentenced in the United States for the first attempt on the World Trade Center) and his sons. The Saudi Hassan as-Sarehi was charged in Saudi Arabia with the 1995 attacks on the National Guard barracks (he denied any involvement). Leaders of the Egyptian Gama'at Islamiya, Fuad Qassim, Mustafa Hamza and Ahmed Taha, are also 'Afghans', as is Ayman al-Zawahiri, leader of Egyptian Islamic Jihad, who cosigned Bin Laden's communiqués in early 1998. Mehat Muhammad Abdel Rahman, suspected of being the leader of the group responsible for the massacre of European tourists in Luxor in September 1997, was also an 'Afghan'. Nevertheless, all the Egyptian 'Afghans', while still claiming to belong to the Gama'at and Islamic Jihad, developed a more radical line, which ended in a split with the parent organisations after 9/11.

The 'Afghans' make up the majority of the Harakat ul-Ansar movement presently fighting in Kashmir, and whose training camps were bombed on 21 August 1998 by US missiles in the Afghan province of Khost, in retaliation for the bombing of the US embassies in East Africa. Sipah-e-Sahaba also sent many of its members for training in Afghanistan (which provided a training group for many Pakistani activists). Spending time in Afghanistan was a kind of rite of passage for young Pakistani students of religion; it was even added to the curriculum by some *madrasas* (such as Haqqaniyya at Akora Khattak in 2001).

Other former 'Afghans' played a role as individuals, not as members or founders of organisations, as did, for example, Abu Messaab (a Syrian), a former writer for the London-based GIA journal *Al Ansar*. Others moved with alacrity into building an international terrorist network, like the cell that perpetrated the first bombing of the World Trade Center in February 1993. Ramzi Ahmed Yousef, Muhammad Salameh, Ahmed Ajjaj and Wadih el-Hage (convicted for the bombing of the US embassy in Nairobi, Kenya) also spent some time in Afghanistan. Others returned to the country in which they were living and started to recruit new members (for example, in France, among second-generation Muslims).

Finally a hard core of veterans remained closely connected with Bin Laden, following him in his peregrinations from Saudi Arabia and Somalia to Yemen and Sudan: Muhammad Atef, alias Abdulaziz Abu Sitta, alias Abu Hafs al-Misri, a former Egyptian police officer (who would become the father-in-law of Bin Laden's son); Sulaiman Abu Ghaith, Bin Laden's spokesman; and Ay-man al-Zawahiri. In any case, many 'Afghans' remained in touch with one another, wherever they went. Such personal connections could at any time be reactivated, or new recruits could be sent to Afghanistan, under the patronage of veterans. Moreover, the volunteers in Afghanistan experienced a concrete internationalisation based on personal contacts, the brotherhoods of comrades in arms, friendships and affinities. They learned to know other people and other languages, and travelled elsewhere to meet their former comrades, as did Ramzi Ahmed Yousef when he travelled to the Philippines. Converts found in Afghanistan a new community and brotherhood with which to identify, as John Walker Lindh stated when he was captured in Kunduz.

But between 1989 and 1996, no individual organised or directed the Arab militants in Afghanistan. Some Islamic NGOs (such as the International Islamic Relief Organisation, or IIRO) had their own centres (in Kunduz, for instance); some local *mujahedin* commanders kept their 'Arabs' with them and received direct support from the Gulf or Pakistan (like commanders Mullah Afzal in Nuristan and Jamil ur-Rahman in the Pech Valley). When the Taliban took Kabul in September 1996, they were quite upset to see the mess in Afghanistan and were happy to hand the monopoly of organising the Arab volunteers to Bin Laden, who, after travelling successively in Yemen and Sudan, had been expelled from Sudan in May 1996 to Jalalabad, in Afghanistan (and was a guest of Haji Qadir, the brother of Abdul Haqq, who would become a key ally of the United States in 2001).[6] It seems the Pakistanis introduced Bin Laden to Mullah Omar. The label 'Arab' was applied to all foreigners who were not Pakistani or Central Asian. These last two groups had their own organisations (such as the Islamic Movement of Uzbekistan, and the many Pakistani groups, including Sipah-e-Sahaba, Harkat-ul-Mujahidin, Lashkar-e-Toiba, and so on). Bin Laden, with the help of al-Zawahiri, reorganised the volunteers, and put them into training camps (Darunta and Khalden) and residential compounds for cadres (and their families). As a result, any Islamic volunteers (except Pakistanis or Central Asians) who went to Afghanistan between 1997 and 2001 were necessarily enlisted by Al Qaeda.

The volunteers were cut off from Afghan society and organised into two categories: an infantry battalion that fought alongside the Taliban against the Northern Alliance, and more gifted Western Muslims were trained to go return to Europe and the United States to perpetrate terrorism. While the initial action of Al Qaeda was the first bombing of the World Trade Center in 1993, it was only in 1998 that it became well known in the West when the creation of the 'World Islamic Front for the Struggle against Jews and Crusaders' was announced, followed by the bombings of US embassies in East Africa.

Al Qaeda's first-generation members shared common traits: all came from a Muslim country and had a previous record of political activism; almost all went directly from the Middle East to Afghanistan. They had little experience of the West, and had a traditional way of life (traditional marriages, and their women kept at home).

From the early 1990s a new breed of militants slowly emerged. The change was embodied by two leading figures who participated in anti-US terrorist attacks, namely the first World Trade Center bombing in February 1993, and the attack on the US embassy in Kenya in August 1998. Ramzi Ahmed Yousef was born in 1968 in Kuwait, of a Pakistani father (from Baluchistan) and a Palestinian mother. He did not identify with a given country (although he used to call himself a Pakistani). His name (an alias) means 'secret'; it is almost a choice of identity. He was educated at a vocational training school in Wales between 1986 and 1989 under the name Adul Basit Mahmoud Kareem, graduated in electronic engineering, and then went in 1990 to Afghanistan to wage *jihad*. There he met the brother of the founder of the Philippine Abu Sayyaf Group (Janjalani), who invited him to his country. Yousef left for Baghdad, acquired an Iraqi passport, returned to Peshawar, met Ahmed Ajjaj (a Palestinian refugee in the United States), and settled in New Jersey. He left the very day of the first attack against the World Trade Center, stayed in Karachi with an extremist Pakistani anti-Shiite group, the Sipah-e-Sahaba, then returned to the Philippines, where he was involved in a plot to hijack aeroplanes and kill the Pope. Finally he was arraigned in Karachi and extradited to the United States.[7] The second example is Mohamed Saddiq Odeh (Awadh or Howeyda), a Jordanian citizen, born in Saudi Arabia of a Palestinian family. He received a degree in architecture in the Philippines in 1990, was trained in Afghanistan in the same year, and went to Somalia in 1992 to join the Sheikh Hassan radical Islamic group. Odeh married a Kenyan wife, acquired a Yemeni passport, settled in Kenya and was involved in the bombing of the US embassy there in 1998.

This new breed was above all largely uprooted and more westernised than its predecessors, had few links (if any) to any particular Muslim country, and moved around the world, travelling from *jihad* to *jihad*. The flying *jihadi* was born, the *jihadi* jet set.

The Second Wave: Western Muslims

The second wave of Al Qaeda militants operating internationally was character-ised by the breaking of their ties with the 'real' Muslim world they claimed to represent. If we exclude most of the Saudis and Yemenis, as well as the 'subcon-tractors' (militants from local organisations that act under the Al Qaeda label in their own country), most Al Qaeda militants left their country of origin to fight or study abroad (usually in the West), breaking with their families. They lived separate from society and rarely integrated with a new community, except around some radical mosques. They were cultural outcasts, in their home coun-tries and their host countries. But they were all westernised in some way (again, except for the Saudis and Yemenis); none had attended a *madrasa,* and all were trained in technical or scientific disciplines and spoke a Western language. If we include the logistical networks, some held Western citizenship (the alleged 9/11 conspirator Zacarias Moussaoui was born in France). Most of them (except, again, the Saudis) became born-again Muslims in the West after living 'normal' lives in their countries of origin. The mosques of Hamburg (Al Quds), London (Finsbury Park), Marseilles and even Montreal played a far greater role in their religious radicalisation than any Saudi *madrasa.*

Thus, far from representing a traditional religious community or culture, these militants broke with their past (and some with traditional Islam altogether). They experienced an individual re-Islamisation in a small cell of uprooted fellows, where they forged their own Islam—as vividly illustrated by Muhammad Atta's refusal to be buried according to tradition, which he dubbed un-Islamic.[8] They did not follow any Islamic school or notable cleric, and sometimes lived according to non-Muslim standards. They were all far more products of a westernised Islam than of traditional Middle Eastern politics. However old-fashioned their theology may seem to Westerners, and whatever they may think of themselves, radical Euro-Islamists are clearly more a postmodern phenomenon than a premodern one.

Even if many of these militants come from the Middle East, they are not linked to or used by any Middle Eastern state, intelligence service or radical movement, as had been the case with the militants of the 1980s. With a single, transitional exception,[9] they are part of the deterritorialised, supranational Islamic networks that operate specifically in the West and at the periphery of the Middle East. Their background has nothing to do with Middle Eastern conflicts. Their groups are often mixtures of educated middle-class leaders and working-class dropouts, a pattern common to most West European radicals of the 1970s and 1980s (Germany's Red Army Faction, Italy's Red Brigades, France's Action Directe). Many became 'born-again' Muslims or gaolhouse converts, sharing a common marginal culture.

Roughly there are three main categories: students, who came from Middle Eastern countries to study in the West; second-generation Muslims, who were either born in the West or came as infants; and converts. The students (for example, the World Trade Center pilots) are usually middle or upper class, and all were educated in technical or scientific disciplines. The second-generation Muslims emanate from the working class and disfranchised urban youths. The converts are a more complex category. Most of the individuals who gravitate towards these three categories are 'new Muslims', either born-again or converts.

We will now try to summarise what these new militants have in common, using a sample based on those individuals involved in or indicted for international terrorism since the 1993 World Trade Center attack.[10] International terrorism is taken to mean attacks that are committed outside the homeland of the perpetrators, and are not state-sponsored.

Deterritorialisation

Our militants operate globally, travelling widely, settling in various countries that have little connection with their homelands and learning foreign languages. Zacarias Moussaoui, a French citizen of Moroccan descent, studied in Montpellier, learnt English and settled in London, where he became a born-again Muslim. Muhammad Atta and the other 9/11 pilots came from the Middle East, settled first in Germany, learnt German, and then went to the United States. Djamel Beghal, who was living in the Paris suburb of Corbeil, settled in Leicester, in the English Midlands. Ahmed Ressam left Algeria, where he was born, for Marseilles and later for Corsica (1992–94), before settling in Montreal, where he scraped a living from casual jobs and theft. He became a born-again Muslim at the As Sunnah mosque and went to Afghanistan in 1998. Back in Montreal, he was contacted by a Mauritanian, Mohambedou Ould Slahi, who funded his preparations to attack Los Angeles International Airport in December 1999. Ould Slahi used to live in Duisburg, Germany, where he attended university and launched an import business.

Al Qaeda is an international organisation, even if its centre till 2001 was in Afghanistan. Its local networks were built with the aim of targeting a specific objective and organised around 'hubs', none of which was in a Middle Eastern country. The 9/11 attacks were prepared in Hamburg, Spain and Kuala Lumpur by four students based in Hamburg (an Egyptian, Muhammad Atta; an Emirati, Marwan al-Shehhi; a Yemeni, Ramzi Binalshibh; and a Lebanese, Ziad Jarrah). The members of the Hamburg support cell for 9/11 fitted the same patterns. They met at the Al Quds mosque in Hamburg. London probably served as the main global centre for propaganda and the recruitment of would-be terrorists who were dispatched to Afghanistan.

Relations between militants and their country of origin are weak or non-existent; we are facing not a diaspora but a truly deterritorialised population. Almost none of the militants fought in his own country, or in his family's country of origin (except some Pakistanis). Two cases are especially relevant: those of the Palestinians and the Algerians. One would expect a Western-based born-again Muslim of Algerian or Palestinian origin to be eager to wage *jihad* in his country of origin, both Algeria and Palestine being battlefields. But I do not know of a single instance of such a return from the diaspora. The French Redouane Hammadi and Stephane Ait Idir, of Algerian origin, carried out a terrorist attack in Morocco (1995); Fateh Kamel and Ahmed Ressam (both Algerians) tried to blow up Los Angeles airport. None of the Algerian militants in Al Qaeda came directly from Algeria. Links with Al Qaeda were built up through Algerian immigration, not by way of the GIA's headquarters or other groups within Algeria. Conversely, the campaign of demonstrations in Algeria, from 1999 onwards, has been carried out in the name of democracy, human rights and defence of the Kabyle (Berber) identity, not of *sharia* or an Islamic state.

All of the Palestinians in Al Qaeda (such as Mohamed Odeh and Abu Zubayda) come from refugee families (either from 1948 or 1967). None of them tried to return to Palestinian-Israeli territory. There is a trend among uprooted Islamic Palestinians towards a 'de-Palestinisation' of their identity in favour of the *ummah,* as is obvious in the Palestinian refugee camp of Ain al-Hilweh, in Lebanon, where Salafi groups are on gaining ground, as we saw previously.

The same is true of the Egyptians: how does one explain the discrepancy between the high number of Egyptians in Al Qaeda's leadership and the decrease in religious violence in Egypt? Clearly this time it is the leadership inside Egypt that has cut links with the internationalists.

Some personal trajectories are particularly instructive in highlighting the internationalisation of Islamist militants. Ramzi Ahmed Yousef's life has already been discussed. Mohammed Mansour Jabarah, who was born in Kuwait, went to Canada when he was twelve years old and later became a Canadian citizen. He was allegedly the intermediary between Al Qaeda and Jemaah Islamiah in Indonesia.[11] It is interesting to note that (as was the case with Khalid Sheikh Mohammed and Abu Zubayda, other Al Qaeda Kuwaitis) he never attempted an operation in Kuwait. Amor Sliti, a Tunisian-born Belgian citizen, was a frequent worshipper at the Finsbury Park mosque in London, spent years in Afghanistan with Bin Laden, and helped the murderers of the anti-Taliban commander Massoud to travel to Afghanistan. Sliti married a Belgian woman and gave his very young daughter in marriage to an Afghan *mujahid.*

Wadih el-Hage, a US citizen, has been indicted for helping in the attacks on the East African US embassies in 1998. A Lebanese Christian who converted to Islam, el-Hage also lived for a while in Kuwait and went to the United States in 1978 to study city planning at South-Western Louisiana University. He married an American, fathered seven children, and went off to help the *mujahedin* fight the Soviet Union. Then, in the early 1990s, he worked in Sudan as Bin Laden's secretary. By 1994 el-Hage had moved to Kenya and helped to establish an Al Qaeda cell in Nairobi—the same unit that allegedly plotted the embassy bombing there. El-Hage returned home in 1997 and took a low-level job as manager of the Lone Star Wheels and Tires shop in Fort Worth, Texas. Also indicted in the case was Ali Mohamed, a major in the Egyptian army. He went to the United States in 1986 and continued his military career. He joined the US army and was eventually assigned to the John F. Kennedy Special Warfare Center at Fort Bragg, North Carolina. Within a year of his 1989 discharge, he was training Al Qaeda members in Afghanistan and Sudan and travelling the world for Bin Laden, delivering messages and conducting financial transactions.

Born March 1960 at El-Harrach, in the suburbs of Algiers, Fateh Kamel moved to France, and later settled in Canada in 1987. He took citizenship, married a woman (Nathalie B.) from Gaspé, Quebec, and opened a business in Montreal, importing Cuban cigars. Kamel went to Afghanistan in 1990 and then to Bosnia, where he met members of the Roubaix gang. He was extradited from Jordan to France in April 1999 for allegedly being the *'emir'* of the Roubaix network.

L'Houssaine Kherchtou, born in Morocco in 1964, went to Corsica after graduating from university, settled in Milan where he headed the Islamic cultural centre, and went to Afghanistan in 1991. He was arrested in Kenya for his role in the 1998 attack on the US embassy there.

Beyond these examples, a general rule is that, except for a few Pakistanis and Yemenis, no Al Qaeda member left Europe or the United States to fight for Islam in his homeland or that of his family.[12] As we have seen, none of the Algerians involved in international Al Qaeda terrorism came from a GIA stronghold in Algeria; they all became radicalised in Europe (like Ahmed Ressam). The foreigners sentenced in Yemen in January 1999 for kidnapping included six British citizens of Pakistani descent (including the son-in-law of Abu Hamza, the Egyptian-born former *imam* of the Finsbury Park mosque) and two French Algerians. No Britons of Yemeni descent were involved in the case. The two young Muslims sentenced in Morocco for shooting tourists in a Marrakech hotel in 1994 were from French Algerian families. Omar Saeed Sheikh, convicted in Pakistan for the kidnapping of Daniel Pearl, is a British-born citizen of the United Kingdom. He is one of the few who returned to his family's country of origin.

All these examples bear out how activists of Middle Eastern origin have hardly ever undertaken missions in the region or with a regional objective. They have struck global targets, in most cases from the West.[13]

Notes

Olivier Roy, "Al Qaeda and the New Terrorists." In *Globalized Islam: The Search for a New Ummah* (New York: Columbia University Press, 2004): 294–307. Used by permission of Columbia University Press.

Allusions to chapters within this piece refer to the original book from which this chapter was taken. References omitted.

1. There have already been many books and papers on Al Qaeda. The most important ones include: Rohan Gunaratna, *Inside Al Qaeda: Global Network of Terror,* London: Hurst, 2002; Jessica Stern, *Terror in the Name of God: Why Religious Militants Kill,* New York: HarperCollins, 2003; Jason Burke, *Al Qaeda: Casting a Shadow of Terror,* London: I.B. Tauris, 2003; and Marc Sageman, *Understanding Terror Networks,* Philadelphia: University of Pennsylvania Press, 2004.

2. For an English translation of Azzam's work, see 'Join the Caravan', http://www.religioscope.com/info/doc/jihad/azzam_caravan_3_part1.htm. Azzam states that *jihad* comes just after *iman* (faith), which makes it a pillar of Islam, but maintains the difference between 'offensive' *jihad,* which is *kifaya* (collective), and 'defensive' *jihad,* which is *ayn* (compulsory for individuals). However, he considers *de facto* that the contemporary *jihad* are all defensive: '*Defensive Jihad*

> This is expelling the Kuffar from our land, and it is Fard Ayn, a compulsory duty upon all. It is the most important of all the compulsory duties and arises in the following conditions:
>
> 1) If the Kuffar enter a land of the Muslims.
> 2) If the rows meet in battle and they begin to approach each other.
> 3) If the Imam calls a person or a people to march forward then they must march.
> 4) If the Kuffar capture and imprison a group of Muslims.'

From 'Defence of the Muslim Lands: The First Obligation after Iman', http://www.religioscope.com/info/doc/jihad/azzam_defence_3_chap1.htm.

3. Azzam, 'Join the Caravan': 'Establishment of the Muslim community on an area of land is a necessity, as vital as water and air. This homeland will not come about without an organised Islamic movement which perseveres consciously and realistically upon Jihad, and which regards fighting as a decisive factor and as a protective wrapping.

The Islamic movement will not be able to establish the Islamic community except through a common, people's Jihad which has the Islamic movement as its beating heart and deliberating mind. It will be like the small spark which ignites a large keg of explosives, for the Islamic movement brings about an eruption of the hidden capabilities of the Ummah, and a gushing forth of the springs of Good stored up in its depth. The Companions of the Prophet were exceedingly few in number compared to the troops who toppled the throne of the Persian Kisra and overthrew the Caesar of Rome.' A well-known website, azzam.com, for years promoted international *jihad,* but after Azzam's death it reflected far more extremist views than those held by Azzam.

4. There is a theory that Azzam was killed by the ISI to prevent first a rapprochement between him and Massoud, and second the appointment of his son-in-law (the Algerian Boujema Bounouar, who went by the *nom de guerre* Abdullah Anas) as his successor. Anas having been trained in Panjshir alongside Massoud, the story could make sense, although there is no evidence other than the testimony of Bounouar, as collected by Judith Miller; see Stephen Engelberg, 'One Man and a Global Web of Violence', *New York Times,* 14 January 2001.

5. There are many contradictory estimates of the number of 'Afghans', but I cannot see how more than 50,000 volunteers could have gone into Afghanistan. It also depends how we define a sojourn in Afghanistan. Some (and not only Islamic volunteers) spent just one day and claim to have participated in the war. For a plausible sample to estimate the proportions of nationalities, the best sources are the many lists of martyrs; see, among others, Imtiaz Hussain, 'Osama Prepares List of Arab Martyrs of Afghan Jihad', *Frontier Post,* 13 May 2000.

6. The expulsion of Bin Laden from Sudan also meant that the United States did not request his extradition; the French had in 1994 taken Carlos from the same Sudanese government.

7. David B. Ottaway and Steve Coll, 'Retracing the Steps of a Terror Suspect', *Washington Post,* 5 June 1995.

8. Muhammad Atta's will in English can be found at http://abcnews.go.com/sections/us/DailyNews/WTC_atta_will.html.

9. Khaled Kelkal's network in France (1995) was set up by an Algerian, Ali Touchent, who might be either an emissary of a GIA *emir* (Zeytuni) or, more probably, an agent of the military security services. (See Samraoui, *Chroniques des années de sang,* p. 230.)

10. In the list referred to (which is pending judicial decisions; inclusion in the list does not necessarily mean an individual is a terrorist) are included: Abdel Sattar, Ahmed; Abderrahman, Ahmed; Ait Idir, Stephane; Akhnouche, Yasin; al-Fadli, Tariq; al-Maqdisi, Sheikh Abu Muhammad; al-Shehhi, Marwan; Amrouche Laurent; Atmani, Said; Atta, Muhammad; Attar; Bahaji, Said; Bakri Omar; Beghal, Djamel; Ben Mustafa Khaled; Bensakhria, Mohamed; Binalshibh, Ramzi; Budiman, Agus; Cazé, Christophe; Dahmane, Abdesattar; Daoudi, Kamel; Darkazanli, Mamoun; Derwish, Kamal (alias Ahmed Hijazi); Djaffo, Xavier; Dumont, Lionel; al-Deek, Khalil; el-Hage, Wadih; al-Mihdar, Zayn al-Abidin Abu Bakr; el-Ouaer, Rachid Bouraoui; Essabar, Zakariya; Hammadi

Redouane; Ibn ul-Khattab; Isamuddin, Riduan; Jabarah, Mohammed Mansour; Jarrah, Ziad; Kamel, Fateh; Kherchtou, L'Houssaine; Khalfaoui, Slimane; Khedr, Ahmed Sayyid; Loudaini, Ahmed; Mohammed, Khalid Sheikh; al-Motassadeq, Munir; Moussaoui, Zacarias; Odeh, Mohamed Saddiq; Omary, Mohammed; Ouldali, Khaled; Rechouane, Abdesslam.; Ressam Ahmed; Sheikh, Omar Saeed; Walker Lindh, John; Yousef, Ramzi Ahmed; Zammar, Mohammed Haydar; Zubayda, Abu.

11. Richard C. Paddock, 'The Making of a Terrorist', *Los Angeles Times*, 22 January 2002.

12. The Yemeni exception is Kamal Derwish from Buffalo, Colorado, of Yemeni descent. Derwish was killed by a CIA missile in October 2002 in Yemen, alongside Ali Qaed Senyan al-Harthi, who masterminded the attack on the destroyer USS *Cole*. But the other members of the so-called Lackawanna group (all US citizens of Yemeni descent) were caught in Pakistan.

13. One partial exception is Abu Mussab al-Zarqawi, a Jordanian. He never went to the West, even if his path in the Middle East is also 'deterritorialised'. He fought in Afghanistan, joined the Kurdish Ansar al Islam pro–Al Qaeda group in Iraq, and killed a US diplomat in Jordan. He has also been accused of having links with two Western Al Qaeda cells in Britain and Germany (http://www.theage.com.au/articles/2003/01/27/1043533989987.html), and in Italy (Risa Molitz, 'Suspected Terrorists Arrested in Italy', ABC News, 3 June 2003). In 2003 he became the figurehead of the internationalist radicals fighting the United States in Iraq.

CHAPTER 13
FROM MARKET GLOBALISM TO IMPERIAL GLOBALISM
IDEOLOGY AND AMERICAN POWER AFTER 9/11

Manfred B. Steger

Introduction

Soon after the collapse of Soviet-style communism in Eastern Europe, various power elites concentrated in the global North stepped up their efforts to sell their neoliberal version of 'globalization' to the public. While not disavowing some of the coercive measures referred to by Joseph Nye as 'hard power'—particularly the application of economic pressure through international lending institutions like the IMF and World Bank—this phalanx of neoliberal forces preferred enhancing the legitimacy of their worldview by means of 'soft power', that is, the use of cultural and ideological appeals to effect their desired outcomes without commanding allegiance.[1] Seeking to make a persuasive case for a new global order based on their values, these power elites constructed and disseminated narratives and images that extolled the virtues of deregulated and globally integrated markets. Throughout the 1990s, they advanced a globalization discourse sufficiently systematic to add up to a comprehensive political

177

ideology. Elsewhere, I have referred to it as 'globalism'—a market ideology endowing the buzzword 'globalization' with norms, values, and meanings that not only legitimate and advance neoliberal interests, but also seek to cultivate consumerist cultural identities in billions of people around the world (Steger, 2002; 2003; 2004).[2]

For most of the decade, this double-pronged strategy of utilizing the persuasive power of ideas and ideals together with the 'sticky power' of international economic policy seemed to minimize ideological dissent.[3] Many people came to accept globalism's core claims, thus internalizing large parts of an overarching normative framework that advocated the deregulation of markets, the liberalization of trade, and the privatization of state-owned enterprises.[4] Representing what Pierre Bourdieu and Zygmunt Bauman have called a 'strong' discourse, globalism was difficult to resist because it relied on the soft power of 'common sense', that is, the widespread belief that its prescriptive program ultimately derived from an accurate description of 'objective reality' (Bauman, 1999, pp. 28–29, 127–28; Bourdieu, 1998, p. 95). As Judith Butler (1996, p. 112) notes, the constant repetition, public recitation, and 'performance' of an ideology's core claims tend to have the capacity to produce what they name.

By the late 1990s, however, a growing divergence between neoliberal ideological claims and the everyday experience of people in many parts of the world undermined globalism's legitimacy. This, in turn, facilitated the production of counterdiscourses powerful enough to seriously challenge the neoliberal worldview. Disseminated by heterogenous social forces on both the political Left and Right, these competing ideological perspectives found their political manifestation in successive waves of worldwide antiglobalist protests. From the spectacular 1999 anti-WTO demonstrations in Seattle to the street protests at the 2001 G-8 Summit in Genoa, these massive displays of popular dissent elicited two major responses from the hegemonic neoliberal forces.

First, and consistent with their original soft-power strategy, some globalists responded with public admissions that globalization did, indeed, require 'minor reforms', particularly 'better management'. These concessions were often followed by highly publicized assurances to put 'a human face' on globalization. Former wizards of globalism like George Soros, Joseph Stiglitz, Jeffrey Sachs, and Paul Krugman publicly bemoaned the 'excesses of market fundamentalism' that had occurred during the 'Roaring Nineties' (see Stiglitz, 2003; 2002; Soros, 2002). At the same time, however, other globalists recommended hard-power tactics to crack down on dissenters. Yet, in order to justify their strange willingness to activate coercive state powers against protesters, these globalists sought to mobilize the corporate-media in fueling the stereotype of the chaotic, cobblestone-throwing antiglobalizer.[5]

As a result, mainstream television images broadcast from Genoa glossed over the fact that the vast majority of demonstrators were committed to nonviolent means of social change. These attempts to stabilize the neoliberal model by means of generating fear and demands for greater security were increasingly reflected in globalist discourse. Globalizing markets were now portrayed as requiring protection against the violent hordes of irrationalism. In other words, the allegedly 'inevitable' and 'irreversible' unfolding of self-regulating markets suddenly needed to be helped along by strong law enforcement measures that would 'beat back' the enemies of democracy and the free market.

After al-Qaeda's devastating attacks on the world's most recognized symbols of a US-dominated globalized economy and culture, this neoliberal tendency to tolerate or endorse hard-power tactics grew even stronger. In the volatile post-9/11 environment in the United States, neoconservative players in the Bush administration drew on the existing climate of fear to promote their vision of a benign American empire leading a coalition of 'allies' in the open-ended War on Terror. President George W. Bush abandoned the mildly isolationist position he espoused during the 2000 election campaign and instead adopted the bellicose views of inveterate hard-power advocates like Dick Cheney and Donald Rumsfeld.[6]

If the liberalization and global integration of markets was to continue as a viable project, many globalists felt they had little choice but to enter into a shaky ideological compromise with the ascending neoconservative forces. If neoliberals accepted that their core ideological claims had to be 'hard-powered' to fit the neoconservative agenda, then, in turn, neoconservatives would continue to support a 'free-market' discourse that also helped to soften their militarism. Indeed, this uneasy and sometimes stormy marriage between the economic neoliberalism of the 1990s and the neoconservative security agenda of the 2000s marked the birth of an 'imperial globalism' with an American face. While the hard-powering of market globalism led to a modification of some of its original claims, it would be a mistake to assume that the neoliberal project came to an end with 9/11. The Bush administration's embrace of hard power has been amply documented and analyzed *on the policy level* in today's raging debates over whether or not the post-9/11 United States actually constitutes an 'empire'—formal or informal.[7] However, little attention has been paid to the corresponding *ideological-discursive shift* from the soft power discourse of persuasion centered on the idea of a 'leaderless market' to the tough imperial language of American dominance. What are the major ideological differences between market globalism and imperial globalism? Seeking to shed light on the precise nature of these morphological changes in the dominant ideology, this essay scrutinizes a number of representative utterances and writings of influential advocates of globalism before and after 9/11. Focusing on what I identify as its six core claims of globalism, I analyze these major ideological changes and raise critical questions of ideological continuity. Ultimately, then, this essay seeks to contribute to the larger project of developing a critical theory of globalization by focusing on the shifting discursive power dynamics (for a more detailed discussion of developing a critical theory of globalization, see Steger, 2004, pp. 10–11; Mittelman, 2004, Chap. 4, pp. 34–44).

Claim No. 1: Globalization Is about the Liberalization and Global Integration of Markets

This foundational claim of market globalism seeks to shape global preferences without resorting to verbal threats—and, therefore, represents the essence of 'soft power' (Nye, 2004, p. 5). It activates the neoliberal ideal of the self-regulating market as the normative basis for a future global order. According to this ideological narrative, the vital functions of the free market—its rationality and efficiency, as well as its alleged ability to bring about greater social integration and material progress—can only be realized in a liberal society that values and protects individual freedom. Let us consider some examples.

A passage in a 1990s *BusinessWeek* article (13 December 1999, p. 212) clearly defines globalization in market terms: 'Globalization is about the triumph of markets over governments. Both proponents and opponents of globalization agree that the driving force today is markets, which are suborning the role of government. The truth is that the size of government has been shrinking relative to the economy almost everywhere.' Joan Spiro, US Undersecretary of State for Economic, Business, and Agricultural Affairs in the Clinton administration, stated that 'One role [of government] is to get out of the way—to remove barriers to the free flow of goods, services, and capital' (Spiro, 1996).

Perhaps the most eloquent exposition of the neoliberal claim that globalization is about the liberalization and global integration of markets can be found in Thomas Friedman's bestseller, *The Lexus and the Olive Tree: Understanding Globalization* and its post-9/11 sequel, *Longitudes and Attitudes: The World in the Age of Terrorism*. Indeed, many commentators have emphasized that Friedman's books provide the 'official narrative of globalization' in the United States today (see, e.g., Bole, 1999, pp. 14–16). The award-winning *New York Times* columnist argues that people ought to accept the following 'truth' about globalization: 'The driving idea behind globalization is free-market capitalism—the more you let market forces rule and the more you open your economy to free trade and competition, the more efficient your economy will be. Globalization means the spread of free-market capitalism to virtually every country in the world' (Friedman, 2000, p. 9).

After 9/11, both neoliberals and their opponents emphasized the continued viability of this foundational globalist claim while acknowledging a hardening of the narrative. For example, the Indian writer Arundhati Roy, one of the most eloquent critics of corporate globalization, argues that the language of neoliberalism appears to have absorbed the aggressive idiom of 'breaking open markets' (Roy, 2004, p. 11). This discursive shift is clearly visible in President Bush's public utterances before and after 9/11. During his 2000 presidential campaign, candidate Bush consistently promised to 'work tirelessly to open up markets all over the world' and 'end tariffs and break down barriers everywhere, entirely, so the whole world trades in freedom' (Bush, 2000). After 9/11, Bush still hoped to 'ignite a new area of global economic growth through free markets and free trade', but his 2002 *National Security Strategy of the United States* (NSSUS) explicitly merges market language with security slogans, culminating in the credo of imperial globalism: 'Free markets and free trade are key priorities of our national security strategy' (Bush, 2002a).

Bush's post-9/11 understanding of the neoliberal project as part of an overarching security agenda has been dutifully echoed in similar remarks by world leaders as different as Paul Martin, Canada's Minister of Finance, and Goh Chok Tong, Prime Minister of Singapore (see Lien, 2003). Moreover, most importantly, a good number of neoliberal globalists went along with the hard-powerization of their market ideology. For example, Thomas Friedman—initially a strong proponent of the Bush administration's global war on terror in Afghanistan and Iraq—admonished his readers to go along with the neoconservative posture of 'aggressive engagement' in the Middle East. In his view, this was the best strategy for 'leading the Arab world into globalization' (Friedman, 2003, pp. 314–315).

Claim No. 2: Globalization Is Inevitable and Irreversible

A study of the utterances of influential globalists in the 1990s reveals their reliance on an economistic narrative of historical inevitability. While disagreeing with Marxists on the final goal of historical development, globalists nonetheless share with their ideological opponents a fondness for such terms as 'irresistable', 'inevitable', and 'irreversible' to describe the projected path of globalization. Let us consider some examples.

In a speech on US foreign policy, President Clinton told his audience: 'Today we must embrace the inexorable logic of globalization ... Globalization is irreversible. Protectionism will only make things worse' (Clinton, 1999; and Clinton cited in Ross, 1997). Frederick W. Smith, chairman and CEO of FedEx Corporation, suggests that 'globalization is inevitable and inexorable and it is accelerating ... Globalization is happening, it's going to happen. It does not matter whether you like it or not, it's happening, it's going to happen' (Smith, 1999). Neoliberal elites in the global South faithfully echoed the globalist language of inevitability. For example, Manuel Villar, the Philippines Speaker of the House of Representatives, insisted that 'We cannot simply wish away the process of globalization. It is a reality of a modern world. The process is irreversible' (Villar, 1998).

Throughout the 1990s, the neoliberal portrayal of globalization as some sort of natural force, like the weather or gravity, made it easier for globalists to convince people that they would have to adapt to the discipline of the market if they were to survive and prosper. Hence, the globalist claim of inevitability neutralized the challenges of antiglobalist opponents by depoliticizing the public discourse about globalization: neoliberal policies were above politics, because they simply carried out what was ordained by nature. This view implied that, instead of acting according to a set of choices, people merely fulfill world-market laws that demanded the elimination of government controls. Since the emergence of a world based on the primacy of market values reflected the dictates of history, resistance would be unnatural, irrational, and dangerous.

In the immediate aftermath of 9/11, this claim came under sustained criticism by commentators who emphasized the 'dark side of globalization'. Some even proclaimed the imminent 'collapse of globalism', worrying that the terrorist attacks would usher in a new age of nationalism (Saul, 2004; see also Roach, 2002, p. 65). Noted neoliberal economists like Robert J. Samuelson argued in his widely read *Newsweek* column that globalization might not be inevitable since previous globalization processes had been stopped by similar cataclysmic events such as the 1914 assassination of the Austrian Archduke Franz Ferdinand in Sarajevo (Samuelson, 2003, p. 41).

On the other hand, the unfolding War on Terror allowed the Bush administration to weave the determinist language of globalism into imperial pronouncements of the inexorable triumph of the forces of 'Good' over the 'Axis of Evil'. The old soft-power discourse of *economic* inevitability reemerged confidently in the new hard-power narrative of *military* inevitability. Constant assurances that the United States and its allies would prevail in the War on Terror reverberated through the media landscape. For example, Christopher Shays, neoliberal Republican Congressman from Connecticut and Chair of the House Subcommittee on National Security, publicly expressed his belief that the 'fight against global terrorism' was bound to end in a 'safer world' characterized by 'broad-based free expression and free markets'. After all, Shays added, the 'toxic zeal' of the terrorists 'can only be defeated by market forces, the relentless inevitability of free peoples pursuing their own enlightened self-interest in common cause' (Shays, 2003).

Claim No. 3: Nobody Is in Charge of Globalization

Market globalism's deterministic language offered its proponents in the 1990s yet another rhetorical advantage. If the natural laws of the market have indeed preordained a neoliberal course of history, then globalization does not reflect the arbitrary agenda of a particular social class or group. In other words, globalists merely carry out the unalterable imperatives of a transcendental force much larger than narrow partisan interests. People are not in charge of globalization; markets and technology are. Here are two examples.

Robert Hormats, vice chairman of Goldman Sachs International, emphasized that 'The great beauty of globalization is that no one is in control. The great beauty of globalization is that it is not controlled by any individual, any government, any institution' (Hormats, 1998). In his usual confident tone, Thomas Friedman, too, alleged that 'the most basic truth about globalization is this: No one is in charge ... We all want to believe that someone is in charge and responsible. But the global marketplace today is an Electronic Herd of often anonymous stock, bond and currency traders and multinational investors, connected by screens and networks' (Friedman, 2000, pp. 112–113).

After 9/11, it became increasingly difficult for market globalists to maintain the position that 'nobody is in charge of globalization'. While a number of corporate leaders still reflexively referred to the 'leaderless market', neoconservatives close to the Bush administration lectured market globalists that global security and a global liberal order 'depend on the United States—that "indispensable nation"—wielding its power' (Kagan, 2002). After all, if America indeed spearheaded the cause of universal principles, then it had a responsibility to make sure that the spread of these values was not hampered by ideological dissenters. The resulting hardening of discourse is obvious in the 2002 NSSUS. For example, Bush ends the preface of this document by glorifying tough US global leadership: 'Today, humanity holds in its hands the opportunity to further freedom's triumph over all these [terrorist] foes. The United States welcomes our [*sic*] responsibility to lead in this great mission' (Bush, 2002a).

If the United States indeed sought to conceal its imperial ambitions in the 1990s behind the soft language of market globalism, then the gloves definitely came off after 9/11, exposing the iron fist of an irate giant. The attacks changed the terms of the globalist discourse in that they enabled neoconservatives to put their global ambitions *explicitly* before a public alarmed by an amorphous terrorist threat and thus vulnerable to what Claes Ryn, Chairman of the National Humanities Institute, calls the 'neo-Jacobin spirit' of the Bush administration (Ryn, 2003, pp. 384–385). The resulting move toward imperial globalism meant that the claim 'nobody is in charge of globalization' had to be abandoned and replaced by Bush's aggressive pronouncement of global leadership.

However, the replacement of claim three with a more aggressive pronouncement of global Anglo-American leadership should not be read as a sign of globalism's ideological weakness. Rather, it reflects its ideational flexibility and growing ability to respond to a new set of political issues. Indeed, like all fullfledged political belief systems, globalism is increasingly bearing the marks of an 'ideational family' broad enough to contain the more economistic variant of the 1990s as well as its more militaristic post-9/11 manifestation.

Claim No. 4: Globalization Benefits Everyone (… in the Long Run)

This claim lies at the very core of market globalism because it provides an affirmative answer to the crucial normative question of whether globalization represents a 'good' or a 'bad' phenomenon. Market globalists in the 1990s frequently connected their arguments in favor of the integration of global markets to the alleged benefits resulting from the liberalization and expansion of world trade. At the 1996 G-7 Summit in Lyon, France, for example, the heads of states of the seven major industrialized democracies issued a joint communiqué that contains the following passage:

> Economic growth and progress in today's interdependent world is bound up with the process of globalization. Globalization provides great opportunities for the future, not only for our countries, but for all others too. Its many positive aspects include an unprecedented expansion of investment and trade; the opening up to international trade of the world's most populous regions and opportunities for more developing countries to improve their standards of living; the increasingly rapid dissemination of information, technological innovation, and the proliferation of skilled jobs. These characteristics of globalization have led to a considerable expansion of wealth and prosperity in the world. Hence we are convinced that the process of globalization is a source of hope for the future. (Economic Communiqué, 1996)

The public discourse on globalization in the 1990s was rife with such generalizations. Even cautious Alan Greenspan, chairman of the US Federal Reserve

Board, insisted that 'there can be little doubt that the extraordinary changes in global finance on balance have been beneficial in facilitating significant improvements in economic structures and living standards throughout the world' (Greenspan, 1997).

In addition, globalists often seek to cement their decontestation of globalization as 'benefits for everyone' by coopting the powerful language of 'science' which claims to separate 'fact' from 'fiction' in a 'neutral' fashion, that is, solely on the basis of 'hard evidence'. And yet, the two most comprehensive empirical assessments of changes in global income distributions in the last decade have arrived at sharply conflicting results.[8] Even those globalists who consider the possibility of unequal global distribution patterns nonetheless insist that the market itself will eventually correct these 'irregularities'. As John Meehan, chairman of the US Public Securities Association, puts it, 'episodic dislocations' such as mass unemployment and reduced social services might be 'necessary in the short run', but, 'in the long run', they will give way to 'quantum leaps in productivity' (Meehan, 1997).

Remarkably resilient after 9/11, this claim nonetheless received hard-power treatment. Indeed, the terrorist attacks actually added to the fervor with which imperial globalists speak of the supposed benefits accruing from the rapid liberalization and global integration of markets. For example, in the NSSUS, Bush consistently mentions the alleged benefits of securing the benefits of free markets: 'Free trade and free markets have proven their ability to lift whole societies out of poverty—so the United States will work with individual nations, entire regions, and the entire global trading community to build a world that trades in freedom and therefore grows in prosperity' (Bush, 2002a).

Claim No. 5: Globalization Furthers the Spread of Democracy in the World

This claim is anchored in the neoliberal assertion that *freedom, free markets, free trade* and *democracy* are synonymous terms. Affirmed as common sense throughout the 1990s, the compatibility of these concepts often went unchallenged in the public discourse. Francis Fukuyama, for example, asserted that there existed a clear correlation between a country's level of economic development and successful democracy. While globalization and capital development did not automatically produce democracies, 'the level of economic development resulting from globalization is conducive to the creation of complex civil societies with a powerful middle class. It is this class and societal structure that facilitates democracy' (Fukuyama, n.d.). Praising the economic transitions towards capitalism in Eastern Europe, US Senator Hillary Rodham Clinton told her Polish audience that the emergence of new businesses and shopping centers in former communist countries should be seen as the 'backbone of democracy' (Rodham Clinton, 1999).

After September 11, this claim, too, became firmly linked to the Bush administration's security agenda. The President did not mince words in 'Securing Freedom's Triumph'—his *New York Times* op-ed piece a year after the attacks: 'As we preserve the peace, America also has an opportunity to extend the benefits of freedom and progress to nations that lack them. We seek a peace where repression, resentment and poverty are replaced with the hope of democracy, development, free markets and free trade' (Bush, 2002b). Fourteen months later, he reaffirmed this 'forward strategy for freedom' by referring to his country's unwavering 'commitment to the global expansion of democracy' as the 'third pillar' of the United States' 'peace and security vision for the world' (Bush, 2003).

This idea of securing 'freedom' through an American-led drive for political and economic 'democratization' around the globe—thus connecting the military objectives of the War on Terror to the neoliberal agenda of liberalizing markets—has emerged as the centerpiece of imperial globalism. And nowhere did these hard discursive dynamics of imperial globalism become as apparent as in the corporate scramble for Iraq following the official end of 'major combat operations' on 1 May 2003. Already during the first days of the Iraq war in late March 2003, globalists with strong ties to the Republican party had suggested that Iraq be subject to a radical neoliberal treatment.

Exemplifying this ideological marriage of convenience between many neoliberals and neoconservatives, Robert McFarlane, former National Security Advisor to President Reagan and current chairman of the Washington, DC–based corporation Energy & Communication Solutions, LLC, together with Michael Bleyzer, CEO and president of SigmaBleyzer, an international equity fund management company, co-authored a remarkably brazen op-ed piece in *The Wall Street Journal* bearing the suggestive title, 'Taking Iraq Private'. Calling on 'major U.S. corporations, jointly with other multinationals', to 'lead the effort to create capital-friendly environments in developing countries', the globalist duo praised the military operations in Iraq as an indispensable tool in establishing the 'political, economic and social stability' necessary for 'building the basic institutions that make democracy possible'. Alleging that recent analyses of the 'economic policies of 128 countries' identified neoliberal measures as the 'key drivers for development', the two men reminded the government that 'the U.S. must demonstrate that it is not only the most powerful military power on the planet, but also the foremost market economy in the world, capable of leading a greater number of developing nations to a more prosperous and stable future' (McFarlane & Bleyzer, 2003).

It did not take a long time for the Bush administration to heed such advice. In what amounted to a concentrated public relations initiative in autumn 2003, Secretary of State Colin Powell conveyed the administration's view of the matter in countless speeches, Internet messages, and television and radio interviews. For example, in his address to an economic conference on the Middle East attended by hundreds of American and Arab-American business executives, Powell emphasized the administration's intention to develop the US–Middle East Free Trade Area (MEFTA) within a decade. Linked to the adminstration's 2002 'US–Middle East Partnership Initiative', the new project also included programs to send Arab college students to work as interns in American corporations (Colin Powell cited in Treaster, 2003; Olivastro, 2002).

In the meantime, in Iraq, the US head of the Coalition Provisional Authority, Ambassador Paul Bremer, had pressured the Governing Council to let Order 39 take effect, permitting complete foreign ownership of Iraqi companies and assets (excluding natural resources) that had hitherto been publicly owned, total remittance of profits, and some of the lowest corporate tax rates in the world (Williams, 2003). No doubt, the military-industrial complex and related enterprises have been the biggest beneficiaries of imperial globalism. For example, in the fiscal year 2002, the 'Big Three' US weapons makers—Lockheed Martin, Boeing, and Northrop Grumman—received a total of more than $42 billion in Pentagon contracts. This was an increase of nearly one-third from 2000, President Clinton's final year in office (Hartung, 2004, pp. 19–21). The Bush adminstration awarded largely without competition or detailed explanations of total costs multi-billion dollar reconstruction contracts to such companies as Bechtel Group Inc., Halliburton Co., and Stevedoring Services of America—all generous contributors to the Republican party with strong personal connections to high-level officials in the two Bush administrations, including Vice President Cheney, former Secretary of State George Shultz, Under Secretary of Defense Douglas Feith, and Defense Policy Board member Richard Perle. Companies headquartered in countries that opposed the Iraq war, like France, Germany, and Russia, were not invited to submit any bids (Mittal, 2003).

Thus, imperial globalism amounts to a neoliberal structural adjustment program by military means. With their economy in complete shambles and burdened with a national debt of nearly $400 billion, the Iraqi people have to come to grips with the emerging reality that debtor countries might be unwilling to write off their loans in their entirety, thus making the privatization of the country's oil industry—either partially or fully—a distinct possibility for fiscal reasons. Moreover, UN Security Council Resolution 1483, adopted on 23 May 2003, incorporated Iraq into the global market, but granted broad power to the United States and United Kingdom to manage Iraq's economic fate for at least a year. It should come as no surprise that Secretary of Defense Donald Rumsfeld has announced that since the American people have already made significant investments in 'liberating and rebuilding Iraq', the administration would turn to the Iraqi regime for funds before further burdening the US taxpayer (Looney, 2003).

In short, the globalist claim of spreading freedom and democracy has become a convenient narrative for the Bush administration and its supporters in Congress to secure and expand its influence and power globally by combining arguments in favor of military interventions with the familiar slogans of market liberalization.

Claim No. 6: Globalization Requires a War on Terror

At this point, it should be obvious why, in the post-9/11 context, it has become necessary for neoliberal globalist forces to make their peace with a hardened narrative. If globalization, understood as the liberalization and global integration of markets, is to remain a viable project then the coercive powers of the state have to be employed against those who threaten it—both internal antiglobalist dissenters and external terrorist foes. Hence the addition of a new globalist claim: globalization requires a war on terror.

Two representative samples of how this new claim has been circulating in the public discourse are Thomas Barnett's 'The Pentagon's New Map', published in the March 2003 issue of *Esquire* magazine, and Robert Kaplan's 'Supremacy by Stealth' featured in the July 2003 issue of *The Atlantic Monthly*. Both publications reach a mass readership and its authors are respected professionals in their fields. Thomas Barnett, a Harvard-educated professor of military strategy at the US Naval War College, has been advising the Office of the Secretary of Defense for some time. Within weeks of September 11, he was called to the Pentagon and installed as the assistant for strategic futures in the Office of Force Transformations. Since then, he has been giving his briefings regularly at the Pentagon, in the intelligence community, and to high-ranking officers from branches of the military.

In his much-debated *Esquire* article, which he later expanded into a best-selling book, Barnett argues that the Iraq War marks 'the moment when Washington takes real ownership of strategic security in the age of globalization'. He breaks the globe down into three distinct regions. The first is characterized by 'globalization thick with network connectivity, financial transactions, liberal media flows, and collective security', yielding nations featuring stable democratic governments, transparency, rising standards of living, and more deaths by suicide than by murder (North America, most of Europe, Australia, New Zealand, and a small part of Latin America). He calls these regions of the world the 'Functioning Core', or 'Core'. Conversely, areas where 'globalization is thinning or just plain absent' constitute a region plagued by repressive political regimes, regulated markets, mass murder, and widespread poverty and disease (the Caribbean Rim, virtually all of Africa, the Balkans, the Caucasus, Central Asia, the Middle East and Southwest Asia, and much of Southeast Asia). The breeding ground of 'global terrorists', Barnett refers to this region as the 'Non-Integrating Gap', or 'Gap'. Between these two regions, one finds 'seam states' that 'lie along the Gap's bloody boundaries' (Mexico, Brazil, South Africa, Morocco, Algeria, Greece, Turkey, Pakistan, Thailand, Malaysia, the Philippines, and Indonesia).

For Barnett, the importance of September 11 is that the attacks forced the United States and its allies to make a long-term military commitment to 'deal with the entire Gap as a strategic threat environment'. In other words, the desired spread of globalization requires a War on Terror. Its three main objectives are: '1) Increase the Core's immune system capabilities for responding to September 11–like system perturbations; 2) Work on the seam states to firewall the Core from the Gap's worst exports, such as terror, drugs, and pandemics; and, most important, 3) *Shrink the Gap* ... The Middle East is the perfect place to start'. The third point is particularly important, because 'the real battlegrounds in the global war on terrorism are still *over there*'. As Barnett emphasizes, 'We ignore the Gap's existence at our own peril, because it will not go away until we as a nation respond to the challenge of making globalization truly global'.

At the end of his article, Barnett offers a nod to neoliberals by conceding 'it will take a whole lot more than the U.S. exporting security to shrink the Gap', because 'the integration of the Gap will ultimately depend more on private investment than anything the Core's public sector can offer. But it all has to begin with security, because free markets and democracy cannot flourish amid chronic conflict' (Barnett, 2003; 2004).

This celebration of hard-power US hegemony is precisely the starting point of Robert D. Kaplan's recent essay. Simply taking for granted that 'the United States now possesses a global empire', the award-winning journalist and bestselling author urges his readership to 'move beyond a statement of the obvious' and instead join him in pondering how America should 'manage an unruly world' after 9/11:

The purpose of [US] power is not power itself; it is the fundamentally liberal purpose of sustaining the key characteristics of an orderly world. Those characteristics include basic political stability; the idea of liberty, pragmatically conceived; respect for property; economic freedom; and representative government, culturally understood. At this moment in time it is American power, and American power only, that can serve as an organizing principle for the worldwide expansion of a liberal civil society. (Kaplan, 2003a)

What does Kaplan mean by 'the idea of liberty, pragmatically conceived'? It turns out that Kaplan's pragmatics of liberty refer chiefly to hard-power military tactics designed to maintain American pre-eminence: fast-track naturalization for foreign-born soldiers fighting for the empire; training special forces to be lethal killers one moment and humanitarians the next; using the military to promote democracy; not to let military missions be compromised by diplomacy; the resolve to 'fight on every front', including the willingness to strike potential enemies pre-emptively on limited evidence, deal with the media 'more strictly', and crack down on internal dissent, especially anti-war demonstrators. Kaplan suggests 'Ten Rules' for running the world, which culminate in the idea that the best way for the United States to maintain and expand its empire is to adopt the 'pagan warrior ethos of second-century Rome'. What Kaplan seems to forget in the heat of his argument, however, is that neither Emperors Trajan nor Hadrian were renowned for their liberal inclinations. This, of course, is the central problem of the uneasy compromise between neoliberalism and neoconservatism: once empire gets hold of market globalism, it may turn it into a very different ideological creature. No wonder, then, that Kaplan closes his article with a panegyric to Winston Churchill and his assessment of the United States as 'a worthy successor to the British Empire, one that would carry on Britain's liberalizing mission' (Kaplan, 2003a).

From Market Globalism to Imperial Globalism: Ideological Continuity or Rift?

As capitalist liberalism reinvented itself in the last two decades, it drew largely on the basic ideas of nineteenth-century British free-market philosophers. Still, it represented a remarkable ideological achievement of neoliberal globalists in the 1990s to re-energize these quaint arguments with the buzzword 'globalization', thereby bestowing new currency upon their antiquated vision. The Anglo-American framers of market globalism spoke softly and persuasively as they sought to attract people worldwide to their vision of globalization as a leaderless, inevitable juggernaut that would ultimately engulf the entire world and produce liberal democracy and material benefits for everyone.

In the harsh political climate following the attacks of September 11, however, many market globalists struggled to maintain the viability of their project. One obvious solution was to toughen up their ideological claims to fit the neoconservative vision of a benign US empire relying on overwhelming military power. As a result, market globalism morphed into imperial globalism. Claims one (globalization is about the liberalization and global integration of markets) and four (globalization benefits everyone)—the backbone of market globalism—are still largely intact but had to undergo hard-power facelifts. The determinist language of claim two found its new expression in the proclaimed 'inevitability' of America's military triumph over its terrorist nemesis. Claim three (nobody is in charge of globalization), however, was dropped in favor of Bush's ostentatious pronouncement of US global leadership. Claim five (globalization furthers the spread of democracy in the world) ascended to new heights with the hard-power mission of 'building democracy' in the Gap regions. The neoconservative commitment to 'American values' of freedom, security, and free markets made it necessary to add claim six (globalization requires a War on Terror) to globalism's discursive arsenal. Robert Kaplan best captures the new logic of imperial globalism: 'You have to have military and economic power behind it, or else your ideas cannot spread' (Kaplan, 2003b).

But this changing morphology of globalism raises the legitimate question of ideological continuity: how much of 'neoliberalism' remains in imperial globalism? After all, in recent years, leading neoliberal voices like George Soros and Paul Krugman fiercely denounced the hard-power approach of neoconservatives. At first glance, then, it appears that there has been more of a split than a convergence between market globalism and imperial globalism, with some neoliberal globalist elites openly expressing both their dislike for and mistrust of the unilaterist imperialist drive of the Bush government. After all, they argued, their 1990s brand of globalism had been very different from its imperial version: fundamentally multilateral, it was strongly committed to the mutual effort of creating military stability, a transnational trade regime, and comprehensive international treaties (see Soros, 2003; Krugman, 2003).

There is no question that a number of prominent neoliberals have refused to make ideological compromises with neoconservatives, especially on the subject of unilateralism. Combining their hands-off attitude toward Big Business with intrusive government action for the regulation of the ordinary citizenry in the name of public security and traditional values, neoconservatives have advocated a more assertive and expansive use of both economic and military power than neoliberals—ostensibly for the purpose of promoting freedom and democracy around the world. These sentiments seem to imply a strong commitment to universalistic principles, but, as one commentator puts it,

> Unlike liberal Wilsonians, their [neoconservatives'] promotion of democracy is not for the sake of democracy and human rights in and of themselves. Rather,

> democracy-promotion is meant to bolster America's security and to further its world preeminence; it is thought to be pragmatically related to the U.S. national interest. The principles of these neocons[ervatives] are universalistic, but not so their policy, which steers clear of international organizations and is nationalist and unilateralist. (Wolfson, 2004; see also Lind, 2004)

On the other hand, it is crucial to bear in mind that neoliberalism and neoconservativism in the United States are not ideological opposites. In fact, they represent variations on the same liberal theme, and their similarities often outweigh their differences. Contemporary American neoconservatives are far removed from classical British traditionalists who expressed a fondness for aristocratic virtues and bemoaned radical social change, disliked egalitarian principles, and distrusted progress and reason. Rather, American neoconservatives subscribe to a variant of liberalism they relate to the world views espoused by Ronald Reagan, Theodore Roosevelt, Abraham Lincoln, and James Madison.

In fact, the militaristic display put on at the 2004 Democratic Convention in Boston showed that despite persisting differences with the Bush administration's crude unilateralism, prominent neoliberals like John Kerry and Hillary Rodham Clinton have embraced large portions of the Republican hard-power security agenda, including the neoconservative dogma that the United States does not 'ask anybody's permission' in pursuit of its national interests. Finally, on major issues of economic globalization such as trade liberalization, deregulation, and privatization, the ideological differences between neoliberals and neoconservatives have been negligible for years. Like the late nineteenth-century context that gave rise to American imperialism, the post-9/11 landscape seems to call for a hard-power globalism that unites the twin goals of global economic and political hegemony in the name of high-sounding ideals like strength, security, just peace, democracy, development, free markets, and free trade.

Overall, then, my argument in favor of considerable ideological continuity between 1990s market globalism and 2000s imperial globalism leaves room for the dangerous possibility of an ideological turn toward US nationalism and right-wing militarism. In my view, claim six best captures this ominous potential. On one hand, the claim that globalization requires a global war on terror attests to globalism's political responsiveness and conceptual flexibility—qualities that characterize mature political belief systems (for possible criteria of 'mature' ideologies, see Freeden, 2003). On the other hand, however, claim six possesses a paradoxical character. If global terror were no longer a major issue, it would disappear without doing damage to the overall conceptual coherence of globalism. Hence, it appears that claim six is a contingent one and thus *less important* than the previous five. If, however, the global War on Terror turns out to be a lengthy and intense engagement—as suggested by the Bush administration—then it would become actually more important over time. No wonder, then, that some commentators who seize upon the second option have claimed to detect a dangerous turn of globalism toward fascism (Falk, 2003).

To be sure, throughout the 1990s there had been sinister warnings on the part of some cultural theorists that globalization was actually 'Americanization' or 'McDonaldization' in universalist and rationalist disguise (see, e.g., Latouche, 1996; Ritzer, 1993). But US unilaterism and belligerence in the wake of 9/11 constitute a much more serious manifestation of the same phenomenon. Indeed, the problem with globalism's turn toward nationalism has been as much conceptual as political. After all, bestowing meaning on 'globalization' by connecting it to the idea of a necessary global War on Terror has created serious logical contradictions. First, the globalists' reliance on the coercive powers of the state to secure their project undermines both the idea of the 'self-regulating market' and the claim of historical 'inevitability'. Second, the belligerent vision of enforcing 'democracy' and 'freedom' at gunpoint conflicts with the common understanding of liberty as absence of coercion. Third, as noted above, the Anglo-American unilateralism contradicts the cosmopolitan, universal spirit associated with the concept 'globalization'—hence the criticism of 'reformed' neoliberals like George Soros.

In short, introducing claim six as an ideological pillar of globalism runs a considerable risk of causing irreparable damage to the political belief system. After all, the celebration of globalization in American imperialist terminology invites a conceptual contradiction that may eventually prove to be fatal to globalism. And yet, if the political issues of our time indeed favor an ideology that boldly arranges seemingly conflicting pieces of three major political belief systems—liberalism, conservatism, and nationalism—around the idea of 'globalization', then imperial globalism might actually achieve a level of ideological dominance unprecedented in modern history.

Notes

Manfred B. Steger, "From Market Globalism to Imperial Globalism: Ideology and American Power After 9/11," *Globalizations* 2, no. 1 (May 2005): 31–46. (Taylor & Francis Ltd., http://www.informaworld.com, reprinted by permission of the publisher.)

1. The terms 'hard power' and 'soft power' have been coined by Joseph S. Nye. However, the power dynamics in question have been described and analyzed in different terms by generations of political thinkers influenced by the writings of Antonio Gramsci. For the latest elaboration of his perspective on power, see Nye (2004).

2. As I point out in these studies, these power elites consist chiefly of corporate managers, executives of large transnational corporations (TNCs), corporate lobbyists, high-level military officers, prominent journalists and public-relations specialists, intellectuals writing to a large public audience, state bureaucrats and influential politicians. It is questionable whether these social elites constitute a coherent 'transnational capitalist class' (in an orthodox Marxist sense), as Leslie Sklair suggests. In my view, Mark Rupert's neo-Gramscian concept of a 'transnational historic bloc of internationally-oriented capitalists, liberal statesman, and their allies' seems to come closer to an accurate description of the loose, heterogeneous, and often disagreeing global alliance of neoliberal forces that I have in mind (see Sklair, 2001; Rupert, 2000, pp. 16–17, 154).

3. A *BusinessWeek*–Harris poll on globalization conducted by Harris Interactive between 7 and 10 April 2000 found that 65% of 1,024 American respondents thought that globalization was a 'good thing' for consumers and businesses in both the United States and the rest of the world. More recent polls are still showing a slim majority holding these views. For example, a 2004 University of Maryland Center on Policy Attitudes poll shows that slightly more than 50% of respondents saw globalization as 'positive' or 'somewhat positive'. At the same time, however, this number confirms a significant decline in positive attitudes since the late 1990s. See http://americans-world.org/digest/global_issues/globalization?gz_summary.cfm.

4. Walter Russell Mead argues rather convincingly that the military and economic dimensions of Nye's 'hard power' concept are sufficiently different to warrant separate terms. Thus he refers to military power as 'sharp power', and to economic power as 'sticky power', which he defines as a more coercive 'sort of soft power' comprised 'by a set of economic institutions and policies that attracts others toward U.S. influence and then traps them in it' (see Mead, 2004, pp. 46–53).

5. For example, at the G-8 Summit in Genoa, the Italian government employed a contingent of over 16,000 police and military troops to 'guarantee the safety' of delegates who pondered new neoliberal measures.

6. Joseph Nye (2004, p. ix) reports that Secretary Rumsfeld responded to a question about the relevance of 'soft power' in the US foreign policy by claiming that he did not know what the term meant.

7. The post-9/11 literature on the power dynamics of 'American Empire' is vast and rapidly growing (see, e.g., Johnson, 2004; Boggs, 2004; Todd, 2003; Soros, 2003; Schmemann, 2003; Mann, 2003; Harvey, 2003). Michael Walzer, for example, suggests that the post-9/11 American empire constitutes a 'new beast' characterized by 'a looser form of rule, less authoritarian than empire is or was, more dependent on the agreement of others'. At the same time, Walzer acknowledges the administration's shift to hard power by conceding that 'George W. Bush's unilateralism is a bid for hegemony without compromise; perhaps he sees America playing an imperial—perhaps also messianic—role in the world' (see Walzer, 2003, pp. 27–30).

8. Columbia University economist Xavier Sala i-Martin argues that his evidence shows that inequality of individuals across the world is declining; but according to World Bank economist Branko Milanovic, global inequality has risen (see Secor, 2003).

References

Barnett, T. P. M. (2003) The Pentagon's new map, *Esquire* (March). Available at http://www.nwc.navy.mil/newrulessets/ThePentagonsNewMap.htm.

Barnett, T. P. M. *The Pentagon's New Map: War and Peace in the 21st Century* (New York: Putnam, 2004).

Bauman, Z. (1999) *In Search of Politics* (Stanford, CA: Stanford University Press).

Boggs, C. (2004) *The New Militarism: U.S. Empire and Endless War* (Lanham, MD: Rowman & Littlefield Publishers).

Bole, W. (1999) Tales of globalization, *America*, 181(18), 4 December, pp. 14–16.

Bourdieu, P. (1998) *Acts of Resistance* (New York: The New Press).

Bush, G. W. (2000) speech at the Republican Primary debate in West Columbia, SC, 7 January. Available at http://www.issues2002.org/Background_Free_Trade.htm.

Bush, G. W. (2002a) *National Security Strategy of the United States* (NSSUS). Available at http://www.whitehouse.gov/nsc/print/nssall.html.

Bush, G. W. (2002b) Securing freedom's triumph, *New York Times*, 11 September.

Bush, G. W. (2003) Speech in London on Iraq and the Mideast, printed in *New York Times*, 19 November.

Butler, J. (1996) Gender as performance, in P. Osborne (Ed) *A Critical Sense: Interviews with Intellectuals* (London: Routledge).

Clinton, W. (1999) Remarks by the president on foreign policy, San Francisco, 26 February. Available at http://www.pub.whitehouse.gov/urires/12R?urn:pdi://oma.eop.gove.us/1999/3/1/3.text.1.html.

Economic Communiqué (1996) G-7 Summit, Lyon, June 28. Available at http://library.utoronto.ca/www/g7/96ecopre.html.

Falk, R. (2003) Will the empire be fascist?, *The Transnational Foundation for Peace and Future Research Forum*, 24 March. Available at http://www.transnational.org/forum/meet/2003/Falk_FascistEmpire.html.

Freeden, M. (2003) Editorial: ideological boundaries and ideological systems, *Journal of Political Ideologies*, 8(1), pp. 1–8.

Friedman, T. (2000) *The Lexus and the Olive Tree: Understanding Globalization* (New York: Anchor Books).

Friedman, T. (2003) *Longitudes and Attitudes: The World in the Age of Terrorism* (New York: Anchor Books).

Fukuyama, F. (n.d.) Economic globalization and culture: a discussion with Dr. Francis Fukuyama. Available at http://www.ml.com/woml/forum/global2.html.

Greenspan, A. (1997) The globalization of finance, 14 October. Available at http://cato.org/pubs/journal/cj17n3-1.html.

Hartung, W. H. (2004) Making money on terrorism, *The Nation*, 23 February, pp. 19–21.

Harvey, D. (2003) *The New Imperialism* (Oxford, UK: Oxford University Press).

Hormats, R. (1998) PBS interview with Danny Schechter, February. Available at http://pbs.org/globalization/hormats1.html.

Johnson, C. (2004) *The Sorrows of Empire: Militarism, Secrecy, and the End of the Republic* (New York: Metropolitan Books).

Kagan, R. (2002) The U.S.-Europe divide, *Washington Post,* 26 May.

Kaplan, R. D. (2003a) Supremacy by stealth, *The Atlantic Monthly* (July/August). Available at http://www.theatlantic.com/issues/2003/07/kaplan.htm.

Kaplan, R. D. (2003b) The hard edge of American values, *The Atlantic Monthly Online,* 18 June. Available at http://www.theatlantic.com/fc … com/unbound/interviews/int2003-06-18.htm.

Krugman, P. (2003) *The Great Unraveling: Losing Our Way in the New Century* (New York: Norton).

Latouche, S. (1996) *The Westernization of the World* (Cambridge: Polity Press).

Lien, J. (2003) Open trade doors in East Asia, *Business Times Singapore,* 9 May.

Lind, M. (2004) A tragedy of errors, *The Nation,* 23 February, pp. 23–32.

Looney, R. (2003) Bean counting in Baghdad: debt, reparations, reconstruction, and resources, *Middle East Review of International Affairs Journal,* 7(3). Available at http://meria.idc.ac.il/journal/2003/issue3/jv7n3a4.html.

Mann, M. (2003) *Incoherent Empire* (London: Verso).

McFarlane, R. & Bleyzer, M. (2003) Taking Iraq private, *The Wall Street Journal,* 27 March.

Mead, W. R. (2004) *Foreign Policy* (March/April), pp. 46–53.

Meehan, J. J. (1997) Globalization and technology at work in the bond markets, speech given in Phoenix, AZ, 1 March. Available at http://www/bondmarkets.com/news/Meehanspeechfinal.html.

Mittal, A. (2003) Open fire and open markets: strategy of an empire, *Common Dreams,* 6 September. Available at http://www.ccmep.org/2003_articles/090603_open_fire_and_open_markets.htm.

Mittelman, J. H. (2004) *Whither Globalization? The Vortex of Knowledge and Ideology* (New York: Routledge).

Nye, J. S. (2004) *Soft Power: The Means to Success in World Politics* (New York: PublicAffairs).

Olivastro, A. (2002) Powell announces U.S.–Middle East partnership initiative, *The Heritage Foundation,* 12 December. Available at http://www.heritage.org/research/middleeast/wm179.cfm.

Ritzer, G. (1993) *The McDonaldization of Society: An Investigation into the Changing Character of Contemporary Social Life* (Thousand Oaks, CA: Pine Forge Press).

Roach, S. (2002) Is it at risk?—globalisation, *The Economist,* 2 February, p. 65.

Rodham Clinton, H. (1999) Growth of democracy in Eastern Europe, Warsaw, 5 October. Available at http://www. whitehouse.gov/WH/EOP/FirstLady/html/generalspeeches/1999/19991005.html.

Ross, S. (1997) Clinton talk of better living, *Associated Press,* 15 October. Available at http://more.abcnews.go.com/sections/world/brazil1014/index.html.

Roy, A. (2004) The new American century, *The Nation,* 9 February, p. 11.

Rupert, M. (2000) *Ideologies of Globalization: Contending Visions of a New World Order* (London: Routledge).

Ryn, C. (2003) The ideology of American empire, *Orbis* (Summer), pp. 384–385.

Samuelson, R. J. (2003) Globalization goes to war, *Newsweek,* 24 February, p. 41.

Saul, J. R. (2004) The collapse of globalism and the rebirth of nationalism, *Harper's Magazine* (March), pp. 33–43.

Schmemann, S. (2003) *America Unbound: The Bush Revolution in Foreign Policy* (Washington: Brookings Institution Press).

Secor, L. (2003) Mind the gap, *The Boston Globe,* 5 January.

Shays, C. (2003) Free markets and fighting terrorism, *The Washington Times,* 10 June.

Sklair, L. (2001) *The Transnational Capitalist Class* (Oxford, UK: Blackwell).

Smith F. W. (1999) cited in International Finance Experts Preview Upcoming Global Economic Forum, 1 April. Available at http://www.econstrat.org/pctranscript.html.

Soros, G. (2002) *George Soros on Globalization* (New York: PublicAffairs).

Soros, G. (2003) *The Bubble of American Supremacy: Correcting the Misuse of American Power* (New York: PublicAffairs).

Spiro, J. E. (1996) The challenges of globalization, speech at the World Economic Development Congress in Washington, DC, 26 September. Available at http://www.state.gov/www/issues/economic/960926.html.

Steger, M. B. (2002) *Globalism: The New Market Ideology* (Lanham, MD: Rowman & Littlefield Publishers).

Steger, M. B. (2003) *Globalization: A Very Short Introduction* (Oxford, UK: Oxford University Press).

Steger, M. B., Ed (2004) *Rethinking Globalism* (Lanham, MD: Rowman & Littlefield Publishers).

Stiglitz, J. (2002) *Globalization and Its Discontents* (New York: Norton).

Stiglitz, J. (2003) *The Roaring Nineties* (New York: Norton).

Todd, E. (2003) *After Empire: The Breakdown of the American Order* (New York: Columbia University Press).

Treaster, J. (2003) Powell tells Arab-Americans of hopes to develop Mideast, *New York Times,* 30 September.

Villar, M., Jr. (1998) High-level dialogue on the theme of the social and economic impact of globalization and interdependence and their policy implications, New York, 17 September. Available at http://www.un.int/philippines/villar.html.

Walzer, M. (2003) Is there an American empire?, *Dissent* (Fall), pp. 27–31.

Williams, S. (2003) The seeds of Iraq's future terror, *The Guardian,* 28 October.

Wolfson, A. (2004) Conservatives and neoconservatives, *The Public Interest* (Winter). Available at http://www.the publicinterest.com/current/article2.html.

CHAPTER 14
THE WORLD AS A POLDER
WHAT DOES IT ALL MEAN TO US TODAY?

Jared Diamond

It seems to me that the most serious environmental problems facing past and present societies fall into a dozen groups. Eight of the 12 were significant already in the past, while four (numbers 5, 7, 8, and 10: energy, the photosynthetic ceiling, toxic chemicals, and atmospheric changes) became serious only recently. The first four of the 12 consist of destruction or losses of natural resources; the next three involve ceilings on natural resources; the three after that consist of harmful things that we produce or move around; and the last two are population issues. Let's begin with the natural resources that we are destroying or losing: natural habitats, wild food sources, biological diversity, and soil.

1. At an accelerating rate, we are destroying natural habitats or else converting them to human-made habitats, such as cities and villages, farmlands and pastures, roads, and golf courses. The natural habitats whose losses have provoked the most discussion are forests, wetlands, coral reefs, and the ocean bottom. As I mentioned in the preceding chapter, more than half of the world's original area

198

of forest has already been converted to other uses, and at present conversion rates one-quarter of the forests that remain will become converted within the next half-century. Those losses of forests represent losses for us humans, especially because forests provide us with timber and other raw materials, and because they provide us with so-called ecosystem services such as protecting our watersheds, protecting soil against erosion, constituting essential steps in the water cycle that generates much of our rainfall, and providing habitat for most terrestrial plant and animal species. Deforestation was a or *the* major factor in all the collapses of past societies described in this book. In addition, as discussed in Chapter 1 in connection with Montana, issues of concern to us are not only forest destruction and conversion, but also changes in the structure of wooded habitats that do remain. Among other things, that changed structure results in changed fire regimes that put forests, chaparral woodlands, and savannahs at greater risk of infrequent but catastrophic fires.

Other valuable natural habitats besides forests are also being destroyed. An even larger fraction of the world's original wetlands than of its forests has already been destroyed, damaged, or converted. Consequences for us arise from wetlands' importance in maintaining the quality of our water supplies and the existence of commercially important freshwater fisheries, while even ocean fisheries depend on mangrove wetlands to provide habitat for the juvenile phase of many fish species. About one-third of the world's coral reefs—the oceanic equivalent of tropical rainforests, because they are home to a disproportionate fraction of the ocean's species—have already been severely damaged. If current trends continue, about half of the remaining reefs would be lost by the year 2030. That damage and destruction result from the growing use of dynamite as a fishing method, reef overgrowth by algae ("seaweeds") when the large herbivorous fish that normally graze on the algae become fished out, effects of sediment runoff and pollutants from adjacent lands cleared or converted to agriculture, and coral bleaching due to rising ocean water temperatures. It has recently become appreciated that fishing by trawling is destroying much or most of the shallow ocean bottom and the species dependent on it.

2. Wild foods, especially fish and to a lesser extent shellfish, contribute a large fraction of the protein consumed by humans. In effect, this is protein that we obtain for free (other than the cost of catching and transporting the fish), and that reduces our needs for animal protein that we have to grow ourselves in the form of domestic livestock. About two billion people, most of them poor, depend on the oceans for protein. If wild fish stocks were managed appropriately, the stock levels could be maintained, and they could be harvested perpetually. Unfortunately, the problem known as the tragedy of the commons (Chapter 14) has regularly undone efforts to manage fisheries sustainably, and the great

majority of valuable fisheries already either have collapsed or are in steep decline (Chapter 15). Past societies that overfished included Easter Island, Mangareva, and Henderson.

Increasingly, fish and shrimp are being grown by aquaculture, which in principle has a promising future as the cheapest way to produce animal protein. In several respects, though, aquaculture as commonly practiced today is making the problem of declining wild fisheries worse rather than better. Fish grown by aquaculture are mostly fed wild-caught fish and thereby usually consume more wild fish meat (up to 20 times more) than they yield in meat of their own. They contain higher toxin levels than do wild-caught fish. Cultured fish regularly escape, interbreed with wild fish, and thereby harm wild fish stocks genetically, because cultured fish strains have been selected for rapid growth at the expense of poor survival in the wild (50 times worse survival for cultured salmon than for wild salmon). Aquaculture runoff causes pollution and eutrophication. The lower costs of aquaculture than of fishing, by driving down fish prices, initially drive fishermen to exploit wild fish stocks even more heavily in order to maintain their incomes constant when they are receiving less money per pound of fish.

3. A significant fraction of wild species, populations, and genetic diversity has already been lost, and at present rates a large fraction of what remains will be lost within the next half-century. Some species, such as big edible animals, or plants with edible fruits or good timber, are of obvious value to us. Among the many past societies that harmed themselves by exterminating such species were the Easter and Henderson Islanders whom we have discussed.

But biodiversity losses of small inedible species often provoke the response, "Who cares? Do you really care less for humans than for some lousy useless little fish or weed, like the snail darter or Furbish lousewort?" This response misses the point that the entire natural world is made up of wild species providing us for free with services that can be very expensive, and in many cases impossible, for us to supply ourselves. Elimination of lots of lousy little species regularly causes big harmful consequences for humans, just as does randomly knocking out many of the lousy little rivets holding together an airplane. The literally innumerable examples include: the role of earthworms in regenerating soil and maintaining its texture (one of the reasons that oxygen levels dropped inside the Biosphere 2 enclosure, harming its human inhabitants and crippling a colleague of mine, was a lack of appropriate earthworms, contributing to altered soil/atmosphere gas exchange); soil bacteria that fix the essential crop nutrient nitrogen, which otherwise we have to spend money to supply in fertilizers; bees and other insect pollinators (they pollinate our crops for free, whereas it's expensive for us to pollinate every crop flower by hand); birds and mammals that disperse wild fruits (foresters still haven't figured out how to grow from seed the most important commercial tree species of the Solomon Islands, whose seeds are naturally dispersed by fruit bats, which are becoming hunted out); elimination of whales, sharks, bears, wolves, and other top predators in the seas and on the land, changing the whole food chain beneath them; and wild plants and animals that decompose wastes and recycle nutrients, ultimately providing us with clean water and air.

4. Soils of farmlands used for growing crops are being carried away by water and wind erosion at rates between 10 and 40 times the rates of soil formation, and between 500 and 10,000 times soil erosion rates on forested land. Because those soil erosion rates are so much higher than soil formation rates, that means a net loss of soil. For instance, about half of the topsoil of Iowa, the state whose agriculture productivity is among the highest in the U.S., has been eroded in the last 150 years. On my most recent visit to Iowa, my hosts showed me a churchyard offering a dramatically visible example of those soil losses. A church was built there in the middle of farmland during the 19th century and has been maintained continuously as a church ever since, while the land around it was being farmed. As a result of soil being eroded much more rapidly from fields than from the churchyard, the yard now stands like a little island raised 10 feet above the surrounding sea of farmland.

Other types of soil damage caused by human agricultural practices include salinization, as discussed for Montana, China, and Australia in Chapters 1, 12, and 13; losses of soil fertility, because farming removes nutrients much more rapidly than they are restored by weathering of the underlying rock; and soil acidification in some areas, or its converse, alkalinization, in other areas. All of these types of harmful impacts have resulted in a fraction of the world's farmland variously estimated at between 20% and 80% having become severely damaged, during an era in which increasing human population has caused us to need more farmland rather than less farmland. Like deforestation, soil problems contributed to the collapses of all past societies discussed in this book.

The next three problems involve ceilings—on energy, freshwater, and photosynthetic capacity. In each case the ceiling is not hard and fixed but soft: we can obtain more of the needed resource, but at increasing costs.

5. The world's major energy sources, especially for industrial societies, are fossil fuels: oil, natural gas, and coal. While there has been much discussion about how many big oil and gas fields remain to be discovered, and while coal reserves are believed to be large, the prevalent view is that known and likely reserves of readily accessible oil and natural gas will last for a few more decades. This view should not be misinterpreted to mean that all of the oil and natural gas within the Earth will have been used up by then. Instead, further reserves will be deeper underground, dirtier, increasingly expensive to extract or process, or will involve

higher environmental costs. Of course, fossil fuels are not our sole energy sources, and I shall consider problems raised by the alternatives below.

6. Most of the world's freshwater in rivers and lakes is already being utilized for irrigation, domestic and industrial water, and in situ uses such as boat transportation corridors, fisheries, and recreation. Rivers and lakes that are not already utilized are mostly far from major population centers and likely users, such as in Northwestern Australia, Siberia, and Iceland. Throughout the world, freshwater underground aquifers are being depleted at rates faster than they are being naturally replenished, so that they will eventually dwindle. Of course, freshwater can be made by desalinization of seawater, but that costs money and energy, as does pumping the resulting desalinized water inland for use. Hence desalinization, while it is useful locally, is too expensive to solve most of the world's water shortages. The Anasazi and Maya were among the past societies to be undone by water problems, while today over a billion people lack access to reliable safe drinking water.

7. It might at first seem that the supply of sunlight is infinite, so one might reason that the Earth's capacity to grow crops and wild plants is also infinite. Within the last 20 years, it has been appreciated that that is not the case, and that's not only because plants grow poorly in the world's Arctic regions and deserts unless one goes to the expense of supplying heat or water. More generally, the amount of solar energy fixed per acre by plant photosynthesis, hence plant growth per acre, depends on temperature and rainfall. At any given temperature and rainfall the plant growth that can be supported by the sunlight falling on an acre is limited by the geometry and biochemistry of plants, even if they take up the sunlight so efficiently that not a single photon of light passes through the plants unabsorbed to reach the ground. The first calculation of this photosynthetic ceiling, carried out in 1986, estimated that humans then already used (e.g., for crops, tree plantations, and golf courses) or diverted or wasted (e.g., light falling on concrete roads and buildings) about half of the Earth's photosynthetic capacity. Given the rate of increase of human population, and especially of population impact (see point 12 below), since 1986, we are projected to be utilizing most of the world's terrestrial photosynthetic capacity by the middle of this century. That is, most energy fixed from sunlight will be used for human purposes, and little will be left over to support the growth of natural plant communities, such as natural forests.

The next three problems involve harmful things that we generate or move around: toxic chemicals, alien species, and atmospheric gases.

8. The chemical industry and many other industries manufacture or release into the air, soil, oceans, lakes, and rivers many toxic chemicals, some of them "unnatural" and synthesized only by humans, others present naturally in tiny

concentrations (e.g., mercury) or else synthesized by living things but synthesized and released by humans in quantities much larger than natural ones (e.g., hormones). The first of these toxic chemicals to achieve wide notice were insecticides, pesticides, and herbicides, whose effects on birds, fish, and other animals were publicized by Rachel Carson's 1962 book *Silent Spring*. Since then, it has been appreciated that the toxic effects of even greater significance for us humans are those on ourselves. The culprits include not only insecticides, pesticides, and herbicides, but also mercury and other metals, fire-retardant chemicals, refrigerator coolants, detergents, and components of plastics. We swallow them in our food and water, breathe them in our air, and absorb them through our skin. Often in very low concentrations, they variously cause birth defects, mental retardation, and temporary or permanent damage to our immune and reproductive systems. Some of them act as endocrine disruptors, i.e., they interfere with our reproductive systems by mimicking or blocking effects of our own sex hormones. They probably make the major contribution to the steep decline in sperm count in many human populations over the last several decades, and to the apparently increasing frequency with which couples are unable to conceive, even when one takes into account the increasing average age of marriage in many societies. In addition, deaths in the U.S. from air pollution alone (without considering soil and water pollution) are conservatively estimated at over 130,000 per year.

Many of these toxic chemicals are broken down in the environment only slowly (e.g., DDT and PCBs) or not at all (mercury), and they persist in the environment for long times before being washed out. Thus, cleanup costs of many polluted sites in the U.S. are measured in the billions of dollars (e.g., Love Canal, the Hudson River, Chesapeake Bay, the *Exxon Valdez* oil spill, and Montana copper mines). But pollution at those worst sites in the U.S. is mild compared to that in the former Soviet Union, China, and many Third World mines, whose cleanup costs no one even dares to think about.

9. The term "alien species" refers to species that we transfer, intentionally or inadvertently, from a place where they are native to another place where they are not native. Some alien species are obviously valuable to us as crops, domestic animals, and landscaping. But others devastate populations of native species with which they come in contact, either by preying on, parasitizing, infecting, or outcompeting them. The aliens cause these big effects because the native species with which they come in contact had no previous evolutionary experience of them and are unable to resist them (like human populations newly exposed to smallpox or AIDS). There are by now literally hundreds of cases in which alien species have caused one-time or annually recurring damages of hundreds of millions of dollars or even billions of dollars. Modern examples include Australia's rabbits and foxes, agricultural weeds like Spotted Knapweed and Leafy Spurge

(Chapter 1), pests and pathogens of trees and crops and livestock (like the blights that wiped out American chestnut trees and devasted American elms), the water hyacinth that chokes waterways, the zebra mussels that choke power plants, and the lampreys that devastated the former commercial fisheries of the North American Great Lakes (Plates 30, 31). Ancient examples include the introduced rats that contributed to the extinction of Easter Island's palm tree by gnawing its nuts, and that ate the eggs and chicks of nesting birds on Easter, Henderson, and all other Pacific islands previously without rats.

10. Human activities produce gases that escape into the atmosphere, where they either damage the protective ozone layer (as do formerly widespread refrigerator coolants) or else act as greenhouse gases that absorb sunlight and thereby lead to global warming. The gases contributing to global warming include carbon dioxide from combustion and respiration, and methane from fermentation in the intestines of ruminant animals. Of course, there have always been natural fires and animal respiration producing carbon dioxide, and wild ruminant animals producing methane, but our burning of firewood and of fossil fuels has greatly increased the former, and our herds of cattle and of sheep have greatly increased the latter.

For many years, scientists debated the reality, cause, and extent of global warming: are world temperatures really historically high now, and, if so, by how much, and are humans the leading cause? Most knowledgeable scientists now agree that, despite year-to-year ups and downs of temperature that necessitate complicated analyses to extract warming trends, the atmosphere really has been undergoing an unusually rapid rise in temperature recently, and that human activities are the or a major cause. The remaining uncertainties mainly concern the future expected magnitude of the effect: e.g., whether average global temperatures will increase by "just" 1.5 degrees Centigrade or by 5 degrees Centigrade over the next century. Those numbers may not sound like a big deal, until one reflects that average global temperatures were "only" 5 degrees cooler at the height of the last Ice Age.

While one might at first think that we should welcome global warming on the grounds that warmer temperatures mean faster plant growth, it turns out that global warming will produce both winners and losers. Crop yields in cool areas with temperatures marginal for agriculture may indeed increase, while crop yields in already warm or dry areas may decrease. In Montana, California, and many other dry climates, the disappearance of mountain snowpacks will decrease the water available for domestic uses, and for irrigation that actually limits crop yields in those areas. The rise in global sea levels as a result of snow and ice melting poses dangers of flooding and coastal erosion for densely populated low-lying coastal plains and river deltas already barely above or even below sea level. The areas thereby threatened include much of the Netherlands, Bangladesh, and the seaboard of the eastern U.S., many low-lying Pacific islands, the deltas of the Nile and Mekong Rivers, and coastal and riverbank cities of the United Kingdom (e.g., London), India, Japan, and the Philippines. Global warming will also produce big secondary effects that are difficult to predict exactly in advance and that are likely to cause huge problems, such as further climate changes resulting from changes in ocean circulation resulting in turn from melting of the Arctic ice cap.

The remaining two problems involve the increase in human population:

11. The world's human population is growing. More people require more food, space, water, energy, and other resources. Rates and even the direction of human population change vary greatly around the world, with the highest rates of population growth (4% per year or higher) in some Third World countries, low rates of growth (1% per year or less) in some First World countries such as Italy and Japan, and negative rates of growth (i.e., decreasing populations) in countries facing major public health crises, such as Russia and AIDS-affected African countries. Everybody agrees that the world population is increasing, but that its annual percentage rate of increase is not as high as it was a decade or two ago. However, there is still disagreement about whether the world's population will stabilize at some value above its present level (double the present population?), and (if so) how many years (30 years? 50 years?) it will take for population to reach that level, or whether population will continue to grow.

There is long built-in momentum to human population growth because of what is termed the "demographic bulge" or "population momentum," i.e., a disproportionate number of children and young reproductive-age people in to-day's population, as a result of recent population growth. That is, suppose that every couple in the world decided tonight to limit themselves to two children, approximately the correct number of children to yield an unchanging population in the long run by exactly replacing their two parents who will eventually die (actually, 2.1 children when one considers childless couples and children who won't marry). The world's population would nevertheless continue to increase for about 70 years, because more people today are of reproductive age or entering reproductive age than are old and post-reproductive. The problem of human population growth has received much attention in recent decades and has given rise to movements such as Zero Population Growth, which aim to slow or halt the increase in the world's population.

12. What really counts is not the number of people alone, but their impact on the environment. If most of the world's 6 billion people today were in cryogenic storage and neither eating, breathing, nor metabolizing, that large population would cause no environmental problems. Instead, our numbers pose problems

insofar as we consume resources and generate wastes. That per-capita impact—the resources consumed, and the wastes put out, by each person—varies greatly around the world, being highest in the First World and lowest in the Third World. On the average, each citizen of the U.S., western Europe, and. Japan consumes 32 times more resources such as fossil fuels, and puts out 32 times more wastes, than do inhabitants of the Third World (Plate 35).

But low-impact people are becoming high-impact people for two reasons: rises in living standards in Third World countries whose inhabitants see and covet First World lifestyles; and immigration, both legal and illegal, of individual Third World inhabitants into the First World, driven by political, economic, and social problems at home. Immigration from low-impact countries is now the main contributor to the increasing populations of the U.S. and Europe. By the same token, the overwhelmingly most important human population problem for the world as a whole is not the high rate of population increase in Kenya, Rwanda, and some other poor Third World countries, although that certainly does pose a problem for Kenya and Rwanda themselves, and although that is the population problem most discussed. Instead, the biggest problem is the increase in total human impact, as the result of rising Third World living standards, and of Third World individuals moving to the First World and adopting First World living standards.

There are many "optimists" who argue that the world could support double its human population, and who consider only the increase in human numbers and not the average increase in per-capita impact. But I have not met anyone who seriously argues that the world could support 12 times its current impact, although an increase of that factor would result from all Third World inhabitants adopting First World living standards. (That factor of 12 is less than the factor of 32 that I mentioned in the preceding paragraph, because there are already First World inhabitants with high-impact lifestyles, although they are greatly outnumbered by Third World inhabitants.) Even if the people of China alone achieved a First World living standard while everyone else's living standard remained constant, that would double our human impact on the world (Chapter 12).

People in the Third World aspire to First World living standards. They develop that aspiration through watching television, seeing advertisements for First World consumer products sold in their countries, and observing First World visitors to their countries. Even in the most remote villages and refugee camps today, people know about the outside world, Third World citizens are encouraged in that aspiration by First World and United Nations development agencies, which hold out to them the prospect of achieving their dream if they will only adopt the right policies, like balancing their national budgets, investing in education and infrastructure, and so on.

But no one at the U.N. or in First World governments is willing to acknowledge the dream's impossibility: the unsustainability of a world in which the Third World's large population were to reach and maintain current First World living standards. It is impossible for the First World to resolve that dilemma by blocking the Third World's efforts to catch up: South Korea, Malaysia, Singapore, Hong Kong, Taiwan, and Mauritius have already succeeded or are close to success; China and India are progressing rapidly by their own efforts; and the 15 rich Western European countries making up the European Union have just extended Union membership to 10 poorer countries of Eastern Europe, in effect thereby pledging to help those 10 countries catch up. Even if the human populations of the Third World did not exist, it would be impossible for the First World alone to maintain its present course, because it is not in a steady state but is depleting its own resources as well as those imported from the Third World. At present, it is untenable politically for First World leaders to propose to their own citizens that they lower their living standards, as measured by lower resource consumption and waste production rates. What will happen when it finally dawns on all those people in the Third World that current First World standards are unreachable for them, and that the First World refuses to abandon those standards for itself? Life is full of agonizing choices based on trade-offs, but that's the cruelest trade-off that we shall have to resolve: encouraging and helping all people to achieve a higher standard of living, without thereby undermining that standard through overstressing global resources.

I have described these 12 sets of problems as separate from each other. In fact, they are linked: one problem exacerbates another or makes its solution more difficult. For example, human population growth affects all 11 other problems: more people means more deforestation, more toxic chemicals, more demand for wild fish, etc. The energy problem is linked to other problems because use of fossil fuels for energy contributes heavily to greenhouse gases, the combating of soil fertility losses by using synthetic fertilizers requires energy to make the fertilizers, fossil fuel scarcity increases our interest in nuclear energy which poses potentially the biggest "toxic" problem of all in case of an accident, and fossil fuel scarcity also makes it more expensive to solve our freshwater problems by using energy to desalinize ocean water. Depletion of fisheries and other wild food sources puts more pressure on livestock, crops, and aquaculture to replace them, thereby leading to more topsoil losses and more eutrophication from agriculture and aquaculture. Problems of deforestation, water shortage, and soil degradation in the Third World foster wars there and drive legal asylum seekers and illegal emigrants to the First World from the Third World.

Our world society is presently on a non-sustainable course, and any of our 12 problems of non-sustainability that we have just summarized would suffice to limit our lifestyle within the next several decades. They are like time bombs with fuses of less than 50 years. For example, destruction of accessible lowland tropical rainforest outside national parks is already virtually complete in Peninsular Malaysia, will be complete at current rates within less than a decade in the Solomon Islands, the Philippines, on Sumatra, and on Sulawesi, and will be complete around the world except perhaps for parts of the Amazon Basin and Congo Basin within 25 years. At current rates, we shall have depleted or destroyed most of the world's remaining marine fisheries, depleted clean or cheap or readily accessible reserves of oil and natural gas, and approached the photosynthetic ceiling within a few decades. Global warming is projected to have reached a degree Centigrade or more, and a substantial fraction of the world's wild animal and plant species are projected to be endangered or past the point of no return, within half a century. People often ask, "What is the single most important environmental/population problem facing the world today?" A flip answer would be, "The single most important problem is our misguided focus on identifying the single most important problem!" That flip answer is essentially correct, because any of the dozen problems if unsolved would do us grave harm, and because they all interact with each other. If we solved 11 of the problems, but not the 12th, we would still be in trouble, whichever was the problem that remained unsolved. We have to solve them all.

Thus, because we are rapidly advancing along this non-sustainable course, the world's environmental problems *will* get resolved, in one way or another, within the lifetimes of the children and young adults alive today. The only question is whether they will become resolved in pleasant ways of our own choice, or in unpleasant ways not of our choice, such as warfare, genocide, starvation, disease epidemics, and collapses of societies. While all of those grim phenomena have been endemic to humanity throughout our history, their frequency increases with environmental degradation, population pressure, and the resulting poverty and political instability.

Notes

Jared Diamond, "The World as a Polder: What Does It All Mean to Us Today?" In *Collapse: How Societies Choose to Fail or Succeed* (New York: Viking Penguin, 2005): 486–498. Used by permission of Viking Penguin, a division of Penguin Group (USA) Inc.

Allusions to chapters and plates within this piece refer to the original book from which this chapter was taken.

Chapter 15

The Spectre That Haunts the Global Economy?

The Challenge of Global Feminism

Valentine Moghadam

"Male-dominated monetary, trade and financial policies are gender blind, resulting in serious costs to all."[1]

"Vigorous global feminism is perhaps the single most effective form of resistance to the systematic degradation of human rights standards worldwide, which makes possible the worst ravages of the transnational economy."[2]

"Another world is possible and women are building it!"[3]

In the previous chapters, we have seen how the twin processes of economic restructuring and religious fundamentalisms in an era of globalization galvanized women around the world, led to a convergence of previously divergent perspectives, and resulted in the formation of transnational feminist networks. In the latter part of the 1980s, the world's women were ready for such mobilization and forms of organization, in part due to socio-demographic changes such as rising educational attainment and employment among women, and female labor incorporation in the world-economy. Since then, women have formed transnational feminist networks and have joined forces with other advocacy networks, civil society groups, and social movement organizations to challenge the neoliberal corporate agenda and to advance the cause of women's human rights. Along with other organizations and networks that are working for an alternative globalization or are engaging with global public policies, TFNs have contributed to the transnational social movement infrastructure and are helping to construct global civil society.

Female labor and women's organizations are integral elements of globalization in its economic, cultural, and political dimensions. The capitalist world-economy functions by means of the deployment of labor that is waged and non-waged, formal and informal, male and female. In recent decades, the involvement of women in various kinds of labor arrangements has been striking. Capitalist accumulation is achieved through the surplus-extraction of labor, and this includes the paid and unpaid economic activities of women, whether in male-headed or female-headed households. The various forms of the deployment of female labor reflect asymmetrical gender relations and patriarchal gender ideologies. Global accumulation as the driving force of the world-system not only hinges on class and regional differences across economic zones, but it is also a gendered process, predicated upon gender differences in the spheres of production and reproduction. In an era of economic globalization, the pressure for greater competitiveness through lower labor and production costs has encouraged the demand for and supply of female labor.

However, in a reflection of the contradictions of capitalism, the incorporation of women in the global economy and in national labor forces has also served to interrogate and modify gender relations and ideologies. Women have been organizing and mobilizing against the hegemonic and particularistic aspects of globalization. Organized and mobilized women—locally, nationally, and transnationally—are raising questions about social and gender arrangements and making demands on employers, governments, patriarchal movements, and international financial institutions. Many feminist organizations have been middle-class and elite, but class lines are increasingly blurred as women professionals and women proletarians find common cause around personal, economic, and social issues, including violence against women, poverty, job security, land rights, the redistribution and socialization of domestic work, reproductive health and rights, and women's roles in decision-making. The transnational feminist networks examined in this book show that the social movement of women has a more radical and transformative vision of the socio-economic and political order than do many of the "new social movements" that have been the focus of much sociological research.

Organizational Dynamics, Strengths and Weaknesses

The case-study chapters have illustrated some of the observations that were made in Chapter 4 concerning women's organizations in general and transnational feminist networks in particular. First, women's organizations reflect women's collective consciousness, identity, experiences, and aspirations. These are forged in labor processes, in domestic experiences, and in political struggles, and give rise to feminist organizations, women's caucuses, and participation in unions. We have seen that some feminist movements and their organizations have grown out of left-wing organizations, national liberation movements, labor movements, and other struggles. Disillusionment with male-dominated organizations and movements or the marginalization of women's movements and concerns often has been the impetus for women's organizations. But feminist networks emerge and make interventions in policy dialogues and debates on national and global levels also because women are convinced that their own, feminist perspectives have value and can make a difference.

When activists form organizations, they may build on pre-existing organizations and networks of women. This pattern has been noted in the social movements and women's movements literatures, and has been confirmed by the case studies here. All the TFNs examined in this book have grown out of personal, professional, and political networks, and many of the founders of the networks had worked together in other organizations or movements. Women's organizations, and TFNs in particular, are not exclusivist; we have seen that they join in coalitions with unions, political parties, and other civil society organizations or advocacy networks as well as with other feminist networks. And like some other civil society or social movement organizations, women's organizations may face state repression and resource constraints. Limited budgets are a perennial problem, but harassment and intimidation are more serious and are not unknown. Of the TFNs examined in this book, WLUML has been the most security-conscious, mainly due to the sensitive nature of its work, whereby it opposes fundamentalists, criticizes regimes, and objects to patriarchal interpretations and applications of Islamic law.

In her study of the Women's International League for Peace and Freedom, Mary Meyer contrasts the longevity of WILPF (founded in 1915) with other women's peace groups which, while often quite radical, disavowed formal organization or dissolved following specific antimilitarist campaigns. She attributes this to the WILPF founders' determination to "institutionalize the international women's peace movement ... through an organizational structure that combined both mainstreaming and disengaging political strategies."[4] Like WILPF, contemporary TFNs combine both an engagement with international organizations and public policy issues with a radical and at times utopian stance on the social order.

Formal organizations, however, have their tensions. Like other types of women's organizations, TFNs face issues of centralization, decentralization, institutionalization, professionalization, as well as charismatic leadership. Professionalization is a double-edged sword, as WIDE discovered and as critics of WEDO maintain. Some activists feel that WEDO's New York office has been too central, that there is a one-way relationship with the contacts in developing countries, and that its lobbying work overwhelms other worthwhile objectives, such as fostering or supporting grassroots women's organizations. The difficulties of effecting change in the global economy to establish gender justice and economic justice have led some feminists to question the strategy of participating in international conferences and lobbying delegates. As one WEDO Board member remarked: "International meetings are too distracting. There's no time to take care of your housekeeping. It's the same people who go to the UN meetings all the time. It's a complex, labor-intensive, technical process." The focus, rather, should be on support for grassroots women's organizations and for the building of the movement. The WEDO Board member continued: "There's been a little tension within the Board regarding advocacy versus movement. Bella was clear; she wanted advocacy and not grassroots work. Now there's recognition of the importance of being more organically connected to grassroots movements that organize and not just advocate. As an NGO we don't have to be a mini-donor. We shouldn't have to limit ourselves to that."[5]

Weaknesses and risks facing transnational feminists also should be acknowledged. Like many women's groups—and as we saw in particular with the AWMR—TFNs lack the necessary financial and other resources for real growth or more effective participation and lobbying. In the absence of a mass membership base, or due to the difficulties and expenses of collecting dues in a variety of currencies, they rely on "soft money" from external grants or foundation assistance, with its attendant problems of sustainability or legitimation.

Another weakness or danger is cooptation. There is always the possibility that states or international agencies can co-opt activists and especially "experts" who work with TFNs. After all, some transnational feminist activists have become UN officials or consultants, and they consult governments as well. The question of possible cooptation has been raised especially in connection with the World Bank's outreach activities, although there is no evidence thus far that involvement with the EGCG or participation in the many gender seminars organized by the World Bank has led to dilution of the critical analysis of those feminist political economists who accept the invitations.[6]

As we have seen with the AWMR, "political purity" or a willful disengagement from multilateral organizations can attenuate the potential effectiveness of a TFN. For example, WLUML leaders have admitted that they were not as effective as they could have been with respect to an issue that has been of central importance to the network—the fate of Algerian women, and especially fellow feminists, during the terrible years of the Algerian civil conflict.[7] WLUML was quite active in supporting Algerian feminists in their encounter with Islamist groups, but the efficacy of their work was hampered by the network's reluctance to engage with UN bodies as extensively as other TFNs have done, in favor of an approach that prioritized networking, solidarity, and appeals to feminists and other progressives around the world. On the other hand, their co-authorship of a shadow report on Algeria, submitted to the CEDAW Committee, did represent a shift in their approach.

I would conclude, nevertheless, that TFN accomplishments outweigh their weaknesses or the risks that they face. Without TFN activity the world would hardly have known about the atrocities facing Algerian and Afghan women in the 1990s. Indeed, the worldwide excoriation of the Taliban, its diplomatic isolation, and the defeat of the UNOCAL oil pipeline project are a success story of transnational feminism. Here, WLUML and its Lahore branch, Shirkat Gah, played a critical role, especially in the early years. In the area of economic policy, the trenchant and sustained critiques of structural adjustment by TFNs compelled the World Bank to retreat from its earlier disregard for the social sectors and to adopt a policy of gender-sensitivity in its research and policy work. The UN, World Bank and international development agencies recognize the role of women's organizations in the development process and in the making of civil society, and they have adopted transnational feminist concepts such as gender approach, gender equality, empowerment, and autonomy.

In fact, the study of TFNs shows that women's organizations have become major non-state political actors on the global, regional, and national scenes. They are in a dynamic relationship with states, the media, inter-governmental organizations, and other TSMOs and TANs. They use the global, inter-governmental arena and the transnational public sphere to accomplish national priorities in the areas of women's human rights (such as violence against women and the rights of women in Muslim societies) and economic policies (such as structural adjustment and the new global trade agenda), as well as to influence international norms and conventions. As such they challenge and engage with the state and global forces alike. They also refute stereotypical notions that women's organizations are local; or that they are concerned primarily with issues of identity and sexuality; or that they do not engage with economic policy issues.

The TFNs that I have described offer a critique of neoliberal capitalism and advocate for the welfare state and for global Keynesianism. They have actively responded to adverse global processes, including economic restructuring and the expansion of fundamentalism, and are offering alternative frameworks. In order to realize their goals of equality and empowerment for women and social justice and democratization in the society and globally, TFNs engage in information exchange, mutual support, and a combination of lobbying, advocacy and (at times) direct action. In so doing they take advantage of other global processes, including the development and spread of information and computer technologies.

TFNs confirm the importance of networks for women—whether in the form of micro-level personal relations that spawn formal groups and organizations, or macro-level organizations which operate transnationally. Transnational feminists have devised an organizational structure that consists of active and autonomous local/national women's groups but that transcends localisms or nationalisms. And as we have seen with all case-study TFNs, including those working on Muslim or Mediterranean women's human rights, their discourses are not particularistic but universalistic; they emphasize solidarity and commonality rather than *difference*. This finding runs counter to some arguments that have been made by feminist scholars situated in postmodernist or postcolonialist frames.

Feminism, Labor, and Human Rights

The global women's movement, and in particular transnational feminist networks, may offer lessons to other social movements and their organizations, not least the labor movement. According to two analysts, "[N]o major American institution changed less than the labor movement. At the end of the twentieth century, American unions are as poorly adapted to the economy and society of their time as were the craft unions of iron puddlers and corwainers to the mass production industries of seventy years ago."[8] This can hardly be said of transnational feminist networks. At the dawn of the new millennium, transnational feminist networks evince the organizational form and supra-national solidarities that socialists had expected of the labor movement in the early 20th century. What is more, they have become remarkably ICT-savvy. In fact, just as the labor movement historically emerged from the involvement of workers in social production and the exploitation they experienced, so has the feminist movement emerged from women's involvement in the labor force and from the exploitation and inequality they experience at the workplace and in society more broadly.

Historically, trade unions and communist and socialist parties were the organizational expressions of the labor movement. The social movement of women has produced women's organizations; moreover, in a reflection of their incorporation in the paid labor force, women are becoming increasingly involved in unions. If the emergence of the workers' movement represented the contradictions of early capitalism, the emergence of the global women's movement and of transnational women's organizations is indicative of the contradictions of late capitalism in an era of globalization. It is worth pointing out that in the early 1990s, when the labor movement and left parties alike were in retreat, it was the emerging transnational women's movement, and specifically a number of TFNs, that were consistently critical of economic globalization. Since then, labor unions have become increasingly skeptical of the neoliberal capitalist agenda; the participation of U.S. unions in the Battle of Seattle and in various anti-war protests could represent the beginnings of "social movement unionism." But it remains to be seen whether the labor movement as a whole—within the United States and across the world-system—will follow the lead of the women's movement in its approach to globalization and collective action.

Indeed, it is my view that a formidable alliance would be one between feminism and labor—that is, between the social movement of women and social movement unionism—along with other elements of the global justice movement. Such an alliance is entirely possible, given global feminism's concern with the exploitation of female labor in the global economy, and given the growing participation of women in trade unions. Trade union women, and especially feminists within trade unions, could bridge the divide between the feminist movement and the labor movement. Such an alliance would call for a more activist and transnational labor movement than we have been accustomed to seeing in recent decades—although a number of commentators feel that social movement unionism and transnational alliances are now on the agenda. There is increasing recognition that unions, social movement organizations, and NGOs will need to work together to counter the dominance of neoliberal economic policies, as a roundtable held in Bangkok concluded.[9] Many trade union activists "are able to recognize their affinity and resemblance to other social movements, while links particularly with women's and democratic movements are now common, accepted and welcomed."[10] Gallin refers to the need for unions and NGOs to coalesce around "a program of radical democracy diametrically opposed to the currently hegemonic neoliberalism," and to "reconstitute the social movement worldwide, with the means provided by globalization and its technologies."[11] A formal alliance among the women's, environmental, and labor movements could help move forward the project of global Keynesianism or transnational socialism.

This is not to say that there are no tensions between the women's movement and other social movements, or tensions within the global women's movement. As we have seen, Mahnaz Afkhami of SIGI and WLP has indicated that human rights organizations do not consistently take gender issues on board; there is sometimes distance and distrust between women's human rights organizations and the non-feminist human rights organizations. DAWN has voiced concern that women's reproductive rights could be sidelined in a broad progressive movement that includes religious groups that are against abortion. DAWN also has raised concerns about divisions between feminist groups in the South and the North concerning trade and labor standards.[12] In 2003, as the global justice movement morphed into a global justice and peace movement and as dozens of Muslim groups in some countries joined antiwar mobilizations in the wake of the American and British invasion of Iraq, secular feminists from Muslim countries and communities began to wonder if women's issues would again be glossed over. Ideally, transnational social movement organizations and the global justice and peace movement will recognize that women's rights are human rights and that the demands, objectives, and methods of the women's movement and of global feminism—encapsulated by the passage below by Peggy Antrobus of DAWN—are essential to the broader project of global change:

> Feminism's tendencies to reject domination and hierarchy and its replacement of the male concept of power (power to dominate and control) with a female concept of power (power to act, or to empower others), its concern for humanistic values, and its questioning of economistic considerations—all can serve as a brake against the corruption of unchallenged male domination and greed, as expressed in the neglect of human welfare in the interest of capital; the materialism of market liberalization that negates spiritual and cultural values associated with women; and, most importantly, the violence that has emerged with the rise of fundamentalism, often wrapped in the flags of identity politics, which has accompanied the deterioration in the quality of life and the threats of globalization to national identity.[13]

Globalization, the State, and Gender Justice

This book has shown that TFNs contribute several new ideas to current discussions of, and collective action around, globalization. One idea pertains to understandings and definitions of globalization. We have seen that transnational feminists are not, strictly speaking, anti-globalization. They are anti-neoliberal capitalism, but they view globalization as a multifaceted phenomenon whose most positive feature is its opportunities for transnational networking and solidarity. They would like to help reinvent globalization and reorient it from a *project of markets* to a *project of peoples.* Their literature is replete with condemnations of the ills of neoliberal capitalism. But their stated solutions and strategies are to remake (democratize and engender) global governance, not to destroy it. After all, they frequently engage with institutions and norms of global governance in order to influence policy-makers or affect legal frameworks at the state level. Thus they endorse redistributive mechanisms and global social policies because these would lead to greater investments in human development, increase the likelihood of gender budgets, reduce social and gender inequalities, and redirect globalization.

A second idea pertains to the state. For transnational feminists, the state remains a key institutional actor—even though they eschew nationalist politics in favor of internationalism and transnational solidarity. The state matters because of women's stakes in the areas of reproductive rights, family law, and social policy; and because transnational feminists oppose the neoliberal and patriarchal state and favor the welfarist, developmentalist form of the state that is also woman-friendly. I have called this the critical realist approach to the state. Thus the focus of TFN activity is simultaneously the state, the region (e.g., Latin America, the European Union, the Mediterranean), and the global economy/institutions of global governance.

A third distinctive idea pertains to the transnational feminist calls for women's human rights and for "gender justice." This call was first made in the context of cooperation with the broader global economic justice movement and campaigns such as Jubilee 2000. To be sure, transnational feminists do not want women's rights, including reproductive rights, to be placed on the back burner or postponed until after the triumph of the anti-globalization movement, as has been the case with so many national political movements. But they also believe that global justice is rendered a meaningless, abstract concept without consideration of the gendered (and racial) make-up of working people—or of "working families."[14] Without due consideration of the sexual division of labor and the care economy, of the traffic in women's bodies, of working women's civil rights (i.e., rights to bodily integrity, reproductive rights), and of their social rights (e.g., paid maternity leaves, paternity leaves, and quality child care), there can in fact be no economic justice for women. As such, the slogan "gender justice *and* economic justice" may be understood as a variation of the slogan "women's rights *are* human rights"—both of which are key concepts of global feminism that have been developed and disseminated by transnational feminist networks.

These are still early days in the study of gender and globalization, of transnational social movements and certainly of transnational feminist networks. This book has drawn on globalization studies, social movements research, and the scholarship on women's organizations to examine global change and the role of transnational feminist networks. I have argued that in an era of globalization, the capitalist world-system is comprised not only of a global economy and unequal nation-states, but also of transnational movements and networks—including transnational feminist networks. By analyzing several representative feminist networks, I hope to have generated a more powerful understanding of their structures and their agency, along with their links to globalization processes. And by discussing the ideas, activities, strategies, and goals of TFNs, I hope to have elucidated what I have called global feminism.

Notes

Valentine Moghadam, "The Specter That Haunts the Global Economy: The Challenge of Global Feminism." In *Globalizing Women: Transnational Feminist Networks* (Baltimore: Johns Hopkins University Press, 2005): 191–202. Reprinted with permission of The Johns Hopkins University Press.

Allusions to chapters within this piece refer to the original book from which this chapter was taken. References omitted.

1. Mpoumou 2000: 6.
2. Spillane 2001.
3. Statement by the Women's Caucus, United Nations International Conference on Financing for Development, Monterrey, Mexico, issued 19 March 2002.
4. Meyer 1999: 108. Meyer notes that while the radical feminist peace groups of the 1980s lost their focus and energy or largely disappeared, WILPF's formal organizational structure allowed it to adapt to new times (p. 119).
5. Personal interview with Rosalind Petchesky, WEDO Board member, New York, 3 March 2002.
6. This statement pertains also to the present author.
7. Marieme Helie-Lucas, in a conversation with the author, Vienna, January 2000.
8. Brecher and Costello 1998: 25.
9. The Bangkok International Roundtable of Unions, Social Movements, and NGOs was organized by Focus on the Global South and the Friedrich Ebert Stiftung, in Bangkok on 11–13 March 2001.
10. Cohen and Rai 2000: 11, citing the works of Sarah Ashwin, Ronaldo Munck, Peter Waterman and others.
11. Gallin 2000: 30–31.
12. See, for example, various articles in *DAWN Informs,* 1999, 2000, 2001, 2002.
13. Antrobus 1996: 66–67.
14. "Justice for working families" is the motto of the AFL-CIO of the United States.

CHAPTER 16
ARGUING GLOBALIZATIONS

PROPOSITIONS TOWARDS AN INVESTIGATION OF GLOBAL FORMATION

Paul James

Across the turn of the millennium, images of planet earth were commodified as corporate icons even as they were used to signify the wonders of local and embodied life. Just as the globalization literature began to focus on the problem of the relationship between globalism and localism, advertising images of the global began actively reclaiming the localized, the embodied and the culturally specific. Some of the examples are extraordinary. The telecommunications transnational Nortel transmogrifies the globe into a spongy human brain divided into eastern and western hemispheres: 'To guarantee our success', they say, 'we source intelligence from both hemispheres.' Energex's naked baby reaches towards a blue heaven, sitting on corporate cloudy-blue earth. Barclays Global Investors uses an image of the globe with the words, 'Events here. Affect your investments here . . . and here . . . and here.' Vectors of penetration pointing to unnamed locations are used to indicate the multitude of places where your personal investments might be affected. Lockheed Martin, the producer of weapons of guided destruction, presents a globe that has been broken into a thousand facets of localized colour or globalized significance. And perhaps in the most strikingly derivative connection of the embodied and disembodied, NEC, under the slogan 'C&C for Human Potential', uses a peacenik-style water-colour-rendered globe around which floating people—all Western, all white—link their bodies to form a kind of global garland.[1] Such advertisements, as bizarre as they are, act as distorting representations within the dominant matrix of subjective representations of globalization today. They present the globe as getting subjectively smaller and people becoming more interconnected even as the nature of that connection becomes objectively more abstract and mediated by techniques and technologies of spatial extension-connection.[2]

That such images can link global capitalism to the putatively grounded expressions of the human without appearing simply ridiculous is indicative of a much bigger issue—the phenomenal experiences (and objective relations) of globalization *are* contradictory. Subjectively, globalization is experienced as an over-bracing phenomenon coming from the outside, but one that affects life on the ground including how we eat, work and acquire knowledge (for two very different accounts of this see Savage et al., 2005; Brennan, 2003). Objectively, globalization works differently at different levels and in different spheres of human activity. In this context, many commentators have taken that experience of globalization and made it into the basis of their definitions and theorizing. Roland Robertson has, for example, coined the concept of 'glocalization', defined as the simultaneous globalizing and localizing of social life, and used it to name one aspect of this matrix of different levels and extensions of social relations.[3] This was a useful first step. However, the concept of 'glocalization' does not in itself explain anything, and I am not sure that George Ritzer's (2003) 'grobalization' takes us any further. Alongside the simultaneous and inconsistent use of such concepts as 'time-space distantiation' and 'time-space compression', it has allowed critics such as Justin Rosenberg (2000) to take apart existing theories of these globalizing tensions and critically dissect their methodological confusions and limitations.

In this context, the present article takes as its core task the problem of reframing the arguments about the formations of globalization. The article suggests that an adequate theory of globalization requires a prior and generalizing social theory, one that is able to take into account the contradictory nature of the various processes that extend social relations across time and space—from the local to global, and everything in-between. In other words, a theory of globalization has to be first and foremost a theory of different social formations. There can be no adequate theory of globalization-in-itself. Such a theory, arguably, has to be part of a broader method that takes into account the contradictory and uneven layering of different practices and subjectivities across all social relations. This is too large a task for one article to do more than take a couple of extra steps, but we need to begin the process somewhere. The discussion is thus organized around a series of interconnected propositions and arguments.

The article begins with the apparently simple issue of defining globalization. It is suggested that definitional issues hide a multitude of methodological questions. This discussion is used to draw out the series of propositions for consideration, followed then by a preliminary presentation of an alternative method of analysis. Finally, the article relates this method to questions of politics as an elaboration on one of the central propositions—namely, that globalization is structured as relations of power.

Towards an Alternative Definition

Too many definitions of globalization are reductive, with a tendency to over-emphasize the economic basis of global relations or to focus on the communication revolution as its defining characteristic. One of the most quoted, broadest and most useful conceptions in the field—a definition that does not have this problem of being reductive—comes from a book called *Global Transformations*. There globalization is defined as

> a process (or set of processes) which embodies a transformation in the spatial organization of social relations and transactions, assessed in terms of their extensity, intensity, velocity and impact—generating transcontinental or inter-regional flows and networks of activity, interaction and the exercise of power. (Held et al., 1999, p. 16)

The first key definitional point being made here is that globalization is a process, not a state of being. Secondly, it is treated as a process that involves organized social connections across space, with that space specified as transcontinental or inter-regional. This is a definition that mostly works; however it is workable partly because of its studied vagueness. We might well ask what degree of extensity, intensity, velocity and impact make for globalization. Or alternatively, why is the inter-regional or even transcontinental reorganization of space sufficient to call it 'globalization'? Why have changes in the mode of organization become the defining basis of globalization? Globalization, in the case that I want to mount, is defined not in terms of inter-regional reorganization. Nor is it, as some other definitions have suggested, the annihilation of space, the end of the nation-state, the overcoming of distance, or an end-state that we will finally reach when the local is subsumed by the global. Globalization may become more totalizing than it is now, but can never be complete—at least while we remain human and bound to some extent by our bodies and immediate relations. Rather, as I will suggest in a moment, it is no more than the extension of matrices of social practice and meaning across *world-space* where the notion of 'world-space' is itself defined in the historically variable terms that it has been practised and understood phenomenally through changing *world-time*. Globalization is thus a layered and uneven process, changing in its form, rather than able to be defined as a specific condition.

Malcolm Waters' approach gives us much more specificity, but also provides an instructive case study of the problems inherent in moving too quickly from definitional to methodological claims. He writes that globalization can be defined as 'A social process in which the constraints of geography on economic, political, social and cultural arrangements recede, in which people become increasingly aware that they are receding and in which people act accordingly' (Waters, 2001, p. 5; emphasis original).[4] This definition is not reductive and it sounds helpful on the face of it. However, it quickly fades into an over-generalized claim that globalization includes every process of abstracting mobility across space—for example, the use of wheeled vehicles in the ancient world after 3000 BCE, spreading across Eurasia from the Fertile Crescent, would fit his definition. Alternatively, beneath the definition remains an under-theorized claim that implies that where people do not believe that the constraints of geography are not lifted, globalization does not exist.

Thus Waters finds himself arguing two contrary points at the same time: firstly, that 'some measure of globalization has always occurred', and secondly that 'globalization could not begin until [the early modern period] because it was only the Copernican revolution that could convince humanity that it inhabited a globe' (Waters, 2001, p. 7).[5] Beyond the historical problems with such a claim, there are methodological issues: the 'constraints of geography' do not simply recede across *all levels* of interchange. The English Channel has not dried up, and the executives of the world's communications-connected corporations still experience jet-lag as they fly to an ever-increasing number of 'face-to-face' meetings. Put in more theoretical terms, what it suggests is the need for a layered rather than one-dimensional approach to understanding the spatial integration of social relations from the local to the global, and from the embodied to the disembodied.

Waters' approach in fact turns to a kind of 'levels' metaphor to attempt to get out of the very problem that his definition of globalization initially sets up. In the end the move fails, but it is instructive for considering what kinds of pitfalls a 'levels' approach needs to avoid. Part of the problem is that he reduces the metaphor of levels into a series of ideal types. He begins by distinguishing three types of exchange: material exchanges from trade to capital accumulation (linked to the economy); power exchanges from elections to the exercises of military control (linked to the polity); and symbolic exchanges from oral communication to data transfer (linked to the culture) (Waters, 2001, p. 19).[6] Already we have a problem here, because, as theorists as dissimilar as Michael Mann and Michel Foucault have suggested, questions of power are relevant across all spheres of social life. Power reaches far beyond the political. Similarly, material relations cannot be limited to economic exchange relations. Both projections of power and symbolic interchange always have a material dimension.

According to Waters (2001), these three types of exchange tend to be associated with three different types of spatially organized social relations: local, international and global. First, ignoring the obvious point that 'material exchanges' such as trade (using his definition of 'material') are in the contemporary period central to the process of globalization, Waters concludes that commodity and labour exchanges tend to bind social arrangements to localized settings. Secondly, 'power exchanges', he says, tend 'to tie social arrangements to extended territories ... indeed they are specifically directed towards controlling the population that occupies a territory'. This is the sphere of nation-states engaged in international relations. Again by a peculiar definitional closure, international relations are not globalizing. The third of his forms of exchange, symbolic exchange, thus becomes the arena of globalization. Such exchanges 'release social arrangements from spatial referents'. He has already forgotten that on the previous page he defined symbolic exchange as including, alongside more abstracted or mediated forms of communication, forms of communication that are often conducted as face-to-face interchanges: oral communication, performance, oratory, ritual and public demonstration. In a reversal of his argument we can say that these forms of exchange often act to bind social arrangements to place and to localize others. The act of talking to someone is a form of symbolic exchange, but it is not usually the stuff of globalization.

Waters' *Globalization,* like a lot of globalization theory, never stops taking new methodological turns to solve the problems of the last turn. 'In summary then', he writes, 'the theorem that underpins the new theoretical paradigm of globalization is that: *material exchanges localize; political exchanges internationalize and symbolic exchanges globalize'* (Waters, 2001; emphasis original)—all of which, I suggest, are both empirically unsustainable and theoretically unhelpful. To get out of the set of problems that this proclamation entails, Waters' (2001) approach takes another helical turn. He writes:

> We need to make a point here which is subtle and complex but which is extremely important. The apparent correspondence between the three arenas of

social life—economy, politics, and culture—and the three types of exchange—material, power and symbolic—should not mislead us into thinking that each type of exchange is restricted to a single arena.

In this case, the writer is onto something, but has twisted himself like a cartoon super-hero in a spiral of increasingly powerful confusion. The key implicit insight for our purposes—though never made explicit—is that processes of embodied integration tend to tie people to localities while disembodied or more abstract processes are potentially associated with the crossing of spatial and temporal boundaries.

This relatively simple point is rarely made in the literature on globalization and the following discussion will attempt to take this further. In terms of the alternative approach that I am arguing for, we can say that in the contemporary world the more abstract the form of relation the more it seems to transcend borders. Put more precisely, the more materially abstract the process of globalization, the more it has in the contemporary period been deregulated and allowed to cross the borders of locales and nation-states. While the movements of bodies, objects of exchange and processes of disembodied inter-relation are all increasingly globalized, what most commentators miss is the relatively obvious point that they are globalized in different ways. In empirical terms, finance capital flies across 'deterritorialized' national borders (albeit made possible by very material processes of exchange and organization), while refugees are administered by states with a heavy-handed vigilance unknown in human history. Drawing out of the previous discussion and taking up the method of the 'constitutive abstraction' approach outlined in more detail elsewhere,[7] this point can be taken further as part of a systematic series of propositions.

Arguing Globalizations

Proposition 1. Globalization is the extension of social relations across world-space, defining that world-space in terms of the historically variable ways that it has been practised and socially understood through changing world-time.

In other words, long before that stunning photograph of the globe, 'Earthrise', 1968, hit us in the face with the obviousness of planet earth, there were different practices and conceptions of world-space. We may not have previously come close to the current condition of self-conscious *globality*—an unprecedented development in human history—but processes of globalization and the subjectivities of globalism were occurring, both intended and unintended, to the extent that social relations and subjectivities (together with their ecological consequences) were being given global reach. For example, subjective and ideological projections of the globe (*globalism*)[8] emerged with the incipient development of a technical-analytical mode of enquiry by the ancient Greek philosophers. An understanding of the inhabited world-space (the *oecumene*) began to be debated during the sixth and fifth centuries BCE, combining information both from phenomenal experience such as oral testimony and from abstract principles such as geometry (Jacob, 1999). Lines of *objective* global extension developed in the traditional empires, arguably, for example, with the Roman Empire as it sought to control the known world.

Proposition 2. The forms of globalization have been, and continue to be, historically changing. This can be analytically understood in terms of 'globalization' taking fundamentally different modes across world history, or even within one historical moment. In any particular period, globalization ranges from embodied extensions of the social, such as through the movements of peoples, to the disembodied extensions, such as through communications on the wings of textual or digital encoding. In terms of the present argument, across human history, and carrying into the present, the dominant forms of globalization range from *traditional* forms (primarily carried by the embodied movement of peoples and the projections of traditional intellectuals) to *modern* and *postmodern* forms (primarily carried by disembodied practices of abstracted extension, in particular the projections and practices of an emergent cosmopolitan class of the intellectually trained.

Proposition 3. The driving structural determinants of contemporary globalization can best be understood in term of modes of practice that relate to social relations in general: production, exchange, communication, organization and enquiry. So that the contemporary dominant form of globalization needs to be understood in terms of *capitalism* (based on an accelerating electronic mode of production and an expanding mode of commodity and financial exchange), *mediatism* (the systemic interconnectivity of a mass-mediated world, based on a mode of electronically networked communication), and *techno-scientism* (based on a new intersection between the mode of production and the mode of enquiry). Contemporary globalization has reached its present stage of relative globality under conditions of the intersection of each of these modes of practice. For example, satellite transmission, cable networking, and the internet were all developed techno-scientifically as means of communication within state-supported capitalist markets that rapidly carried globalization to a new dominant level of technological mediation (Briggs & Burke, 2002).

Proposition 4. Globalization is structured as relations of power. If it can be argued that disembodied power, borne across the various modes of practice, has the greatest capacity to effect generalized change at a distance, this proposition can be made more explicit. The dominant form of contemporary globalization is structured as relations of disembodied power that bear back upon the bodies of the people across the world with increasing intensity and systematicity.

Proposition 5. Globalization does not inevitably sweep all before it. All that is solid does not melt into air. For example, processes of globalization may eventually undermine the sovereignty of the nation-state, but there is no inevitability about such an outcome, either in logic or reality.

It is salutary to remember that the institutions and structures of modern globalization and the modern nation-state were born during the same period; they were formed through concurrent processes, with the tension between these two phenomena being over boundary formation and sovereignty rather than in general. This argument goes directly against those who would treat nation formation and global formation as the antithetical outcomes of respectively a 'first and second modernity', or those who would narrowly define globalization as that which undermines the nation-state.[9] In the context of contemporary globalization we have seen both nationalist revivals and reassertions of tribalism. As Michael Freeman argues:

> The impact of technological and economic globalization is more complex than simplistic 'end-of-nation-state' prophecies allow, but it is reordering of the world in such a way that many feel excluded and insecure. In this situation the so-called 'new tribalism' (which we have seen is not really new nor tribalism) appears to offer security and a measure of self-determination. As decision-making power moves away to trans-state or supra-state agencies, so sub-state ethnonationalist groups are encouraged to bypass what they perceive to be their unresponsive nation-states and seek solutions either at higher levels, where the real power is thought to be located, and/or at more local levels, where autonomy seems possible. Globalism and 'tribalism' may, therefore, not only co-exist but mutually support each other. (Freeman, 1998, p. 27)

All of this suggests a very different approach from positing a 'world of flows'—of ethnoscapes, mediascapes, technoscapes, financescapes and ideoscapes—such as presented by Arjun Appadurai (1996). It also suggests the need to go beyond the claims about a one-dimensional 'network society' as presented by Manuel Castells (see Sharp, 1997). Globalization is not simply a process of disorder, fragmentation or rupture. Nor, on the other hand, is it simply a force of homogenization. Writers as sophisticated and concerned about the structures of the 'social whole' as Fredric Jameson and David Harvey have found themselves arguing that the postmodern world has become increasingly fragmented without having an account of the level at which fragmentation takes place and the level at which reintegration is occurring.[10] A similar problem of positing a social whole based on fragmentation is found in the argument about a shift from 'organized' to 'disorganized capitalism' (Lash & Urry, 1987; Offe, 1985). World capitalism has not recently become disorganized—and it was not uniquely *organized* in the first place; certainly not when Rudolf Hilferding first coined the term at the beginning of this century. It is true that the pace of change has accelerated and the life-world is experienced as increasingly in flux, but this does not mean that generalizable patterns cannot be ascertained. Both the critics of postmodernity and the postmodernists themselves may be right to point to the subjective *experience* of fragmentation. However, they have done very little to theorize the relationship between the increasing interconnection of social relations at a more abstract level (able to be generalized when viewed from afar) and the confusing, variable pastiche of fragmented practices and counter-practices apparent when viewed at close hand.

How then do we take the next step? By explicitly recognizing how the nature of our analysis depends upon the place from which we begin the analysis (in other words, the level of abstraction taken by the theory), we can usefully move across a manifold of theoretical levels from on-the-ground detailed description to generalizations about modes of practice and forms of social being without privileging any one level.[11] In doing so, it becomes possible to say that the world is becoming increasingly interconnected at the most abstract level of integration—for example, by the disembodying networks of electronic mass communication—even as social difference and social disruption at the level of the face-to-face are accented in and through that same process.

Towards an Alternative Methodology

Empirical Analysis

It is generally accepted that any theory of globalization has to be built on a foundation of extensive empirical research. However, problems usually arise over either describing different things or partial versions of the same thing—hence the aptness of Manfred Steger's (2002, p. 17) use of the Buddhist parable of the blind scholars attempting to describe an animal they have never encountered before by groping at its various body parts. As such the debates over the process of globalization are full of unhelpful proclamations. Either it is said that it does not exist *as such* (Hirst & Thompson, 1999), or that it is all-embracing or epochal

(Waters, 2001; Albrow, 1996); that an earlier stage of globalization was brought to an end by the Great Depression (James, 2001), or that the dominance of market globalization ended with the attack on the World Trade Center towers.[12] By moving to a more abstract level of analysis the all-or-nothing style of these interpretative claims can be avoided.

Conjunctural Analysis

At the more abstract level of conjunctural analysis, one useful way of examining the nature of globalization is through tracking the networks of social interchange in relation to analytically distinguishable modes of practice. Many writers already make this move partially and implicitly, some more successfully than others. Richard Langhorne's writing is well grounded, but it illustrates the limitations of concentrating on one mode of practice. He begins with the tautologous claim that globalization is made possible by '*global* communications'. This is expressed dramatically as a single determinative: the 'communications revolution is *the* cause of globalization' (Langhorne, 2001, p. 2; emphasis added). Descending into reductionist technological determinism, he writes: 'the real beginning of the globalizing process came when the steam locomotive revolutionized the transport of people, goods and information, particularly newspapers, and at much the same time, the electric telegraph first divorced verbal communication from whatever was the speed of terrestrial transport' (Langhorne, 2001, pp. xi–xii). Anthony Giddens vacillates between the same emphasis on communications technologies as the key and saying singularly vague things such as 'Globalisation is thus a complex set of processes, not a single one ... Globalisation not only pulls upwards, but also pushes downwards ... Globalisation also squeezes sideways' (Giddens, 2002, pp. 10, 12–13).[13]

Working from a quite different perspective that at once avoids the tendencies in the literature to over-emphasize the mode of communications and/or lose specificity of focus, Susan Strange (1996, chs. 1–2) takes the categories of security, credit, knowledge, and production as her basis for analysing the systems of power in globalization. Strange's categories are adequate for what she wants to understand—namely, the control of who-gets-what in the world of finance capital—but her categories leave out too much for a broader understanding. Even if it is not the single determinative basis of globalization, changes in the mode of communication have to be recognized in the matrix of explanation somewhere. Arguably, by working across modes of production, exchange, communication, organization and enquiry we are in a better position to engage in a fuller range of questions across the spectrum of concerns about globalization and localization.[14] A summary of the dominant determinative pressures in the world today would thus look something like the following. In the contemporary period, the dominant *mode of production* has become computer-mediated and less dependent on labour-in-place or single-site integration; *exchange* has become increasingly dominated by the manifold processes of commodity marketing and abstracted capital trading; *enquiry* has become techno-scientific and rationally decontextualizing of locality and specific nature; *organization* has become abstract rational-bureaucratic and centred on the institutions of the state and the transnational corporation; and *communication* has become dominated by electronic interchange, including mass broadcasting with the content sourced across the globe, but control either centred in corporate America or organized relative to it. All of these processes contribute to the extensions of globalization.

Focusing for a moment on the mode of communication, and providing an illustration for Proposition 3, we can bring together empirical and conjunctural analyses. In April 2003 Rupert Murdoch closed a $US6.6 billion contract to buy US pay-television group DirecTV, thus giving the News Corporation–Fox Entertainment nexus the first global pay-TV satellite network, including Star Asia, Star Plus (India) and British Sky. This is empirically a powerful illustration of globalization in action, but it does not tell us much about the nature of the process. What does it mean in relation to evidence that this globalizing corporation is part of promoting the new nationalism? Fox News succeeded in winning the largest cable-audience share in the United States during 'Operation Freedom for Iraq' predicated on presenting the war through the matrix of gung-ho nationalism. The stars-and-stripes fluttered in the top left-hand corner of the screen and presenters such as Bill O'Reilly spoke in the language of 'us' and 'them', the 'good' and the 'evil'. *The O'Reilly Factor* had a daily American audience of 5.4 million viewers in the first week of April 2003. Despite the global reach of Fox News, this is evidence that might be equally taken as substantiating claims about counter-globalization tendencies and suggesting a return to the boundaries of the nation-state. The point here, however, is that we are not talking about content, but about the social form of communication. Whatever the force of the content—localizing, nationalizing or globalizing—the form of the media is globalizing in its interconnections, points of reference and technological sourcing. Whether it is Fox News, CNN, or even Al-Jazeera, the dominant telecommunications systems are satellite-based, cross-referential, and watched by more than their local or national audiences. Fox News, like all of the news groups, has a globally accessible website. Neilsen/NetRatings reported that in the week ending 23 March 2003, over 2.3 million persons accessed Fox News, 8.3 million persons accessed MSNBC and over 10 million persons accessed CNN. Across the month of March 2003, Nielsen gave the 'active internet universe' as 247.5 million users, a massive expansion from that time in March 1994 when the US Vice-President Al Gore presented 'his' project for a network of networks—the Global Information Infrastructure.

Integrational Analysis

Layered across an analysis of modes of practice we can move to another level of analysis to examine the nature of the relations in which those patterns of practice occur. It is only at this more abstract level of analysis that the argument previously made about power being carried by the most abstracted-mediated forms of global movement and global interconnection can be directly addressed. At this level we can thus distinguish between different dominant kinds of globalism expressed in terms of different modes of integration from the embodied to the disembodied or abstract-mediated.

- Embodied globalism—the movements of peoples across the world, the oldest form of globalism, but still current in the movements of refugees, emigrants, travellers and tourists.
- Object-extended globalism—the movements of objects, in particular traded commodities, as well as those most ubiquitous objects of exchange and communication: coins, notes, stamps and postcards. It is no small irony that Nike is at once the (traditional) Greek goddess of victory and also the name of a (modern/postmodern) globalized consumption object. Traded global commodities today range from pre-loved pairs of Levis to the relics and treasures of antiquity such as Cleopatra's Needle and the Ram in the Thicket from Ur, a statue representing a deity from 2600 BC, reported as stolen from the Iraq National Museum during the collapse of Saddam Hussein's regime.
- Agency-extended globalism—the movements of agents of institutions such as corporations and states, but beginning with the expansionist empire of Rome and the proselytizing of the agents of Christendom.
- Disembodied globalism—the movements of immaterial things and processes including images, electronic texts and encoded capital. This is the really new phenomenon, but it has taken on a new generality with the intersection of electronic communications, computerized exchange, techno-science and late capitalism.

It is at this level of analysis that *Proposition 2* can best be understood. Put most directly, the argument here is that embodied globalism is not the defining condition of contemporary globalization, although it is still present. Despite interesting work by writers such as Stephen Castles (2000) and Robin Cohen (1987) on the post-war changes in migration patterns, the statistical evidence suggests that in terms of sheer numbers and proportions the century after 1815 rather than the present century was *the* period of embodied global resettlement.

The century from 1915 saw a sharp decrease in transnational migration between the world wars and then an upsurge after 1945; however, in relative terms, global migration was constrained by increasingly restrictive immigration laws (Hirst & Thompson, 1999, ch. 2; Held et al., 1999, ch. 6). What is new in relation to migration in the last few decades, I would argue, is the increased diversity and spread of immigrant destinations across the globe, not the fact of massive movement. However, in this argument, what is really novel, and perhaps the defining dominant condition of contemporary globalization, is the movement of abstracted capital and culture through processes of disembodied interchange.

These different modes of integration can in turn be better understood in terms of how they are framed by basic conditions of existence such as temporality. Hence we need to take the analysis through one last level of increased abstraction.

Categorical Analysis

This level of analysis emphasizes the changing nature of the various categories of being including temporality and spatiality, embodiment and epistemology. Here we are interested, for example, in the *nature* of the space that people move in, relate across, and set up systems to manage or transcend. While globalization by definition involves the extension of social relations across world space, it does not mean that globalization can be explained in terms of the abstraction of spatiality in itself. This point relates to *Proposition 1* and parallels Justin Rosenberg's argument (2000, p. 63):

> It is not only space and time which partake of these qualities of uniformity and abstraction. On the contrary, for classical social theory, it was precisely the generalising of these properties across the totality of forms of social reproduction (mental and material) which define the key question—the question of modernity itself. Abstraction of individuals as 'individuals', of space and time as 'emptiable', of states as 'sovereign', of things as 'exchange-values'—we moderns, wrote Marx, 'are now ruled by *abstractions*'.

One of the most telling processes of abstraction of space can be illustrated by linking back to the early discussion of the changing patterns of the mode of exchange. As Saskia Sassen documents, the foreign-currency exchange market led the way with increasingly globalized transactions from the mid-1970s with a daily turnover of US$15 billion. The escalation in itself was extraordinary: $60 billion in the early 1980s; US$1.3 trillion in the late 1990s. Over and above this, however, the point is that these more abstract forms of exchange outpaced more concrete exchange transactions such as commodity trading, which itself was greatly increasing in volume: foreign currency exchange was 10 times world trade in 1983, 60 times in 1992 and 70 times in 1999 (Sassen, 2000; see also Arnoldi, 2004). For all the substantial facts and figures that Paul Hirst and Grahame Thompson accumulate in order to dismiss the significance of this change and to show the continuities in the international integration of the economy from the 1870s to the present, they reduce the differences in form to the kind of empirical generalizations that an accountant might make. For example, the change in character for them is reduced to 'a switch to short-term capital' from the longer-term capital of the gold standard period. Some of 'the capital flows of the present, they suggest, 'could thus be accounted for by significant differences in the pattern of interest rate variation' (Hirst & Thompson, 1999, p. 29). This hides so much, including the recurrent themes of contemporary globalization: the speed of transactions (at one level, challenging the modern idea of regulating temporality for social return) and the transversal of jurisdictional bases (at one level, challenging the modern idea of the nation-state regulating territoriality) (see e.g., Frankman, 2002; Mandle, 2000, Amin, 2004; Paris, 2003; Edwards, 2002). The volume of traded derivatives, in this respect, abstracts from and carries forward the power of older kinds of capital movement such as direct foreign-currency exchange. Traded derivatives developed from the 1970s and grew exponentially from the mid-1980s. By the turn of the century, they amounted to an estimated US$70 trillion or eight times the annual GDP of the United States. The vagueness of the figures are testament to the abstraction of the process: derivative exchanges are conducted 'Over the Counter' on private digital networks as the exchange of the temporally projected value of value-units that do not yet exist.

This methodological conversation, as brief as it is, is intended to be only indicative of the kind of research needed in relation to the changing forms of globalization and how they are bound up with the most basic conditions of how we live spatially and temporarily. There is a final task to which we still have to attend—namely, as an extension of *Proposition 4,* to put into theoretical context what is happening to the 'wretched of the earth' in these changed circumstances. If you read the tracts put out by conservative think-tanks and governments, globalization is simply a 'great force for good'.[15] According to a recent Australian government report, 'Over the past 30 years, mainly due to strong growth in globalising East Asia, world poverty has declined. However, poverty increased significantly in more inward looking economies, many of which also were poorly governed economies' (Department of Foreign Affairs and Trade, 2003, p. 1). Presumably the second sentence of that pronouncement is intended to cover the fact that over the 1990s more than 50 countries suffered declining living standards as measured in conventional terms.

Globalism and the Politics of Subjection[16]

Each day, around the world, 30,000 children die of preventable diseases. Across the last decade 13,000,000 children were killed by diarrhoea, a number that exceeds the count of all the people killed in armed combat since World War II.[17] Despite an increasing global division of wealth and poverty, avant-garde theory tends to be consumed by post-structural questions about globalism as a chaotic process and neo-colonial identity as an ambivalent subject-position. Mainstream theory in its various guises—conservative, liberal and radical—now takes for granted the very structures of global capitalism that earlier theories of dependency and imperialism, in all their faltering over-confident dogmatism, tried to criticize. In general, amorphous conceptions of 'interdependency' and 'the borderless world' have tended to replace the hard-edged connotations of imperialism, dependency, underdevelopment and structured subjugation.[18] This two-fold softening of the theories of structured subjugation is mirrored darkly by Western mass-cultural representations of the Global South. It also brings us back to the advertising images of the globe with which the article began. Counterposed to the unremittingly positive images of the global *oecumene* discussed earlier, the images of the Global South take two major forms: firstly, as an aestheticized theatre of horror in which only a few can be rescued from amongst the mass of unredeemable; and, secondly, as a romanticized location of Otherness. The global electronic media has enhanced the possibility of us witnessing tsunamis, famines and floods on the other side of the world. However, in one of those tragic contradictions of globalism, the images of Third World poverty and exploitation are far more likely to be anaesthetized in the form of advertisements for World Vision, the Body Shop or Benetton, than they are to be systematically examined on the evening television news.

The second form taken by popular images, romanticization, can be found everywhere. They range from the ridiculous—for example, IBM's postmodern advertising campaign 'Solutions for a small planet™' depicted Buddhist monks in saffron robes meditating on the side of a mountain and telepathically anticipating the joy of being able to communicate globally—to the commodified sublime, including the marketing of World Music and the conferencing of novels by Salman Rushdie. One issue of *Studio Bambini*, 'Out of Africa', featured 100 pages of winter fashion photographed in Africa, with its front-cover image depicting an African boy dressed in safari leather-gear protectively embracing a European girl wearing a delicate turtle-neck knit. Hermès Paris advertised its silk twill scarf featuring African masks using a photograph of a European woman bearing an African baby on her back: 'Africa. Mother and Earth.'

With the problems of the dispossessed of the Third World brought into soft focus in our mediated memory banks, the virtues of the poorer regions of the world as sources of interesting anguished literature, as producers of rainforest timber, and as tourist destinations (that is, at least the unspoilt, unlogged bits), can be presented without fear of too much guilt. Commentators such as Peter Bauer no longer write tomes of expiation on 'Western guilt and Third World Poverty' (Bauer, 1981, title of ch. 4). Instead, in the late twentieth century a conservative liberal, Francis Fukuyama, comfortably pronounced the victory of market-oriented liberal democracy and wrote a book on *Trust: The Social Virtues and the Creation of Prosperity*. Why are significant parts of the Third World poverty-stricken? Implicitly in Fukuyama's account it is because they have low levels of abstract trust—that is, trust in strangers and systems, the 'spontaneous sociability, which constitutes a subset of social capital' (Fukuyama, 1995, p. 27; emphasis original. See also Fukuyama, 1992).

New attempts to understand empire have their own problems, particularly given the issue that the increasingly abstract dominant nature of power as discussed earlier does not mean that it is any less structured. This is a premise close to the hearts of writers such as Hardt and Negri: structure is the patterned instantiation of people doing things. The present essay however parts company with their attempt to bring back the concept of 'empire' as 'a single power that over-determines them all, structures them in a unitary way, and treats them under one common notion of right that is decidedly postcolonial and postimperialist' (Hardt & Negri, 2000, p. 9. See also Hardt & Negri, 2005). This goes directly against *Propositions 1–5* that suggest that globalization and thus global subjection should be treated as socially contingent, historically specific and spatially layered processes, usefully understood within a 'levels' framework which continues to take seriously the Marxist notion that people make history but not under conditions of their own choosing. Global capitalism is the dominant condition of our time. In that context, *global subjection* is a relational process, defined as a condition of subjection (used in both senses of that word) within a dominant pattern of social practices or institutional framework(s). This argument then extends upon our series of interconnected propositions about globalization outlined earlier. For example, as an extension upon Proposition 4 on the nature of power at a distance we can talk about the nature of domination across different degrees of extension.

Proposition 6. Domination and subjection operate differently across various degrees of geographical extension—local, regional, nation-state and global relations—and across various levels of social integration—from the embodied to the disembodied. Over the last couple of decades, a framework of globalizing connections has emerged as the dominant form of geographical extension through which power is exercised.

To say that we have seen the emerging dominance and increasing penetration of various modes of practice including production and communication conducted across a global reach is not to imply that the immediacy and efficacy of other levels of extension from the local to the regional are simply subordinated within what some theorists have ontologically flattened out as 'the global flow'. This simple proposition has not been handled well in the literature. Dependency theory, for example, became self-contradictory by statistically documenting dependency and subjection in terms of state-bounded development, and simultaneously treating the world-system as the primary object of enquiry. World-system theory countered this problem by designating 'the region' as the primary subunit of the world economy; however, this overly restricts the analysis while at the same time problematically leaving the category 'world economy' as a definitional totality characterized by a single mode of production.

In response it is worth repeating the point that the geo-political designations—locale, region, nation-state and global relations—can usefully be deployed as descriptive of various overlaying levels of spatial extension so long as the approach goes beyond a proposition about spatial reach. This kind of argument allows us to show how cultural contradictions and tensions of interest emerge in the overlaying of levels.[19] The corporate and communications culture of globalism is the most obvious area where we can see the levels of extension being ideologically collapsed into each other while continuing in practice to raise questions of power. On the one hand, transnational corporations increasingly present themselves as bridging the local and the global. In his introduction to the *News Corporation Annual Report, 2002*, Rupert Murdoch writes:

> Our efforts have always been driven by a fierce egalitarian spirit, by a deep belief in fair play and the rights of individuals. This is the spirit that guided our diverse operations as we've catered for audiences from Britain to Bangalore; as our newspapers have earned one loyal reader at a time from New York to New Guinea ... (p. 6)

On the other hand, this kind of presentation allows the anti-corporate globalization movement to point up the hypocrisy of such a claim given that the corporations are so obviously oriented to globalizing their profit. 'Therefore, I am pleased to report', Rupert Murdoch continues, 'revenues rose 10 per cent to US$15.2 billion.' We can also take this further to make one last claim:

Proposition 7. The changing structures of capitalism, a racing globalization and an enhanced sense of comparative place and comparative identity have both subjectively and objectively reframed (though not necessarily replaced) the old imperial connections.

Subjection is no longer predominantly based upon the old lines of imperial exploitation and domination. Globalizing disembodied capitalism, not classical imperialism, I suggest, now frames the various forms of dependency and exploitation. However, in making this argument the concept of 'framing' is intended to emphasize the reconstitutive and delimiting processes of social reproduction, not to suggest that historically long-term institutions such as colonialism or imperialism are magically irrelevant to the picture of the present. It is certainly not to agree with the post-structuralist Gianni Vattimo (1992, p. 4) that we have seen 'the end of colonialism and imperialism'.[20]

Within this emerging global (postmodern) setting at the turn of the twenty-first century, acts of imperially driven (modernizing) activity continue to occur with unfortunate regularity. When the 'Coalition of the Willing' invaded the territory of Iraq in 2002 it was clear that they were not doing so only to liberate the Iraqi people from Saddam Hussein. Just as with one of the predominant determinations of the United States' precipitous involvement in the first Gulf War of 1991—with a heavier bombing of Iraq in 43 days than in Vietnam in eight years—one driver of the invasion was preventing the anticipated destabilizing of the world's oil production. Nevertheless, despite the regularity of such acts in which imperial power still plays a part, state-based imperialism no longer constitutes a way of life. It no longer dominates the structures of world politics. Acts of domination for extending national interest claims now have to be socially legitimated, politically rationalized and ethically defended against ever-more acerbic scrutiny. Increasingly, they have become ethically ambiguous and half-thought-through reactionary attempts to ameliorate problems exacerbated by earlier activities of modern imperialism.

Despite the carry-overs, much has changed. Classical imperialism, from the ancient and traditional empires to early twentieth century colonialism and mid-century neo-colonialism was based largely upon a control of territory (however uneven that might have been) and the relatively direct exploitation of the production and trading of material commodities. It entailed forms of agency-extension, that is, the presence on the ground of agents of the empire. With the development of electronic trading, computerized storage of information, and an exponentially increasing movement of capital, there has been an abstraction of the possibilities of control and exploitation, an abstraction of the relationship between territory and power, and an abstraction of the dominant level of integration. The term 'casino capitalism' (Susan Strange's [1996] term) partly captures this process, but together with terms such as 'fictitious capital formation' (that is, capital produced without a growth in production of material objects) it gives the misleading impression that this abstraction is less real than gunboat diplomacy, more ethereal than factory production. To the contrary, when for example global electronic markets sell futures options on agricultural goods not yet produced and transnational corporations speculate on the basis of satellite weather-forecasting, both the relations and the power-effects are very real. Interests other than the importance of feeding people are framing production choices.

In over-accentuating the capitalist mode of production or exchange as the basic determinant of contemporary international relations, dependency theory, world-system theory and some of their recent variants present us with a thoroughly reductive account of social practice.[21] One problem, as I began to discuss earlier, is that capitalism is treated as a system of economics that reconfigures and replaces everything that came before it. Dependency theory gave market capitalism the upper hand centuries before it came to be the predominant formation of practice, but even in the present period it is important not to turn globalizing late capitalism into a one-dimensional system. If we accept that late capitalism has completely replaced prior modes of production then we have no way of understanding why the penetration of capitalism, as extensive and intensive as it is, has not produced a homogenization of cultures and economies. Practices of resistance keep occurring in the Third World and the First, but even that is not the answer. In the same way that the article argues for an alternative analytic scheme based on the metaphor of overlaying (or imbricating) levels of extension, here I am suggesting that modes of production, indeed all modes of practice, should be treated in the same way—that is as overlaying modes with the dominant mode of practice setting the framing conditions for subordinate modes.

This discussion is intended as only a beginning, leaving as many questions to be explored as it has answered. As the questions of method compound upon each other, it is worth returning to the underlying political concern of the article. One of its key premises has been that major discrepancies of power operate across the supposedly free and open flow of global exchange and interdependence. Alongside these lines of interconnection, contemporary globalization has also brought with it heightening inequalities and increasing political violence. It is this very ambiguity that the proponents of globalization find so hard to admit. In this context, developing a coherent theory of globalization becomes even more imperative. In the meantime, we will continue to see images of globalization fluctuate between the 'global garland' and the 'pockets of horror' as if the two are not connected.

Notes

Paul James, "Arguing Globalizations: Propositions towards an Investigation of Global Formation," *Globalizations* 2, no. 2 (September 2005): 193–209. (Taylor & Francis Ltd., http://www.informaworld.com, reprinted with permission of the publisher).

1. Earlier examples of the commodification of pictures of planet earth can be found, particularly from travel companies. For example, advertisements from Thomas Cook, Shaw Savill Lines, and Nippon Yusen Kaisya at the beginning of *The Geographical Magazine Atlas* (Philip, 1938) use images of the globe. However, they are quite limited in their generalization. For more recent examples see Cosgrove (1994).

2. Abstraction is used here as a social-relational term in the material sense of 'drawn away' from the immediacy of embodied or face-to-face relations. Capitalist exchange is, for example, more abstract than reciprocal exchange in the sense that the particularities of the persons involved in the exchange process become less and less relevant to the nature of that exchange. It is still material rather than virtual in the sense that it is practised in patterned ways by people doing or effecting things, however mediated.

3. In the early 1990s, Robertson (1992, pp. 173–174) used the concept advisedly. However, by the middle of the decade it unreservedly took a central place in his writings (Robertson, 1995).

4. I concentrate on this book because it is so widely used in university courses and prominent in the field, but also because it boldly attempts to get beyond the usual range of vague or reductive definitions.

5. See by contrast Cosgrove (2003). Rather than attributing the subjectivity of globalization to a single revolution in science he documents the deep history of globalism back through Ortelius to the Classical Romans and Greeks.

6. All the following quotes from Waters (2001) are from pp. 19–20.

7. The first sustained development of this approach was Sharp's (1985). Most recently see also Nairn and James (2005), and James (2005).

8. My definition of 'globalism' as the subjectivity or ideology framing the projection of the globe is therefore broader than Manfred Steger's (2002) when he emphasizes the intersection of globalism and neo-liberalism. Subjectivities and ideologies of globalism in the definition of this article have taken many forms from heliocentrism to classical imperialism and cosmopolitanism, as well as neo-liberal globalism.

9. See, for example, Ulrich Beck's presumptive and therefore unhelpful definition of globalization as denoting 'the processes through which sovereign national states are criss-crossed and undermined' (Beck, 2000, p. 11).

10. The classic early statement on the fragmentations of postmodernity by a structuralist is Fredric Jameson's (1991). Similarly, David Harvey's (1989) is a brilliant attempt to theorize the structures of the changing world, but he still falls back upon the postmodernist language of fragmentation without providing us with an account of the levels at which fragmentation actually occurs.

11. This is to shift gear and talk of levels of epistemological abstraction; not the

broader category of levels of ontological abstraction that the earlier part of the essay briefly addressed.

12. John Gray, London School of Economics, cited in *The Economist*, 29 September 2001.

13. This descent into methodological incoherence does not compare well with his overall position presented in the two volumes of *A Critique of Historical Materialism*. There he posited a gently modified mode-of-production argument in intersection with an emphasis on the mode of organisation: the extension of allocative resources under conditions of capitalism/industrialism.

14. For example, security is a social theme rather than a mode of practice, but we can analyze the different historical forms that generating security has taken through examining the dominant modalities of organization or exchange that it has taken.

15. From the opening article of the special lift-out on globalization by *The Economist*, 29 September 2001.

16. The following section recontextualizes research that I first did for a chapter in Darby (1997).

17. UN annual development report figures reported in *The Guardian*, 9 July 2003.

18. Going back to the early period of writings on globalization, see, for example, Robert Keohane's (1984) highly regarded text, *After Hegemony: Co-operation and Discord in the World Economy*. Despite the title of his book, he devotes a grand total of two paragraphs to what he calls 'negative reciprocity', that is, 'attempts to maximize utility at the expense of others' (p. 128). There are of course exceptions. See for example, Amin (1990).

19. For a discussion of levels of extension in relation to the changing form of the economy see Hinkson (1993, pp. 23–44).

20. Cf. the writings of Walter D. Mignolo (2000) who rightly continues to emphasize the continuing relevance of colonialism.

21. For a useful discussion of the relevance of a non-reductive 'modes of production' approach to the study of international relations see Cox (1987).

References

Albrow, M. (1996) *The Global Age: State and Society Beyond Modernity* (Cambridge: Polity Press).

Amin, A. (2004) Regulating economic globalization, *Transactions of the Institute of British Geographers*, new series, no. 29, pp. 217–233.

Amin, S. (1990) *Maldevelopment: Anatomy of a Global Failure* (London: Zed Books).

Appadurai, A. (1996) *Modernity at Large: Cultural Dimensions of Globalization* (Minneapolis: University of Minnesota Press).

Arnoldi, J. (2004) Derivatives: virtual values and real risks, *Theory, Culture and Society*, 21(6), pp. 23–42.

Bauer, P. T. (1981) *Equality, the Third World and Economic Delusion* (London: Weidenfeld and Nicolson).

Beck, U. (2000) *What Is Globalization?* (Cambridge: Polity Press).

Brennan, T. (2003) *Globalization and Its Terrors: Daily Life in the West* (London: Routledge).

Briggs, A. & Burke, P. (2002) *A Social History of the Media: From Gutenberg to the Internet* (Cambridge: Polity Press).

Castles, S. (2000) *Ethnicity and Globalization* (London: Sage Publications).

Cohen, R. (1987) *The New Helots: Migrants in the International Division of Labour* (Aldershot: Gower).

Cosgrove, D. (1994) Contested global visions: One-World, Whole-Earth, and the Apollo space photographs, *Annals of the Association of American Geographers*, 84(2), pp. 270–294.

Cosgrove, D. (2003) Globalism and tolerance in early modern geography, *Annals of the Association of American Geographers*, 93(4), pp. 852–870.

Cox, R. (1987) *Production, Power and World Order: Social Forces in the Making of History* (New York: Columbia University Press).

Darby, P. (ed) (1997) *At the Edge of International Relations: Postcolonialism, Gender and Dependency* (London: Pinter).

Department of Foreign Affairs and Trade (2003) *Globalisation: Keeping the Gains* (Canberra: Commonwealth of Australia).

Frankman, M. (2002) Beyond the Tobin Tax: global democracy and a global currency, *Annals of the American Academy*, no. 581, pp. 61–73.

Freeman, M. (1998) Theories of ethnicity, tribalism and nationalism, in Kenneth Christie (ed) *Ethnic Conflict, Tribal Politics: A Global Perspective* (Richmond: Curzon Press).

Edwards, S. (2002) Capital mobility, capital controls, and globalization in the twenty-first century, *The Annals of the American Academy*, no. 579, pp. 261–270.

Fukuyama, F. (1992) *The End of History and the Last Man* (New York: Free Press).

Fukuyama, F. (1995) *Trust* (London: Hamish Hamilton).

Giddens, A. (2002) *Runaway World: How Globalisation Is Reshaping Our Lives*, 2nd edn (London: Profile Books).

Hardt, M. & Negri, A. (2000) *Empire* (Cambridge: Harvard University Press).

Hardt, M. & Negri, A. (2005) *Multitude* (London: Hamish Hamilton).

Harvey, D. (1989) *The Condition of Postmodernity* (Oxford: Basil Blackwell).

Held, D., McGrew, A., Goldblatt, D. & Perraton, J. (1999) *Global Transformations* (Cambridge: Polity Press).

Hinkson, J. (1993) Postmodern economy: value, self-formation and intellectual practice, *Arena Journal*, new series no. 1, pp. 23–44.

Hirst, P. & Thompson, G. (1999) *Globalization in Question*, 2nd edn (Cambridge: Polity Press).

Jacob, C. (1999) Mapping in the mind: the earth from ancient Alexandria, in D. Cosgrove (ed) *Mappings* (London: Reaktion Books).

James, H. (2001) *The End of Globalisation: Lessons from the Great Depression* (Cambridge: Harvard University Press).

James, P. (2005) *Globalism, Nationalism and Tribalism: Bringing Theory Back In* (London: Sage Publications), forthcoming.

Jameson, F. (1991) *Postmodernism or, the Cultural Logic of Late Capitalism* (London: Verso).

Keohane, R. (1984) *After Hegemony: Co-operation and Discord in the World Economy* (Princeton: Princeton University Press).

Langhorne, R. (2001) *The Coming of Globalization: Its Evolutionary and Contemporary Consequences* (Basingstoke: Palgrave).

Lash, S. & Urry, J. (1987) *The End of Organized Capitalism* (Cambridge: Polity Press).

Mandle, J. (2000) Globalization and justice, *Annals of the American Academy*, no. 570, pp. 126–139.

Mignolo, W. D. (2000) *Local Histories/Global Designs: Coloniality, Subaltern Knowledges and Border Thinking* (Princeton: Princeton University Press).

Nairn, T. & James, P. (2005) *Global Matrix: Nationalism, Globalism and State-Terrorism* (London: Pluto Press).

Offe, C. (1985) *Disorganized Capitalism* (Cambridge: Polity Press).

Paris, R. (2003) The globalization of taxation? Electronic commerce and the transformation of the state, *International Studies Quarterly*, 47, pp. 153–182.

Philip, G. (1938) *The Geographical Magazine Atlas* (published by the *Geographical Magazine* and George Philip & Son, London, no date but circa 1938).

Ritzer, G. (2003) Rethinking globalization: glocalization/grobalization and something/nothing, *Sociological Theory*, 21(3), pp. 193–209.

Robertson, R. (1992) *Globalization: Social Theory and Global Culture* (London: Sage Publications).

Robertson, R. (1995) Glocalization: time-space and homogeneity-heterogeneity, in M. Featherstone, S. Lash, & R. Robertson (eds) *Global Modernities* (London: Sage).

Rosenberg, J. (2000) *The Follies of Globalisation Theory* (London: Verso).

Sassen, S. (2000) Digital networks and the state, *Theory, Culture and Society*, 17(4), pp. 19–33.

Savage, M., Bagnall, G. & Longhurst, B. (2005) *Globalization and Belonging* (London: Sage Publications).

Sharp, G. (1985) Constitutive abstraction and social practice, *Arena*, 70, pp. 48–82.

Sharp, G. (1987) An overview for the next millennium, *Arena Journal*, new series no. 9, pp. 1–8.

Steger, M. B. (2002) *Globalism: The New Market Ideology* (Lanham: Rowman and Littlefield).

Strange, S. (1996) *The Retreat of the State: The Diffusion of Power in the World Economy* (Cambridge: Cambridge University Press).

Vattimo, G. (1992) *The Transparent Society* (Cambridge: Polity Press).

Waters, M. (2001) *Globalization*, 2nd edn (London: Routledge).

CHAPTER 17
THE URBAN CLIMACTERIC

Mike Davis

We live in the age of the city. The city is everything to us—it
consumes us, and for that reason we glorify it.

Onookome Okome[1]

Sometime in the next year or two, a woman will give birth in the Lagos slum of
Ajegunle, a young man will flee his village in west Java for the bright lights of
Jakarta, or a farmer will move his impoverished family into one of Lima's innumerable *pueblos jovenes*. The exact event is unimportant and it will pass entirely unnoticed. Nonetheless it will constitute a watershed in human history, comparable
to the Neolithic or Industrial revolutions. For the first time the urban population
of the earth will outnumber the rural. Indeed, given the imprecisions of Third
World censuses, this epochal transition has probably already occurred.

The earth has urbanized even faster than originally predicted by the Club
of Rome in its notoriously Malthusian 1972 report *Limits of Growth*. In 1950
there were 86 cities in the world with a population of more than one million;
today there are 400, and by 2015 there will be at least 550.[2] Cities, indeed,

have absorbed nearly two-thirds of the global population explosion since 1950, and are currently growing by a million babies and migrants each week.[3] The world's urban labor force has more than doubled since 1980, and the present urban population—3.2 billion—is larger than the total population of the world when John F. Kennedy was inaugurated.[4] The global countryside, meanwhile, has reached its maximum population and will begin to shrink after 2020. As a result, cities will account for virtually all future world population growth, which is expected to peak at about 10 billion in 2050.[5]

Megacities and *Desakotas*

Ninety-five percent of this final buildout of humanity will occur in the urban areas of developing countries, whose populations will double to nearly 4 billion over the next generation.[6] Indeed, the combined urban population of China, India, and Brazil already roughly equals that of Europe and North America. The scale and velocity of Third World urbanization, moreover, utterly dwarfs that of Victorian Europe. London in 1910 was seven times larger than it had been in 1800, but Dhaka, Kinshasa, and Lagos today are each approximately *forty* times larger than they were in 1950. China—urbanizing "at a speed unprecedented in human history"—added more city-dwellers in the 1980s than did all of Europe (including Russia) in the entire nineteenth century![7]

The most celebrated phenomenon, of course, is the burgeoning of new megacities with populations in excess of 8 million and, even more spectacularly, hypercities with more than 20 million inhabitants—the estimated urban population of the world at the time of the French Revolution. In 2000, according to the UN Population Division, only metropolitan Tokyo had incontestably passed that threshold (although Mexico City, New York, and Seoul-Injon made other lists).[8] The *Far Eastern Economic Review* estimates that by 2025 Asia alone might have ten or eleven conurbations that large, including Jakarta (24.9 million), Dhaka (25 million), and Karachi (26.5 million). Shanghai, whose growth was frozen for decades by Maoist policies of deliberate underurbanization, could have as many as 27 million residents in its huge estuarial metro-region. Mumbai (Bombay), meanwhile, is projected to attain a population of 33 million, although no one knows whether such gigantic concentrations of poverty are biologically or ecologically sustainable.[9]

The exploding cities of the developing world are also weaving extraordinary new urban networks, corridors, and hierarchies. In the Americas, geographers already talk about a leviathan known as the Rio/São Paulo Extended Metropolitan Region (RSPER) which includes the medium-sized cities on the

Figure 17.1 World Population Growth

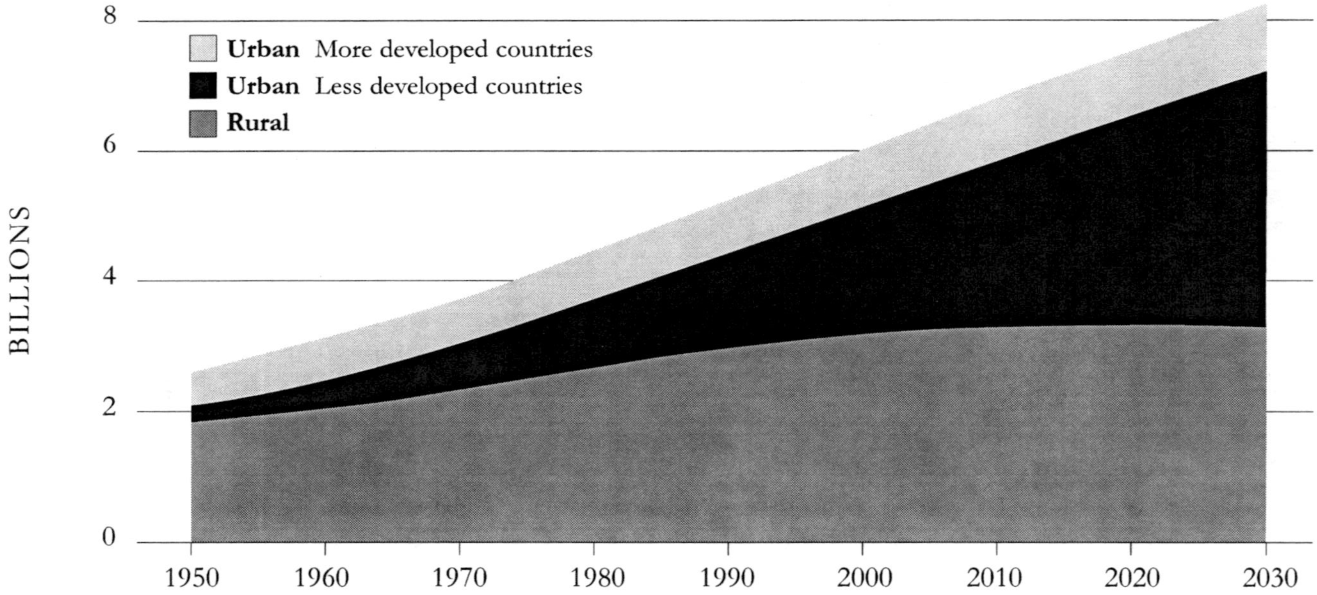

Source: United Nations, World Urbanization Prospects: The 2001 Revision (2002): tables A.3 and A.4

Table 17.1[10]   **Third World Megacities (population in millions)**

	1950	2004
Mexico City	2.9	22.1
Seoul-Injon	1.0	21.9
(New York	12.3	21.9)
São Paulo	2.4	19.9
Mumbai (Bombay)	2.9	19.1
Delhi	1.4	18.6
Jakarta	1.5	16.0
Dhaka	0.4	15.9
Kolkata (Calcutta)	4.4	15.1
Cairo	2.4	15.1
Manila	1.5	14.3
Karachi	1.0	13.5
Lagos	0.3	13.4
Shanghai	5.3	13.2
Buenos Aires	4.6	12.6
Rio de Janeiro	3.0	11.9
Tehran	1.0	11.5
Istanbul	1.1	11.1
Beijing	3.9	10.8
Krung Thep (Bangkok)	1.4	9.1
Gauteng (Witwatersrand)	1.2	9.0
Kinshasa/Brazzaville	0.2	8.9
Lima	0.6	8.2
Bogotá	0.7	8.0

500-kilometer-long transport axis between Brazil's two largest metropolises, as well as the important industrial area dominated by Campinas; with a current population of 37 million, this embryonic megalopolis is already larger than Tokyo-Yokohama.[11] Likewise, the giant amoeba of Mexico City, already having consumed Toluca, is extending pseudopods that will eventually incorporate much of central Mexico, including the cities of Cuernavaca, Puebla, Cuautla, Pachuca, and Queretaro, into a single megalopolis with a mid-twenty-first-century population of approximately 50 million—about 40 percent of the national total.[12]

Even more surprising is the vast West African conurbation rapidly coalescing along the Gulf of Guinea with Lagos (23 million people by 2015 according to one estimate) as its fulcrum. By 2020, according to an OECD study, this network of 300 cities larger than 100,000 will "have a population comparable to the U.S. east coast, with five cities of over one million ... [and] a total of more than 60 million inhabitants along a strip of land 600 kilometers long, running

Table 17.2[13] Urbanization of the Gulf of Guinea			
Cities	1960	1990	2020
over 100,000	17	90	300
over 5000	600	3500	6000

east to west between Benin City and Accra."[14] Tragically, it probably will also be the biggest single footprint of urban poverty on earth.

The largest-scale posturban structures, however, are emerging in East Asia. The Pearl River (Hong Kong–Guangzhou)[15] and the Yangze River (Shanghai) deltas, along with the Beijing-Tianjin corridor, are well on their way to becoming urban-industrial megapolises comparable to Tokyo-Osaka, the lower Rhine, or New York–Philadelphia. Indeed, China, unique amongst developing countries, is aggressively planning urban development at a super-regional scale using Tokyo-Yokohama and the US eastern seaboard as its templates. Created in 1983, the Shanghai Economic Zone is the biggest subnational planning entity in the world, encompassing the metropolis and five adjoining provinces with an aggregate population almost as large as that of the United States.[16]

These new Chinese megalopolises, according to two leading researchers, may be only the first stage in the emergence of "a continuous urban corridor stretching from Japan/North Korea to West Java."[17] As it takes shape over the next century, this great dragon-like sprawl of cities will constitute the physical and demographic culmination of millennia of urban evolution. The ascendency of coastal East Asia, in turn, will surely promote a Tokyo-Shanghai "world city" dipole to equality with the New York–London axis in the control of global flows of capital and information.

The price of this new urban order, however, will be increasing inequality within and between cities of different sizes and economic specializations. Chinese experts, indeed, are currently debating whether the ancient income-and-development chasm between city and countryside is now being replaced by an equally fundamental gap between small, particularly inland cities and the giant coastal metropolises.[18] However, the smaller cities are precisely where most of Asia will soon live. If megacities are the brightest stars in the urban firmament, three-quarters of the burden of future world population growth will be borne by faintly visible second-tier cities and smaller urban areas: places where, as UN researchers emphasize, "there is little or no planning to accommodate these people or provide them with services."[19] In China—officially, 43 percent urban in 1993—the number of official "cities" has soared from 193 to 640 since 1978, but the great metropolises, despite extraordinary growth, have actually declined in relative share of urban population. It is, instead, the small- to medium-sized cities and recently "city-ized" towns that have absorbed the majority of the rural labor-power made redundant by post-1979 market reforms.[20] In part, this is the result of conscious planning: since the 1970s the Chinese state has embraced policies designed to promote a more balanced urban hierarchy of industrial investment and population.[21]

In India, by contrast, small cities and towns have lost economic traction and demographic share in the recent neoliberal transition—there is little evidence of Chinese-style "dual-track" urbanization. But as the urban ratio soared in the 1990s from one quarter to one third of total population, medium-sized cities, such as Saharanpur in Uttar Pradesh, Ludhiana in the Punjab, and, most famously, Visakhapatnam in Andhra Pradesh, have burgeoned. Hyderabad, growing almost 5 percent per annum over the last quarter century, is predicted to become a megacity of 10.5 million by 2015. According to the most recent census, 35 Indian cities are now above the one million threshold, accounting for a total population of nearly 110 million.[22]

In Africa, the supernova growth of a few cities like Lagos (from 300,000 in 1950 to 13.5 million today) has been matched by the transformation of several dozen small towns and oases like Ouagadougou, Nouakchott, Douala, Kampala, Tanta, Conakry, Ndjamena, Lumumbashi, Mogadishu, Antananarivo, and Bamako into sprawling cities larger than San Francisco or Manchester. (Most spectacular, perhaps, has been the transformation of the bleak Congolese diamond-trading center of Mbuji-Mayi from a small town of 25,000 in 1960 into a contemporary metropolis of 2 million, with growth occurring mostly in the last decade.[23]) In Latin America, where primary cities long monopolized growth, secondary cities such as Santa Cruz, Valencia, Tijuana, Curitiba, Temuco, Maracay, Bucaramanga, Salvador, and Belém are now booming, with the most rapid increase in cities of fewer than 500,000 people.[24]

Moreover, as anthropologist Gregory Guldin has emphasized, urbanization must be conceptualized as structural transformation along, and intensified interaction between, every point of an urban-rural continuum. In Guldin's case study of southern China, he found that the countryside is urbanizing *in situ* as well as generating epochal migrations; "Villages become more like market and *xiang* towns, and county towns and small cities become more like large cities." Indeed, in many cases, rural people no longer have to migrate to the city: it migrates to them.[25]

This is also true in Malaysia, where journalist Jeremy Seabrook describes the fate of Penang fishermen "engulfed by urbanization without migrating, their lives overturned, even while remaining on the spot where they were born." After the fishermen's homes were cut off from the sea by a new highway, their fishing grounds polluted by urban waste, and neighboring hillsides deforested to build apartment blocks, they had little choice but to send their daughters into nearby Japanese-owned sweatshop factories. "It was the destruction," Seabrook emphasizes, "not only of the livelihood of people who had always lived symbiotically with the sea, but also of the psyche and spirit of the fishing people."[26]

The result of this collision between the rural and the urban in China, much of Southeast Asia, India, Egypt, and perhaps West Africa is a hermaphroditic landscape, a partially urbanized countryside that Guldin argues may be "a significant new path of human settlement and development ... a form neither rural nor urban but a blending of the two wherein a dense web of transactions ties large urban cores to their surrounding regions."[27] German architect and urban theorist Thomas Sieverts proposes that this diffuse urbanism, which he calls *Zwischenstadt* ("in-between city"), is rapidly becoming the defining landscape of the twenty-first century in rich as well as poor countries, regardless of earlier urban histories. Unlike Guldin, however, Sieverts conceptualizes these new conurbations as polycentric webs with neither traditional cores nor recognizable peripheries.

> Across all cultures of the entire world, they share specific common characteristics: a structure of completely different urban environments which at first sight is diffuse and disorganized with individual islands of geometrically structured patterns, a structure without a clear centre, but therefore with many more or less sharply functionally specialized areas, networks and nodes.[28]

Such "extended metropolitan regions," writes geographer David Drakakis-Smith, referring specifically to Delhi, "represent a fusion of urban and regional development in which the distinction between what is urban and rural has become blurred as cities expand along corridors of communication, by-passing or surrounding small towns and villages which subsequently experience *in situ* changes in function and occupation."[29] In Indonesia, where a similar process of rural/urban hybridization is far advanced in Jabotabek (the greater Jakarta region), researchers call these novel landuse patterns *desakotas* ("city villages") and argue whether they are transitional landscapes or a dramatic new species of urbanism.[30]

An analogous debate is taking place amongst Latin American urbanists as they confront the emergence of polycentric urban systems without clear rural/urban boundaries. Geographers Adrian Aguilar and Peter Ward advance the concept of "region-based urbanization" to characterize contemporary peri-urban development around Mexico City, São Paulo, Santiago, and Buenos Aires. "Lower rates of metropolitan growth have coincided with a more intense circulation of commodities, people and capital between the city center and its hinterland, with ever more diffuse frontiers between the urban and the rural, and a manufacturing deconcentration towards the metropolitan periphery, and in particular beyond into the peri-urban spaces or penumbra that surround mega-cities." Aguilar and Ward believe that "it is in this peri-urban space that the reproduction of labor is most likely to be concentrated in the world's largest cities in the 21st century."[31]

In any case, the new and old don't easily mix, and on the *desakota* outskirts of Colombo "communities are divided, with the outsiders and insiders unable to build relationships and coherent communities."[32] But the process, as anthropologist Magdalena Nock points out in regard to Mexico, is irreversible: "Globalization has increased the movement of people, goods, services, information, news, products, and money, and thereby the presence of urban characteristics in rural areas and of rural traits in urban centers."[33]

Back to Dickens

The dynamics of Third World urbanization both recapitulate and confound the precedents of nineteenth- and early-twentieth-century Europe and North America. In China the greatest industrial revolution in history is the Archimedean lever shifting a population the size of Europe's from rural villages to smog-choked, sky-climbing cities: since the market reforms of the late 1970s it is estimated that more than 200 million Chinese have moved from rural areas to cities. Another 250 or 300 million people—the next "peasant flood"—are expected to follow in coming decades.[34] As a result of this staggering influx, 166 Chinese cities in 2005 (as compared to only 9 US cities) had populations of more than 1 million.[35] Industrial boomtowns such as Dongguan, Shenzhen, Fushan City, and Chengchow are the postmodern Sheffields and Pittsburghs. As the *Financial Times* recently pointed out, within a decade "China [will] cease to be the predominantly rural country it has been for millennia."[36] Indeed, the great oculus of the Shanghai World Financial Centre may soon look out upon a vast urban world little imagined by Mao or, for that matter, Le Corbusier.

It is also unlikely that anyone fifty years ago could have envisioned that the squatter camps and war ruins of Seoul would metamorphose at breakneck speed (a staggering 11.4 percent per annum during the 1960s) into a megalopolis as large as greater New York—but, then again, what Victorian could have envisioned a city like Los Angeles in 1920? However, as unpredictable as its specific local histories and urban miracles, contemporary East Asian urbanization, accompanied by a tripling of per capita GDP since 1965, preserves a quasi-classical relationship

Table 17.3[37]   China's Industrial Urbanization (percent urban)

	Population	GDP
1949	11	—
1978	13	—
2003	38	54
2020 (projected)	63	85

between manufacturing growth and urban migration. Eighty percent of Marx's industrial proletariat now lives in China or somewhere outside of Western Europe and the United States.[38]

In most of the developing world, however, city growth lacks the powerful manufacturing export engines of China, Korea, and Taiwan, as well as China's vast inflow of foreign capital (currently equal to half of total foreign investment in the entire developing world). Since the mid-1980s, the great industrial cities of the South—Bombay, Johannesburg, Buenos Aires, Belo Horizonte, and São Paulo—have all suffered massive plant closures and tendential deindustrialization. Elsewhere, urbanization has been more radically decoupled from industrialization, even from development *per se* and, in sub-Saharan Africa, from that supposed *sine qua non* of urbanization, rising agricultural productivity. The size of a city's economy, as a result, often bears surprisingly little relationship to its population size, and vice versa. Table 17.4 illustrates this disparity between population and GDP rankings for the largest metropolitan areas.

Some would argue that urbanization without industrialization is an expression of an inexorable trend: the inherent tendency of silicon capitalism to delink the growth of production from that of employment. But in Africa, Latin America, the Middle East and much of South Asia, urbanization without growth, as we shall see later, is more obviously the legacy of a global political conjuncture—the worldwide debt crisis of the late 1970s and the subsequent IMF-led restructuring of Third World economies in the 1980s—than any iron law of advancing technology.

Third World urbanization, moreover, continued its breakneck pace (3.8 percent per annum from 1960 to 1993) throughout the locust years of the 1980s and early 1990s, in spite of falling real wages, soaring prices, and skyrocketing urban unemployment.[39] This perverse urban boom surprised most experts and contradicted orthodox economic models that predicted that the negative feedback of urban recession would slow or even reverse migration from the countryside.[40] "It appears," marveled developmental economist Nigel Harris in 1990, "that for low-income countries, a significant fall in urban incomes may not necessarily produce in the short term a decline in rural-urban migration."[41]

Table 17.4[42]   Population versus GDP: Ten Largest Cities

(1) by 2000 population	(2) by 1996 GDP (2000 pop. rank)
1. Tokyo	Tokyo (1)
2. Mexico City	New York (3)
3. New York	Los Angeles (7)
4. Seoul	Osaka (8)
5. São Paulo	Paris (25)
6. Mumbai	London (19)
7. Delhi	Chicago (26)
8. Los Angeles	San Francisco (35)
9. Osaka	Dusseldorf (46)
10. Jakarta	Boston (48)

The situation in Africa was particularly paradoxical: How could cities in Côte d'Ivoire, Tanzania, Congo-Kinshasa, Gabon, Angola, and elsewhere—where economies were contracting by 2 to 5 percent per year—still support annual population growth of 4 to 8 percent?[43] How could Lagos in the 1980s grow twice as fast as the Nigerian population, while its urban economy was in deep recession?[44] Indeed, how has Africa as a whole, currently in a dark age of stagnant urban employment and stalled agricultural productivity, been able to sustain an annual urbanization rate (3.5 to 4.0 percent) considerably higher than the average of most European cities (2.1 percent) during peak Victorian growth years?[45]

Part of the secret, of course, was that policies of agricultural deregulation and financial discipline enforced by the IMF and World Bank continued to generate an exodus of surplus rural labor to urban slums even as cities ceased to be job machines. As Deborah Bryceson, a leading European Africanist, emphasizes in her summary of recent agrarian research, the 1980s and 1990s were a generation of unprecedented upheaval in the global countryside:

> One by one national governments, gripped in debt, became subject to structural adjustment programmes (SAPs) and International Monetary Fund (IMF) conditionality. Subsidized, improved agricultural input packages and rural infrastructural building were drastically reduced. As the peasant "modernization" effort in Latin American and African nations was abandoned, peasant farmers were subjected to the international financial institutions' "sink-or-swim" economic strategy. National market deregulation pushed agricultural producers into global commodity markets where middle as well as poor peasants found it hard to compete. SAPs and economic liberalization policies represented the convergence of the worldwide forces of de-agrarianization and national policies promoting de-peasantization.[46]

As local safety nets disappeared, poor farmers became increasingly vulnerable to any exogenous shock: drought, inflation, rising interest rates, or falling commodity prices. (Or illness: an estimated 60 percent of Cambodian small peasants who sell their land and move to the city are forced to do so by medical debts.[47])

At the same time, rapacious warlords and chronic civil wars, often spurred by the economic dislocations of debt-imposed structural adjustment or foreign economic predators (as in the Congo and Angola), were uprooting whole countrysides. Cities—in spite of their stagnant or negative economic growth, and without necessary investment in new infrastructure, educational facilities or public-health systems—have simply harvested this world agrarian crisis. Rather than the classical stereotype of the labor-intensive countryside and the capital-intensive industrial metropolis, the Third World now contains many examples of capital-intensive countrysides and labor-intensive deindustrialized cities. "Overurbanization," in other words, is driven by the reproduction of poverty, not by the supply of jobs. This is one of the unexpected tracks down which a neoliberal world order is shunting the future.[48]

From Karl Marx to Max Weber, classical social theory believed that the great cities of the future would follow in the industrializing footsteps of Manchester, Berlin, and Chicago—and indeed Los Angeles, São Paulo, Pusan, and today, Ciudad Juárez, Bangalore, and Guangzhou have roughly approximated this canonical trajectory. Most cities of the South, however, more closely resemble Victorian Dublin, which, as historian Emmet Larkin has stressed, was unique amongst "all the slumdoms produced in the western world in the nineteenth century ... [because] its slums were not a product of the industrial revolution. Dublin, in fact, suffered more from the problems of de-industrialization than industrialization between 1800 and 1850."[49]

Likewise, Kinshasa, Luanda, Khartoum, Dar-es-Salaam, Guayaquil, and Lima continue to grow prodigiously despite ruined import-substitution industries, shrunken public sectors, and downwardly mobile middle classes. The global forces "pushing" people from the countryside—mechanization of agriculture in Java and India, food imports in Mexico, Haiti, and Kenya, civil war and drought throughout Africa, and everywhere the consolidation of small holdings into large ones and the competition of industrial-scale agribusiness—seem to sustain urbanization even when the "pull" of the city is drastically weakened by debt and economic depression. As a result, rapid urban growth in the context of structural adjustment, currency devaluation, and state retrenchment has been an inevitable recipe for the mass production of slums. An International Labour Organization (ILO) researcher has estimated that the formal housing markets in the Third World rarely supply more than 20 percent of new housing stock, so out of necessity, people turn to self-built shanties, informal rentals, pirate subdivisions, or the sidewalks.[50] "Illegal or informal land markets," says the UN, "have provided the land sites for most additions to the housing stock in most cities of the South over the last 30 or 40 years."[51]

Since 1970, slum growth everywhere in the South has outpaced urbanization *per se*. Thus, looking back at late-twentieth-century Mexico City, urban planner Priscilla Connolly observes that "as much as 60 percent of the city's growth is the result of people, especially women, heroically building their own dwellings on unserviced peripheral land, while informal subsistence work has always accounted for a large proportion of total employment."[52] São Paulo's *favelas*—a mere 1.2 percent of total population in 1973, but 19.8 percent in 1993—grew throughout the 1990s at the explosive rate of 16.4 percent per year.[53] In the Amazon, one of the world's fastest-growing urban frontiers, 80 percent of city growth has been in shantytowns largely unserved by established utilities and municipal transport, thus making "urbanization" and "favelization" synonymous.[54]

The same trends are visible everywhere in Asia. Beijing police authorities estimate that 200,000 "floaters" (unregistered rural migrants) arrive each year, many of them crowded into illegal slums on the southern edge of the capital.[55] In South Asia, meanwhile, a study of the late 1980s showed that up to 90 percent of urban household growth took place in slums.[56] Karachi's sprawling *katchi abadi* (squatter) population doubles every decade, and Indian slums continue to grow 250 percent faster than overall population.[57] Mumbai's estimated annual housing deficit of 45,000 formal-sector units translates into a corresponding increase in informal slum dwellings.[58] Of the 500,000 people who migrate to Delhi each year, it is estimated that fully 400,000 end up in slums; by 2015 India's capital will have a slum population of more than 10 million. "If such a trend continues unabated," warns planning expert Gautam Chatterjee, "we will have only slums and no cities."[59]

The African situation, of course, is even more extreme. Africa's slums are growing at twice the speed of the continent's exploding cities. Indeed, an incredible 85 percent of Kenya's population growth between 1989 and 1999 was absorbed in the fetid, densely packed slums of Nairobi and Mombasa.[60] Meanwhile any realistic hope for the mitigation of Africa's urban poverty has faded from the official horizon. At the annual joint meeting of the IMF and World Bank in October 2004, Gordon Brown, UK Chancellor of the Exchequer and heir apparent to Tony Blair, observed that the UN's Millennium Development Goals for Africa, originally projected to be achieved by 2015, would not be attained for generations: "Sub-Saharan Africa will not achieve universal primary education until 2130, a 50 percent reduction in poverty in 2150 and the elimination of avoidable infant deaths until 2165."[61] By 2015 Black Africa will have 332 million slum-dwellers, a number that will continue to double every fifteen years.[62]

Thus, the cities of the future, rather than being made out of glass and steel as envisioned by earlier generations of urbanists, are instead largely constructed out of crude brick, straw, recycled plastic, cement blocks, and scrap wood. Instead of cities of light soaring toward heaven, much of the twenty-first-century urban world squats in squalor, surrounded by pollution, excrement, and decay. Indeed, the one billion city-dwellers who inhabit postmodern slums might well look back with envy at the ruins of the sturdy mud homes of Çfatal Hiiydk in Anatolia, erected at the very dawn of city life nine thousand years ago.

Notes

Mike Davis, "The Urban Climacteric." In *Planet of Slums* (London; New York: Verso, 2006): 1–19. Reprinted with permission of Verso.

1. Onookome Okome, "Writing the Anxious City: Images of Lagos in Nigerian Home Video Films," in Okwui Enwezor et al. (eds), *Under Siege: Four African Cities— Freetown, Johannesburg, Kinshasa, Lagos,* Ostfildern-Ruit 2002, p. 316.
2. UN Department of Economic and Social Affairs, Population Division, *World Urbanization Prospects,* the 2001 Revision, New York 2002.
3. Population Information Program, Center for Communication Programs, the Johns Hopkins Bloomburg School of Public Health, *Meeting the Urban Challenge,* Population Reports, vol. 30, no. 4, Baltimore 2002 (Fall), p. 1.
4. Dennis Rondinelli and John Kasarda, "Job Creation Needs in Third World Cities," in John D. Kasarda and Allan M. Parnell (eds), *Third World Cities: Problems, Policies and Prospects,* Newbury Park 1993, p. 101.
5. Wolfgang Lutz, Warren Sanderson, and Sergei Scherbov, "Doubling of World Population Unlikely," *Nature* 387 (19 June 1997), pp. 803–04. However, the populations of sub-Saharan Africa will triple, and of India, double.
6. Although the velocity of global urbanization is not in doubt, the growth rates of specific cities may brake abruptly as they encounter the frictions of size and congestion. A famous instance of such a "polarization reversal" is Mexico City, widely predicted to achieve a population of 25 million during the 1990s (the current population is between 19 and 22 million). See Yue-man Yeung, "Geography in an Age of Mega-Cities," *International Social Sciences Journal* 151 (1997), p. 93.
7. *Financial Times,* 27 July 2004; David Drakakis-Smith, *Third World Cities,* 2nd ed., London 2000.
8. UN-HABITAT Urban Indicators Database (2002).
9. *Far Eastern Economic Review,* Asia 1998 Yearbook, p. 63.
10. Composite of UN-HABITAT Urban Indicators Database (2002); Thomas Brinkhoff, "The Principal Agglomerations of the World," www.citypopulation.de/ World.html (May 2004).

11. Hamilton Tolosa, "The Rio/São Paulo Extended Metropolitan Region: A Quest for Global Integration," *The Annals of Regional Science* 37:2 (September 2003), pp. 480, 485.

12. Gustavo Garza, "Global Economy, Metropolitan Dynamics and Urban Policies in Mexico," *Cities* 16:3 (1999), p. 154.

13. Jean-Marie Cour and Serge Snrech (eds), *Preparing for the Future: A Vision of West Africa in the Year 2020*, Paris 1998, p. 48.

14. Ibid., p. 94.

15. See Yue-man Yeung, "Viewpoint: Integration of the Pearl River Delta," *International Development Planning Review* 25:3 (2003).

16. Aprodicio Laquian, "The Effects of National Urban Strategy and Regional Development Policy on Patterns of Urban Growth in China," in Gavin Jones and Pravin Visaria (eds), *Urbanization in Large Developing Countries: China, Indonesia, Brazil, and India*, Oxford 1997, pp. 62–63.

17. Yue-man Yeung and Fu-chen Lo, "Global restructuring and emerging urban corridors in Pacific Asia," in Lo and Yeung (eds), *Emerging World Cities in Pacific Asia*, Tokyo 1996, p. 41.

18. Gregory Guldin, *What's a Peasant to Do? Village Becoming Town in Southern China*, Boulder 2001, p. 13.

19. UN-HABITAT, *The Challenge of Slums: Global Report on Human Settlements 2003* [henceforth: *Challenge*], London 2003, p. 3.

20. Guldin, *What's a Peasant to Do?*

21. Sidney Goldstein, "Levels of Urbanization in China," in Mattei Dogon and John Kasarda (eds), *The Metropolis Era: Volume One—A World of Giant Cities*, Newbury Park 1988, pp. 210–21.

22. *Census 2001*, Office of the Registrar General and Census Commissioner, India; and Alain Durand-Lasserve and Lauren Royston, "International Trends and Country Contexts," in Alain Durand-Lasserve and Lauren Royston (eds), *Holding Their Ground: Secure Land Tenure for the Urban Poor in Developing Countries*, London 2002, p. 20.

23. Mbuji-Mayi is the center of the "ultimate company state" in the Kaasai region run by the Société Minière de Bakwanga. See Michela Wrong, *In the Footsteps of Mr. Kurtz: Living on the Brink of Disaster in the Congo*, London 2000, pp. 121–23.

24. Miguel Villa and Jorge Rodríguez, "Demographic Trends in Latin America's Metropolises, 1950–1990," in Alan Gilbert (ed), *The Mega-City in Latin America*, Tokyo and New York 1996, pp. 33–34.

25. Guldin, *What's a Peasant to Do?*, pp. 14–17.

26. Jeremy Seabrook, *In the Cities of the South: Scenes from a Developing World*, London 1996, pp. 16–17.

27. Guldin, *What's a Peasant to Do?*, pp. 14–17. See also Jing Neng Li, "Structural and Spatial Economic Changes and Their Effects on Recent Urbanization in China," in Jones and Visaria, *Urbanization in Large Developing Countries*, p. 44. Ian Yeboah finds a *desakota* ("city village") pattern developing around Accra, whose sprawling form (188 percent increase in surface area in 1990s) and recent automobilization he attributes to the

impact of structural adjustment policies. Yeboah, "Demographic and Housing Aspects of Structural Adjustment and Emerging Urban Form in Accra, Ghana," *Africa Today,* 50:1 (2003), pp. 108, 116–17.

28. Thomas Sieverts, *Cities Without Cities: An Interpretation of the Zwischenstadt,* London 2003, p. 3.

29. Drakakis-Smith, *Third World Cities,* p. 21.

30. See overview in T. G. McGee, "The Emergence of *Desakota* Regions in Asia: Expanding a Hypothesis," in Norton Ginsburg, Bruce Koppel, and T. G. McGee (eds), *The Extended Metropolis: Settlement Transition in Asia,* Honolulu 1991. Philip Kelly, in his book on Manila, agrees with McGee about the specificity of the Southeast Asian path of urbanization, but argues that *desakota* landscapes are unstable, with agriculture slowly being squeezed out. Kelly, *Everyday Urbanization: The Social Dynamics of Development in Manila's Extended Metropolitan Region,* London 1999, pp. 284–86.

31. Adrián Aguilar and Peter Ward, "Globalization, Regional Development, and Mega-City Expansion in Latin America: Analyzing Mexico City's Peri-Urban Hinter-land," *Cities* 20:1 (2003), pp. 4, 18. The authors claim that *desakota*-like development does not occur in Africa: "Instead city growth tends to be firmly urban and large-city based, and is contained within clearly defined boundaries. There is not meta-urban or peri-urban development that is tied to, and driven by, processes, in the urban core," p. 5. But certainly Gauteng (Witwatersrand) must be accounted as an example of "regional urbanization" fully analogous to Latin American examples.

32. Ranjith Dayaratne and Raja Samarawickrama, "Empowering Communities: The Peri-Urban Areas of Colombo," *Environment and Urbanization* 15:1 (April 2003), p. 102. (See also, in the same issue, L. van den Berg, M. van Wijk, and Pham Van Hoi, "The Transformation of Agricultural and Rural Life Downsteam of Hanoi.")

33. Magdalena Nock, "The Mexican Peasantry and the *Ejido* in the Neo-liberal Period," in Deborah Bryceson, Cristobal Kay, and Jos Mooij (eds), *Disappearing Peasantries? Rural Labour in Africa, Asia and Latin America,* London 2000, p. 173.

34. *Financial Times,* 16 December 2003, 27 July 2004.

35. *New York Times,* 28 July 2004.

36. Wang Mengkui, Director of the Development Research Center of the State Council, quoted in the *Financial Times,* 26 November 2003.

37. Goldstein, "Levels of Urbanizaton in China," table 7.1, p. 201; 1978 figure from Guilhem Fabre, "La Chine," in Thierry Paquot, *Les Monde des Villes: Panorama Urbain de la Planète,* Brussels 1996, p. 187. It is important to note that the World Bank's time series differs from Fabre's, with a 1978 urbanization rate of 18 percent, not 13 percent. (See World Bank, *World Development Indicators,* 2001, CD-ROM version.)

38. World Bank, *World Development Report 1995: Workers in an Integrating World,* New York 1995, p. 170.

39. Josef Gugler, "Introduction—II. Rural-Urban Migration," in Gugler (ed), *Cities in the Developing World: Issues, Theory and Policy,* Oxford 1997, p. 43.

40. Sally Findley emphasizes that everyone in the 1980s underestimated levels of continuing rural-urban migration and resulting rates of urbanization. Findley, "The Third World City," in Kasarda and Parnell, *Third World Cities: Problems,* p. 14.

41. Nigel Harris, "Urbanization, Economic Development and Policy in Developing Countries," *Habitat International* 14:4 (1990), pp. 21–22.

42. Population rank from Thomas Brinkhoff (www.citypopulation.de); GDP rank from Denise Pumain, "Scaling Laws and Urban Systems," *Santa Fe Institute Working Paper* 04-02-002, Santa Fe 2002, p. 4.

43. David Simon, "Urbanization, Globalization and Economic Crisis in Africa," in Carole Rakodi (ed), *The Urban Challenge in Africa: Growth and Management in Its Large Cities,* Tokyo 1997, p. 95. For growth rates of English industrial cities 1800–50, see Adna Weber, *The Growth of Cities in the Nineteenth Century: A Study in Statistics,* New York 1899, pp. 44, 52–53.

44. A. S. Oberai, *Population Growth, Employment and Poverty in Third-World Mega-Cities: Analytical Policy Issues,* London 1993, p. 165.

45. United Nations Economic Programme (UNEP), *African Environment Outlook: Past, Present and Future Perspectives,* quoted in *Al Ahram Weekly* (Cairo), 2–8 October 2003; Alain Jacquemin, *Urban Development and New Towns in the Third World: Lessons from the New Bombay Experience,* Aldershot 1999, p. 28.

46. Deborah Bryceson, "Disappearing Peasantries? Rural Labour Redundancy in the Neo-Liberal Era and Beyond," in Bryceson, Kay, and Mooij, *Disappearing Peasantries?,* pp. 304–05.

47. Sébastien de Dianous, "Les Damnés de la Terre du Cambodge," *Le Monde diplomatique* (September 2004), p. 20.

48. See Josef Gugler, "Overurbanization Reconsidered," in Gugler, *Cities in the Developing World,* pp. 114–23.

49. Foreword to Jacinta Prunty, *Dublin Slums, 1800–1925: A Study in Urban Geography,* Dublin 1998, p. ix. Larkin, of course, forgets Dublin's Mediterranean counterpart: Naples.

50. Oberai, *Population Growth, Employment and Poverty in Third-World and Mega-Cities,* p. 13.

51. UN-HABITAT, *An Urbanising World: Global Report on Human Settlements,* Oxford 1996, p. 239.

52. Priscilla Connolly, "Mexico City: Our Common Future?," *Environment and Urbanization* 11:1 (April 1999), p. 56.

53. Ivo Imparato and Jeff Ruster, *Slum Upgrading and Participation: Lessons from Latin America,* Washington, D.C. 2003, p. 333.

54. John Browder and Brian Godfrey, *Rainforest Cities: Urbanization, Development, and Globalization of the Brazilian Amazon,* New York 1997, p. 130.

55. Yang Wenzhong and Wang Gongfan, "Peasant Movement: A Police Perspective," in Michael Dutton (ed), *Streetlife China,* Cambridge 1998, p. 89.

56. Dileni Gunewardena, "Urban Poverty in South Asia: What Do We Know? What Do We Need to Know?," working paper, Conference on Poverty Reduction and Social Progress, Rajendrapur, Bangladesh, April 1999, p. 1.

57. Arif Hasan, "Introduction," in Akhtar Hameed Khan, *Orangi Pilot Project: Reminiscences and Reflections,* Karachi 1996, p. xxxiv.

58. Suketu Mehta, *Maximum City: Bombay Lost and Found,* New York 2004, p. 117.

59. Gautam Chatterjee, "Consensus versus Confrontation," *Habitat Debate* 8:2 (June 2002), p. 11. Statistic for Delhi from Rakesh K. Sinha, "New Delhi: The World's Shanty Capital in the Making," *OneWorld South Asia*, 26 August 2003.

60. Harvey Herr and Guenter Karl, "Estimating Global Slum Dwellers: Monitoring the Millenium Development Goal 7, Target 11," UN-HABITAT working paper, Nairobi 2003, p. 19.

61. Gordon Brown quoted in *Los Angeles Times*, 4 October 2004.

62. UN statistics quoted in John Vidal, "Cities Are Now the Frontline of Poverty," *Guardian*, 2 February 2005.

CHAPTER 18

THE NEW PUBLIC SPHERE

GLOBAL CIVIL SOCIETY, COMMUNICATION NETWORKS, AND GLOBAL GOVERNANCE

Manuel Castells

The Public Sphere and the Constitution of Society

Between the state and society lies the public sphere, "a network for communicating information and points of view" (Habermas 1996, 360). The public sphere is an essential component of sociopolitical organization because it is the space where people come together as citizens and articulate their autonomous views to influence the political institutions of society. Civil society is the organized expression of these views; and the relationship between the state and civil society is the cornerstone of democracy. Without an effective civil society capable of structuring and channeling citizen debates over diverse ideas and conflicting interests, the state drifts away from its subjects. The state's interaction with its citizenry is reduced to election periods largely shaped by political marketing and special interest groups and characterized by choice within a narrow spectrum of political option.

259

The material expression of the public sphere varies with context, history, and technology, but in its current practice, it is certainly different from the ideal type of eighteenth-century bourgeois public sphere around which Habermas (1989) formulated his theory. Physical space—particularly public space in cities as well as universities—cultural institutions, and informal networks of public opinion formation have always been important elements in shaping the development of the public sphere (Low and Smith 2006). And of course, as John Thompson (2000) has argued, media have become the major component of the public sphere in the industrial society. Furthermore, if communication networks of any kind form the public sphere, then our society, the network society (Castells 1996, 2004a), organizes its public sphere, more than any other historical form of organization, on the basis of media communication networks (Lull 2007; Cardoso 2006; Chester 2007). In the digital era, this includes the diversity of both the mass media and Internet and wireless communication networks (McChesney 2007).

However, if the concept of the public sphere has heuristic value, it is because it is inseparable from two other key dimensions of the institutional construction of modern societies: civil society and the state. The public sphere is not just the media or the sociospatial sites of public interaction. It is the cultural/informational repository of the ideas and projects that feed public debate. It is through the public sphere that diverse forms of civil society enact this public debate, ultimately influencing the decisions of the state (Stewart 2001). On the other hand, the political institutions of society set the constitutional rules by which the debate is kept orderly and organizationally productive. It is the interaction between citizens, civil society, and the state, communicating through the public sphere, that ensures that the balance between stability and social change is maintained in the conduct of public affairs. If citizens, civil society, or the state fail to fulfill the demands of this interaction, or if the channels of communication between two or more of the key components of the process are blocked, the whole system of representation and decision making comes to a stalemate. A crisis of legitimacy follows (Habermas 1976) because citizens do not recognize themselves in the institutions of society. This leads to a crisis of authority, which ultimately leads to a redefinition of power relationships embodied in the state (Sassen 2006).

As Habermas (1976) himself acknowledged, his theorization of democracy was in fact an idealized situation that never survived capitalism's penetration of the state. But the terms of the political equation he proposed remain a useful intellectual construct—a way of representing the contradictory relationships between the conflictive interests of social actors, the social construction of cultural meaning, and the institutions of the state. The notion of the public sphere as a neutral space for the production of meaning runs against all historical evidence (Mann 1986, 1993). But we can still emphasize the critical role of the cultural arena in which representations and opinions of society are formed, de-formed, and re-formed to provide the ideational materials that construct the basis upon which politics and policies operate (Giddens 1979).

Therefore, the issue that I would like to bring to the forefront of this analysis is that sociopolitical forms and processes are built upon cultural materials and that these materials are either unilaterally produced by political institutions as an expression of domination or, alternatively, are coproduced within the public sphere by individuals, interest groups, civic associations of various kinds (the civil society), and the state. How this public sphere is constituted and how it operates largely define the structure and dynamics of any given polity.

Furthermore, it can be argued that there is a public sphere in the international arena (Volkmer 2003). It exists within the political/institutional space that is not subject to any particular sovereign power but, instead, is shaped by the variable geometry of relationships between states and global nonstate actors (Guidry, Kennedy, and Zald 2000). It is widely recognized that a variety of social interests express themselves in this international arena: multinational business, world religions, cultural creators, public intellectuals, and self-defined global cosmopolitans (Beck 2006). There is also a global civil society (Kaldor 2003), as I will try to argue below, and ad hoc forms of global governance enacted by international, conational, and supranational political institutions (Nye and Donahue 2000; Keohane 2002). For all these actors and institutions to interact in a nondisruptive manner, the same kind of common ideational ground that developed in the national public sphere should emerge. Otherwise, codestruction substitutes for cooperation, and sheer domination takes precedence over governance. However, the forms and processes of construction of the international public sphere are far from clear. This is because a number of simultaneous crises have blurred the relationships between national public spheres and the state, between states and civil society, between states and their citizens, and between the states themselves (Bauman 1999; Caputo 2004; Arsenault 2007). The crisis of the national public sphere makes the emergence of an international public sphere particularly relevant. Without a flourishing international public sphere, the global sociopolitical order becomes defined by the realpolitik of nation-states that cling to the illusion of sovereignty despite the realities wrought by globalization (Held 2004).

Globalization and the Nation-State

We live in a world marked by globalization (Held et al. 1999; Giddens and Hutton 2000; Held and McGrew 2007). Globalization is the process that constitutes a social system with the capacity to work as a unit on a planetary scale in real or chosen time. *Capacity* refers to technological capacity, institutional capacity, and organizational capacity. New information and communication technologies, including rapid long-distance transportation and computer networks, allow global networks to selectively connect anyone and anything throughout the world. *Institutional capacity* refers to deregulation, liberalization, and privatization of the rules and procedures used by a nation-state to keep control over the activities within its territory. *Organizational capacity* refers to the ability to use networking as the flexible, interactive, borderless form of structuration of whatever activity in whatever domain. Not everything or everyone is globalized, but the global networks that structure the planet affect everything and everyone. This is because all the core economic, communicative, and cultural activities are globalized. That is, they are dependent on strategic nodes connected around the world. These include global financial markets; global production and distribution of goods and services; international trade; global networks of science and technology; a global skilled labor force; selective global integration of labor markets by migration of labor and direct foreign investment; global media; global interactive networks of communication, primarily the Internet, but also dedicated computer networks; and global cultures associated with the growth of diverse global cultural industries. Not everyone is globalized: networks connect and disconnect at the same time. They connect everything that is valuable, or that which could become valuable, according to the values programmed in the networks. They bypass and exclude anything or anyone that does not add value to the network and/ or disorganizes the efficient processing of the network's programs. The social, economic, and cultural geography of our world follows the variable geometry of the global networks that embody the logic of multidimensional globalization (Beck 2000; Price 2002).

Furthermore, a number of issues faced by humankind are global in their manifestations and in their treatment (Jacquet, Pisani-Ferry, and Tubiana 2002). Among these issues are the management of the environment as a planetary issue characterized by the damage caused by unsustainable development (e.g., global warming) and the need to counter this deterioration with a global, long-term conservation strategy (Grundmann 2001); the globalization of human rights and the emergence of the issue of social justice for the planet at large (Forsythe 2000); and global security as a shared problem, including the proliferation of weapons of mass destruction, global terrorism, and the practice of the politics of fear under the pretext of fighting terrorism (Nye 2002).

Overall, as Ulrich Beck (2006) has analyzed in his book *Power in the Global Age,* the critical issues conditioning everyday life for people and their governments in every country are largely produced and shaped by globally interdependent processes that move beyond the realm of ostensibly sovereign state territories.

In Beck's formulation, the meta-power of global business challenges the power of the state in the global age, and "accordingly, the state can no longer be seen as a pre-given political unit" (p. 51). State power is also undermined by the counterpower strategies of the global civil society that seek a redefinition of the global system. Thus,

> What we are witnessing in the global age is not the end of politics but rather its migration elsewhere.... The structure of opportunities for political action is no longer defined by the national/international dualism but is now located in the "global" arena. Global politics have turned into global domestic politics, which rob national politics of their boundaries and foundations. (p. 249)

The growing gap between the space where the issues arise (global) and the space where the issues are managed (the nation-state) is at the source of four distinct, but interrelated, political crises that affect the institutions of governance:

1. *Crisis of efficiency:* Problems cannot be adequately managed (e.g., major environmental issues, such as global warming, regulation of financial markets, or counterterrorism intelligence; Nye and Donahue 2000; Soros 2006).

2. *Crisis of legitimacy:* Political representation based on democracy in the nation-state becomes simply a vote of confidence on the ability of the nation-state to manage the interests of the nation in the global web of policy making. Election to office no longer denotes a specific mandate, given the variable geometry of policy making and the unpredictability of the issues that must be dealt with. Thus, increasing distance and opacity between citizens and their representatives follows (Dalton 2005, 2006). This crisis of legitimacy is deepened by the practice of media politics and the politics of scandal, while image-making substitutes for issue delib- eration as the privileged mechanism to access power (Thompson 2000). In the past decade, surveys of political attitudes around the world have revealed widespread and growing distrust of citizens vis-à-vis political parties, politicians, and the institutions of representative democracy (Caputo 2004; Catterberg and Moreno 2005; Arsenault 2007; Gallup International 2006).

3. *Crisis of identity:* As people see their nation and their culture increasingly disjointed from the mechanisms of political decision making in a global, multinational network, their claim of autonomy takes the form of resis- tance identity and cultural identity politics as opposed to their political identity as citizens (Barber 1995; Castells 2004b; Lull 2007).

4. *Crisis of equity:* The process of globalization led by market forces in the framework of deregulation often increases inequality between countries and between social groups within countries (Held and Kaya 2006). In the absence of a global regulatory environment that compensates for growing inequality, the demands of economic competition undermine existing welfare states. The shrinking of welfare states makes it increasingly difficult for national governments to compensate for structurally induced inequality because of the decreased capacity of national institutions to act as corrective mechanisms (Gilbert 2002).

As a result of these crises and the decreased ability of governments to mitigate them, nongovernmental actors become the advocates of the needs, interests, and values of people at large, thus further undermining the role of governments in response to challenges posed by globalization and structural transformation.

The Global Civil Society

The decreased ability of nationally based political systems to manage the world's problems on a global scale has induced the rise of a global civil society. However, the term *civil society* is a generic label that lumps together several disparate and often contradictory and competitive forms of organization and action. A distinction must be made between different types of organizations.

In every country, there are *local civil society actors* who defend local or sectoral interests, as well as specific values against or beyond the formal political process. Examples of this subset of civil society include grassroots organizations, community groups, labor unions, interest groups, religious groups, and civic associations. This is a very old social practice in all societies, and some analysts, particularly Putnam (2000), even argue that this form of civic engagement is on the decline, as individualism becomes the predominant culture of our societies. In fact, the health of these groups varies widely according to country and region. For instance, in almost every country of Latin America, community organizations have become a very important part of the social landscape (Calderón 2003). The difference between these groups in varying nations is that the sources of social organization are increasingly diversified: religion, for instance, plays a major role in Latin America, particularly non-Catholic Christian religious groups. Student movements remain an influential source of social change in East Asia, particularly in South Korea. In some cases, criminal organizations build their networks of support in the poor communities in exchange for patronage and forced protection. Elsewhere, people in the community, women's groups, ecologists, or ethnic groups organize themselves to make their voices heard and to assert their identity. However, traditional forms of politics and ideological sources of voluntary associations seem to be on the decline almost everywhere, although the patronage system continues to exist around each major political party. Overall, this variegated process amounts to a shift from the institutional political system to informal and formal associations of interests and values as the source of collective action and sociopolitical influence. This empowers local civil society to face the social problems resulting from unfettered globalization. Properly speaking, this is not the global civil society, although it constitutes a milieu of organization, projects, and practices that nurtures the growth of the global civil society.

A second trend is represented by *the rise of nongovernmental organizations (NGOs) with a global or international frame of reference in their action and goals.* This is what most analysts refer to as "global civil society" (Kaldor 2003). These are private organizations (albeit often supported or partly financed by public institutions) that act outside government channels to address global problems. Often they affirm values that are universally recognized but politically manipu-lated in their own interest by political agencies, including governments. In other words, international NGOs claim to be the enforcers of unenforced human rights. A case in point is Amnesty International, whose influence comes from the fact that it is an equal-opportunity critic of all cases of political, ideologi-cal, or religious repression, regardless of the political interests at stake. These organizations typically espouse basic principles and/or uncompromising values. For instance, torture is universally decried even as a means of combating greater "evils." The affirmation of human rights on a comprehensive, global scale gives birth to tens of thousands of NGOs that cover the entire span of the human experience, from poverty to illnesses, from hunger to epidemics, from women's rights to the defense of children, and from banning land mines to saving the whales. Examples of global civil society groups include Médecins Sans Frontières, Oxfam, Greenpeace, and thousands of others. *The Global Civil Society Yearbook* series, an annual report produced by the London School of Economics Centre for Global Governance and under the direction of Mary Kaldor, provides ample evidence of the quantitative importance and qualitative relevance of these global civil society actors and illustrates how they have already altered the social and political management of global and local issues around the world (e.g., Anheier, Glasius, and Kaldor 2004; Glasius, Kaldor, and Anheier 2005; Kaldor, Anheier, and Glasius 2006).

To understand the characteristics of the international NGOs, three features must be emphasized: In contrast to political parties, these NGOs have consid-erable popularity and legitimacy, and this translates into substantial funding both via donations and volunteerism. Their activity focuses on practical matters, specific cases, and concrete expressions of human solidarity: saving children from famine, freeing political prisoners, stopping the lapidation of women, and ameliorating the impact of unsustainable development on indigenous cultures. What is fundamental here is that the classical political argument of rationalizing decisions in terms of the overall context of politics is denied. Goals do not justify the means. The purpose is to undo evil or to do good in one specific instance. The positive output must be considered in itself, not as a way of moving in a positive direction. Because people have come to distrust the logic of instrumental politics, the method of direct action on direct outputs finds increasing support. Finally, the key tactics of NGOs to achieve results and build support for their causes is media politics (Dean, Anderson, and Lovink 2006; Gillmor 2004). It is through the media that these organizations reach the public and mobilize people in support of these causes. In so doing, they eventually put pressure on governments threatened by the voters or on corporations fearful of consumers' reactions. Thus, the media become the battleground for an NGO's campaign. Since these are global campaigns, global media are the key target. The globalization of communication leads to the globalization of media politics (Costanza-Chock 2006).

Social movements that aim to control the process of globalization constitute a third type of civil society actor. In attempting to shape the forces of globalization, these social movements build networks of action and organization to induce a global social movement for global justice (what the media labeled, incorrectly, as the antiglobalization movement) (Keck and Sikkink 1998; Juris forthcoming). The Zapatistas, for instance, formed a social movement opposed to the economic, social, and cultural effects of globalization (represented by NAFTA) on the Mexican Indians and on the Mexican people at large (Castells, Yawaza, and Kiselyova 1996). To survive and assert their rights, they called for global solidarity, and they ended up being one of the harbingers of the global network of indigenous movements, itself a component of the much broader global movement. The connection between many of these movements in a global network of debate and coordination of action and the formalization of some of these movements in a permanent network of social initiatives aimed at altering the processes of globalization are processes that are redefining the sociopolitical landscape of the world. Yet the movement for global justice, inspired by the motto that "another world is possible," is not the sum of nationally bound struggles. It is a global network of opposition to the values and interests that are currently dominant in the globalization process (Juris 2004). Its nodes grow and shrink alternately, depending on the conditions under which each society relates to globalization and its political manifestations. This is a movement that, in spite of the attempts by some leaders to build a program for a new world order, is better described by what it opposes than by a unified ideology. It is essentially a democratic movement, a movement that calls for new forms of political representation of people's will and interests in the process of global governance. In spite of its extreme internal diversity, there is indeed a shared critique of the management of the world by international institutions made up exclusively of national governments. It is an expression of the crisis of legitimacy, transformed into oppositional political action.

There is a fourth type of expression of global civil society. This is *the movement of public opinion,* made up of turbulences of information in a diversified media system, and of the emergence of spontaneous, ad hoc mobilizations using horizontal, autonomous networks of communication. The implications of this phenomenon at the global level—that were first exemplified by the simultaneous peace demonstrations around the world on February 15, 2003, against the imminent Iraq war—are full of political meaning. Internet and wireless communication, by enacting a global, horizontal network of communication, provide both an organizing tool and a means for debate, dialogue, and collective decision making. Case studies of local sociopolitical mobilizations organized by means of the Internet and mobile communication in South Korea, the Philippines, Spain, Ukraine, Ecuador, Nepal, and Thailand, among many other countries, illustrate the new capacity of movements to organize and mobilize citizens in their country while calling for solidarity in the world at large (Castells et al. 2006). The mobilization against the military junta in Myanmar in October 2007 is a case in point (Mydans 2007). The first demonstrations, mainly led by students, were relatively small, but they were filmed with video cell phones and immediately uploaded on YouTube. The vision of the determination of the demonstrators and of the brutality of the military regime amplified the movement. It became a movement of the majority of society when the Buddhist monks took to the streets to express their moral outrage. The violent repression that followed was also filmed and distributed over the Internet because the ability to record and connect through wireless communication by simple devices in the hands of hundreds of people made it possible to record everything. Burmese people connected among themselves and to the world relentlessly, using short message service (SMS) and e-mails, posting daily blogs, notices on Facebook, and videos on YouTube. The mainstream media rebroadcast and repackaged these citizen journalists' reports, made from the front line, around the world. By the time the dictatorship closed down all Internet providers, cut off mobile phone operators, and confiscated video-recording devices found on the streets, the brutality of the Myanmar regime had been globally exposed. This exposure embarrassed their Chinese sponsors and induced the United States and the European Union to increase diplomatic pressure on the junta (although they refrained from suspending the lucrative oil and gas deals between the junta and European and American companies). In sum, the global civil society now has the technological means to exist independently from political institutions and from the mass media. However, the capacity of social movements to change the public mind still depends, to a large extent, on their ability to shape the debate in the public sphere. In this context, at this instance of human history, how is governance articulated in social practice and institutions?

Global Governance and the Network State

The increasing inability of nation-states to confront and manage the processes of globalization of the issues that are the object of their governance leads to ad hoc forms of global governance and, ultimately, to a new form of state. Nation-states, in spite of their multidimensional crisis, do not disappear; they transform themselves to adapt to the new context. Their pragmatic transformation is what really changes the contemporary landscape of politics and policy making. By nation-states, I mean the institutional set comprising the whole state (i.e., national governments, the parliament, the political party system, the judiciary, and the state bureaucracy). As a nation-state experiences crises wrought by globalization, this system transforms itself by three main mechanisms:

1. Nation-states associate with each other, forming networks of states. Some of these networks are multipurpose and constitutionally defined, such as the European Union; others focus on a set of issues, generally related to trade (e.g., Mercosur or NAFTA); while still others are spaces of coordination and debate (e.g., the Asia-Pacific Economic Cooperation or APEC and the Association of South East Asian Nations known as ASEAN). In the strongest networks, participating states explicitly share sovereignty. In weaker networks, states cooperate via implicit or de facto sovereignty-sharing mechanisms.

2. States may build an increasingly dense network of international institutions and supranational organizations to deal with global issues—from general-purpose institutions (e.g., the United Nations) to specialized ones (e.g., the International Monetary Fund, World Bank, NATO, the European Security Conference, and the International Atomic Energy Agency). There are also ad hoc international agencies defined around a specific set of issues (e.g., environmental treaties).

3. States may also decentralize power and resources in an effort to increase legitimacy and/or attempt to tap other forms of cultural or political allegiance through the devolution of power to local or regional governments and to NGOs that extend the decision-making process in civil society.

From this multipronged process emerges a new form of state, the network state, which is characterized by shared sovereignty and responsibility, flexibility of procedures of governance, and greater diversity in the relationship between governments and citizens in terms of time and space. The whole system develops pragmatically via ad hoc decisions, ushering in sometimes contradictory rules and institutions and obscuring and removing the system of political representation from political control. In the network state, efficiency improves, but the ensuing gains in legitimacy by the nation-state deepen its crisis, although overall political legitimacy may improve if local and regional institutions play their role. Yet the growing autonomy of the local and regional state may bring the different levels of the state into competition against one another.

The practice of global governance through ad hoc networks confronts a number of major problems that evolve out of the contradiction between the historically constructed nature of the institutions that come into the network and the new functions and mechanisms they have to assume to perform in the network while still relating to their nation-bound societies. The network state faces a *coordination problem* with three aspects: organizational, technical, and political. The state faces organizational problems because agencies that previously flourished via territoriality and authority vis-à-vis their societies cannot have the same structure, reward systems, and operational principles as agencies whose fundamental role is to find synergy with other agencies. Technical coordination problems take place because protocols of communication do not work. The introduction of the Internet and computer networks often disorganizes agencies rather than facilitating synergies. Agencies often resist networking technology. Political coordination problems evolve not only horizontally between agencies but also vertically because networking between agencies and supervisory bodies necessitates a loss of bureaucratic autonomy. Moreover, agencies must also network with their citizen constituencies, thus bringing pressure on the bureaucracies to be more responsive to the citizen-clients.

The development of the network state also needs to confront an ideological problem: coordinating a common policy means a common language and a set of shared values. Examples include opposition to market fundamentalism in the regulation of markets, acceptance of sustainable development in environmental policy, or the prioritization of human rights over the *raison d'état* in security policy. More often than not, governments do not share the same principles or the same interpretation of common principles.

There is also a lingering geopolitical problem. Nation-states still see the networks of governance as a negotiating table upon which to impose their specific interests. There is a stalemate in the intergovernmental decision-making processes because the culture of cooperation is lacking. The overarching principles are the interests of the nation-state and the domination of the personal/political/social interests in service of each nation-state. Governments see the global state as an opportunity to maximize their own interests, rather than a new context in which political institutions have to govern together. In fact, the more the globalization process proceeds, the more contradictions it generates (e.g., identity crises, economic crises, and security crises), leading to a revival of nationalism and to the primacy of sovereignty. These tensions underlie the attempts by various governments to pursue unilateralism in their policies in spite of the objective multilateralism that results from global interdependence in our world (Nye 2002).

As long as these contradictions persist, it is difficult, if not impossible, for the world's geopolitical actors to shift from the practice of a pragmatic, ad hoc networking form of negotiated decision making to a system of constitutionally accepted networked global governance (Habermas 1998).

The New Public Sphere

The new political system in a globalized world emerges from the processes of the formation of a global civil society and a global network state that supersedes and integrates the preexisting nation-states without dissolving them into a global government. There is a process of the emergence of de facto global governance without a global government. The transition from these pragmatic forms of sociopolitical organization and decision making to a more elaborate global institutional system requires the coproduction of meaning and the sharing of values between global civil society and the global network state. This transformation is influenced and fought over by cultural/ideational materials through which the political and social interests work to enact the transformation of the state. In the last analysis, the will of the people emerges from people's minds. And people make up their minds on the issues that affect their lives, as well as the future of humankind, from the messages and debates that take place in the public sphere. The contemporary global public sphere is largely dependent on the global/local communication media system. This media system includes television, radio, and the print press, as well as a variety of multimedia and communications systems, among which the Internet and horizontal networks of communication now play a decisive role (Bennett 2004; Dahlgren 2005; Tremayne 2007). There is a shift from a public sphere anchored around the national institutions of territorially bound societies to a public sphere constituted around the media system (Volkmer 1999; El-Nawawy and Iskander 2002; Paterson and Sreberny 2004). This media system includes what I have conceptualized as mass self-communication, that is, networks of communication that relate many-to-many in the sending and receiving of messages in a multimodal form of communication that bypasses mass media and often escapes government control (Castells 2007).

The current media system is local and global at the same time. It is organized around a core formed by media business groups with global reach and their networks (Arsenault and Castells forthcoming). But at the same time, it is dependent on state regulations and focused on narrowcasting to specific audiences (Price 2002). By acting on the media system, particularly by creating events that send powerful images and messages, transnational activists induce a debate on the hows, whys, and whats of globalization and on related societal choices (Juris forthcoming). It is through the media, both mass media and horizontal networks of communication, that nonstate actors influence people's minds and foster social change. Ultimately, the transformation of consciousness does have consequences on political behavior, on voting patterns, and on the decisions of governments. It is at the level of media politics where it appears that societies can be moved in a direction that diverges from the values and interests institutionalized in the political system.

Thus, it is essential for state actors, and for intergovernmental institutions, such as the United Nations, to relate to civil society not only around institutional mechanisms and procedures of political representation but in public debates in the global public sphere. That global public sphere is built around the media communication system and Internet networks, particularly in the social spaces of the Web 2.0, as exemplified by YouTube, MySpace, Facebook, and the growing blogosphere that by mid-2007 counted 70 million blogs and was doubling in size every six months (Tremayne 2007). A series of major conferences was organized by the UN during the 1990s on issues pertinent to humankind (from the condition of women to environmental conservation). While not very effective in terms of designing policy, these conferences were essential in fostering a global dialogue, in raising public awareness, and in providing the platform on which the global civil society could move to the forefront of the policy debate. Therefore, stimulating the consolidation of this communication-based public sphere is one key mechanism with which states and international institutions can engage with the demands and projects of the global civil society. This can take place by stimulating dialogue regarding specific initiatives and recording, on an ongoing basis, the contributions of this dialogue so that it can inform policy making in the international arena. To harness the power of the world's public opinion through global media and Internet networks is the most effective form of broadening political participation on a global scale, by inducing a fruitful, synergistic connection between the government-based international institutions and the global civil society. This multimodal communication space is what constitutes the new global public sphere.

Conclusion: Public Diplomacy and the Global Public Sphere

Public diplomacy is not propaganda. And it is not government diplomacy. We do not need to use a new concept to designate the traditional practices of diplomacy. Public diplomacy is the diplomacy of the public, that is, the projection in the international arena of the values and ideas of the public. The public is not the government because it is not formalized in the institutions of the state. By *the public*, we usually mean what is common to a given social organization that transcends the private. The private is the domain of self-defined interests and values, while the public is the domain of the shared interests and values (Dewey 1954). The implicit project behind the idea of public diplomacy is not to assert the power of a state or of a social actor in the form of "soft power." It is, instead, to harness the dialogue between different social collectives and their cultures in the hope of sharing meaning and understanding. The aim of the practice of public diplomacy is not to convince but to communicate, not to declare but to listen. Public diplomacy seeks to build a public sphere in which diverse voices can be heard in spite of their various origins, distinct values, and often contradictory interests. The goal of public diplomacy, in contrast to government diplomacy, is not to assert power or to negotiate a rearrangement of power relationships. It is to induce a communication space in which a new, common language could emerge as a precondition for diplomacy, so that when the time for diplomacy comes, it reflects not only interests and power making but also meaning and sharing. In this sense, public diplomacy intervenes in the global space equivalent to what has been traditionally conceived as the public sphere in the national system. It is a terrain of cultural engagement in which ideational materials are produced and confronted by various social actors, creating the conditions under which different projects can be channeled by the global civil society and the political institutions of global governance toward an informed process of decision making that respects the differences and weighs policy alternatives.

Because we live in a globalized, interdependent world, the space of political codecision is necessarily global. And the choice that we face is either to construct the global political system as an expression of power relationships without cultural mediation or else to develop a global public sphere around the global networks of communication, from which the public debate could inform the emergence of a new form of consensual global governance. If the choice is the latter, public diplomacy, understood as networked communication and shared meaning, becomes a decisive tool for the attainment of a sustainable world order.

Note

Manuel Castells, "The New Public Sphere: Global Civil Society, Communication, Networks, and Global Governance," *The ANNALS of the American Academy of Political Science* 616, no. 1 (March 2008): 78–93. Reprinted by permission of Sage Publications.

References

Anheier, Helmut, Marlies Glasius, and Mary Kaldor, eds. 2004. *Global civil society 2004/5.* London: Sage.

Arsenault, Amelia. 2007. The international crisis of legitimacy. Unpublished working paper.

Arsenault, Amelia, and Manuel Castells. Forthcoming. Structure and dynamics of global multimedia business networks. *International Journal of Communication.*

Barber, Benjamin R. 1995. *Jihad vs. McWorld.* New York: Times Books.

Bauman, Zygmunt. 1999. *In search of politics.* Stanford, CA: Stanford University Press.

Beck, Ulrich. 2000. *What is globalization?* Malden, MA: Polity.

———. 2006. *Power in the global age.* Cambridge, UK: Polity.

Bennett, W. Lance. 2004. Global media and politics: Transnational communication regimes and civic cultures. *Annual Review of Political Science* 7 (1): 125–48.

Calderón, G., Fernando, ed. 2003. *Es sostenible la globalización en América Latina?* Santiago, Chile: Fondo de Cultura Económica PNUD-Bolivia.

Caputo, Dante, ed. 2004. *La democracia en America Latina.* Pograma de Naciones Unidas para el Desarrollo. Buenos Aires, Argentina: Aguilar, Altea, Alfaguara.

Cardoso, Gustavo. 2006. *The media in the network society.* Lisbon, Portugal: Center for Research and Studies in Sociology.

Castells, Manuel. 1996. *The rise of the network society.* Oxford, UK: Blackwell.

———, ed. 2004a. *The network society: A cross-cultural perspective.* Northampton, MA: Edward Elgar.

———. 2004b. The power of identity. Malden, MA: Blackwell.

———. 2007. Communication, power and counter-power in the network society. *International Journal of Communication* 1:238–66.

Castells, Manuel, Mireia Fernandez-Ardevol, Jack Linchuan Qui, and Araba Sey. 2006. *Mobile communication and society: A global perspective.* Cambridge, MA: MIT Press.

Castells, Manuel, Shujiro Yazawa, and Emma Kiselyova. 1996. Insurgents against the new global order: A comparative analysis of Mexico's Zapatistas, the American militia, and Japan's Aum Shinrikyo. *Berkeley Journal of Sociology* 40:21–59.

Catterberg, Gabriela, and Alejandro Moreno. 2005. The individual bases of political trust: Trends in new and established democracies. *International Journal of Public Opinion Research* 18 (1): 31–48.

Chester, Jeff. 2007. *Digital destiny. New media and the future of democracy.* New York: New Press.

Costanza-Chock, Sasha. 2006. *Analytical note: Horizontal communication and social movements.* Los Angeles: Annenberg School of Communication.

Dahlgren, Peter. 2005. The Internet, public spheres, and political communication: Dispersion and deliberation. *Political Communication* 22:147–62.

Dalton, Russell J. 2005. The social transformation of trust in government. *International Review of Sociology* 15 (1): 133–54.

———. 2006. *Citizen politics: Public opinion and political parties in advanced industrial democracies.* Washington, DC: CQ Press.

Dean, Jodi, Jon W. Anderson, and Geert Lovink, eds. 2006. *Reformatting politics: Information technology and global civil society.* New York: Routledge.

Dewey, John. 1954. *The public and its problems.* Chicago: Swallow Press.

El-Nawawy, Mohammed, and Adel Iskander. 2002. *Al-jazeera: How the free Arab news network scooped the world and changed the Middle East.* Cambridge, MA: Westview.

Forsythe, David P. 2000. *Human rights in international relations.* Cambridge: Cambridge University Press.

Gallup International. 2006. The voice of the people. International survey conducted for the World Economic Forum. http://www.gallup-international.com/.

Giddens, Anthony. 1979. *Central problems in social theory: Action, structure, and contradiction in social analysis.* Berkeley: University of California Press.

Giddens, Anthony, and Will Hutton. 2000. *On the edge: Living with global capitalism.* London: Jonathan Cape.

Gilbert, Neil. 2002. *Transformation of the welfare state: The silent surrender of public responsibility.* Oxford: Oxford University Press.

Gillmor, Dan. 2004. *We the media: Grassroots journalism by the people for the people.* Sebastopol, CA: O'Reilly.

Glasius, Marlies, Mary Kaldor, and Helmut Anheier, eds. 2005. *Global civil society 2005/6.* London: Sage.

Grundmann, Reiner. 2001. Transnational environmental policy: Reconstructing ozone. London: Routledge.

Guidry, John A., Michael D. Kennedy, and Mayer N. Zald. 2000. *Globalizations and social movements: Culture, power, and the transnational public sphere.* Ann Arbor: University of Michigan Press.

Habermas, Jürgen. 1976. *Legitimation crisis.* London: Heinemann Educational Books.

———. 1989. *The structural transformation of the public sphere.* Cambridge, UK: Polity.

———. 1996. *Between facts and norms: Contributions to a discourse theory of law and democracy.* Cambridge, MA: MIT Press.

———. 1998. *Die postnationale konstellation: Politische essays.* Frankfurt am Main, Germany: Suhrkamp.

Held, David. 2004. *Global covenant: The social democratic alternative to the Washington consensus.* Malden, MA: Polity.

Held, David, and Ayse Kaya. 2006. *Global inequality: Patterns and explanations.* Cambridge, UK: Polity.

Held, David, and Anthony G. McGrew, eds. 2007. Globalization theory: Approaches and controversies. London: Polity.

Held, David, Anthony G. McGrew, David Goldblatt, and Jonathan Perraton, eds. 1999. *Global transformations: Politics, economics and culture.* Cambridge, UK: Polity.

Jacquet, Pierre, Jean Pisani-Ferry, and Laurence Tubiana, eds. 2002. *Gouvernance mondiale.* Paris: Documentation Française.

Juris, Jeffrey. 2004. Networked social movements: The movement against corporate globalization. In *The network society: A cross-cultural perspective,* ed. Manuel Castells, 341–62. Cheltenham, UK: Edward Elgar.

———. Forthcoming. Networking futures: The movements against corporate globalization. Durham, NC: Duke University Press.

Kaldor, Mary. 2003. *Global civil society: An answer to war.* Malden, MA: Polity.

Kaldor, Mary, Helmut Anheier, and Marlies Glasius, eds. 2006. *Global civil society 2006/7.* London: Sage.

Keck, Margaret E., and Kathryn Sikkink. 1998. *Activists beyond borders: Advocacy networks in international politics.* Ithaca, NY: Cornell University Press.

Keohane, Robert O. 2002. *Power and governance in a partially globalized world.* London: Routledge.

Low, Setha M., and Neil Smith, eds. 2006. *The politics of public space.* New York: Routledge.

Lull, James. 2007. *Culture-on-demand: Communication in a crisis world.* Malden, MA: Blackwell.

Mann, Michael. 1986. *The sources of social power,* vol. I, *A history of power from the beginning to A.D. 1760.* Cambridge: Cambridge University Press.

———. 1993. *The sources of social power,* vol. II, *The rise of classes and nation-states, 1760–1914.* Cambridge: Cambridge University Press.

McChesney, Robert Waterman. 2007. *Communication revolution: Critical junctures and the future of media.* New York: New Press.

Mydans, Seth. 2007. Myanmar comes face to face with a technology revolution. *International Herald Tribune,* October 3.

Nye, Joseph S. 2002. *The paradox of American power: Why the world's only superpower can't go it alone.* New York: Oxford University Press.

Nye, Joseph S., and John D. Donahue, eds. 2000. *Governance in a globalizing world.* Washington, DC: Brookings Institution Press.

Paterson, Chris A., and Annabelle Sreberny. 2004. *International news in the 21st century.* Eastleigh, UK: University of Luton Press.

Price, Monroe E. 2002. *Media and sovereignty: The global information revolution and its challenge to state power.* Cambridge, MA: MIT Press.

Putnam, Robert D. 2000. *Bowling alone: The collapse and revival of American community.* New York: Simon & Schuster.

Sassen, Saskia. 2006. *Territory, authority, rights: From medieval to global assemblages.* Princeton, NJ: Princeton University Press.

Soros, George. 2006. *The age of fallibility: The consequences of the war on terror.* New York: PublicAffairs.

Stewart, Angus. 2001. *Theories of power and domination: The politics of empowerment in late modernity.* London: Sage.

Thompson, John B. 2000. *Political scandal: Power and visibility in the media age.* Cambridge, UK: Polity.

Tremayne, Mark, ed. 2007. *Blogging, citizenship, and the future of media.* London: Routledge.

Volkmer, Ingrid. 1999. *News in the global sphere: A study of CNN and its impact on global communication.* Eastleigh, UK: University of Luton Press.

———. 2003. The global network society and the global public sphere. *Journal of Development* 46 (4): 9–16.

CHAPTER 19
GLOBALIZATION AND THE EMERGENCE OF THE WORLD SOCIAL FORUMS

Jackie Smith and Marina Karides et al.

In the 1970s and 1980s, protests against the lending policies of the International Monetary Fund (IMF) emerged in the global south. By the late 1990s, tens of thousands of protesters were gathering wherever the world's political and economic elite met, raising criticisms of global economic policies and calling for more just and equitable economic policies. As the numbers of protesters grew, so did the violence with which governments responded. Governments spent millions and arrested hundreds of nonviolent protesters to ensure their meetings could take place. Italian police killed Carlo Giuliani, a twenty-three-year-old protester, at the meeting of the Group of 8 (G8) in Genoa in 2001, dramatizing for activists in the global north the brutal repression against activists that is common in the global south. The size of police mobilizations against these overwhelmingly nonviolent protests was unprecedented in Western democracies, and it signaled the declining legitimacy of the system of economic globalization promoted by the world's most powerful governments. After years of such protests against the world's most powerful economic institutions—the World Bank, the International

Monetary Fund, the World Trade Organization (WTO), and the G8—a team of Latin American and French activists launched the first World Social Forum (WSF) in January 2001.

Over just a few short years, the WSF has become the largest political gathering in modern history and a major focal point of global efforts to promote an alternative vision of global integration. Mobilizing around the slogan "Another World Is Possible," the WSF began as both a protest against the annual World Economic Forum (WEF) in Davos, Switzerland, and as an effort to develop a shared vision of alternatives to the predominant, market-based model of globalization. Many see the WSF as a crucial process for the development of a global civil society that can help democratize the global political and economic order, and some would argue that it is the most important political development of our time. This book aims to introduce readers to the WSF process—by which we mean the networked, repeated, interconnected, and multilevel gatherings of diverse groups of people around the aim of bringing about a more just and humane world—and the possibilities and challenges this process holds. In this chapter we describe the political and economic conditions that gave rise to the global justice movement and the WSF.

The first WSF was held in Porto Alegre, Brazil, in late January 2001. The timing of the WSF was strategically chosen to coincide with the WEF, an annual meeting of global political and economic elites typically held in Davos, Switzerland. The WEF is a private interest group that has worked since its founding in 1971 to promote dialogue among business leaders and governments and to shape the global economy. Over the years an ever-more-impressive list of political leaders have participated in this private event, for which corporate members pay upward of $15,000 for the opportunity to schmooze with the global power elite. Civil society has been largely shut out of the process of planning an increasingly powerful global economy.

The WEF is widely criticized for providing a space where the future of the world is decided while excluding the democratic participation of most of the globe's population. French and Latin American activist groups and political organizations were among the first to protest the WEF in 1999. This eventually blossomed into the idea of a WSF that received sponsorship in Brazil from the Worker's Party, a political party that won government elections in the city of Porto Alegre, supported the principles of global economic justice, and was willing to work with social change activists to coordinate the first WSF.

This first meeting in Porto Alegre, Brazil, drew more than twice the 4,000 people organizers anticipated, and the global meeting now regularly attracts more than 150,000 registered participants. Its first attempt to move outside of Porto Alegre was in 2004 when the WSF met in Mumbai, India. After a return to Porto Alegre in 2005, it moved to Africa (Nairobi) in 2007 in an effort to expand opportunities for different activists to participate. Inspired by the call for open discussions of and organizing around visions of "another world," activists launched regional and local counterparts to the WSF around the world. This expanded opportunities for citizens to become part of the WSF process and helped sustain and energize local organizing efforts.

The WSF has become an important, but certainly not the only, focal point for the global justice movement. It is a setting where activists can meet their counterparts from other parts of the world, expand their understandings of globalization and of the interdependencies among the world's peoples, and plan joint campaigns to promote their common aims. It allows people to actively debate proposals for organizing global policy while nurturing values of tolerance, equality, and participation. And it has generated some common ideas about other visions for a better world. Unlike the WEF, the activities of the WSF are crucial to cultivating a foundation for a more democratic global economic and political order.

The WSF not only fosters networking among activists from different places, but it also plays a critical role in supporting what might be called a transnational counterpublic (Olesen 2005; cf. Fraser 1992). Democracy requires public spaces for the articulation of different interests and visions of desirable futures. If we are to have a more democratic global system, we need to enable more citizens to become active participants in global policy discussions. Without a global public sphere, there can be no plural discussion of global issues. Even the most democratic governments lack public input and accountability for actions that influence the living conditions of people in other parts of the world.

Just as the WSF serves as a foundation for a more democratic global polity, it also provides routine contact among the countless individuals and organizations working to address common grievances against global economic and political structures. This contact is essential for helping activists share analyses and coordinate strategies, but it is also indispensable as a means of reaffirming a common commitment to and vision of "another world," especially when day-to-day struggles often dampen such hope. Isolated groups lack information and creative input needed to innovate and adapt their strategies. In the face of repression, exclusion, and ignorance, this transnational solidarity helps energize those who challenge the structures of global capitalism. While many activists will never have the chance to attend the global WSF meeting, they see themselves as part of the process and know they are not alone in their struggles. Aided by the Internet and an increasingly dense web of transnational citizens' networks, the WSF and its regional and local counterparts dramatize the unity among diverse local struggles and encourage coordination among activists working at local, national, and transnational levels.

The Global Scene: Politics and Economy in the Neoliberal Era

Globally and nationally, the logic of the relationship between governments and corporations changed somewhere between the late 1970s and the early 1980s (McMichael 2003; Brunelle 2007). The global justice movement and the WSF challenge the economic and political restructuring initiated during this period, which is seen as increasing social inequalities, environmental degradation, and political injustices worldwide. In this section, we review how global economic restructuring taking hold in the mid-1980s undermined democracy and transformed the globe.

Changes in the World's Economic Principles

For fifty years up until the mid-1980s the ideas of John Maynard Keynes dominated economic policymaking. The principles of Keynes, or Keynesianism, included two very important features that informed economic policies in the United States and the world in the aftermath of the Great Depression. First, government involvement in economic development was encouraged as vital to successful capitalist industrialization (Portes 1997; McMichael 2003). Government duties included providing a buffer against cyclical economic downturns and planning and developing various economic sectors (Kiely 1998; Portes 1997; McMichael 2003). Second, government was also needed to reduce the inevitable inequalities produced by capitalist development. Such redistribution and assistance would not—according to Keynesian principles—interfere with economic growth, but rather it would help foster it.

The Keynesian era and the organization of the global political economy on these principles ended in the mid-1980s and were replaced with what is widely referred to as the Washington Consensus (Williamson 1997), or neoliberalism. Former U.S. president Ronald Reagan and former U.K. prime minister Margaret Thatcher are two leading politicians responsible for ushering in the neoliberal era. Neoliberals argue that prioritizing the interest of capital is the only assurance for national economic success. Governments were required to drastically reduce their involvement with the economy, and good governance was measured by the extent to which a state could promote development through market forces. Government attempts at poverty alleviation and the reduction of social inequality were viewed as detrimental to economic growth. Neoliberal proponents view all regulations on corporate activity, such as those that protect the environment from toxic dumping or workers from unsafe and unhealthy working conditions, as a hindrance to economic growth.

Proponents of economic globalization like to argue that if governments enact policies to encourage international trade and economic growth (profits) for corporations, the benefits will automatically "trickle down" to all sectors of society. One of the claims made by those advocating a free-market model for global economic governance is that, if progress is to be achieved, *there is no alternative* (TINA) to the global expansion of capitalism. Margaret Thatcher made precisely this claim. Neoliberals have shaped the policies of global institutions like the World Bank, the International Monetary Fund, and the World Trade Organization to promote this particular vision of global economic integration. Because those adopting this model of economic development occupied positions of power within the world's richest and most powerful countries, they were able to effectively impose the neoliberal model of globalization from above. They did this through the terms of international aid and loans and through unequal trading arrangements (McMichael 2003; Peet 2003; Robinson 2004; Babb 2003).

Critics of economic globalization argue that markets alone are not able to achieve many important social goals, such as ensuring a humane standard of living for all people, protecting the natural environment, and limiting inequality. Markets sometimes aid economic growth, and they have succeeded in generating vast amounts of wealth and technological innovation, but they also have contributed to rising global inequalities. Moreover, many experts argue that the recent decades of rapid globalization have not generated economic benefits for most of the world's poor. They point to World Bank and United Nations statistics to demonstrate that, for instance, the poorest 100 countries are actually worse off economically than they were before the 1980s, and that the costs of global economic restructuring have disproportionately affected the world's poorest people (see, e.g., UNDP 2005).

Political Participation on a Global Scale

Given these failures of market-oriented approaches to governing the world economy, participants in the WSF criticize the "democratic deficit" in global institutions. They argue that we need a model of global integration that allows a wider range of people—not just financial experts—to be involved in shaping decisions about how our economic and social lives are organized. Yet along with the economic principles of neoliberalism guiding the current world order is the elite strategy of *depoliticization,* or the deliberate effort to exclude civil society from political participation in global governance.

Depoliticization is driven by the belief that democracy muddles leadership and economic efficiency. This crisis of democracy is reflected in the proliferation of public protests and other forms of citizen political participation, which are seen by the neoliberals as resulting from excessive citizen participation in democracy.

In other words, states and governments have been overburdened by democratic demands that increase their involvement in social and economic programs. Through the depoliticization of society, citizens and their organizations, either for profit or nonprofit, are forced through measures such as the privatization of public spaces and political repression to withdraw from a shrinking public sphere. Instead, they are encouraged to operate on their own through market forces. States and governments are not only deemed incapable of tackling issues such as homelessness, housing shortages, or environmental pollution, they are also rendered powerless. Therefore, under neoliberalism, the governance of democracies is not the sole responsibility of elected and accountable governments but, rather, of markets.

How have we come to a world stage where the problems we face are not attributed to faulty economic reasoning and corporate profiteering but to the influence of "nonexpert" citizens on economic and social policy decisions? The crisis of democracy was a diagnosis developed by political and economic elites in the 1970s, a time when the WEF was first launched. Two reports had a profound impact on how governments came to redefine their relations with their citizens and social organizations in the ensuing years. The first was a report made to the Trilateral Commission in 1975, and the second was a 1995 Commission on Global Governance report.

The Trilateral Commission

David Rockefeller, president of the Chase Manhattan Bank, founded the Trilateral Commission in 1973 (Sklar 1980). This initiative was prompted by three sets of events. The first and foremost event was the deterioration of relations among the three economic poles of the capitalist economy (e.g., North America—basically the United States and Canada at the time, the European Community, and Japan) after former U.S. president Nixon removed the U.S. dollar from the gold standard, changing one of the major foundations of the global economy as it was structured since the Bretton Woods Agreement of 1944.

The second event was the growing politicization of Third World nations and the process of decolonization that shattered the control of colonial empires over many regions of the globe. In particular, the Bandung Conference, a meeting in 1955 of newly independent nations that had not officially aligned themselves with either the capitalist or socialist nations, and the founding of the Organization for Solidarity with the Peoples of Africa, Asia, and Latin America (OSPAAAL) in 1966 represented to U.S. economic leaders a potential threat to the country's influence around the globe. The third event that triggered the creation of the Trilateral Commission was the growing student unrest throughout the world in the late 1960s, which was fueled in part by the social revolutions in the Third World and by the growing social opposition to the war in Vietnam.

Soon after its creation, the Trilateral Commission conducted a study to assess what they saw as the ills that were plaguing democracy. The report, *The Crisis of Democracy: Report on the Governability of Democracies to the Trilateral Commission,* provided a framework accepted by many politicians and academics to define and explain the crisis of democracy (Crozier et al. 1975). The report spells out a theory of cycles according to which increasing participation on the part of citizens in political affairs leads to social polarization. In turn, this polarization fosters distrust toward the political process, which leads to a weakening of its efficacy and efficiency, and ultimately, to lower political participation. Consequently, governments should encourage political passivity so that prevailing excessive citizen democratic participation can be reduced. Instead reliance on expertise, experience, and seniority was emphasized as the best model for effective governance.

The Commission on Global Governance

The context leading to the creation of the Commission on Global Governance in 1995 is quite different from the one that gave birth to the Trilateral Commission. However, some of the underlying issues are similar and can help us understand the movement toward depoliticization. Two important precursors were the end of the Cold War and the mission to chart a new course for the United Nations for its fiftieth anniversary.

The growing participation of civil society organizations in UN-sponsored conferences reflected the need for some form of global governance in an increasingly interlinked global economy. For instance, the first Earth Summit, held in Stockholm in 1972, which a large number of nongovernmental organizations (NGOs) attended, gained more international prominence than had previous conferences.[1] Running parallel to the official conference was an NGO Forum, which included a daily newspaper providing immediate and often critical coverage of negotiations inside. The summit otherwise would have been much less open to public scrutiny. The Stockholm pattern was repeated, and expanded, at subsequent UN conferences on issues such as population, food, human rights, development, and women (Rice and Ritchie 1995).

Although the first Earth Summit set a precedent for international decisionmaking and global participation, it was the second Earth Summit in 1992 that revealed the difficulties besetting world governance and eventually led to the Commission on Global Governance. The commission report, *Our Global Neighborhood,* acknowledged that national governments had become less and less able to deal with a growing array of global problems. It argued that the international system should be renewed for three basic reasons: to weave a tighter fabric of international norms, to expand the rule of law worldwide, and to enable citizens to exert their democratic influence on global processes (Carlsson and Ramphal 1995). To reach these goals, the commission proposed a set of "radical" recommendations, most notably the reform and expansion of the UN Security Council, the replacement of ECOSOC by an Economic Security Council (ESC), and an annual meeting of a Forum of Civil Society that would allow the people and their organizations, as part of "an international civil society," to play a larger role in addressing global concerns.

The commission report recognized that global governance operates through a complex set of venues at the world level, including the International Monetary Fund, the World Bank, the World Trade Organization, and major partners such as the then Group of 7 (G7), the Organisation for Economic Co-operation and Development (OECD), as well as regional organizations such as the European Union (EU), North American Free Trade Agreement (NAFTA), and Mercosur (the Southern Common Market). The proposed Economic Security Council was to provide a focal point for global economic and social policy, mirroring the intergovernmental structure of the UN Security Council. In one of the most profound statements of the dilemmas with respect to global governance, the report stated:

> At a global level, what model of decision-making should an emerging system of economic governance adopt? It will have to draw on lessons from regional and national levels and from business organizations where inflexible, centralized command-and-control structures have been shown to be unsustainable. Multilayered decision-making systems are emerging that depend on consultation, consensus, and flexible "rules of the games." Intergovernmental organizations, however, still face basic questions as to who should set the rules and according to what principles. (Commission on Global Governance 1995:146–147)

Significantly, the report also stated that global governance cannot rest on governments or public sector activity alone, but should rely on transnational corporations—which "account for a substantial and growing slice of economic activity" (Commission on Global Governance 1995:153). Whereas it recognized a need for civil society and NGOs to be active in global governance, the report supported the increased role of market forces and the expansion of neoliberal agents of globalization such as the WTO. In effect, it endorsed the notion that business and private enterprise should take a dominant role in global governance, while NGOs and civil society should play a subordinate role assisting governments and business in (market-oriented) development at the local level.

Like the report presented by the Trilateral Commission twenty years prior, the report of the Commission of Global Governance also fails to provide a meaningful role for civil society in global governance. In both reports, society and citizens remain a depoliticized entity. However, our analysis highlights a fundamental contradiction in the globalization program envisioned by the authors of these reports. Although both seek to remove civil society from playing a substantive role in the development of global policy, the Commission on Global Governance recognized that civil society needed to have some role if the institutions of governance were to be seen as legitimate. Without popular legitimacy, the stability of this new international order would be compromised. This tension between the desire to exclude most of the population from policymaking while also strengthening the possibilities for global governance created opportunities for challenges by those denied a voice in shaping the direction of globalization (Markoff 1999).

The WSF: A New Principle of Global Politics

If we consider the increasing privatization, commercialization, and depoliticization of social life and the underlying rational mechanism of efficiency, profit, and accumulation, it appears as if the wheels of history were set in the mid-1980s on an inexorable path toward the dominance of corporations and the eradication of social equality, justice, and political freedom. Given this panorama it would have been difficult to predict the emergence of the WSF as a political body running in a radically different direction. How could we have thought the WSF was possible? Yet contrary to Thatcher's claim that there is no alternative, the WSF arose as a global force, powered by transnational social movements that would have to be reckoned with by governments and corporations. The WSF is an arena for the practice of a democratic form of globalization and a common public space where previously excluded voices can speak and act together to challenge the TINA claim.

The WSF is not simply (or even mainly) a reaction against neoliberal globalization. Instead, it grows from the work of many people throughout history working to advance a just and equitable global order (see Smith 2008). In this sense, it constitutes a new body politic, a common public space where previously excluded voices can speak and act in plurality. With the help of the ideas of noted political theorist Hannah Arendt, we propose to see the WSF not as the logical consequence of global capitalism but rather as the foundation for a new form of politics that breaks with the historical sequence of events that led to the dominance of neoliberal globalization. Arendt viewed the political as a sphere that is not ruled by processes and where the unexpected can happen:

It is not in the least superstitious, it is even a counsel of realism, to look for the unforeseeable and unpredictable, to be prepared for and to expect "miracles" in the political realm. And the more heavily the scales are weighted in favor of disaster, the more miraculous will the deed done in freedom appear; for it is disaster, not salvation, which always happens automatically and therefore always must appear to be irresistible. (1993:170)

Precursors to the WSF

If our understanding of the WSF is to be set apart from the processes of neoliberal globalization, we need to see more concretely the unexpected events that sit at the beginning of this break in our political history. The WSF is a culmination of political actions for social justice, peace, human rights, labor rights, and ecological preservation that resist neoliberal globalization and its attempts to depoliticize the world's citizens. We identify four key factors that interacted to help set the WSF in motion. These factors include:

- Third World protests against international institutions;
- Transnational networks and global mobilizations that challenged the logic of depoliticization (such as those in Seattle in 1999 and Chiapas in 1994);
- Civil society dissatisfaction with the UN system;
- The rise of a transnational feminist and women's movement.

More than any other global actions or transnational networking, the Zapatista uprising in Chiapas, beginning January 1, 1994, and the anti-WTO protests in Seattle in November 1999 were perhaps the most direct precursors to the WSF. After discussing the factors listed above, we showcase these two events to highlight their roles in helping to bring about the WSF process.

Protests in the Global South

The origins of the WSF lie in the countries that have been most deeply impacted by globalization—the countries of the global south. In the 1970s and 1980s, those countries found themselves increasingly squeezed by growing international debts and decreasing prices for the goods they export. They had borrowed money from the World Bank and International Monetary Fund both to cover large-scale industrial development projects as well as to meet the rising costs of fuel during the 1970s successive oil crises. Now these loans were coming due, and they found themselves unable to service their debts while also continuing to develop their national economies and meet the needs of their citizens. Furthermore, the World Bank and IMF began attaching strict conditions to the loans they made, forcing Third World governments to cut government spending and raise interest rates in order to obtain international financing (McMichael 2003). They reasoned that these policies—though painful in the short term—would allow long-term economic growth and, more importantly, ensure that debtor countries could pay back their loans. Essentially, governments had to force their citizens to bear the brunt of the costs of the debt. In many poor countries, this led to what have been called "IMF riots," where citizens protested against the policies of global financial institutions as well as the actions of their own governments (Walton and Seddon 1994).

The IMF riots demonstrated that people in the Third World saw international institutions as a major cause of their economic hardships. Moreover, they saw that their own governments were part of the problem, as their governments were limited in their ability to pursue policies at odds with those favored by the World Bank and IMF. The people also saw that their governments held little sway in those institutions.

Transnational Networks and Global Mobilizations

Meanwhile, in the global north, or the rich Western countries, citizens were organizing around a growing number of environmental problems. Environmentalists and unionists joined forces with each other, and across nations, to contest proposed international free trade agreements, such as the North American Free Trade Agreement (NAFTA) and the Multilateral Agreement on Investment (Ayres 1998; Smith and Smythe 2001). Meanwhile, workers and their allies organized transnational campaigns against the practices of transnational corporations (see, e.g., Sikkink 1986). Northern citizens also became more interested in how the policies of their governments were affecting people elsewhere in the world. Some of this interest grew from the peace and solidarity movements of the 1970s and 1980s (Rucht 2000). The interventionist policies of Western governments encouraged transnational solidarity campaigns between northern activists and their counterparts in the Third World (Gerhards and Rucht 1992; Smith 2008).

At the same time, the United Nations was sponsoring a number of global conferences on issues such as women's rights, environmental protection, and peace that provided opportunities for citizen activists from around the world to meet, exchange stories about their work, and compare analyses of the global and local problems they faced. Aided by advances in technology and reduced costs of transnational communication and travel, these efforts generated more long-term and sustained transnational cooperation than was possible in earlier decades. Beginning in the 1970s there was a tremendous growth in the numbers of formally organized groups working across national borders to promote some kind of social or political change. Thus, between the early 1970s and the late 1990s, the number of transnationally organized social change groups rose from less than 200 to nearly 1,000 (Smith 2004a). Many more transnational citizens' groups were formed around other goals, such as encouraging recreational activities and supporting religious or professional identities, among others. These groups were not only building their own memberships, but they were also forging relationships with other nongovernmental actors and with international agencies, including the United Nations. In the process, they nurtured transnational identities and a broader world culture (Boli and Thomas 1999).

NGO Dissatisfaction with UN Conferences

A third factor that fueled the idea of an alternative venue was the growing dissatisfaction among NGO participants with the mediocre results, if not setbacks, coming out of the conferences convened by the UN—especially the 1992 Conference on Environment and Development (UNCED) in Rio de Janeiro, Brazil; the 1995 Fourth World Conference on Women in Beijing; and the 1995 World Summit on Social Development in Copenhagen. For a number of NGOs that participated in these UN conferences, dissatisfaction changed into disillusionment at the five-year review (dubbed "Rio/Beijing/Copenhagen plus five") conferences aimed at assessing governments' follow-through on the commitments they made at these world conferences. Activists at the review meetings called these the "Rio [or Beijing or Copenhagen] minus five" conferences, highlighting governments' failures to fulfill their conference promises.

Besides their disappointment with the inability of UN conferences to affect the practices of governments, civil society groups that worked hard to influence the texts of the conference agreements felt that much of their efforts in the UN were futile. The real obstacle, they realized, was not the absence of multilateral agreements, but rather the structure of the UN system and the refusal of major countries to address key global issues. Moreover, they saw that many environmental and human rights agreements were being superseded by the WTO, which was formed in 1994 and which privileged international trade law over other international agreements. Agreements made in the UN were thus made irrelevant by the new global trade order, in which increasingly powerful transnational corporations held sway (Smith 2008).

The Global Women's Movement and Feminist Participation

Women's social movement organizations throughout the world have been very effective in establishing networks to promote international responses to gender injustices and violence against women (Moghadam 2005). While women's organizations continue to participate in UN-led conferences, many are also very active in the WSF. The first of the Feminist Dialogues was held in 2003 in Mumbai, India, as a follow-up to the Women's Strategy Meeting held at the 2002 WSF in Porto Alegre, Brazil, in which feminists from around the world came together to discuss their dissatisfaction with men dominating the WSF. In 2005 and 2007 the Feminist Dialogues preceded the WSF event to provide a space to consider feminist concerns, which many organizations feel are sidelined at the WSF, and to collectively influence the forum (Macdonald 2005). Nevertheless, one of the main contributions of feminist political organizations has been their promotion of the participatory processes that refuse to prioritize one issue over another.

While focusing on gender, feminist activists (especially those from the global south) emphasize the intersection of inequalities such as race, gender, nation, class, and sexuality. In addition, feminist activism challenges hierarchical organizational structures that establish formal leadership that tend to silence the voices of the majority. The history of transnational feminist organizing provided important models for fostering decentralized, respectful dialogue and cooperation that helped inform other social movements seeking to bridge national and other differences (see, e.g., Rupp 1997; Alvarez et al. 2004; Polletta 2002; Gibson-Graham 2006). In fact, the model of the "encuentro," a meeting that is organized around a collectivity of interests without hierarchy, on which the Zapatistas and later the WSF process built, emerged from transnational feminist organizing in Latin America (Sternbach et al. 1992; Smith 2008).

Zapatismo and the Battle of Seattle

Many accounts of the 1994 Zapatistas' uprising in Chiapas, Mexico, and the so-called Battle of Seattle during the WTO ministerial meetings of December 1999 speak of their implications for global democracy and for citizens' mobilizations around the world (Burbach 1994; Harvey 1998; Bello 2000; Gill 2000; Halliday 2000; Kaldor 2000; Seoane and Taddei 2002; Scholte 2000). These two key events helped break the continuity of the processes of neoliberal globalization and, therefore, helped open the possibility for the WSF to emerge as an alternative political body (see Escobar 2004a).The events of Chiapas and Seattle reflect not simply resistance to globalized capitalism, but rather they were catalysts to a new political dynamic within the global landscape.

Zapatismo

In 1994 indigenous people in Mexico took up arms to protest their governments' acceptance of the North American Free Trade Agreement. The Zapatistas quickly emerged as one of the first globally networked groups to resist economic globalization. Their struggle inspired many activists in all parts of the world to more actively resist the growing global trade regime. For many, the emergence of a global citizens' movement is credited to the appearance of the Ejercito Zapatista de Liberación Nacional (EZLN, Zapatista National Liberation Army) on the world scene, January 1, 1994, the same day that NAFTA came into force (Amin et al. 2002; Benasayag and Sztulwark 2002). According to Samir Amin and others, the EZLN ushered in an era of "new radicality" fundamentally different from that which prevailed before then.

Worldwide supporters of the EZLN helped popularize some of the writings of the Zapatista leader, Subcomandante Marcos, which were becoming widely known among activists during the 1990s. When the 1999 Seattle and subsequent protests generated complaints from movement critics that "we know what you're against, but what are you *for*?" Marcos's words proved fruitful in inspiring activists to focus on the quest for alternatives. He argued that one of the main problems of economic globalization is that it does not allow other forms of economic and social organization to coexist. Its need to continually expand and conquer makes it incompatible with the desire for diversity in either nature or society. Marcos argued that we can have "one world with room for many worlds" if we can rein in the movement toward economic globalization. A tolerance for diverse forms of economic organization, a respect for local autonomy and participation in economic decisions, and a celebration of the possibilities for innovation and adaptation fostered by diversity were values that Marcos encouraged (Olesen 2005). The widespread attention to his work demonstrates the transnational resonance of his ideas (Khasnabish 2005).

Following the 1994 EZLN uprising, the Zapatistas used the Internet strategically to call on others to join their struggle for a new sort of world (Cleaver 1995; Ronfeldt et al. 1998). Many around the world responded to their call, and they traveled to Chiapas to participate in international meetings, or "encuentros," on how to confront economic globalization. Many more organized in their local communities in support of Zapatista goals: "against neoliberalism and for humanity" (Schultz 1998). Marcos's analysis of the problems of economic globalization and the possibilities for popular liberation inspired the "political imaginations" of many people facing common experiences in the global neoliberal order (Khasnabish 2005).

The Zapatista uprising and subsequent mobilization are without doubt a cornerstone of the global justice movement. They established and disseminated a pattern of transnational mobilization that continues to inspire and inform activists throughout the world. Moreover, the writings of Marcos and the approach to organizing he promoted provided a focal point that helped bring activists together around a shared understanding of their values and organizing capacities. The networks Zapatismo inspired—including an important grassroots formation called Peoples Global Action—provided an infrastructure of people, organizations, and ideas required for the WSF's emergence. These groups helped catalyze global resistance to the G8 and WTO during the late 1990s, including the June 1999 Global Day of Action Against Capitalism and the November 1999 protests in Seattle (Juris 2008; Notes from Nowhere 2003; Starr 2005).

The Battle of Seattle

As we have seen, the preconditions for the emergence of global justice movements included increasing capacity for globally coordinated action, a growing recognition of the limitations of the UN, the diffusion of feminist organizing principles, and resistance in the global south to international institutions. While these factors percolated in various nations at different rates in numerous social justice organizations, by 1999 the stage was set for the entrance of a new form of political participation.

Unexpectedly for many, the global justice movement seemed to explode on the scene in Seattle in 1999. Tens of thousands of college students, labor union members, educators, public health workers, unemployed workers, environmental activists, feminists, immigrants, and other concerned citizens came to protest the ministerial meetings of the World Trade Organization. The vast majority of activists engaged in peaceful protest, and some sought to nonviolently disrupt the meeting by occupying the streets surrounding the conference hall where WTO delegates were to meet. But police were unprepared for the volume of protesters, and they responded with brutality, triggering what was called "the Battle of Seattle." Although subsequent inquiries showed that the police were at fault by instigating violence against protesters and bystanders, the mainstream media portrayed the protesters as violent and unreasonable (Smith 2002).

A key feature of the organization behind the Seattle protest was the lack of formalized leadership. Rather than a single organization or political body representing the protesters as a single entity, smaller units referred to as affinity groups came together around shared values and identities, uniting with others to forge a common front against the meetings of the WTO. While some affinity groups blocked traffic and engaged in other acts of civil disobedience, trade unionists and other activists marched along preordained march routes and gave passionate speeches denouncing the WTO's policies before a stadium full of supporters. The actions held that day in Seattle were not directed by a single person, group, or organizing unit. Rather they happened organically from the context of protest in which they were situated and from each organization's own traditions of protest.

Global mobilizations like the one in Seattle also present opportunities for learning about the struggles of other groups and understanding the relationship among the organizations attending. For instance, many church members who participated in the Seattle protests learned about the damaging effects of global economic policies through their interactions with other church members around the world. They marched to demand greater equity and justice for all members of their faith (and presumably other faiths as well), regardless of where they were from. Students and teachers that found their schools increasingly impoverished by cuts in public budgets see a connection between their experiences and the changes in the global economy. Unions and professional associations have also been motivated by both threats to their members' interests as well as their solidarity with their counterparts around the world.

Given this rapid growth of transnational networking, by the time of the Seattle WTO meeting many participants had already learned a great deal from each other and had cultivated skills for organizing protests at the local, national, and increasingly the transnational levels. Moreover, subsequent global mobilizations in cities such as Prague, Quebec City, Genoa, Barcelona, and Washington, D.C., continued to provide critical spaces for learning, coalition building, and action. At the same time, many activists felt global protests alone were insufficient. Rather than simply denouncing what they were *against*, it was also important to articulate a clear vision of what they were fighting *for*. In January 2001, the first ever WSF was organized precisely to provide a space for developing concrete alternatives to corporate globalization. Indeed, the WSF process is an important place for popular education about the injustices occurring all over the world as a result of the policies of economic globalization. At the same time, the process creates opportunities for groups to learn about and articulate economic and political alternatives and plan future mobilizations.

Conclusion

Protesters in Seattle and elsewhere and participants in the social forums have challenged people to ask whether the world's major economic institutions are producing the kind of world in which they want to live. The answer, activists argue, is that we cannot govern by markets. Rather, we need political institutions that can help balance competing social interests and goals. By separating trade and other economic policy decisions from other policy areas (such as human rights, public safety, or environmental protection), governments have undermined their own legitimacy and introduced untenable contradictions into international law. Social forum participants argue that the goal of reducing restrictions on international trade must not be allowed to trump other social values and goals.

Governments gain their legitimacy from popular elections and recognition by their populations as their representatives. But with globalization, governments are delegating more policy decisions to international institutions such as the WTO or the European Union. While global interdependence requires some policy coordination to ensure peace and common security, the way governments have managed international policy has created a "democratic deficit" in global institutions. Many of those protesting economic globalization argue for greater government accountability and responsiveness in both domestic and international policy arenas. As they have pursued their particular aims—such as environmental protection, human rights, and equitable development—civil society groups have found themselves uniting behind demands for a more democratic global polity. The protests against economic globalization are really wider battles about whether people and democratic institutions or technical experts and markets should govern the global system.

Understanding the WSF process as a fundamentally new form of politics challenges the visions of history that emphasize chronological chains of processes where all that happens is the logical consequence of its context and its immediate past. Although growing out of a long tradition of struggle, the process of rebellion made visible in Chiapas and Seattle has begun to fracture the historical process of neoliberal domination. The continuity of corporate globalization is now in question. By challenging the relentless progression of privatization, trade liberalization, consumption, and individuation, the rebellion has created another temporality within which the WSF is clearly situated.

Note

Jackie Smith and Marina Karides et al. in "Globalization and the Emergence of World Social Forums." In *Global Democracy and World Social Forums*, by Jackie Smith and Marina Karides et al. (Boulder, CO: Paradigm Publishers, 2008): 1–25. Reprinted by permission of Paradigm Publishers. References omitted.

1. "The 1972 Stockholm Conference institutionalized the environment as a legitimate concern of government, and it institutionalized NGOs as the instruments through which government could varnish its agenda with the appearance of public support. The primary outcome of the conference was a recommendation to create the United Nations Environment Programme (UNEP) which became a reality in 1973" (Lamb 1997).

Chapter 20

Globalization

Long Term Process or New Era in Human Affairs?

William H. McNeill

Globalization refers to the way recent changes in transport and communication have tied humankind in all parts of the earth together more closely than ever before. One effect, the widespread breakup of older forms of village life after 1950, changed the daily experience of innumerable persons so drastically that those years may plausibly claim to mark a new era in human history. New and more capacious transport and communication were primarily responsible for that change, powerfully seconded by population growth that made older ways of life unsustainable in many rural landscapes. Massive migrations from village to city were the principal manifestations of the new order, and affected all the inhabited parts of the earth.

Yet sporadic increases in the capacity of transport and communication are age-old among humankind and have always changed behavior. That process began when our proto-human ancestors learned to control fire and to dance. Fire eventually allowed humans to accelerate the recycling of organic vegetation by deliberately setting grass and brush alight in dry seasons of the year; and to survive sub-freezing temperatures even in the Arctic. Control of fire was so valuable that all surviving humans acquired that skill, beginning as long ago as 400,000 B.C.E.[1]

Dancing aroused a different kind of warmth by communicating a sense of commonality to participants that dissipated inter-personal frictions. That, in turn, allowed human bands to expand in size beyond the limits our chimpanzee relatives sustain today. The advantages of larger numbers of cooperating individuals were so great that all surviving humans learned to dance. But dancing leaves no archaeological trace, so dating is completely unknowable. Yet like control of fire, all humans learned to dance; and in all probability it was among bands enlarged and sustained by dancing on festival occasions that language, the principal vehicle of subsequent human communication, developed between 90,000 and 50,000 B.C.E.[2] Language, too, was so advantageous that it also became universal among humankind.

These three capabilities remain unique to our species; and of the three, language is the most amazing. It proved capable of sustaining agreed upon meanings among indefinite numbers of persons—by now even among hundreds of millions. More particularly, it freed humans from the limitations of acting in response to sense experience in a rather narrow present as other animals do. By talking about things remembered and about what might happen in times to come our ancestors became able to agree on what to do tomorrow and even further into the future. Moreover, when planned actions met disappointment, they were stimulated, indeed required, to talk things over again, seeking to change what they had done in hope of achieving better results.

That process of trial and error induced systematic change in human behavior as never before, since discrepancy between hopes, plans and actual experience was perennial and only increased as new skills and knowledge enlarged human impact on the diverse environments into which they soon penetrated.[3] We live with the result—an ever accelerating pace of social change that strains our capability for successful adjustment.

The subsequent human past can plausibly be understood as a series of thresholds when new conditions of life rather abruptly accelerated the pace of resulting change. Control of fire, which antedated language, had particularly drastic effects, allowing humans to transform local plant life by deliberately burning grass and brush wherever they went. Mastery of movement across water by use of rafts and boats much facilitated human dispersal from their ancestral cradle in Africa. The earliest clear evidence for this capability is the initial occupation of Australia in about 40,000 B.C.E., which required crossing miles of open water.

Resort to agriculture was the next major accelerant of social change. As they spread to different parts of the earth, humans discovered a wide variety of different plants to feed on. Ways to multiply the number of such plants by weeding and seeding and transplanting roots that grew naturally may well have been familiar to many hunters and gatherers long before they ever thought of settling down in a single spot and raising food crops in fields where they did not grow of their own accord.

Why our ancestors did so remains unsure. Hunters and gatherers enjoyed a more variegated and more dependable diet than early farmers; and tilling fields was far more laborious than wandering in search of game and wild-growing plant foods. But farming did produce far more food per acre and sustained far denser populations than hunting and gathering could do. That meant that wherever farmers settled down, superior numbers soon assured them against attack by hunter-gatherers and allowed them to encroach upon hunting grounds wherever cultivable land attracted their attention.

Dense populations raising different crops in diverse landscapes arose independently in several parts of the earth between 8000 B.C.E. and 4000 B.C.E. From the start, deliberate selection of seeds and roots prevailed, sometimes changing food plants radically, as when wild teosinte turned into maize in Mexico. As food supplies increased, farming populations multiplied and established new villages wherever suitable land lay within reach. More people distributed over varying landscapes soon generated divergences of local customs and skills, so that even sporadic contacts with strangers, arriving on foot or by sea, brought attractive novelties to the attention of local communities more and more often.

Consequently, the pace of social change accelerated systematically within each of the major centers of agriculture because more people made more inventions; and some advantageous inventions and discoveries traveled well—new varieties of seeds for example and preciosities like mood-altering drugs, gems for decoration, and obsidian or flint to give cutting tools a sharp edge.

In Eurasia, an impressive array of domesticated animals diversified the agricultural complex of evolving plants and people still further—dogs, cats, donkeys, cattle, horses, water buffalo, camels and still others. Cattle, horses and camels were particularly significant, for their size and strength far surpassed that of human beings and could be used to plow the soil and to transport heavy loads. The Americas lacked a comparable array of large-bodied domesticable animals and much of Africa was inhospitable to them. Overland transport in those parts of the earth therefore remained more slender than in Eurasia.

Accordingly, in the Americas and sub-Saharan Africa social change in general, largely dependent on contacts with strangers, fell behind the pace of Eurasian developments. Other factors, especially the prevalence of lethal infectious diseases in much of Africa, also handicapped human populations more than in Eurasia, which therefore remained the principal setting for further advances of human power and skill.

The appearance of cities and civilizations after 3500 B.C.E. accelerated social changes still further. Cities existed only by virtue of occupational differentiation and systematic exchanges of goods and services between urban populations and their rural hinterlands. Urban specialists persistently improved their skills and extended their reach further and further, as professional traders began to spend their lives traveling to and fro across long distances.

When cities started to arise in Eurasia, merchants were already sailing overseas in ships and traveling overland with caravans of pack animals. It was not accidental that where land and sea transport routes met in the land of Sumer (southernmost Iraq) was where the first cities and civilizations appeared. Other civilizations too arose at locations where strangers mingled more than usual, exchanging skills and ideas coming from extensive hinterlands. Consequently, wherever they existed, cities and civilizations circulated goods, skills and ideas more quickly and more widely than before.

The earliest civilizations of Mesopotamia and Egypt were in slender contact from the start; and successive West Asian empires and civilizations remained constantly in touch with Mediterranean cities and civilizations thereafter. Indian and Chinese civilizations were geographically distant; and climate as well as cultural differences limited what could travel from western Asia and Europe to India and China, and vice versa, even after merchant, military and missionary contacts did begin to connect them loosely together. That became a reality by about 100 B.C.E. and made all of Eurasia into a single interacting web, with tentacles reaching into sub-Saharan Africa, the frozen north and among the far-flung Pacific islands off South East Asia.

The vastness and variety of peoples and landscapes within that circle far exceeded similar interacting webs in other parts of the earth. It is therefore not surprising that the Eurasian web evolved levels of skill and power superior to what people elsewhere had at their command when new advances in transport and communication exposed them to Old World accomplishments after 1500 C.E.

Biological resistance to a long array of infectious diseases, from the common cold to small pox, measles, plague and others, was the single most decisive factor in compelling previously isolated populations to submit to intruders from the disease-experienced Eurasian web. The most lethal of these diseases were transfers from animal herds. Eurasia's uniquely complex array of domesticated—and some wild—animals had exposed civilized Eurasian peoples to these diseases across millennia, not without wreaking serious damages along the way. But when one epidemic after another started to rage in rapid succession among inexperienced populations in America and other newly-contacted lands, resulting die-offs were crippling. The newcomers remained little affected, thanks to immunities in their bloodstreams, partly inherited, and partly acquired or reinforced by exposure in early childhood.[4]

The human destruction that followed the opening of the oceans to sustained navigation in the decades immediately after Columbus's famous voyage of 1492 was greater than ever before, since European explorers and conquistadors encountered populous, civilized lands in both Mexico and Peru where millions of persons died of new diseases within a few decades. That massive die-off in turn provoked the trade in African slaves that carried millions of Africans across the Atlantic in subsequent centuries. Accordingly, Europeans, Africans and Amerindians mingled in the Americas earlier and more extensively than anywhere else.

In Eurasia itself after 1500 the pace of change also accelerated. New phenomena, like the flood of silver from American mines, upset prices and social-political patterns in China as well as in Europe, and the spread of new crops from America—especially maize, potatoes and sweet potatoes—enlarged food supplies very significantly as well.

The global pace of change accelerated yet again with the introduction of steam transport on both land and sea, together with instantaneous electrical communication after 1850. One manifestation was the spread of European empires across much of Asia and Africa. Everywhere weavers and other artisans suffered severely from a flood of cheap, machine-made goods coming from newfangled European factories, powered first by flowing water, then by steam and later by electricity. But before very long Asian factories, especially in Japan, China and India, began to produce cheaper and, more recently, also better goods than Europeans (and Americans) did; and European empires all collapsed soon after World War II.

From the long term point of view, therefore, recent mass migrations and widespread disruption of village patterns of life by roads, trucks, buses, radio, TV and computers look more like another wave of intensified human interaction, comparable to its predecessors and far from unique.

Argument about whether continuity or uniqueness prevails among us today is really pointless. Each moment is unique in every human life; yet continuities are strong and undeniable, both privately and publicly. It is always tempting to exaggerate the unprecedented character of the problems we face. My personal cast of mind prefers to seek commonality; and one such indisputable commonality is that in recent centuries, as social change accelerated, each generation felt uniquely challenged, yet survived in greater numbers than before. No clear end of that process is yet in view, unsustainable though it is sure to be across any lengthy future.

Really basic is the fact that human numbers recently surpassed 6 billions, after having quadrupled in the course of the 20th century. An equally amazing fact is that more people now live in towns and cities than labor to produce food in the countryside. Both these facts are unprecedented and, despite a margin of inexactitude in all demographic data, are also undisputed.[5] Yet the massive flow of information, goods, services and human migrants that sustains our cities and keeps us alive remains precarious, for political, environmental and sociological reasons.

Politically, the threat of nuclear proliferation and reckless resort to weapons of mass destruction hangs over a world of divided sovereignties. Atomic, supplemented by biological and chemical warfare may break out suddenly and wreak enormous, perhaps paralyzing destruction around the globe in a very short period of time. Religious fanaticism and other ideological hatreds may even provoke governments to actions that might make the whole earth uninhabitable.

The risk is old hat by now. Having safely survived the Cold War, we seldom worry much about it. But with suicidal bombers at work in Iraq and neighboring lands every day, and with several beleaguered governments trying to build atomic warheads to threaten others and protect themselves, political risks of sudden disaster seem to be rising rather than diminishing.

Ecological catastrophe is a vaguer, multiplex threat. Industrial factories, mines and transport vehicles are changing the chemical composition of soil, air and water at unprecedented rates. Global temperatures are rising and climates are changing very fast. The result for human and other forms of life remains uncertain, but may reach critical levels locally, or even globally some time soon. No one knows. Human capacity to alter natural environments has increased so rapidly in recent decades that the stability of the world's ecosystems can no longer be taken for granted. That, I think, is all one can say for sure.[6]

A less familiar instability in human affairs rests on the fact that across millennia, cities nearly always failed to reproduce themselves biologically and depended on immigrants from surrounding healthier countrysides to maintain their numbers. Intensified exposure to disease in cities was the traditional reason for urban die-off. In the nineteenth and twentieth centuries sanitation and medical advances seemed to have conquered most lethal infections. Yet new lethal infections, most notably AIDS, have now emerged; and some old ones are coming back thanks to the emergence of germs resistant to antibiotics and other once-decisive forms of treatment.

So far, however, the introduction of cheap and effective methods of birth control has proved more significant for human affairs. Most women in rich urbanized countries like the United States and Europe quickly began to use contraceptive pills when they became available after 1960; and their birth rates soon shrank below the figure of 2.1 per woman needed to sustain existing populations. This is a new phenomenon. Women and men, in effect, became able to insulate sex from reproduction at will, and began to give birth to fewer children with no diminution of sexual gratification.

This capability was enhanced by changes of family life in urban settings that increased the cost of raising children and diminished parental satisfactions. Beginning as far back as the 18th century, in more and more instances, work among city dwellers began to mean leaving home and spending day-time hours in a factory, store or office. To begin with it was mostly men who left their homes to work, leaving women behind to keep house and look after small children.

But in the twentieth century, modern conveniences—packaged food, vacuum cleaners, dish washers, refrigerators and the like—made housekeeping into a part-time job. Then during World War II labor shortages brought more and more women into factories and offices. Looking after small children at home became increasingly irksome for those who stayed behind, for their work remained unpaid.

Simultaneously, prolonged schooling and prohibition of child labor, often dictated by law, lengthened the time before children could contribute to family income; and the rise of distinctive, and often rebellious, forms of youth culture among adolescents strained family relations yet further. Finally, government pensions for the elderly meant that children were no longer needed to support their parents in old age.

All these changes diminished the satisfactions and increased the cost of raising children among urban dwellers everywhere, especially in Europe and other highly industrialized lands. For a while rural populations lagged behind and continued to reproduce themselves in traditional fashion. But as radio, TV and other exposure to urban styles of life penetrated the rural hinterland in the more highly urbanized countries, old-fashioned family patterns of behavior among rural dwellers were strained to the breaking point, and village birth rates also began to fall.

That opened wide the door for millions of migrants from lands where rapid population growth persisted. Consequently, Europe, the United States and other countries of European settlement overseas are now increasingly divided between newcomers, with different languages, religions and physical appearance from those of older inhabitants.

In such circumstances, mutual accommodation is inescapable, and behavioral changes run both ways. Eventual assimilation to a single norm cannot be assumed. In the past, cities regularly accommodated diverse ethnic groups, some of which were confined to ghettos; and our recent rates of migration seem sure to sustain ethnic and cultural plurality as long as they continue.

The co-existence of lands where family patterns and economic conditions sustain rapid population growth with countries and classes who are failing to reproduce themselves is not unprecedented. As I said before, throughout history cities have usually failed to reproduce themselves biologically. As long as nearby villages supplied the deficit, and as long as something approximating ethnic and cultural homogeneity prevailed regionally, European nations could be built on the premise of a common biological and cultural heritage.

But that was exceptional. Empires bulk far larger in the historic record; and they were always multi-ethnic. Imperial capitals and large provincial cities attracted populations who maintained distinct and different ways of life indefinitely, often helped by limited rights of ethnic self-government, diverse religious institutions and, not infrequently, by occupational specialization as well. In a sense, therefore, the recent expansion of urban polyethnicity in European lands is a return to normal for Europeans. Nation-wide ethnic uniformity was always somewhat mythical. Today's ethnic mixing is more massive and, obviously, not new.

An unanswered question for the longer future, however, is whether the recent disruption of traditional rural life will affect birth rates among all the peoples of the earth in the same way that it did after about 1960 in Europe and in lands of European settlement overseas. It is already true that cities of China, India, Latin America and even of Africa seem to be becoming population sink holes. Some always were, and it is in these cities that infectious diseases have made their greatest comeback from the effect of antibiotics and other medical advances of the twentieth century.

But whether the sociological changes that make child rearing more difficult and less satisfying among richer populations will spread to the rest of the world is not sure. Rural reservoirs of poor farmers remain vast, incentives to migration remain strong, and rural birth rates in Latin America, India, Africa and the Moslem lands of Asia have diminished only slightly. Consequently, world population is still growing rapidly and may precipitate some sort of ecological and/or political disaster before changes in private family life and birth control pills make much difference in the poorer and still mainly rural countries of the world.

Yet such changes come quickly. The collapse of French Canadian birth rates immediately after World War II to a level below that of English-speaking Canada is a case in point. No one knows whether Mexico, Nigeria and other such countries will follow the French Canadian example, but it is worth realizing that sometime late in the 21st century, say about 2075, declining human populations might become general throughout the world. If so, consequences are likely to be as baffling as those our recent extraordinary population growth still continues to provoke.

Future demographic stability, allowing time to adjust to ever-accelerating social change, is most unlikely. Human numbers have tended to increase over time throughout our career on earth. Local die-offs and sharp decreases happened often enough. But globally speaking, new ecological and technological discoveries that sustained population increases soon overtook even the most massive regional losses.

We may or may not be nearing an end to that age-old process of expanding the human niche in earth's ecosystem. But we will not know ahead of time. And even if global catastrophe takes over, even a small human remnant might be able to start all over again, even in a radically different environment, and maintain our privileged place at the top of the food chain.

Language, endowing us with unparalleled capabilities for cooperation, innovation and adaptability, makes us unique among the forms of life that ever existed. As long as humankind retains such capabilities, we will continue to disturb the world around us and fumble towards an uncertain, changing and always precarious future.

That realization seems to me more important than trying to isolate changes of the past fifty years from the deeper past by emphasizing their uniqueness. All ages are unique; each moment and every person is unique. So is each atom and sub-atomic particle for that matter. But continuities and commonalities also prevail, and recognizing them is what historians and scientists focus on when trying to understand the ever-changing world of which we are a part.

I conclude that the world is indeed one interacting whole and always has been. Human wealth and power have sporadically increased, spurting towards unexampled heights lately. Limits to that spurt may now be close at hand. But ingenuity and invention remain alive among us as much as ever. So we and our successors may perhaps continue to stumble onward like all preceding human generations, meeting with painful disappointments and changing behavior accordingly, only to provoke new risks and meet fresh disappointments. That has always been the human condition, and seems likely to last as long as we do.

Notes

William H. McNeill, "Globalization: Long Term Process or New Era in Human Affairs?," *New Global Studies* 2, no. 1 (2008): 1–9. Used by permission of Berkeley Electronic Press.

1. Johan Goudsblom, *Fire and Civilization*. (Middlesex, England, 1992), p. 17.
2. William H. McNeill, *Keeping Together in Time*. (Cambridge, MA, 1995), p. 31.

3. J. R. McNeill and William H. McNeill, *The Human Web*. (New York, 2003), pp. 11–14 and passim.

4. William H. McNeill, *Plagues and Peoples*.(New York, 1976), passim.

5. Paul Demeny and Geoffrey McNicoll, editors, "The Political Economy of Global Population Change, 1950–2050," *Population and Development Review, Supplement* to vol. 32, 2006, offers a convenient and authoritative discussion of these phenomena.

6. J. R. McNeill, *Something New Under the Sun: An Environmental History of the Twentieth Century World*. (New York, 2000), passim.

About the Editor and Authors

Manfred B. Steger is Professor of Global Studies and head of the School of International and Community Studies at the Royal Melbourne Institute of Technology (RMIT), Australia. He is also research fellow at the Globalization Research Center at the University of Hawaii—Manoa. His academic fields of expertise include global studies, political and social theory, and theories of nonviolence. His most recent publications include *Globalization: A Very Short Introduction* (Oxford University Press, 2009: 1st ed. 2003); *The Rise of the Global Imaginary: Political Ideologies from the French Revolution to the Global War on Terror* (Oxford University Press, 2008); *Globalism: Market Ideology Meets Terrorism* (Rowman & Littlefield, 2005: 1st ed. 2002); *Judging Nonviolence: The Dispute Between Realists and Idealists* (Routledge, 2003); *Gandhi's Dilemma: Nonviolent Principles and Nationalist Power* (St. Martin's Press, 2000); and *The Quest for Evolutionary Socialism: Eduard Bernstein and Social Democracy* (Cambridge University Press, 1997).

Dennis Altman is Professor of Politics and International Relations in the School of Social Sciences at La Trobe University Victoria, Australia.

Arjun Appadurai is Senior Advisor for Global Initiatives at the New School for Social Research, New York.

Manuel Castells is Professor of Communication at the Annenberg School of Communication, University of Southern California–Los Angeles.

Mike Davis is Distinguished Professor in the Department of Creative Writing at the University of California, Riverside.

Jared Diamond is a professor in the Department of Geography at the University of California—Los Angeles.

Anthony Giddens is Professor Emeritus at The Centre for the Study of Global Governance at the London School of Economics.

Michael Hardt is Professor of Literature and Italian in the Department of Romance Studies at Duke University.

Paul Hirst was, until his death, Professor of Social Theory in the Birkbeck College of the University of London.

Paul James is Professor of Globalization and Cultural Diversity and Director of the Global Cities Research Institute at RMIT University.

Mary Kaldor is Professor of Global Governance and Co-Director of The Centre for the Study of Global Governance at the London School of Economics.

Marina Karides is Assistant Professor of Sociology at Florida Atlantic University.

Theodore Levitt was, until his death, Edward W. Carter Professor of Business Administration and head of the marketing area at the Harvard Business School.

James H. Mittelman is Professor of International Affairs in the School of International Service at the American University.

Valentine Moghadam is Professor of Sociology and Women's Studies and Co-Director of the Women's Studies Program at Purdue University.

Antonio Negri is an Italian political philosopher and former member of the radical Italian Organized Worker's Autonomy movement.

Roland Robertson is Chair in Sociology and Global Society in the School of Social Science at the University of Aberdeen in Scotland.

Olivier Roy is Professor and Research Director (CNRS) for the National Center for Scientific Research, School of Advanced Studies in Social Sciences in Paris.

Saskia Sassen is Robert S. Lynd Professor of Sociology and serves on the Committee of Global Thought at Columbia University.

Jackie Smith is Associate Professor of Sociology and Peace Studies at the University of Notre Dame.

Joseph Stiglitz is Chair of The Committee on Global Thought and University Professor of International Affairs in the School of International and Public Affairs at Columbia University.

Grahame Thompson is a professor of political economy in politics and international studies at the Open University in England.

INDEX

CPSIA information can be obtained at www.ICGtesting.com
Printed in the USA
BVOW01s0957071113

335614BV00009B/170/P